ALEX ZANARDI

MY SWEETEST VICTORY

A Memoir Of
Racing Success,
Adversity, and Courage

Alex Zanardi, Two-Time CART Champion
with Gianluca Gasparini

Foreword by Mario Andretti

B | BentleyPublishers™
.com

This book is dedicated to all my U.S. fans and to their wonderful country, where anything is possible and where many of my own dreams came true.

CONTENTS

Foreword by Mario Andretti v

1 The Darkest Day 1

2 Childhood Days..5

3 Getting Started in Karts 15

4 World Championship Karting 33

Color Photos 1–16.. after page 52

5 Racing in Formula 3 and 3000.....................................57

6 Formula 1—At Last 91

7 The Lotus Years 111

8 Time Out, and an Introduction to IndyCar........................131

Color Photos 17–32 .... after page 148

9 A Good Start in CART, and Marriage 153

10 CART Championship Victory Number One 189

11 CART Championship Again, and a Son is Born 215

Color Photos 33–51 .... after page 244

12 A Return to Formula 1 255

13 A Sabbatical and Back to CART 267

14 The Big One 293

15 The Road to Recovery 311

16 The Race Completed 333

Color Photos 52–66 .... after page 340

Afterword..347

Author's Note 363

Alex Zanardi Chronology 366

Map of Italy...372

Map of Germany 373

Index...374

Art Credits..387

B BENTLEY PUBLISHERS™ | Automotive Reference™

Bentley Publishers, a division of Robert Bentley, Inc.
1734 Massachusetts Avenue
Cambridge, MA 02138 USA
800-423-4595 / 617-547-4170   Information that makes
                                the difference®
BentleyPublishers™
.com

Copies of this book may be purchased from booksellers or directly from the publisher.

Bentley Stock No. GDAZ
ISBN 0-8376-1249-7
08 07 06 05 04   10 9 8 7 6 5 4 3 2 1

The paper used in this publication is acid-free and meets the requirements of the National Standard for Information Sciences-Permanence of Paper for Printed Library Materials. ∞

Library of Congress Cataloging-in-Publication Data
Zanardi, Alex.
[--Pero, Zanardi da Castel Maggiore! English]
Alex Zanardi : my sweetest victory / Alex Zanardi with Gianluca Gasparini ; foreword by Mario Andretti.
   p. cm.
Includes index.
ISBN 0-8376-1249-7 (alk. paper)
1. Zanardi, Alex. 2. Automobile racing drivers--Italy--Biography.
I. Gasparini, Gianluca. II. Title.
GV1032.Z36A3 2004
796.72'092--dc22
                        2004021401

Alex Zanardi: My Sweetest Victory by Alex Zanardi with Gianluca Gasparini
©2004 Robert Bentley, Inc., North American edition.
Bentley Publishers is a trademark of Robert Bentley, Inc.

Originally published as *…però, Zanardi da Castel Maggiore!* by Alex Zanardi and Gianluca Gasparini. © 2003 Baldini Castoldi Dalai *editore* S.p.A, Milano

Bentley Publishers and Baldini Castoldi Dalai *editore* would like to thank Mediabuy USA, Inc., and Gabriele Pedone for being instrumental in the publication of this edition. Chapters 1–16 and Author's Note translated from the original Italian by Valencia Haynes and Ottavia Mazzoni. Afterword translated from the original Italian by Jeffrey M. Barnes.

Manufactured in the United States of America

Foreword
by Mario Andretti

Mario Andretti (left) with Alex Zanardi at the Marlboro Grand Prix of Miami, March 2000.

The story of Alex Zanardi is extraordinary. It isn't only about one of the greatest race drivers the world ever saw. It's also about Alex the man, dealing with one of the most harsh and heart-breaking realities of auto racing—a bad accident—and his life afterward with no legs. What is it like to be Alex Zanardi? Well, he comes complete with a sack full of valuable lessons. And these aren't lessons just for racers. This is a crash course in rebuilding life.

I met Alex when he was taking American racing by storm in 1996, 1997 and 1998, winning 15 races for the Ganassi Team and two straight CART championships. Alex was a factor on every track. He could win on a short oval, a superspeedway, a street circuit or a regular road course. His versatility was testimony to his multiple skills and the fact that he was a complete driver. Alex wasn't just a good driver, but a great driver. A good driver wins the race by starting from pole position; a great driver wins regardless of the conditions. Alex was superb if everything was perfect, but even better if everything wasn't.

I am an Alex Zanardi fan. And so are millions of others across the globe. Alex is a star: respected by drivers, adored by fans, embraced by sponsors. He has charisma, the sharpest wit, extreme intelligence and a gift of gab enjoyed especially by the media. That's why the tragedy that befell him on an oval in Lausitz, Germany, on September 15, 2001, resonated around the world.

With 13 laps remaining in that race and Alex in the lead, his car spun coming out of pit lane and stalled on the track. Canadian driver Tagliani had nowhere to go but straight and the nose of his car severed Alex's legs mid-thigh at 190 mph. That Alex is back today, completely adjusted to life with prosthetic legs, only makes his story more poignant. There simply aren't too many people like him. He is still the guy most loved, most admired, most charming, most magnetic.

When I called Alex after the accident, I had mixed emotions—pity for him, anger for his plight, depressed about his future. And in true Alex form, he asked me if I wanted to drive Daytona with him. He's gone mad, I thought. And each time I would call, it was the same thing. Once he said my call was very timely. "I was just about to place an order for legs," he said. "How tall do you think I should be this time?" And on one occasion when I spoke to his wife Daniela, she said "Alex isn't home right now; he's always gone; in fact he's carrying on as though he simply had his appendix out. I think the only way he'll slow down is if I kill him."

In his book, Alex tells the whole gripping story: About growing up in a small village in Italy, falling asleep to the hum of his mother's sewing machine, building a model of the Indianapolis Motor Speedway for a school project and his first attempt at technology, which was painting his bicycle red and having his dad weld half-inch pipes onto the sides. He talks about his sister's tragic death when he was only 12, when her boyfriend's Fiat crashed with a BMW. And later, Alex talks about becoming a professional racer, about the business side of racing, about forbidding his father to come to the race track, and about the critics that said he raced with all heart and no brain. He talks candidly about his dealings with people like Chip Ganassi, Mo Nunn, Frank Williams, Eddie Jordan and Michael Schumacher. You find out about two buddies named Filippo and Titano who are responsible for a pile of shenanigans—and also about Alex's closeness 'like a brother' to

Foreword

Jimmy Vasser. Alex talks about marrying Daniela in Las Vegas and about his beloved son, Niccolò. Yes, this is the picture of what it was like for Alex when he was living life on top of the world.

And suddenly the accident, and Alex wakes up without his legs. He tells the story—public and private—about what was going on in that Berlin hospital for a month and a half. He weaves stories about incredible pain with inconceivable humor. You see him tired, humiliated, and then you laugh out loud. You meet the clan who stayed near him for 20 days and clearly find out where his inspiration came from after Berlin. One gent is Sandro, who is married to Daniela's sister. Sandro spends nights in the hospital to help Alex maneuver around the various tubes. The two bicker about a number of things, mostly over who is the better son-in-law. "You're a brown-nose," Sandro says when Alex sweet-talks their mother-in-law.

This book is not only for race fans. It's for people who love to laugh, cry and cheer and who want to know the intimate side of one of racing's most colorful characters. Alex's stories are not about this rotten, unfair thing that happened to him. They are about having the power to adapt to change and about scoring a victory over, rather then becoming a victim of, the accident. Alex admits that new passions have replaced racing, but he still has the makeup of a great driver—one who wins regardless of the conditions. His ultimate battle truly proved him the champion he always had been.

Alex, *caro amico, Ti saluto.*

Mario Andretti
September 2004
Nazareth, Pennsylvania

CHAPTER 1

The Darkest Day

It was the week of September 11, 2001. Tuesday was the day of the terrorist attacks. Like everyone, I was very upset and angry. I remember thinking about the meaning of the word "evil," and how something worse can then happen, forcing you to reconsider it. I kept asking myself, "What can be worse than this?"

I learned of the attacks when, returning to my home in Monaco with my wife Daniela, I found my mother in front of the television staring at the images from New York. I sat there for half an hour, my mouth gaping, almost paralyzed at the sight of the second airplane crashing into the tower. I then took my son Niccolò, put him on my shoulders and walked to the supermarket, just to get away from the horror of watching the tragedy unfold. I sought out my son's eyes, looking for his innocence. My instinct was to run away from what I couldn't bear to see, or didn't want to see; the instinct to survive.

Wednesday I set off for Berlin and to the Luasitzring circuit, where the first of two European rounds of the championship were taking place. The whole of CART was in shock. Under a gray and gloomy sky, we never stopped talking about what had happened in New York. For hours and hours we discussed, "Is it right to race after all that's happened? Should we cancel the race?" In the United States, all sporting events had been suspended out of respect for those who'd lost their lives in the tragedy. "Is it right to race on the other side of the Atlantic?" In the end, we decided that it was best to stand up and fight—there would be no better message to send than this. We decided to put stars and stripes banners on the nose or sides of all the cars, and to hold a minute's silence to honor the victims before the start.

On Thursday we began our first day of practice. It was a great session. My teammate, Brazilian Tony Kanaan, and I were the fastest, which is always good news. But on Friday, while qualifying was determining the starting line-up, it began to rain. When your average speed is 185 mph with peaks of 250 mph on an oval, you don't race if it rains. This means no qualifying, and therefore no front row of the grid. The rules in this situation say that the racer's current ranking in the championship determines the line-up. Not good news, as I would be starting in the 23rd position.

It had been a tough year. After a particularly unhappy season in Formula 1 with Williams in 1999, I'd decided to take some time off. But I soon succumbed to the flattery of Morris Nunn, or "Mo" as he's known in motor racing. He had been my track engineer when I won the CART titles in 1997 and 1998 and became a racing idol in America. Now Mo had his own team and had persuaded me to come back, but to be honest, it was my passion more than his persuasion that ultimately convinced me to return. This was the same passion that I'd had when I first jumped into a kart. But things did not go that well. The team was very young and still needed to learn how to work together while Mo, who was almost 64 years old, was tired and lacking the energy and enthusiasm that he'd once had. And although we appeared to improve in recent races, we had yet to achieve anything notable. We hoped the Lausitzring circuit, which was new to everybody, might represent a sort of turning point. The first practice session proved it might.

The only problem was actually being able to race. Yes, once again it was raining. It was Saturday morning and if the circuit failed to dry in time, they would postpone the race until Sunday. However, the rain stopped and the race was able to begin, despite the foreboding gray skies. We didn't even have time to concentrate on the race before the one-minute's silence. You can't imagine the impression complete silence makes on a place that is usually roaring with noise. The silence, that silence, was unforgettable. The race started, and it finally seemed to be my race as I slowly worked my way towards the front. I could feel the car going faster and steadier, and I loved this feeling of having everything under control. This sense of control, master of my destiny, was the same enjoyment I'd felt during many successful races such as this.

Thirteen laps to go and I was leading. I only had one more refueling stop to go, which was necessary for everybody because of the extremely high pace of the race. We call it a "splash and go"— just a few drops of fuel to finish the race. With all of the team cheering me on, I tore out of the pits. I was certain that there were no more obstacles and while coming out of the pit lane which runs parallel with the circuit, I was thinking, "I've done it!" Then, for some reason, halfway down the strip of asphalt, the car started to spin. I crossed the grass and ended up back on the track, trying to regain control of the spinning vehicle, while the group of cars was coming at me at 210 mph. Then suddenly, the darkness fell.

CHAPTER 2

Childhood Days

Unlike many children, I was never afraid of the dark. For me this was a sort of testimony of my bravery—a weapon to fight my fears and lack of self-confidence. I was a rather chubby child, which also didn't help. For example, whenever my friends played soccer, I was always the last to be chosen. I was so untalented that I eventually decided that it wasn't that soccer didn't like me, but I didn't like soccer! From then on I was always trying to prove my courage, which is the one thing I never lacked. That's why I was always telling everybody that I wasn't afraid of the dark. "With my light-colored eyes," I used to tell my friends, "I can see really well, like a cat." Just to prove my point, I even got a few bumps on my head trying to demonstrate my feline dexterity. I was always a very determined child and have remained equally determined to this day.

I was born in Bologna, Italy. My parents' lives were similar to many other couples in Italy in the 1960s. Although they didn't have a lot of money, they had a great desire to settle down, have a nice home and raise their children—my sister Cristina and me. I wasn't quite four when we moved to Castel Maggiore, a small village on the outskirts of Bologna where life was, and still is, very comfortable. Although I don't have many memories of the first four years in Bologna, I do have a few images that are still fixed in my mind like photographs. We used to live in a fourth floor flat in a very nice area called Casaglia, at the bottom of the hill just above an area called Saragozza. Even at this age, I was already heedless. For example, I was obsessed with missiles. To me, any object could be transformed into a missile. One day, a lady came up to our flat carrying a tuna fish can. She knocked on our door and said to my mother, "This must be yours—it just missed my head by an inch!" Until I was three, I drank sugar water from a baby's bottle before going to sleep, a habit which my mother tried desperately to make me stop. One day, unable to find any other missile, I threw the bottle from the window. My mother yelled, "What are you going to do now?" and I replied quietly, "I'll simply drink from a glass."

Back then, we didn't watch television, but instead enjoyed socializing at the local bar. There was one bar just below our house with an old-fashioned platform scale outside. Everyone used to go there, including the local drunk who was in the scrap business and carried around a load of junk in his horse-drawn cart. The bartender always complained about the man parking his cart on the weighing machine, so one night my father and his friends came up with a fantastic prank. My dad, a plumber, had a welding kit in his car. So he and his friends quietly welded the horse's shoes to the weighing bridge. When the drunken old man came out of the bar, he jumped on the cart and starting shouting, "Giddyup!" The horse just wouldn't move. As a crowd gathered, the old man explained, "Oh, he's just so stubborn!" He then jumped off the cart, set fire to some newspaper and held it under the poor horse's belly while the horse struggled to free its hooves from the scale.

Another time, a man came to the bar riding a Demm, a small motorbike on which the engine cylinders are mounted at a 45-degree angle. While the motorcyclist enjoyed a glass of red wine in the bar, the locals, returning from a hunt, took out his spark plugs and put some gunpowder in the engine. The drunken motorcyclist staggered out of the bar, jumped on his bike and said goodbye. But as soon as he hit the ignition, there was a huge explosion. Engine parts were flung everywhere. He stood in disbelief, saying, "My God, My God, it backfired!" They were in fits of laughter.

My mother, Anna, was a seamstress and a housewife. She learned how to sew from her mother and her aunt—a job that allowed her to work from home. The house was always full of clients coming for fittings. I remember she used to put us to bed and I would fall asleep to the humming of her sewing machine. She started very early in the morning, especially on Tuesdays when she would make the button holes and sew buttons on the shirts that she had prepared the day before. She had to do this by hand, which took ages, so she started working at four am. Quite often I would wake up and see her sewing away under the glow of a small bulb in her room. I would go to her, carrying a blanket, and she would arrange two chairs to form a little bed for me and sing a lullaby until I fell asleep again, my head on her lap while she kept working.

My father, Dino, was a terrific man. He's no longer alive, but worked just as hard as my mother. Many times I woke up to go to school and he'd already gone to work and often I would go to bed at night and he'd still not be home. He was always teasing my mother, who was very gullible. He was always trying to wind her up, and to be fair, she took it quite well. I can remember a story about a cuckoo telephone. My mom had a friend who was always bragging about her telephone which was red instead of being beige like other people's. My father said, "Well, I've got a friend whose phone makes a cuckoo sound instead of a ring." My mother immediately told her friend about the cuckoo phone. My dad and I couldn't stop laughing about it, but they loved each other very much. They got married before dad left for the army. They didn't get married in order to leave home, but because dad was going into the army, my mother had to go straight from her family's home to my father's.

We moved to Castel Maggiore when I was almost four years old. My sister and I attended the local nursery but she was miserable there. My mother, who always treated us equally, pulled us both out of nursery, which is a shame because I quite liked the food. The nuns gave their affection to the children with the biggest appetites, so naturally I was well looked-after. Despite being a somewhat reckless child, I was very easy-going and independent. I used to play by myself and wasn't afraid of trying something new.

A few days after we moved in, a little girl who lived in our building invited me to a party at her grandmother's who lived around the corner on a busy street. I thought the girl would still be there the following day, so I set off on my tricycle to find her. But at a certain point I got lost, turning left instead of right. I ended up in the next town, which was nearly a mile away. After pushing the tricycle for more than an hour, I was in floods of tears. Fortunately, I managed to explain to someone where I lived and they took me home. My mother was busy sewing and had thought I was with my father, while my father was out in the garden and thought I was in the house with my mother. My first great adventure, and they didn't even realize I was gone.

Then came the courtyard years. It's such a shame that my son will never experience the joy of playing freely outside. As in all big cities today, you can no longer leave your children alone outside, not even in the summertime. But years ago you would always see children wandering around the area and playing in the courtyards of the flats. After school, you had dinner and then ran downstairs to play with the neighborhood children. Every day we tried something new, building small cabins, climbing trees and hurdling wire fences. It was a world with no borders, despite being geographically small. The end of my road was my own Pillars of Hercules, beyond which no one would venture. The inhabitants of that world were my best friends. Alberto was my closest friend, even if we often fought over a beautiful girl named Roberta. Then there was Lorenzo whom I used to greet with a Tarzan cry, and Gianluca, who had an enviable two boxes full of Lego toys. In fact, I could often be found at his house building strange airplanes. I didn't have many toys and the few that I had, I didn't take good care of. One time my grandfather gave me a toy motorbike with a wind-up rear wheel and my first thought was to take a screwdriver and open it up, just to see how it worked. Poor Grandpa, he wasn't too happy about that.

We met at the following places in town: the school, the courtyard and the cinema. On Sunday afternoons, we always went to my favorite cinema, The Rivoli. If the film starred Terence Hill and Bud Spencer, it was a particularly special day. I was seated in the front row, close to the central aisle. I liked the idea of being in front of everybody else and no one next to me. Perhaps I was already dreaming of being in that pole position, who knows, but I do know that it was a wonderful feeling. I remember one Sunday, when they were showing *Taxi Driver* starring Robert De Niro. The film was rated unsuitable for anyone under the age of 14, so I couldn't get in. That was a miserable afternoon; my father was out fishing with friends, my mother was working, and nobody was in the courtyard. All of the shutters were closed which meant that the kids were probably out with their parents, or visiting their grandparents, or doing something else wonderful. I wandered around feeling miserable with not a clue what to do. I soon found myself sitting in a small garden that was directly behind our building, twiddling with a stone and stick. I looked around and remember vividly the feeling of desolation, emptiness and silence. At that moment I decided that in the future, I was going to travel. I was only eight years old, but I knew that whatever I did in my life, I would have to see the world.

My sister Cristina was just over two years older than me. She was very mature for her age, and certainly more mature than me. At ten she was already organized, responsible and able to multi-task. She was also very good in school and in sports, even qualifying for the Olympic swim team trials. She was naturally talented, and I must admit that I was a bit envious. My parents constantly compared us which was very distressing. But overall I had a wonderful childhood, despite the annoying comparisons between my sister and me. Unlike her, I was a bit of rascal who knew how to use my charm to gain forgiveness for a very long list of naughty deeds. But eventually I got my comeuppance and had to pay for all the trouble I was causing. At times I was smacked. My sister, on the other hand, was much more serious, balanced and charismatic than I was. She had loads of friends who would always seek her advice and support. She was very influential and her friends respected her enormously. I'd always wished that my friends respected me in the same way, but there was simply no comparison. She stood out in every way.

Given our age difference, she was also the first to start any new activity, which I then had to take on as well. She was a very good swimmer, so I had to swim too. But I wasn't interested. I remember diving into the pool in Castel Maggiore and sinking. My belly scraped the bottom and I swam along like this for ten yards or so, ignoring the instructors who were yelling at me. Nonetheless, swimming gave me my first character-building experience at the mere age of five. One night after my first swimming lesson, I interrupted the grown-ups' conversation with a proud, "I can swim too!" My father said, "That's not possible, you've only just had your first lesson today." "Oh yeah," I said, "well I can swim without a life vest too, I swear." Actually, the swimming instructor gave me a deflated life vest at the end of the lesson, and I still managed to float. As soon as I got home, I was determined to tell this story, being the show-off that I was, and I wanted to prove to my family that I could swim. My father said simply, "OK then, tomorrow I'll come and see you," and he did. At the beginning of the lesson, I went to the instructor, Roberta, and told her that I didn't want the life vest. "But you need it," she said. "No, the life vest you gave me yesterday was deflated so I could have managed without it." So while my father looked on, I dived in, swam for three or four yards then started to sink, arms flailing like mad. I came back up huffing and puffing, then went back down again, and finally re-emerged and started to swim without any problem. From that day on, I've never needed a life vest. Just to prove something to my father, I accomplished this minor feat without a moment's hesitation. My father laughed a lot about this incident, but I can imagine that he must have been very proud. Now that I'm a father, I think about how my father must have felt that day and am always moved when I see my son do something special.

I was starting to discover just how determined I was. All I needed was a spark of inspiration and I could do almost anything. But the flip side was that I lost interest easily. The following day, without my father to challenge me, I completely lost interest in swimming. A few months later I was told to swim two lengths of the pool doing the crawl, two lengths of backstroke, two lengths of breaststroke and two of butterfly. But I had to do it my own way, one breaststroke, one crawl, and then a few butterfly strokes. "What the hell are you doing?" the instructor asked. "Mixed style!" I replied, making them all laugh. I didn't like sports much, other than making an occasional effort at school. Once I took part in the cross-country competition and finished in the first 50 out of 300 by taking a huge shortcut. Not surprisingly, as soon as I arrived home I bragged about my results. My parents, desperate for me to be good in sports, immediately went out and bought me a pair of extra-light running shoes—quite a luxury back then. I felt terrible that they sacrificed so much to buy me an expensive pair of shoes when in fact, it was all in vain … at least until karting came along.

The only sporting event that I liked to watch on television was the Formula 1 Grand Prix. My father was a big fan and we used to watch the races together. I tried to build a go-kart with pipes, some discarded wheels and other items stolen from his garage. But no joy—instead, I created a vaguely square-shaped thing with four holes drilled in for the wheels. I had always been ingenious and several years earlier, I had built a wagon using roller skates, wood and nails, which I then had our dog, Mita, pull behind her. By dangling a steak at the end of a fishing rod in front of her nose, I was able to sit in the back and get a free ride. But poor Mita was exhausted by the experiment, so I gave her the steak anyway and went on to invent something new.

At school, for example, I used to build complicated toys. While my schoolmates were busy making puppets and houses, I made a model of the Indianapolis racetrack, equipped with the pits and tower and which my mother still has today. I've always been good with my hands, and for a short time applied this to bicycles. I'd go to a junk dealer and with my savings, buy a few Graziella bikes that I rebuilt and repainted. Things got even better when they started selling longer saddles for mopeds, especially for the *Ciao* model. My sister put one on her moped and started carrying her friends around. But after several fines, my father made her dismantle it. I'd been eyeing that seat for a long time, so I surreptitiously put it on my fire-red bicycle with half-inch pipes on the hubs and *TGM* stickers on the side. I rode my bike to school and it was the envy of all my friends, and yet it was just a Graziella. These technological adventures of mine had quite a high rate of failure, but it didn't stop me taking advantage of my father's garage full of equipment and his skill on the welding machine. The best bikes were those that I made myself, with the exception of the very first one, which I joyfully found parked next to my bed on my fifth birthday.

I was a real rascal and if my parents had had to take out insurance on me and my many escapades, it would have cost them dearly. For example, when I was eight years old, I climbed the façade of the building in front of our house—all the way up to the fourth floor—just to see my friend Gianluca's sister, Elisabetta. I climbed up the window awning and her mother only found out once I was on my way back down. She immediately called my mother who could not believe her eyes as I was hanging on the wall, like a spider.

I was 12 years old when my sister had the accident. She was 15 years old and attending high school in Bologna. All of her hopes and ambitions were quashed—first by getting mononucleosis, and then by breaking her thighbone on a moped, thus obliterating any hopes of a sporting career. She continued swimming, but was no longer thinking about going professional. She was dating a nice fellow named Maurizio, although I hated it when he came over and our room became "off-limits." They had been dating for two or three years and he often came to our house. My mother adored him and although my father tried to play the tough guy, he liked him too. One night, Maurizio and Cristina went out for an ice cream. On the way to the cafe, they ran into a friend who had just got his driving license and they decided to go together in his Fiat 127 to see a sick friend. "She'll be glad to see us," they said. They never saw her. They had an accident and Maurizio and Cristina both tragically died.

It was never really clear what happened but it appears that a BMW had stopped at a filling station and while pulling out, cut in front of the oncoming Fiat. The speed limit was 30 mph and the Fiat was probably doing more than this. The boy who was driving the Fiat survived, but has never got over what happened. He was full of remorse and still is, and sadly nobody has really been able to help him move on in life. These are the kind of things that can happen when you're 18 years old; usually everything goes well, but there is a high price to pay when things go terribly wrong.

I can remember the night that Cristina died all too well. It was October 1, 1979, and while I was asleep, a neighbor came by and said, "Look, there's been an accident. I've stopped by … and hope it's not true, but I think Cristina may be involved." Another neighbor came over to look after me while my parents started going around the hospitals. There was no computer network like they have today and they searched all night long. The last place they went to was the morgue where they found Cristina, waiting to be identified. When they came home, I woke up and will never forget what I saw. My mother was like a mummy, she didn't talk, she didn't cry, she didn't react. She just sat in a daze. Meanwhile, my father was wailing—his desperate cries waking me out of bed.

I was just a child and didn't know how to deal with such a tragedy. As paradoxical as it may seem, I didn't miss my sister until much later. It was this bitter twist of fate that pushed me into kart racing. After the accident, my parents became extremely overprotective. They probably thought that sooner or later something would happen to their only other child, who was much more restless than his sister had ever been. When I was a child, I was always covered with cuts and bruises or getting bumps on the head. I was absolutely fearless and tried desperately to keep their spirits up after the accident. But in fact their suffering confused me; they would try to behave as normally as possible, but inside the pain was clearly insurmountable. Now that I understand what really happened it is too painful for me to even think about. I was 12 years old and I stopped everything that I was doing—I no longer went out on my bike with my friends because I knew that my parents were living in constant fear of losing me. I wanted to find something to ease their pain—to help them put things back together again. Soon after that, the kart arrived.

CHAPTER 3

Getting Started in Karts

My father had a *Si*, one of the mopeds which were really popular at the time. Returning from Bologna, he was passed by four guys so quickly that he decided to stop in the village garage, which was run by an old childhood friend. The garage sign said, "Bonini Engines and Modification." There was a wonderful ad on Radio Bologna: "Vroom, vroom—what a sound, listen to the roar of the engines with Bonini Engines and Modifications." The modifications went on until the police stopped by and arrested a few kids with illegally modified mopeds. After the kids admitted that the mopeds had been tampered with, he changed the sign to simply "Bonini Engines." When my father popped into Bonini's shop to see if it was possible to boost up the *Si* he immediately caught sight of a go-kart. A boy named Glauco, who later became a friend of mine, had bought the kart and was keeping it in the shop while his grandfather sponsored him, not telling his father. My father was immediately curious about it, and Bonini teased him a bit and then suggested, "Why don't you buy one for your son?" My father replied abruptly, "Are you crazy? It's too dangerous." Bonini replied, "Dangerous? Isn't it better to let off steam on a racetrack? Not only that, but it comes with a helmet and overalls, everyone is going in the same direction, and you don't have to worry about little old ladies crossing the road." He then concluded, "You can buy it as an alternative to the moped and also spend the weekend camping with your son." I imagine that my father tried to be rational about it but couldn't resist the idea because as soon as he arrived home, he suggested the exchange. I agreed without giving it a second's thought. A kart! I was in seventh heaven with this kart. It was April 1980 and I was not yet 14 years old.

Starting out in racing was traumatic, even before I touched the steering wheel. Out of curiosity, my father and I immediately bought *Autosprint* magazine to look for a race in the area. There was one near Parma, at San Pancrazio. When we arrived, the drivers were already at the starting grid. We sat down in the front of the bend, the green flag went up and suddenly the drivers were coming towards us at an incredible speed. But, to my amazement, they managed to turn, miss hitting me and quickly take the corner. I jumped out of my seat—it seemed unbelievable. "I would never go that fast," I said to myself. "After all, I just want to have fun." The whole world of driving seemed so alien to me.

We actually had to wait three months for that beloved kart, which was torture for a young boy. Bonini didn't actually sell karts so we had to order ours from Mr. Buratti who owned a garage in town. Every time we called to find out what was happening, he answered, "I should have it next week." I couldn't sleep at night. I remember it was July and my father was joining us on holiday, having promised to bring the kart if it arrived. I was so disappointed when I ran to his van, opened the door and didn't find it in there. Finally, Buratti called Bonini to tell him that the kart had arrived. The next day we set off to collect it with every intention of testing it on the new track in Vado, near Sasso Marconi. It was the morning of August 2, 1980—the day of the terrorist attack in Bologna in which 80 people died. We were trying to reach the garage, but we couldn't. There were policemen and roadblocks everywhere, and we didn't understand why. It seemed that I would never get my hands on that damned kart. My father took a very long detour and entered the city from the other side, and we finally found Buratti's. Only later, while going to the circuit, did we hear on the radio what had happened. The irony is that one of the best days of my life fell on that tragic day in Bologna. When we heard the news about the massacre, my father was in shock, but I couldn't get my head around the enormity of what had happened. Still a child at 13 years old, I was not yet capable of comprehending events such as this. All I was thinking about was the kart. My happiness was uncontrollable and I wouldn't let anything get in the way. Only years later did I understand why we shouldn't forget that day in Bologna.

I can still remember the red and white curbs on the first bend of the track in Vado, whizzing by at remarkable speed. Glauco already had his kart, the one left with Bonini. My kart arrived with one for Dante and Massimo, who were the sons of the local baker. From then on, the four of us raced together. We later became known as Team *Sfighé*—the unlucky team—as christened by my father. My father was crazy about boats—rubber dinghies to be exact. But when we needed something to haul the karts, he sold all his boats and let us use his old boat trailer.

I made a very unusual debut on the track. I went so slowly around the corners that my engine kept cutting out. This was due to the excitement of it all, and the fact that in my mind, I was already going fast enough, but then "Bonny," the team's nickname for Bonini, offered to take the kart for a few laps and test out the carburetor. Given that he used to race professionally, he was the expert, and I respected him for this, but when I saw him take the curves with such incredible speed and finesse, I admired him even more. As soon as he stepped out of the kart, I said to myself, "Good Lord, I wonder if I'll ever be able to go as fast as him." Then I looked at my kart and realized, "Boy, this kart can really move!" My first confrontation with speed had completely caught me off guard. Before that, I had only been on a bicycle. If on that day, someone were to predict which of the four of us was to become a professional driver, the driver who would pass on the Corkscrew at Laguna Seca or go from last to first at Long Beach and Cleveland, they certainly wouldn't have chosen me.

Although it was a very clumsy beginning, it was the start of my extraordinary adventure. As soon as I sat behind that steering wheel for the first time, I was breathless from the excitement. From that moment on, I decided that I wanted to be a driver, which probably sounds ridiculous given the way the day was unfolding. Although I was going very slowly, I ended up outside the track lanes whenever I tried to push it, but despite this disaster, there were no limitations in my head, just an unyielding optimism that I could become one of the greats. But this attitude shouldn't be surprising, given how my entire career has been characterized by stubbornness. To believe in this fantasy—that I could become a great driver—was my life's manifesto. Even the most voracious of dreamers would have buckled in the face of such disappointment. Instead, while tens of karts were passing me, I had only one thought, "Go, go. I will soon catch up with you all!"

Under the house there was a very large garage where we kept all the karts. Dante and Massimo were real characters, twins who looked nothing alike and could have walked right out of a Fellini film. They were a couple of years older—and several pounds heavier—than me and although this initially intimidated me, we soon became inseparable. As soon as they finished their bakery deliveries, they would race to my house in their pokey three-wheeled delivery van. Our flat was on the upper floor and during the summer the door to the garden was always open. The twins would be going so fast that I could hear the noise of their engine, the screech of their brakes and their squeaky wheels from down the road. This would announce that they were on their way and indeed a few seconds later, I would hear their horn. "Sandro, come open the garage!" Even though they worked all night at the bakery, they'd still show up. Each one of us would start cleaning and tinkering with the karts—it was wonderful. I was always there, polishing, attaching stickers and moving the banners. I didn't even treat my wife this well! My garage was the center of my world. It was summer, school was over and the morning would fly by between my regular chores and helping my mother. It was all about that.

The Public Ambulance sponsored our first race. Given the risks involved in racing, we should have touched our balls (what Italian men do for good luck) when asking what was involved with the sponsorship—perhaps CPR and IVs! All four of us, Team *Sfighé*, were together at the track at Vado. At that time there were six racing categories at the national levels: three for 125cc karts with single gear, 100cc engine size, and three for karts with gears and clutch. It wasn't a formal rule, but it was common knowledge that the single-gear category was more challenging than the 125cc. Each mistake without a gear would cost you dearly, but as a consequence it would teach you something. In addition, it would create a natural selection between those who had talent and those who didn't. Therefore the norm was to try to get by in the 100cc category, starting in the *Cadetti* class (which was for very young drivers), or go directly into the *Nazionale* class (senior class) for older drivers like me. It wasn't possible to get a permit to start directly in the *100 Avenir*, which was the arrival point at the national level. You could only access this level by achieving exceptionally good results in either *Cadetti* or *Nazionale*.

The various categories were basically similar, only differing in the following ways: engine performance level, the diameter of the carburetor, and most importantly, the tires. *Cadetti* tires were hard with a narrow section; *Nazionale* tires were a bit larger and softer; while those for the *100 Avenir*, to the eyes of a young child like me, seemed incredibly huge and ferocious. Generally, there were more drivers participating in the 100cc category than in the 125cc. Drivers would upgrade to the 125cc only if they wanted to take it easy, or if they didn't want to watch their weight. In the 100cc, you needed to be almost as light as a jockey, which was ultimately the reason that Dante changed class, but that is another story.

Going back to that day at Vado, the race wasn't organized on the basis of the categories, but into two simple groupings, A and B. The alphabetical order would suggest the opposite, but in reality, "A" stood for "amateurs" (the Sunday drivers without permits) and "B," in the Bolognese way, stood for the "Best." Once we told my father this, he famously replied, "OK, then today we will see what category you actually belong to." Then he went on to explain, "The best are divided into three groups, the best, the almost best and the best compared to nothing." We burst out laughing, but I must admit that I was also very nervous. Regardless of the fact that he was only joking, I remember the impact this statement had on me. I was more nervous during that first silly race than during any of my future important races. In addition to all this pressure, I almost missed the chance to race because of a broken brake disc. We didn't have a spare and there wasn't time to get a replacement. The only reason that I was able to race was because Glauco, who was the fastest of us four in the qualification, didn't make the final. Glauco got into an argument with his mechanic (Bonini's son) and ended up slapping him. Bonini's son got revenge by dismantling Glauco's engine. At that point, Glauco came to me and said, "Oh, he's really pissed off. He took it really badly, so if you want to use my kart frame, I don't need it anymore." I raced and finished ninth. "Not too bad, not too good," my father said to me when I finished the race.

That Sunday, we met a very funny tire dealer whom we later nicknamed Corazon. He raced in 125cc and had a very strong local accent. With the help of his Spanish girlfriend, he always repeated the Spanish saying, "In the straight, I have no water in the heart." What he meant was that in the straight part of the racetrack, his ability (I still wonder what that was) allowed him to accelerate at full speed, but on the corners he was admittedly slow. He was the one who let us know about the following race at Fossa, a small town near Modena. "Come to Fossa on Sunday," he said, "It's a nice town track, and you even get a prosciutto ham if you win." The race would take place at night and the track was in the town square which only had two street lamps. The organizers decided to make the track more exciting by adding two chicanes near the streetlights. As it was the only place where you could see properly, it was incredibly dangerous and a miracle that nobody got seriously hurt. A driver in the 125cc senior class crashed into one of the streetlights after hitting one of the other karts. He wasn't hurt, but his kart certainly was—it was less than a yard long after impact! I managed to come in fourth (out of five) in my class and brought home the first trophy of my career. It was sponsored by the Salvioli Bakery and had a plaque saying "Fossa Country Fair, '80." This was the Holy Grail of my career. Since then, I've kept it right in the middle of all the other trophies as my most prized possession.

I completed numerous trials at Vado with a kart that was really badly treated by a variety of incompetent people. We got into racing without any specific knowledge or experience and simply treated the kart like a car. One after another, family and friends used the kart. After numerous off-road excursions and a variety of heavy loads, the frame started to show signs of cracking. We went all the way to the manufacturer in Milan to complain to the DAP factory. After listening to us rant for an hour, the factory owner looked at us in complete awe. Only later did I realize that his look was something between disbelief and compassion. There he had a group of complete idiots standing in front of him who had absolutely no clue as to what they were talking about. He got so fed up with trying to understand us that he yelled, "What the hell, give them a new frame—I can't stand it anymore." They replaced it with a new frame, and also threw in some new tires. I had only changed one tire the entire season. It was one of the rear tires which was in such a poor condition that I returned to the dealer explaining, "The tire must be faulty—look how bald it is already." He just stood there shaking his head in disbelief. "It's useless to try and explain—you wouldn't even begin to understand!" He exchanged the tires just to get rid of us.

I spent a lot of time racing with Dante who, by the way, had a little stammer. He was always up for a challenge, "C-c-come on, Ale-Alessandro, le-let's go five r-r-rounds and whoever arr-arrives first wi-wins." "You're on," I replied. As soon as we took off, I would get in Dante's slipstream, and then overtake him on the next curve. He would accelerate in an attempt to pass from the outside and end up in the grass every time. It was hilarious. I would stop in the middle of the track and say to him, "Dante, what are you doing?" And he would reply angrily, "Ale-Alessandro, if I ca-ca-catch you…!" My father would try to calm him down by saying, "You challenged him, so why should Sandro let you pass?" Dante replied angelically, "Because we-we are fr-friends." During this period we were like wild horses, running about freely. This freedom helped me a lot; I taught myself how to race, and more importantly, how to be in control of a situation. I was soon able to tackle problems logically and with a strength that doesn't come from a textbook or an expert. Whereas others relied on family or a racing friend, we only had my father. We thought we knew all there was to know, but actually we didn't know anything at all.

A clear example of this was during our third race. It was late October when we showed up at a rather important industrial tournament in Parma. Only Dante and I were racing this time. We came in last and second to last in the trials, so when it came to the final, we ended up racing against each other. All of the other drivers lapped us about thirty times, but it didn't matter to us. Just as it didn't matter that our opponents had luxurious caravans and trailers while we only had our second-hand boat trailer. The only thing that mattered to me was seeing Dante in the last bend of the last lap. This was obviously not for the ranking, but was merely to have a good laugh with friends while recounting the expression on his big face as I passed him. For him everything turned into a joke, and his version of the race would always end up, "I wa-was al-almost at the fi-fi-finish line and this bas-bastard zi-zipped up from behind!" He was always pretending that he wanted to beat me. These were such happy times and some of the best moments of my career. Everything would surprise us. The day before the race, we went to the checkpoint to scrutinize the kart and they asked us for the spare engine's serial number. "What? Since when can you have a spare engine?" We were so naïve. I still had the same set of tires that I'd bought in August! And then there was Dante—he was a story in himself. We arrived in Parma on Saturday afternoon when he was still on a "double"—a double shift making bread at the bakery—and hadn't slept a wink. On the Friday, knowing what was in store for him, he arrived at my place with a leather cushion that he had stolen from his mother's sofa. He attached it to his kart seat explaining, "In Parma, I want to be comfortable." But he was now too close to the steering wheel—almost stuck to it—and couldn't drive. He adjusted the seat, tweaking the attachments. As a result, once on the track and he'd reached the straight, his bum ended up scraping the asphalt. Trying to accelerate, Dante sunk even further into his seat with the big leather cushion while the kart would stop and go, dragging forward inch by inch. We caught up with him at the end of the straight and he started shouting, "Di-dino, wh-what did you do t-to my cl-clutch?" Obviously we all knew that there were no clutches on those karts. Once again one of us was trying to hide our complete lack of experience.

Usually before the race, my father would tune the engine by using a needle valve on the carburetor; turning it one way made the mixture lean, and the other way made it rich. As a starting point he would always run the engine rich to avoid seizing it. He would stand at the end of the main straight, saying, "If you pass me and I'm waving my hands, it means that the mixture is lean, therefore open the screw. If I give you an OK sign, that means it is fine, and if I wave a yellow rag [to be honest it was the size of a double bedsheet] the mixture is too rich and you'll need to tighten the screw." During the first lap he waved the yellow rag, so I tightened the screw. On the second lap it was fine and he gave me the OK. My father waved the yellow rag at Dante but he looked the other way. Each lap, he did the same thing. At the end of the race my father came running towards Dante, shouting and swearing, "I was waving at you and you just ignored me, you damn idiot!" Dante replied, "I did see you but I c-c-couldn't remember wh-which way to t-t-urn the screw." Poor Dante. Among all of these professionals, we were so naïve and foolish.

All four of us showed up at the fourth meeting at Jesolo, which was another important race. My father immediately said, "You should go one at time to test out the track. I have to look after four karts, so take it easy. Don't cause any trouble and please, don't give me any extra work to do. I'll call each one of you into the paddock, make the proper adjustments and then you can go for it." Great—everybody agreed. There was a very nice fellow named Arvedo who, despite having a limp from a childhood illness, helped everyone push off. Ironically he called himself the "official pusher." The kart, in fact, didn't have a clutch or gears so we had to push-start it by lifting the back off the ground. At that point, the driver jumped in, accelerated and took off. Anyway, Arvedo helped Dante push off first, but after a few seconds he came running back to my father, his voice trembling, "Dino, Dino—Dante has capsized!" We all laughed at his choice of words. Actually Dante had flipped into the tire barrier, destroying the kart. "I l-lost control of the kart," he explained. He was such a mess. He was trying to be careful, but in reality he was pushing it way too much.

Each race was a hilarious adventure. The main characters were always the same, the four of us and my father. Dante and Massimo's father was never there because he worked all week in the bakery and rested on Sunday. He did show up once—in Vado—and decided to tweak his sons' kart. Dante ran up to me saying, "San-

Sandrooo, look how well my-my fa-father has tuned the throttle cable!" It was tight as a string. I asked, "Isn't it a bit too tight?" He replied, "Come on, it's perfect—it's more responsive this way!" Well indeed it was because during the parade lap, we were all in a single file when suddenly I saw someone shoot by like a human bullet. It was Dante, of course. The throttle jammed fully opened and he spun out, so he got out to push-start the kart but it shot off with him hanging on the bumper like in a cartoon. Jumping and bouncing out of control, he crossed the track in the middle of the starting line-up. For the Team *Sfighé,* the Unlucky Team, these were normal events.

There was also the story of the numbers. I was number 3, Massimo was number 7 like his idol Barry Sheene, Glauco was number 12, and Dante (eventually) was number 61. For fun, he had originally given himself the number "69." His kart was the last on the trailer—the one that motorists saw on the motorway. During one of our first outings, we stopped at a roadside café when my father saw this number 69 hanging out the back of the trailer. In those days, people were much more prudish. Dad got so angry that he ripped off the nine, which was made out of tape, and made a number 61. Since then, Dante has raced as number 61.

My father was a robust man and proudly defined himself as a monster. He was 5 feet, 9 inches tall and 198 pounds of pure muscle. Years of tightening small pipes with a wrench sculpted his impressive physique. One day a doctor diagnosed him with tendonitis (tennis elbow). The doctor asked him, "Do you play tennis a lot?" Thirty years ago tennis was an elite sport, so you can imagine my father's reaction. He couldn't stop laughing. "What do you mean, tennis, doctor?" he said. "This is from hard manual labor." He recounted the story saying, "Oh, kids, can you believe that doctor called me a tennis player?!" My father had beautiful, intense green eyes, was terribly charismatic and always had a huge smile on his face. Because of his unorthodox approach to managing the karts, I gave him the name "*Grezzo* (rough) Man." He even applied his plumbing techniques to his management, "It doesn't matter if the toilet is a quarter-inch to the left or a quarter-inch to the right, you can still do your business in it." But in motor racing, where every quarter-inch is crucial, precision makes a difference. That's not to say he wasn't efficient. For example, he would cover the kart with chicken wire, which was extremely useful in case of a crash—not very elegant, but very resilient. Even better, sometimes the wire would accidentally puncture our opponent's tires and work to our amused advantage!

You didn't need to see my father's muscles to get a sense of his strength. He was one of those men of whom you immediately thought, "Better not mess with him." But he never took advantage of his size unless he was provoked. It was easy to get in arguments while racing, but my father always tried to stay out of it. I was the runt of the group, but Dante and Massimo were not afraid of anybody; in fact, I think they liked looking for trouble. Massimo was the worst and had a terrible mean streak. While in Vado, Dante got in an argument with someone from Ferrara. This guy was quite big and therefore Dante was careful not to mess with him. When Massimo arrived he said, "I'll deal with him. You go get me an ice cream." Massimo beat up the guy and was pissed off at his brother when he returned without his ice cream. He would have beaten him up too if he wasn't his brother. But if anything got out of control, my father would always intervene to calm the situation. One day, once again in Vado, I was driving rather slowly. When this happens in the kart, you go to the side and indicate with one finger that the others can pass. There was a driver behind me who was obviously less experienced and assumed I was trying to change lanes. He ended spinning out and was furious. He was 30 years old and I was just a kid, so he started threatening me, "You'll never make it home—I'll teach you and your family a lesson." He wouldn't shut up. He just went on threatening me until my father arrived. He put his hand on the guy's shoulder and said, "If my son has done something stupid, I'm the first one to tell him that he's an idiot, but *I'm* his family, so you'd better think twice about what you're saying." He immediately changed his attitude.

For a couple of years, things went on like this. But I was getting older and more established. I was now the best driver in the group and was showing the greatest potential. Maybe Glauco could have made it if he'd had a father like mine, maybe even Dante and Massimo … who knows. But by the end of 1981, I was really fast. Once again there was the Public Ambulance-sponsored race in Vado and like the previous year, the only two 100cc categories were the A and B classes. Just my dad and I went to the race, sharing the same kart. I won the *100 Avenir B* ("The Best") class even though my starts weren't very good. Thanks to a timing error, my father was in pole position. He delighted in telling me, "Today I'm going to show you how to start the race." He was first off the grid and ended up blocking everyone else from passing and won the *100 Avenir A* ("The Amateurs"). My father would take up the whole track and shove off anyone who tried to pass him.

There was an old man who lived nearby who hated the noise from the track. But he liked my father a lot because he would always bring him a bottle of Pignoletto, a white wine from Bologna. There were people who would take the entire week off to practice and test karts. The old man, tipsy from the wine, would tell them, "Look, you've been here for a week making a racket and being a pain in the ass, and here these two have just arrived this morning and have won everything—with the same car!" while toasting the Zanardi family. Calling the kart a car, with his heavy dialect, made us all laugh.

Anyway, I was becoming really competitive and having more and more arguments with my father. I had the utmost respect for him, but there were moments in which I hated him. Maybe hate isn't the right word, but he could be tricky. My father was adored by everybody and always made people laugh. He was a charmer and an entertainer, but with me he could be very demanding. Together with the fun there were also the demands of racing. For example, at the end of each race I had to clean and organize all the tools, polishing one wrench at a time. "Can't I do it tomorrow?" I would ask. My father would reply, "No, it has to be done now." Although he pissed me off, he taught me to have rules and principles—without which I would be unfocused and irresponsible. His attitude caused quite a few arguments and more than once I said myself, "That's enough, I'm going to quit." He was always reminding me that I should be grateful to him. It's true that he did a lot for me, but it came at a price. Nevertheless, he was a very good father. He bought the kart as an alternative to the moped, but one of these also came later, as did a motorbike and then a new car. Even when I flipped the car after only having it a month, he had it repaired by his friend Mauro, a mechanic with a great talent for telling jokes, and who is still a friend today.

Time heals everything. After my sister's accident, my life was influenced by my parents' fear of losing me. The kart enabled me to let off steam but was something that they could use to control me. While the others were going to the disco, I never asked my father if I could go because I hated to see the pain and sadness in his eyes when he said no. I would often come home on a Saturday night after a long day at the track and then get ready for the race the next day. I'd find my friends at the bar, all decked out in their white trousers that were so popular at the time, and on their mopeds for the evening. I really fancied the thought of that lifestyle, but not having a social life was the price to pay for the trauma that had hit my family, as well the sacrifice of wanting to do something with all my heart and soul as I did. I took this passion for granted and was unaware that people envied me.

My mother followed us everywhere. She was responsible for keeping time, preparing food and organizing our accommodation. She never looked particularly annoyed or anxious while I was racing. We were very similar and both were a bit impulsive and daring. She became the point person for Team *Sfighé*, not only for her timekeeping, but she'd also keep an eye on the competition. She was able to spot where we were losing ground and where we improved. I remember one of the few times that she didn't come with us. I remember it because we saw a pig on the motorway. Seriously, it was in the fast lane. We were going to Siena in our van and suddenly when we were going downhill. My father said, "Did you see a pig?" I had heard so many jokes from him I just dismissed it, assuming that it was just another one. Then, right before my eyes, we passed an enormous sow. Further down the road, we saw three fellows with ropes and lassos going in reverse on the emergency lane. They stopped and asked us, "Have you by any chance seen a pig?" It felt like we were in the Middle Ages.

In 1982 I made a huge leap and started racing at a completely different level. I was third in the Italian championships for the *100 Nazionale* at Parma. I went from a complete unknown to one of the key drivers and won several races in Jesolo and other places. I would still see Dante, Massimo and Glauco, but we started to go separate ways. I was taking my game to a professional level, but unfortunately they couldn't keep up with the time and money demands. The twins were busy with the bakery and Glauco was broke. His grandfather realized that keeping a kart "was more expensive than fattening a pig with biscuits." In addition to this, Glauco was in school in Germany. His father worked with a German firm and wanted him to learn the language. Sometimes I'd run into Dante who, being very big, had changed classes. I was on a diet because I'd got a bit chubby. I was almost overweight as a teenager but thanks to my will power, I was now fit instead of fat. I became taller and lost a lot of weight for the love of that kart. I ate very little, which I would have never done for any other reason.

After middle school, I went to a private technical school. My parents made the decision because they knew the head of the school. The headmaster convinced my parents that "even though I didn't have any catch-up to do, they could keep an eye on me and get me to take my exam at the end of each year." My parents thought this was a good thing, but I couldn't care less. I was hanging around with a group of guys who didn't want to study either. Because of this I wasted a lot of time and now wish that I had studied more. But I'm sure it's the same for a lot of people. At the middle school, I spent a lot of time drawing robots from Japanese cartoons like Goldrake or Mazinga. I made up for my lack of studying by using other things. I wasn't brilliant at subjects like history and geography, which require studying, but I was good at writing essays—thanks to my charm—and in math, where I could rely on my intuition and ability to focus. I later made up lost time by learning languages, reading a lot, and confronting life's difficulties. But in those years my real job was to race the kart. Thinking about it now, it was crazy. It was like someone sitting around doing nothing until he or she turns 20, relying on the hope of winning the lottery.

My career continued as the costs spiraled. For a family like mine, it wasn't easy. My mother gave up sewing and started a new job, still from home, which my father found for her. The job was assembling a carburetor for converting engines from gasoline to LPG. She was provided with numerous components that she had to assemble. I worked on the kart and then would lend her a hand. Her income was used exclusively to pay for my racing season, and my father helped out too. Traveling around Italy, lodging and maintaining the kart were very expensive. In addition to this, the price of a full chassis was more than 1 million lire (approximately $800 in 1982), the tires cost 100,000 lire a set (and I needed at least a couple of sets per race) and then there were the spare parts, spark plugs, oil and fuel. An accident or a broken engine would amount to a small tragedy. Already back then, a season could cost close to 30 million lire.

My results in 1982 would have placed me in the top category, the *100 Avenir*. And if I ranked among the top ten in the Italian Championship, I could also qualify for the international races. This was a dream of mine, but from a financial point of view, it was a nightmare. There was an unbelievable lack of rules in the international and qualifying races, so the costs were much higher. In the *Super 100*, the engines and chassis frames didn't have any restrictions and you could choose whatever type of tires you wanted. The potential cost of international success hit us hard. We talked about it endlessly; should we just be satisfied with what we have and have fun, or would we regret not moving up, given our luck in the past.

The *Tricolore* race at Parma was the turning point. I covered my kart with "4 Star" stickers—the company that made the tires for the *100 Nazionale*. I did that just because I liked the stickers. After coming in third place, a tiny, sophisticated man came to our pit and said, "Good. You are the only ones who put the stickers on—I'll give you four tires as a present." I had no idea who he was. It turned out that he was the owner of 4 Star. He was about to leave when he turned and asked if we had a mechanic. "Yes, that one—my father." He asked my father, "Would you mind coming to Milan, I'd like to talk to you." He wanted to improve his tires so that they could be used on the international circuit dominated by Bridgestone and Dunlop and wanted to do this quietly and without having to hire a famous racer. "I need someone who can drive with passion and verve. Someone who's young so when he's ready, our tires will be ready, and we can aim to win together." He continued, "Your son's a good driver, a hard worker and grounded, and if you agree, I can pay for the frames and the engine and cover all the costs of spare parts." My father was impressed. He went on, "In addition to this, I will donate 25 million lire a year to cover the rest of the costs." I wasn't there but I believe that my father came out with a classic line, "Sonofabitch!" He couldn't believe it.

When he came home and told me the story, I was in shock for a week. Thanks to this man, Sergio Mantese, I was able to continue racing. The company that was known as 4 Star became Vega, the name of a star. I can count on two hands the people who have really helped me in my career. Mantese was the first to push me toward the professional level, all because of my obsessive habit of covering my kart with stickers.

CHAPTER 4

World Championship Karting

I made the big leap. For the occasion I chose an easy debut, signing up for the winter tournament at the Pista Del Sole in Florence. I won all four races on the program in *100 Avenir*. I was psyched up and went to the first race in Super 100 feeling very confident. The Federation had created a tournament consisting of four trials, called Club Azzurro, which had the same rules as the internationals, which is to say, almost none at all. You could participate only if you had achieved a certain merit in the previous seasons, so therefore an invitation for this was a big honor. I was officially considered one of the top 50 drivers in Italy and ranked amongst the first 12 in the Club Azzurro. I could have even raced for Italy on the international circuit. I never thought that it would be possible, but to my surprise, I won the first race at Pinarella di Cervia. On the podium, I thought, "Wow, Zanardi from Castel Maggiore—I put you all in your place!" The following races brought me back to earth.

I was racing with Vega tires that actually bore the Pirelli name. Back then Mr. Mantese was a small manufacturer and didn't have sufficient machinery so he had to use an old Pirelli mold. He made everything at home and didn't quite understand how racing tires were made. Maybe that day there was a magical combination between the asphalt, the weather and something else that fell into the mix. Because to produce tires is a bit like making pasta. You mix the rubber like flour: the oil and other various binding elements represent the egg. The outcome of the recipe depends a lot on how the ingredients are combined. I remember that the following year, while preparing tires for the European championship, Mantese lost a finger in the machine. It was blended in with the mix, and those tires were excellent. So much so, that jokingly, Mantese said, "We still have nine more to go, so let's choose our races well." Anyway, going back to 1983; in the following months, that "pasta" didn't turn out as well. Nonetheless, I had arrived on the scene with a victory that enabled me to automatically enter the class among the first 12—six Italians and six San Marinos. Several other lower placings were enough to grant me entrance into the internationals.

Even in that first year, when confronted with the best, I had fighting spirit and boundless passion. As a matter of fact, my nickname was "The Parisian" because of my polished driving style. But I could be a real son of a bitch. Although I never hit anyone on purpose or sent someone off the track without a reason, if I were provoked, I wouldn't let it go. In terms of this quality, I was already very "American." In close competition, I was able to keep a clear head, which I discovered was a very important quality. The difference between a great champion and a very good driver is quite subtle. They can both be talented. The good driver wins the race by starting in pole position, while the great driver wins regardless of the conditions. The champion is someone who looks back and realizes that he made his decision within a split second. While this may come naturally to some, it doesn't to others.

This difference was clearly visible between David Coulthard and Mika Häkkinen. Coulthard is an extremely intelligent driver, but he has committed several obvious mistakes in his career. Psychologically, it has probably cost David a lot to be a Formula 1 driver. Häkkinen, on the other hand, might appear clumsy compared to Coulthard outside the cockpit, but once behind the wheel, Mika is utterly determined and focused. Driving is such a natural thing for him that he could calculate incredible moves while focusing on the bigger picture.

I guess you could say that I was good at managing the race, but it doesn't mean that I was immune to emotions. Only after many years did I learn to temper my emotions. Even with 100,000 spectators in the oval, the metamorphosis was just beginning. I would make sure that if I made contact with another driver, it was he who would go off the track. And if my kart were damaged with a flat tire or a bent wheel, I'd make sure that I could adapt my driving style to the situation and somehow make it to the finish line.

For this reason, my idol has always been Nigel Mansell. Ayrton Senna was very fast and Alain Prost was tactically phenomenal. They were all inspirations and I tried to emulate their skills, but Nigel was something else. I felt we shared the same characteristics: those of a racer who was able to perform superbly if everything was perfect—but even better so if everything wasn't. Nigel was a bit of ham and if stuck in a tough situation, he would do something ridiculous in order to create something fabulous. This kept happening to me. If I came in second or third, I would mentally stay stuck in that position. But if, for example, I was hit, or was shoved out or made a mistake, or was in last place, then the psychological barrier would disappear, there was nothing else to lose, and I would push like mad. I often won because of this.

Because I was so similar to Mansell, it's no coincidence that I was the only one of my friends to notice one of his most unforgettable moments. It happened at Imola in 1990, his second year with Ferrari. We were all sitting around the television, mesmerized by Mansell's incredible charge. He was absolutely mad. While passing Berger in the McLaren at Tamburello, Mansell was pushed out and spun on to the grass while going more than 150 mph. He spun 360 degrees, but managed to put the car straight again. "He's still in the race!" Regaining control could be a matter of luck, but not with what happened later, which left me breathless. I was racing Formula 3 that year and thought, "He's flat-spotted his tires, what's he going to do now?" To my amazement he ran the fastest lap to that point of the grand prix. Even talking about it ten years later, I still get chills. Despite everything that happened to his Ferrari, Mansell became one with his car and was so focused that he managed to push it beyond the limit. He put such force into his driving that he was actually able to improve his performance. Then he broke the engine and had to pull out, which was typical of Mansell. But that lap left a lasting impression on me.

Despite the highs and lows of 1983, I finally took part in my first international race, on the European Team. I represented San Marino together with Fabio Tassi, a very talented guy from Parma, Alessandro Bugatti, and Tamara Vidali. The race was at Gestaach near Hamburg, but it felt more like a film set in a Western adventure. During the preliminaries, our German hosts had forced Vidali, Bugatti and most of the Italians off the track. I decided to take revenge by single-handedly eliminating three Germans in the finals. I even sent Otto Rensing full speed into the bank. As he bounced back on to the track, another driver immediately crashed into him. It looked like a pinball game!

Frustratingly, I couldn't get great results at the international level because my tires weren't up to scratch. On the other hand, in Italy, where the tires were all the same, I was doing really well. I won several races and almost won the Italian Championship, the *Tricolore*, at Viverone, near Vercelli. I won the first three races on Saturday. However on Sunday, Sandro Montani, who now races in the Ferrari Challenge and flies airplanes between Rome and Milan, seemed to find the synergy between the tires and the engine, and was unbeatable. I was convinced that he had put on new tires, which was forbidden. In addition, his engine broke down at the end of the race, so it was impossible to prove whether it had been tampered with. He was also a good friend of a Mr. Cimatti, who was the inspection supervisor, so therefore people were becoming suspicious.

But the 1983 *Tricolore* will always remain in the annals of history, at least in mine. During the free practice day on that Thursday I was the fastest, coming in at least one second ahead of the group. A Sicilian guy named Giovanni Bonanno was also racing and his father was convinced, because I was the official international driver for Vega, that I had been given special tires for racing in Italy. At the end of the practice he said, "If you are really clean and have nothing to hide, give me your tires and I'll give you mine." That was out of the question. I usually went to the Vega factory and Mr. Mantese would point to the shelves and say, "Here are the tires for the next race—choose what you want." I would start measuring all of them, selecting the sets and checking even the smallest details. There is a small arrow, for instance, which is marked on each tire before vulcanization. If the manufacturer gets it right, the arrow stays at the center of the tire. Otherwise it moves to the side and when the tire warms up, it becomes pear shaped. Therefore my tires seemed the best that I could have chosen and the thought of having to give them away was dreadful. Also, I was going very fast and it was the Italian Championship and not just any race.

The situation got out of control with Mr. Bonanno getting more and more pissed off. Every once in a while I can be explosive and we started arguing. We were swearing at each other and somehow I called him a son of a bitch. I should have never done that to a Sicilian. He started running after me. "I'm going to kill you!" he screamed as he chased me around the track. I took off running but halfway down the straight I thought, "Why am I running, I'm younger and bigger than him!" I suddenly turned around and started after him. He immediately stopped in his tracks and took off running. That was an unbelievable scene about which people still talk. At the end of it my mechanic, whom I hired to help out my father, started to cry from the stress of the situation. I was so angry that I threw the four tires—literally threw them—at Bonanno and agreed to use his stupid tires.

The next day at the end of practice, I went to check the times and saw that I had gone even faster. His tires were fantastic, much better than mine, which ended up having strange bubbles on the surface. I immediately called Mantese, "How is this possible?" I asked. I assumed the tires were of a different stock or a new process, but he answered innocently, "The ones you're using are seconds—you took them from the seconds pile." I said, "What?!" He kept on, "You know, sometimes the mixture doesn't come out well and there will be a few trapped air bubbles which later will burst." I said indignantly, "But Mantese—you gave them to me!" He said, "If I don't give them to you for free, who's going to buy them?" I couldn't believe that I had almost punched out a 50-year-old Sicilian over a bunch of faulty tires! When Bonanno realized that I was even faster with his tires, he apologized unreservedly. He said, "You were clean and I was wrong. I owe you an apology." He was a real man of honor and became a big supporter of mine.

Towards the end of 1983 DAP, the company which had built my first kart, asked me to come to Milan to talk. When I arrived they said, "We'd be delighted if you could race for us. We already have Stefano Modena who is about to move up, so as this will be his last season racing karts, we'll need to find a replacement. We can't follow you everywhere, but we can offer you all the equipment for free and a small salary." They offered me 600,000 lire a month which was quite good money at the time. They also said, "In the international races you'll be free to race with the Vega tires if they're fast enough, but if Bridgestone or Dunlop are better, you'll have to use them." Mr. Mantese, despite having some problems during the year, was a real gentleman. He said, "It's OK Alessandro, you can't jeopardize your career because of my tires, but I'd like you to keep developing them for me." And so I did.

It was a dreadful year in 1984. Although I was very fast, for one ridiculous reason after another I never seemed to finish a race. For example, during a Club Azzurro race at Lido di Pomposa, I was first in the group when the throttle of the carburetor broke and it remained completely open. I spun off the track, but was able to start again with one hand while closing the air inlet of the carburetor with the other. By doing this I was once again in first place, but two laps from the end, the carburetor finally gave up on me because of a ruptured membrane and Vincenzo Sospiri won. I remember my father stomping on the stopwatch and breaking it into pieces. During the European Championships at Fano, I was on pole position after each qualifying race. I even won the pre-final but during the finals, the carb's needle valve broke completely and I had to stop after just a few yards.

If my racing career was in a dire state, my personal life wasn't any better. I had to pull out of school because of truancy, and I couldn't be bothered with making up for it. That year was full of other small disappointments, like my driving test. It is such a funny story that it inspired Honda to use it in a television ad in 1998 in the United States. I had turned 18 years old and decided that it was time to get a driver's license. I assumed it would be a piece of cake and indeed passed the written test without any problem. But the day before my actual driving test, I had an argument with my father. I thought the driving test would be just a formality and went ahead and offered to drive my friends to a skiing resort that weekend. My father was absolutely opposed to the idea, "You're an idiot—why do you want to go driving in the snow when you've only just got a license?!" I insisted, "What, don't you think I can manage?" As the conversation got more heated, my grandmother Gisella asked, "What's all this racket?" And my father said contentiously, "He wants to drive to the mountains on Sunday—isn't he crazy?" My grandmother said, "Oh, I'm sure you won't pass the exam." I stared at her in amused disbelief—as if I could fail. Shrugging my shoulders, I left with a smug, "Let's see tomorrow."

The following day I was very careful, although I feigned total confidence. To illustrate my ease behind the wheel to the instructor, I kept talking while driving to the point that he told me to just concentrate on the driving. Everything was going well when he said, "Do you mind parking between those two cars— it's a bit tight." I looked at him and thought, "Do you know who you're talking to?" I parked the car and asked smiling, "Is this OK?" He said, "Yes, you can go." I proudly opened the door and the heavens punished me. An old man on a bicycle was directly behind me and I whacked him. I had been too busy looking at the instructor rather than watching to see if anything was coming. The cyclist fell on the ground and, although unhurt, he went crazy and started swearing. The examiner said smugly, "I'll see you again in 40 days." Now I can laugh about it, but my friends were counting on me and I, the professional driver, managed to fail my driving test. I didn't speak to my grandmother for a month, while my father kept rubbing it in: "Oh, what am I going to do with the snow chains I bought you for skiing!"

Towards the end of the year, Achille Parilla, the owner of DAP, invited me to the Nationals. He was superstitious and followed the stars, unfortunately spotting me as an unlucky driver. "I want to see if things change while you are with me," he said. He took me to Viverone, where I was on pole position but during the race something broke—I think it was the chain. I didn't say a word. But after a few days, my telephone rang and Walter Masini was on the other end. He was a very good person and prepared karts out of passion rather than for financial gain. "How's everything going with Achille?" he asked. "I'm racing with him," I answered. Walter replied, "I'm not sure about that. He's in Pomposa and Sospiri is with him." I immediately called Parilla who explained, "Dear Zanardi, you are very fast but very unlucky. A company can't allow itself to lose a race for that reason so we've decided to take on Sospiri, but we'd be happy to keep you on and give you the equipment for free, paying for a mechanic of your choice and giving you 800,000 lire a month." So basically I'd almost be an official driver, however they weren't going to promote me officially. I was very offended by this. In my opinion Achille Parilla was to karts what Frank Williams was to Formula 1. Achille was very respected and I was excited to be around him; he followed Ayrton Senna and then Stefano Modena who were both gods in the racing world.

I accepted the deal because it was the most logical thing to do, but it was hugely disappointing. They did, however, have the best equipment, and I found a terrific mechanic, Mauro Villa (his uncle Walter was the ex-world motorcycle champion) as my collaborator. He was very good and I thought he'd be great at prepping my engine. Or maybe Achille was right? Maybe this was all simply down to the stars? But I ended up winning the first race in 1985, the Champion's Cup at Jesolo, one of the most important international races of the year. And then I won the second, third, fourth and so on. I had Sospiri and Achille as direct rivals that season, and I still came in first. This occurred 23 out of the 24 times, and even when the one time I broke a motor, the same thing would happen to Sospiri. Who knows, maybe it was Achille and his superstitions? In fact, the situation soon became quite tense because Achille was very competitive and very determined to win. In the beginning of 1985, my successes suited him. From the company's point of view, it was great. One would assume that if the unofficial driver won, he had the best equipment and therefore there couldn't possibly be any favoritism. The message was clear: anybody buying their chassis and prepping their engines could succeed. But as time went on the situation must have become annoying.

This time I won the European Championship, just as I'd won the Italian Championship a few months earlier. I also won the prestigious race in Hong Kong, which was icing on the cake. It was actually this trip to the Far East that was the first breaking point with DAP. They already had started a subtle war against me; there would be a part missing, other times no spare parts, or not enough equipment. Before the Hong Kong race, Achille decided,

"We will not send them equipment because they have enough left from last year." We almost had heart attacks when we opened the box containing the chassis. The local retailer, who had supposedly been storing the chassis, had in fact been using it for the entire season. Now I was stuck with a chassis in horrible condition. I was furious—I couldn't show up at such an important international event with cracked equipment. Even though we brought the engines with us from Italy, they weighed only ten kilograms and we carried them as hand luggage, with frames like this there was no way that we could race.

But my father was there and made a plumb line with a rope and a stone and used a kart palate and some rocks to improvise a homemade jig to straighten the chassis. He found a transformer and by inverting the polarities, he used it as a welding machine. Wires stolen from a fence became the improvised electrodes. This is how we got rid of all the cracks. The welding burned the red paint and made the chassis look even worse, but I knew it would be fine when he gave it the finishing touch. My father said, "Rough around the edges, but efficient—just the way you like." My father's eyes lit up with his irresistible laugh, something I now miss a lot. Using the crown of the spare chain, by cutting and shaping it, he managed to straighten the useless seat. It was very enterprising of him. But he was like that. He taught me a big lesson, never surrender in the face of obstacles and always use your brain to look for a solution. With the wobbly chassis and broken seat, I won the final, winning the most important race of the year. When I broke through the finish line, I saw my father on his knees, kissing the asphalt. He then started kissing everyone and everything around him, including the kart, which was so hot that it blistered his lips. The sight of his puffy lips gave us all a very good laugh.

In 1986 I was still racing with DAP, but we started the season on bad terms. My mechanic and I were still having problems with the team. The battle was getting less subtle and more obvious.

Mauro Villa kept explaining, "I asked them for the pistons, and they didn't have them, I asked for connecting rods and they didn't have them. When I need bearings, they give me the ones that blow up the engine after ten laps." This went on until he received an offer from Iame, our competitor, and asked me to go with him. I am fundamentally a loyal person, so I couldn't believe DAP would screw us like this. I rejected the offer and we ended up going separate ways. I found a new mechanic, Walter Masini, the chap who'd called me about Sospiri. He was very nice, almost too kind, but nothing changed around the paddock. I continued to win, but the internal rivalry didn't stop. To make matters worse, the team was surrounded by a lot of arrogant Milanese who really got on my nerves. Every time I asked for equipment and complained a little, they would say the same thing, "Zanardi, don't be a pain in the ass or otherwise we'll send you to race with Kali," an unrespected rival kart manufacturer. Driving karts for Kali would be like driving a Yugo in Formula 1.

The final stage of this fight took place during the qualifications for the 1986 European Championship. The drivers from the southern area were competing at Laval, France, in order to determine who would race in Germany. I was on pole and won the qualifying race, which meant that I would start first in the pre-final. The track was very sticky, so I was looking for a different set of tires. Until then, I had been using soft tires, but I needed harder ones. Starting with the original set would have been suicidal because they would have worn out after a few laps. The Bridgestone soft tires were called IBQ and the hard ones, IBR. I was desperately scouring the paddock for a set of four IBRs, but they were nowhere to be found. I went to Achille and said, "I need a hand. I need a set of hard tires and I'm starting on pole position, but with soft tires, I've already lost." He replied, "Look Zanardi, there's nothing I can do for you. Even Sospiri races with the IBQs which are the only ones available." Sospiri was next to me on the starting line when I noticed that he had IBRs. I looked towards Achille and he seemed very nonchalant. I figured that they must have found the tires at the last moment, so I set off. It was no surprise that I didn't do well; after ten laps in the lead, the kart slowed down and the others caught up with me. Bouchut bumped me off the track, and that was the end of that.

After the race I had to check the carburetor, so I went to the DAP pits and asked for Achille, who was on the truck checking a carburetor. I thought, "Perfect, I'll go right away so that he can have a look at mine." As soon as I entered, Achille froze. I didn't make much of it and we started chatting while he checked a carburetor for the Italian Championship at Empoli the following week. Then I noticed there were some Bridgestones among the other tires. Bridgestone tires always fascinated me; when they are new they're very easy to shape and can be squeezed in half. I took one and started messing around with it and I suddenly noticed that it was an IBR as were all of them. There were IBR yellow specials, IBR blue specials, etc. The whole time in that truck, were the tires that caused me to lose the race. I stared at Achille and he started making excuses, saying that they were experimental tires that Bridgestone had given him and that Sospiri was testing them the following day. I got the impression that he was trying to dig himself out of a hole.

I took my carburetor and left. During the short walk to the pit, more pissed off than disappointed, I only had one thought in my head, "My relationship with DAP is over!" I went to my father and told him everything. Together, without a word, we went to Giancarlo Vanaria from Kali. "I want to race for you," I said. Maybe there were other options, other stronger constructors, but I was too bitter. Pride dictated my reaction. "Now I'm going to race with Kali and show you all what I'm made of—I will, I will," I said to myself resolutely.

Kali could not believe it. "Giancarlo, I want to race with you," I repeated calmly. "The appointment is next Tuesday in Parma," he said. We had to return from France, clean the karts and go straight to practice because the *Tricolore* was on the following Sunday in Empoli.

Two days later I was in San Pancrazio wearing different racing overalls (they used Iame engines) and collaborating with my old mechanic, Mauro Villa. In addition, Vanaria's brother Roberto, and brother-in-law Giancarlo Tinini, were both there. Everybody was very upbeat, including me. We tried all the available equipment, but after a day of hard work with the best possible combination of new tires and faster engines, we only managed to race in 49.9 seconds. The average on that circuit was around 48 seconds.

It wasn't going very well and there were a lot of long faces. We went to the bar to get a coffee and Giancarlo said, "Listen, I want to explain something. Mike Wilson, a world champion, raced for me and left saying that my chassis is like a 'gate' [a disaster in kart language]. And then Colciago and Morbidelli left saying the same thing." He continued, "Now Zanardi, who won the whole of last year and most of this year, is racing with us and if he doesn't win, my chassis will automatically be considered a gate. I understand your commitment because you want to defend your Italian Championship title, but the race is in just four days so let's think about it properly. The European Championship takes place in a month so we better get ready, but it's not worth thinking about Empoli." My father agreed. So with our heads down, we accepted the decision and returned home.

The following Wednesday, my father went to work while I went to the garage. I had brought home the chassis from Parma and wanted to have a closer look. I put it on the bench which my father had built using a sheet of glass. I circled the frame and started studying the position of the seat, the incline of the wheel hubs and several other details. I still had the DAP chassis at home and I compared it with the one from Kali. I realized the strengths of the one and the flaws of the other, and quickly identified what needed fixing. When my father came home from work, I made him come downstairs to the garage, "Look what I've found—it's obvious why this frame doesn't work! See how they've placed the steering. See how they've mounted this seat? And here, it is too wide in the front which makes it too hard to turn." I could not stop myself, explaining to my father all the changes that needed to be made, "We can't narrow the front of chassis—it should be made from scratch—but the other parts can be fixed and we should try." He said, "We could give it a go. It would probably drive much better this way." And then I let slip, "And then we can go to Empoli?" My father went ballistic! "You idiot—you are a fool! You don't understand a thing!" He stormed upstairs, had dinner and a glass of wine, and went to bed without saying goodnight. I kept on working on the chassis. When my father came home, he said nonchalantly, "What about that chassis over there?" He was intrigued after all. "But we need to get on with it," I interrupted, "—so that we can go to Empoli!" He blew up, "No damn way!"

Anything that I could fix on my own I did. That evening, feeling a bit down I stayed to chat with my friends in the garage which also substituted as our bar and meeting place. The following morning at five o'clock, I heard someone calling me, "Sandro, Sandro." I was too sleepy to realize that it was my father, "Load up the truck, we are going to Empoli!" I got Mauro Villa out of bed. "Be at the track with everything that you've got. We're going!" I needed no other explanation. Then I called the Kali chaps, waking them up as well. I gave them a speech, "Now guys, I discovered a whole series of small and big problems. I think that the chassis is much better now and if I didn't race, I'd feel like a coward. I need to go to defend my title. I'm going. For two other important modifications the whole frame needs to be rebuilt. If you can get a new chassis for the race I will be in Empoli." They started working immediately—from the bare metal—and created a completely new chassis. They worked non-stop to get the kart ready and finally arrived at the track on Friday morning at 11:00, thirty minutes before the free practice ended. From a professional point of view, this was Kali's last chance. They arrived in a Peugeot 205 and unloaded everything and mounted the chassis and engine. With the chassis that I had modified in my garage, I was already doing quite well and was among the top five. With the new chassis I managed to do a few laps in the final minutes of the free trials. I got off the kart and winked to everyone that it was going to be OK. Everything ended up like a fairytale; I got pole position, won all the qualifying, the pre-finals and the finals—I was the Italian Champion! From the second to the seventh places, they were all racing DAP karts but I won the *Tricolore* with Kali.

This relationship led to many more victories and enabled Kali, later renamed CRG, to make huge improvements. Their factory was originally a bakery so the cars would often turn up at the race covered with flour; today it is one the world's biggest manufacturers of karts. When I crossed the finishing line in Empoli, everyone was delirious. The Vanaria clan was a hot-blooded family. They were famous in the world of karting primarily because of the father Calogero, who was now concentrating on the 125cc class. The old man was endowed with a great big belly that threw him off balance, so much so that despite a belt, during the summer he was always showing his butt crack. He had also a been a boxer so you knew not to mess with him.

The 125cc class consisted mostly of older professionals—the youngest being 30 years old—who argued over everything. On one occasion, a group of four men from Tuscany started arguing with Calogero. They surrounded him and started to threaten him with a beating. But after five minutes, it was Calogero doing the beating. The four men escaped and took refuge in an old Fiat 242 van, locking themselves inside. Calogero started punching the bodywork, violently transforming the van into a colander. Not happy with his handiwork, he went back to his truck, grabbed a crowbar and then peeled the van door open like a can of tuna. He jumped inside and gave them a good thrashing. I remembered the scene vividly; he climbed out of what was left of the van, shouting, "God damn it—they shouldn't have pissed me off."

Calogero's son Roberto inherited his father's same build and fighting spirit, whereas his brother Giancarlo was very easy-going. Roberto was a semi-professional boxer in bantam and flyweight, and one tough cat to skin, and, with my father around, you can understand why everyone kept their distance from them. From a physical point of view, we were a very good team. Our third team-mate at Kali was Giancarlo Tinini, who was a hard worker and the real soul of the group.

Those were good years, working together with a passionate, enthusiastic group of friends. I finished the 1986 season still winning quite a lot. However, during the European races in Germany, the race after Empoli, things didn't go so well. I had a good lap time, but due to the rain I wasn't able to finish the race. The funniest memory is that during the eliminations I came in first and Michael Schumacher was second. During the last few laps, I had a bald tire with the wrong pressure, and Schumacher soon caught up with me. But when the race was due to end, the German organizers indicated there was another lap to go in order to give Schumacher the chance to overtake me. Schumacher tried to overtake, but I held my position and blocked him so he couldn't pass, sending him into the gravel. I won the race, but Schumacher was given second place even though he pulled out, because the judges claimed that there was "accidentally" an extra lap and the race should have finished earlier.

Meanwhile, I kept developing the tires for Vega. By the end of the summer, we'd got to the bottom of the problem, my father providing the final clue. We were in the bar at the track after a day of trials in Parma. I'd tested at least 30 types of tires, but the results were terrible. Mantese was really depressed when my father broke the silence, "Mantese, there is something wrong here. Two years ago you started making tires with the basics. Now you use very expensive material and elaborate procedures and you still go slow, even with 30 different types of tires!" Mantese asked, "What do you mean?" My father explained, "I mean, how much would you have to sell those tires for in order to make a profit?" Mantese paused and answered, "At least a million lire each set." My father continued, "Then explain to me how Bridgestone can produce good tires in Japan, ship them across the ocean, pay import tax and still keep the price at 160,000 lire? In my opinion you get the vulcanization wrong—why don't you try to put four Bridgestones in your molds and see what happens when you use your same process, then we can get to the bottom of this." Mantese's face lit up and he agreed to give it a shot.

The following week, we experimented with a set of conventional Bridgestone tires, which came in two seconds slower than they should have. This test was the turning point. Mantese started working in a different direction and his tires really started to shift. With his Vega tires, I came in second in the last race of 1986 at the Grand Prix in Hong Kong. After the race Mantese, lifting a glass of wine, toasted my father and proclaimed, "I never thought I'd have to learn how to make tires from a plumber!"

Halfway though 1986, something major happened. I made friends with several drivers, including Massimiliano Papis. I was only 19 years old and I was racing at the senior level in international races whereas Massimiliano (Max) was racing in the junior. It wasn't a direct rivalry—we were actually great fans of one other and helped each other on the karts. We often parked our vans next to each other, and would have a sandwich and hang out together after practice. There was always something to do, work on the chassis, change the tires, clean and check the engines, and all the usual preparations to get ready for the race. Several times we'd spend the night in our vans at the track, sleeping in our overalls and with our hands covered in dirt and oil. I think that roughing it like this taught two young boys some valuable lessons about life.

These are great memories enhanced by the fact that nobody forced us to be there—it was all out of the love of karting. Mechanics and drivers often organized evening races (thanks to night lighting) using rental karts at the tracks. The tracks were open to the public, so we would often race with the bystanders.

One night in Pinarella di Cervia, Max had a particularly tough time when he accidentally hit a German bystander's kart. The German was older, bigger, and most worryingly, drunk. We got off the karts, laughing about the race, when the German started yelling at Max. Poor Max was just a kid and could go from smiles to tears at the drop of a coin. The German ended up slapping Max and made him cry. My father arrived and tried to calm the situation by talking to the German in a Bolognese dialect, "Take it easy, he's just a kid!" The German then tried to punch my father. I thought that this kind of thing only happened in spaghetti Westerns, but I was wrong. My father picked him up by the straps of his overalls and lifted him a foot off the ground. As he wriggled in pain, my father roared, "First of all, you are so ugly that if you were ever in a movie, the director would kill you off in the first act just to please the audience. And now get out of here or I'll kill you." It was not the tone of his voice but the look in his eyes that really scared the German, who immediately understood exactly what my father said, despite the heavy dialect, and took off.

We always had a good time though. Obviously, we would race aggressively on Sundays, but there was always time for our friendship. Having said that, one day in Parma Max told me, "Alex, my father is coming to see me today and he wants to speak to you." He didn't say anything else, leaving me rather curious. His father, Cesare Papis, arrived in the afternoon, chatted with my father and then came to see me, changing my life with a few words. "So Alessandro, when will you start racing in a car?" I replied, "I haven't really thought about it. It's so out of the question financially that I just haven't had a chance to consider it." He replied, "I'd like to help you—even if it's to help pave the way for Max. You get along very well. I hope that one day you two will race together in Formula 3 and he can learn from you." I asked, "What kind of help are you talking about?" He said, "I don't know exactly, but if I find half the budget, can you see what you could do about the rest?" I was stunned. Could this be happening? But I kept thinking, "It's possible!" All of a sudden the outlook was very rosy and for the entire season, I was obsessed with the idea of racing in Formula 3.

Given this prospect of moving on, there was still something that I wanted to do in karting. I thought to myself, this is my last year, so I'll upgrade to 135cc so that I can race in the World Championship. The 135 was a special category that the International Federation decided to create in 1981 as the Formula 1 of karting. But not all the teams liked the initiative because they had to build a special engine that would be used for only five of the European Championship races, and one of the World Championship events. There were a lot of problems between the Federation and the constructors. Teams like DAP used to tell the drivers week by week where they'd be racing. They did this to maximize their exposure and to advertise their products by choosing the most strategic race. The Italian races were often as important to them as the official ones. Obviously they wouldn't prevent the drivers from racing in 135, but it was generally offered to those who needed to get their feet wet for the World Championship. For this reason the Federation had decided to grant a "super license" to all the drivers who raced in 135 and qualified for the final. But once you had a super license, you couldn't go back to the 100cc at any level. Therefore, a driver would end up having only six or seven races a year and miss the opportunity to participate in the national races. The Federation was furious when the constructors started asking the drivers to forgo the World

Championship, but it seemed like the perfect moment to make my debut at the highest level. In addition, there was the fact that the previous year's championship had taken place in Jacksonville, Florida, which the European drivers felt was absolutely unsuitable for racing. To make matters worse, the American drivers were clearly going faster because they were using a clutch that we didn't have in Europe. After the trials, the Europeans refused to race, packed their bags and went back home. The European Federation, instead of protecting them, disqualified them for six months. As a consequence, the 1987 European Championship for 135cc was missing the best drivers. By the time they were allowed to re-enter the championship, there were only two races left for the European title, and one for the World title. Many drivers agreed with me that this was perhaps the right moment to move on.

I made my debut with a Kali chassis, Vega tires and a Komet engine prepared by Mauro Villa. I dominated the first three races of the program. When you are new to an environment and you perform reasonably well, it is easy to attract interest and generosity. But when you are too good, you become a target. People started making predictions, "We want to see Zanardi in Belgium when the good drivers are back—that'll put him in his place." I arrived in Genk, Belgium, and immediately took pole position and won all the elimination heats, the pre-final and the final. In the final, I had almost lapped the rest of the group, including the good ones who were supposed to be "putting me in my place." It was incredibly satisfying, like the *Tricolore* at Empoli. Although I was already statistically the European Champion, I went to Valance for the last race. I won there too, becoming the first champion to conquer the European Championship by winning all the races in the program, and I'm still the only one to have done this.

The day before setting off for Fontenay Le Comte, where the second of the five races was taking place, I had a go on an old, rickety kart, with some friends just for a laugh. That kart

1. Me at the age of one, with my father, Dino, on the Rivabella beach in Rimini.

2. The Zanardi family: dad, mom, my sister Cristina in the driver's seat and me in the sidecar.

3. Aloha! Cristina and I wearing grass skirts and ready to rock and roll on Rivabella beach.

4. Imola, September 1980 at age 13—my first kart race with a Federation licence.

5. In 1985, preparing to start the European
kart race at Gestaach, which I won. Look at
the determined stare of my dad—"Grezzo
(rough) Man"—by my side!

6. I left DAP to join Kali in
the middle of the 1986 season.
With Kali I won the European
Championship just ahead of
Michael Schumacher.

7. My first Formula 3 test: me,
team owner Coperchini, and dad
at Varano in the winter of 1988.

8. Before the start of the Formula 3000 race at
Pau, France, in 1991, with Roberto Trevisan. I
didn't finish this race due to a broken driveshaft,
but I finished second in the 1991 Formula 3000
Championship behind Christian Fittipaldi.

9. My first shot at Formula 1, driving for Jordan in the last three F1 races of the 1991 season. I replaced fellow F1 rookie Michael Schumacher who had been lured over to the Benetton team. This picture was taken at the last race of the season, in Adelaide, Australia, just before a series of encounters with the wall.

10. Here I am pushing to get the best from the Minardi M192 Lamborghini during qualifying for the F1 German Grand Prix at Hockenheim in 1992. I was a test driver for Benetton in 1992, but ended up driving for Minardi at the end of the season as replacement for an injured Christian Fittipaldi.

11. Talking with Peter Wright (technical director), Peter Collins (team manager) and Chris Murphy in the Lotus pit in 1993 during the first of my two F1 seasons with Lotus.

12. Battling with the troublesome active-suspension Lotus 107B during the 1993 Spanish Grand Prix. I retired from fifth position during the next-to-last lap when my engine blew up.

13. Making a hasty exit from the Lotus 109 Mugen-Honda at the 1994 French Grand Prix. I only discovered that my engine had caught fire when fellow racer David Brabham pulled alongside and pointed it out.

14. Although the press claimed I was "praying for guidance" in this photo, I was actually cursing my luck as it started to rain during the Portland Grand Prix in 1996. Despite the rain, this was my first IndyCar victory.

15. Making a pass on polesitter André Ribeiro at the start of the IndyCar Grand Prix at Toronto in 1996.

16. Happy Birthday, boss! Jimmy Vasser and I present Chip Ganassi with a suitable birthday cake during practice for the US 500 at Michigan International Speedway in 1996.

had a finned engine and the carburetor was in front of the driveshaft, which I wasn't used to. As soon as the kart lost power, I immediately started to look for the needle valve when I heard this loud noise and felt a shooting pain. One of my fingers was stuck in the chain! I ended up with 14 stitches in my hand, but still went to Fontenay Le Comte. In order to race, I made a special glove by cutting out the middle finger and replacing it with a plastic tube. It worked great, but halfway through the race, the vibration and lack of circulation got the better of me and I was in a lot of pain. I supported my hand in the chest pocket of my overalls and drove with my other hand. Because I'm such a show-off, in the following years I embellished the story each time I told it.

Done and dusted with the European 135, I went to race in the *100 Avenir* in Gothenburg, Sweden. It was an unforgettable race, partly because Michael Schumacher won, and partly because of what had happened a few yards from the finish line. Throughout the race, I was just inches from Massimiliano Orsini, but ended up with a reasonable lead by the last corner. He tried a desperate move and rear-ended me, sending us both off. For Max, this was the end of the race. Given my advantage on the others, I could have easily won the race. Right in front of my eyes, I saw the incredulous track official just waiting to wave the checkered flag. But like in a nightmare, I wasn't able to reach him because Orsini's father had jumped on to the track. He was blocking me in order to give his son a chance to win. But instead, Schumacher, who was third with a huge, 28-second delay, made it to the finish line first. He was in such a state of disbelief, that he didn't even smile when he crossed the line and they waved the checkered flag at him.

That day something magical ended. After that race, even the Italian Championship went badly for me, but I won the first two races for the *Tricolore* at the Pista d'Oro in Rome. I arrived at the second race thinking my only competition were the drivers who made it to the podium with me, but the rules were changed at the last minute. The points earned in the Lido di Pomposa were now to be doubled, which meant that even the drivers who had performed poorly in Rome were back in the game, including Orsini who was facing an eight-month ban after Gothenburg. Donzelli, who was responsible for Italian drivers during international races, asked me to withdraw my complaint against Orsini, as it wasn't fair that he had to pay for the stupidity of his father's actions. I had every right to be angry—I had lost the European title—but it wasn't really Orsini's fault. I agreed, but never benefited from this decision.

Thanks to the changes in the points system, all the DAP drivers got together in the second race to help Orsini, who was now the highest ranking driver. He was doing really well in the final, but I had a few problems. Nonetheless, even in third place, I still stood a chance to win the championship. I was racing against the Swiss driver, Glauser, and in a strong position with only ten laps remaining. I used a few tricks to overtake him, and was given the black flag for blocking my opponent. In reality, there was no contact and I was just closing the gap around the corner, but the flag was waved. Because the flag was waved without a number, I kept going and arrived third. I ended up disqualified, despite complaining to the officials. My complaint would have been accepted if it hadn't been caught up in endless Italian bureaucracy. We ran out of time and I lost the Italian Championship.

This bad luck continued all year. In the World Championship, I qualified with the third best time. I won several of the elimination heats and was in the lead in the pre-final, but in the final, after just two laps, a piece of rubber as big as a tennis ball got stuck in the engine. I went as I fast as I could but it didn't matter, I still ended up 10th or 12th, I can't really remember. I couldn't even beat the same drivers whom I'd destroyed in the five European races. I ended the season in Hong Kong, coming home with second place.

In the winter, I worked towards obtaining my half of Cesare Papis's proposal. Mantese introduced me to some local businessmen and I found three or four small sponsors. Thanks to their donations together with my savings, I had 65 million lire which went directly into my career. I finally had saved enough money to race one season in Formula 3. I went straight to my parents and said, "I've signed. I'm going to race in Formula 3."

My parents were shocked—this was a possibility that they'd never considered. Karting was, after all, a game with very limited risks. But Formula 3 represented the end of a dream for them, and the end of my protective bubble. Now they would have a son who would control his own life without their influence. On one hand their role started to come to an end, but on the other it was the beginning. Their son was starting his inevitable journey ... the road to professional motor racing—and it was full of danger. I can imagine the guilt and worry they must have felt, considering what had happened to my sister. It was almost impossible for them to accept my decision. It took a month for us to even talk about it, but I wanted their opinion and involvement. It was easier with my mother, but with my father ... it was very hard work. Nevertheless, on the first test drive of a Formula 3 car, he was there—and the photograph of him on that morning, smiling, has been in my wallet ever since.

CHAPTER 5

Racing in Formula 3 and 3000

I never thought that I could actually make the jump to motor racing, or that my career would go beyond karting. With the help of Papis's father, Cesare, my dream was transformed into a reality. It was an incredibly generous offer to a young boy whom he believed in, and to my father whom he respected. I don't think that my father appreciated it at the time though. He and my mother not only had to accept the risks, but they had to re-invent their lives for themselves. They lost touch with many of their friends and gave up many of their hobbies during the years on the track.

Initially my father helped a few other boys for old times' sake but he soon realized he no longer had the same passion. In the meantime, I looked around and started talking to Mario Coperchini's team, which was based in Parma. In 1987, Roberto Colciago and Mauro Martini raced for them and had fantastic results. Believing that they would be an excellent choice, I immediately signed with them.

They didn't have any sponsorship ready for me, so I needed to finance the entire budget myself. To keep the cost down, the team began to cut spending on the winter practice sessions. I found myself racing for the first time in Formula 3 with just two afternoon practice sessions at Varano, two days at Vallelunga and one day at Misano. These sessions were performed in an unusual way. Our team truck would arrive well after the other teams had got there, and the car didn't arrive in the pit lane until almost 11 am. We would start the practice session, do a few test laps before stopping for lunch. After lunch, we would begin working again and then wait until late afternoon for the track to warm up and get faster. Two or three fast laps with new tires and then we'd stop because we needed the same tires for the next practice. Because of this, I never really got used to the feel of the car that winter.

At the time of signing on, I gave the sponsors an extremely positive description of Coperchini's team, but it was Max Papis who had the best assessment of the team. After coming to see me at the trial in Misano, he said, "Alex, this Mr. Coperchini is probably a good person and he certainly has a great organization, but when the other teams' cars have finished practicing, their mechanics work feverishly to dismantle, measure and check everything on the car. On the other hand, when your mechanics finish, your car is brought under the canopy and the guys pull out some bread, knives and half a ham and start preparing lunch. They have a sandwich, some wine, a coffee at the bar and then finally clean the car before quickly loading it on the truck and saying goodbye." Maybe Max was right. I could see this happening, but didn't want to admit it.

The value of the team was not the issue. Although my teammate, Mauro Martini, who had come in second in the championship, was happy, I started having some doubts. The team was very focused on him. He was in his third year racing Formula 3, while I had been taken on for the experience. To make matters worse, whenever I tried to discuss a problem, no one really paid attention to what I said. Because Mauro drove the car with a certain set-up, the mechanics in turn set up my car in the same way and expected me to learn how to drive that way.

I was really frustrated at the fact that I ended up with a team like this when I could have had so many other teams … teams that were equally interested and required less money. Who knows, perhaps I could have found another team who would have been determined to help establish a beginner driver like myself. But my choice, right or wrong, was made in complete ignorance. A little bit like when my wife sends me to do the shopping and says, "Bring home some extra virgin olive oil." How am I supposed to know which one is the best? So I buy the most expensive in order not to make a mistake and put my mind at rest.

I had a very mediocre start with the team. At the time, the Pedrazzani brothers' Novamotor engine nearly monopolized the engine supply. There was this theory that a driver would spend at least three years in Formula 3. During the first year he would go slowly in order to gain experience; during the second, he would bring in some results; and in the third, he would be ready to win the title. This theory didn't work that well for me. In the first race at Vallelunga, I finished in 13th place. At the last race, at Imola, I came in 26th place. During a roller coaster season, I would always land somewhere in the middle.

Instead of improving, I was getting worse. I couldn't understand why this was happening and became more and more disillusioned. This is exactly what happened at Misano, a summer race, where I was unable to improve on my time because of an understeering problem. I pestered Mario Coperchini to modify the set-up on my car, but he wouldn't listen. He said that the car had to be driven in that particular way. That is how Mauro drove it, he entered the corner with his foot on the brake, thus loading the front end, and immediately accelerated to keep the car grounded. Mario reminded me that in the future, I would be able to automatically make the same moves. I remember begging him from the cockpit, "Mario, the future is one thing, but I have an understeering problem *now*—give me at least two holes in the front wing." I knew that this would have helped increase the load on the front wing. Eventually Mario gave in and said to his mechanic, "Give him what he wants or I'll never hear the end of it!" I improved my time by a few tenths of a second and ended up qualifying in a dignified 11th place.

All of the people on the team congratulated me with an affectionate pat on the shoulders, as if to say, "Not bad for a beginner." But something wasn't right. I just couldn't understand why it was so difficult to get at the front half of the starting grid when my teammate was always on the first line without any problem. I had great respect for my opponents and, although I knew I was a decent driver, I was never convinced that I was the best. My father used to say, "The best doesn't exist—everybody learns something from somebody else." But in this case the distance between me and my teammate was too great. The following year, I changed teams and engine types and by the first race in Vallelunga, I ended up in pole position. It is still a mystery to me where I magically gained all of that experience, given that I spent the whole winter at home on the sofa, but things were finally working in my favor.

In 1991 when I won the first race in Formula 3000, the Pedrazzani brothers stopped by to pay me a compliment. Oreste Pedrazzani said, "It's obvious that you need more horsepower," alluding to the fact that the more powerful Formula 3000 cars were more suitable to my driving style than the Formula 3. Remembering my year with Coperchini, I asked him, "Then why didn't you give it to me?"

I'd almost lost my passion in 1988, doubting whether I would ever be good enough to race in a car. I tried everything to improve my time, but my teammate was still much faster. I would push too hard in order to keep up with him and end up making mistakes. These accidents were expensive, and unfortunately the team would have to compensate for the costs. The situation was difficult because in addition to the money from Papis's father, I was spending all of my own money. It was very painful to watch that kind of money go down the drain. Eventually that season's fate was down to the timing of the keyboard. The official timing system was still manual and a bit amateurish. The most organized teams had computers with photocells on the pit walls and timing officials who recorded everybody during the trials. On the keyboard there were 30 keys corresponding to each driver. But in 1988, there were 32 drivers. Daniela Manni, who was the manager of the Venturini team (and eventually became my wife), had left me off the keyboard along with another driver. I never forgave her for this.

I started wondering whether I was any good—a possibility I took seriously—or if I simply wasn't suited to the team's dynamics. My pride made me opt for the latter, which was confirmed when my racing improved immensely the following year. In 1988 I met Ruggero Zamagna who, despite the surname, was from Austria. He launched the brand Racing For Italy, which spawned from the idea of Azzurra, the Italian racing boat. Racing For Italy was a pool of sponsors who wanted to be seen investing in motorsport. I'm not sure how much of this was an official sponsorship and how much just a way of moving money, but I do know that Zamagna had a lot of run-ins with the law after that.

At the time, I was still naïve and was offered a management contract that stated that all I had to do was drive—Zamagna would take care of everything else. He was a fascinating man. He spoke Italian perfectly and was a born salesman. I believed in him and thought that I had found my guardian angel. Zamagna wanted to create his own Formula 3 team. After Mauro Martini went to race in the Japanese Formula 3000, I became Zamagna's main driver in 1989. The new racing team was put together in a second. By an amazing coincidence, one of the best technicians, Roberto Trevisan, had put himself and his team on the market. On his team were Daniela and a group of excellent mechanics. Until then, they had managed the cars for Venturini from their workshop in Padova.

Venturini planned to transfer the whole lot to Langhirano, near Parma, whereas the rest of the group wanted to stay put. Therefore a new team was created using Ralt chassis and Toyota engines. A good part of the budget was covered by Zamagna and his pool of sponsors. Ralt, who were keen to break into Italy, gave us the chassis at a very low price while Toyota Italia took over the cost of the engine repairs as a form of sponsorship. Max Papis became my teammate, as we had always planned. It was a great time. I was getting along well with the whole team, especially Roberto. He and I really complemented each other and he was exceptionally good at getting the best out of me. In the years to follow, he became a great friend whom I have always respected and cared about a great deal. After a long day on the track, a driver usually returns to his hotel or goes out to eat, but it was a pleasure to stay behind in the pits with Roberto while he was working. Obviously there was another reason. I really fancied the team manager, Daniela! I would look for any excuse to spend time with her—meetings, work issues, chatting over a coffee. Her long, blonde curly hair and her blue eyes, which she later explained were made still brighter by contact lenses, fascinated me. But apart from her beauty, there was something unique about her … more womanly than the others.

In the past I had a couple of serious romances. Annamaria was my first girlfriend. She was the sister of Max Angelelli who raced karts and Formula 3 when I did. I met her in the paddock, paid her a few compliments and by the next race we were together. She lived 25 kilometers from Castel Maggiore and I would visit her on my bicycle in order to keep fit for racing, but I'd always have to ask her mom for a lift home. The relationship went on for a couple of years and we really cared about each other, but one day she said, "You are never around on the weekends because of these kart races, and Luca's always asking me out to the movies." I told her, "Be patient—you're dating an athlete—and the sacrifices will be worthwhile." I explained to her that I didn't want to limit my kart career, so she'd have to choose. She chose the movies with Luca.

In the beginning of 1986, I met Susan, a Swedish girl who was at the international kart debut with her brother, another racer. I was a bit shy, but she gave me a huge smile when she saw me in the paddock. All the other guys spent the weekend following her around and exchanging opinions about what they could do with someone like her. I didn't understand why she was smiling at me. I didn't even speak English at the time, other than managing a quick "hello." I went on to win that race and during the award ceremony that night she came up with a friend and introduced herself. I spent the 24-hour journey home on the plane wondering why she liked me.

At the end of the year, I saw her again in Hong Kong. After I won the race, we kissed for the first time. Afterwards, she invited me to her place for Christmas. I showed up in Sweden on my own with a panettone Christmas cake in my hand, not understanding a word of Swedish. Meeting her parents over dinner was dramatic. I was terribly embarrassed and unable to speak. In addition, thanks to the proverbial Nordic lack of inhibitions, they let me sleep in her bedroom. Every now and then, her father would pop his head in—too much freedom for my liking! Needless to say, I couldn't perform at all. I could see in her eyes that she was very disappointed. But I later made up for it and salvaged the honor of my fellow Italians, and the relationship went on quite happily.

A lovely girl, she would often visit me. She quickly learned to speak Italian and by the end of 1988, she started to talk about marriage. I didn't want to plan my future, as I was still very young. Although I really cared about her, we split up. I remember her well. She was 5 feet, 7 inches of pure Swedish beauty and had a sleek, athletic body that tanned remarkably well. She tanned so easily that even my Italian friends envied her, but she was eventually adopted into our group without any problem.

Yes, the group. About 20 of us would meet up every night on our mopeds or cars in a park in Castel Maggiore. We'd hang around some benches under a couple of lights and hence were called the "Benchers." The group included Bonza (his real name was Bonzagni) and Sciopero (which means Striker in Italian, because every time there was an official strike, he would miss school and join in). Then there was Dante, who was always a good laugh; Glauco, who was often away in Germany; and Chicco, whose real name was Enrico Serafini. We were like brothers and people would call us soulmates. We were always up to something.

I met Chicco at a race in Jesolo in 1987 and was immediately impressed by his passion for food. He was 5 feet, 5 inches tall, very slim and had a surprisingly massive appetite. He offered to pick up lunch from the racetrack café and came back with a stack of trays towering over him. Nobody could finish their food, especially the girls who just nibbled on the salads and desserts. Chicco, after devouring his own meal, finished off everyone else's, licking the plates clean. The races didn't go very well. That evening, I wasn't up for going out—my friends had to drag me to the restaurant. I was the last to order and asked for a pizza with everything … a sort of consolation prize. I was irked when Chicco changed his order and asked for the same. He didn't have a problem with his, but I spent the whole night in the john.

The day after the race in Jesolo, I noticed Chicco working on his red VW Golf in the road near my house. I had no idea that we were neighbors but it wasn't long before we became inseparable. Anything connected to motoring and engines captured our interests. Apart from karting, we liked motocross. He already had a motorbike, so I bought a second-hand one from Glauco that had 14 previous owners. Even Glauco gave motocross a shot on it. We used to go riding around the local tracks on the few Sundays when I wasn't karting. And I was always hiding from my parents. Chicco's garage was added to mine as a lab to work on everything. Not to mention what we did when I began in Formula 3. We discovered that with a bit of effort, my used racing car tires could be mounted on the Golf wheel rims. They were ridiculously pear-shaped, but enabled us to do some fantastic stunts. We had great fun going around the park in the middle of the night, and even managed to put the car on two wheels like Holer Togni. We perfected the technique, and today there is still someone in town who remembers a red Golf showing its underbelly around the bends of Castel Maggiore after midnight. We were those jokers.

Our mutual interest was not only motor racing, but also all other sporting events. We jogged together, skied together and went mountain biking. When mountain biking first became fashionable, we used to set out after dinner from Castel Maggiore, ride nine kilometers to the bottom of San Luca hill, climb up it and then return via an off-road path. We would go the whole way without any lights, with Bonza swearing because he was covered with scratches. He would always try to get down the mountain without braking and inevitably fell. He'd say, "Sooner or later, I'll make it," and he did. He didn't do this for his ego—he ended up joining the Italian championship of downhill mountain biking. He came second and received thousands of offers from various clubs who wanted to sponsor him, convinced that they had found a new star. Bonza showed up at the bar the following evening saying, "Hey guys, they want me to train with them, and race for them next Sunday, everything paid." Chicco asks, "What did you say?" Bonza said, "I'm 18 years old and 18-year-olds go after girls not bikes."

That evening finished Bonza's mountain bike career and the day after, instead of bike training, we happily set off skiing. The tires on Chicco's Golf were almost bald and therefore once the snow chains were attached on the front wheels the car was oversteering. He was having a lot of fun showing off in the snowy roads of the Appenino Mountains. He kept saying, "See, you steer a bit, give it a bit of gas and you go." And the following bend he said, "See how fast we're going." We came to a village called Montecreto where there was a bakery that made fantastic pastries. We planned to stop there for breakfast. Chicco took the last corner a bit too eagerly, and clearly didn't have everything under control as he wanted us to believe. The car spun twice and, in a moment that seemed like a lifetime, the scenery changed from the mountains to the valley below but we somehow ended up directly in front of the bakery. I was scared stiff. Chicco was as white as a ghost. But Bonza wasn't the least bit fazed, and casually stepped out of the car and said to three old men who ran to the scene, "Chicco always drives like that. As soon as we have breakfast and do some shopping, if you can bear with us, we'll show you again!" I almost wet myself with laughter, and even more so when trying to unzip those damned ski trousers ....

All of these adventures strengthened our friendship. If I wasn't sleeping over at Chicco's, he was sleeping over at mine. I much preferred the former because his sister was rather hot. Not to mention her girlfriends. But in 1988, this almost came to an end over a funny misunderstanding. We were at the Formula 3 race in Magione. We were sharing a double bed and wearing nothing but our underpants because it was so warm that evening. After chatting for a while with the lights off, I confessed to him, "Chicco, I have something to tell you and it's not that easy. We have a very good friendship and I wouldn't want to ruin it." Chicco seemed concerned. I tried to explain, "What I'm about to say might make things awkward. I respect you and have to tell you everything, and I can't keep these things inside me." You can guess what he thought. I realized he had the wrong idea when I sensed him edging away. I yelled, "I'm trying to tell you that I'd like to go out with your sister, and don't want to do it without you knowing!" Chicco was incredibly relieved and replied, "Do whatever you want with that ugly beast!" He was not known for his graciousness.

Chicco signed up for university but it didn't work out very well. Although endowed with a great mind, he wasn't great at studying. Instead, he went to work for his grandfather's company, producing machines to clean metal. To his credit, it was because of his talent, not family connections, that he was able to lead the technical aspects of the company.

5: Racing in Formula 3 and 3000

Those years we spent together were great, but the idyllic friendship sadly ended over a woman. In 1991 I met a girl who soon joined our group. She was one of those people who, rather than avoid problems, would purposely create them. She was basically a nice girl, but sincerity was never her strong point. I think she fancied me and, in order to send little messages to me, she befriended Chicco. She didn't hide her feeling for me in front of him, at least in the beginning. But when Chicco started to fall for her, I was put in an extremely difficult situation. She would confide in me about how she wasn't interested in Chicco. Nonetheless she led him on. The situation got even worse when she eventually slept with Chicco, yet was still coming on to me. I was already in love with Daniela and, out of respect for Chicco, had to warn him about the girl. It was a horrible situation. I was dragged into the middle of it and became the bad guy. Chicco desperately wanted to believe her and she didn't want to lose him, so she defended herself by saying I was jealous because she had chosen Chicco, not me. Chicco's sister, Michela, who had become a good friend of mine, immediately figured her out. Michela suggested that the girl, after seeing all of Chicco's wealth, including an expensive Porsche, decided that she had better not let him go.

During this time, I got to know Michela—or "Miki" as I used to call her—and we are still close. She's like the sister I'd lost, and I have wonderful memories of the afternoons we spent together. I think that Daniela was suspicious that perhaps something was going on. I felt badly about this but don't regret the time I spent with Michela because she helped me get over my disappointment with Chicco and proved to be a very good friend.

My bond with Chicco ended so suddenly, and I really suffered. I know that it was the same for him because years later, after his relationship with the girl ended, he called and apologized. But it was difficult to forget what had happened and swallow my pride. I had been hoping for a reconciliation before this, and I too made mistakes. Now I see things much more clearly. I never forgot his number and called him after writing this book and said, "Hey Chicco, how are you?" He is a true friend who waited far too long for my forgiveness.

Returning to the beginning of 1989, I couldn't stop thinking about Daniela, but I didn't want to fool myself into believing we would ever be more than friends. I was really smitten with her even though the keyboard incident still pissed me off. But when the new car arrived and I started the winter practices, I found my confidence again. The environment was ideal, even psychologically I couldn't ask for anything better. I also realized that I wasn't the crap driver I once thought. We were going very fast in the practice sessions, although a few people insinuated that we were driving underweight. Although untrue, those rumors haunted me and I had to wait until the first race to verify our time.

At Vallelunga, there were several episodes that contributed to my unique relationship with Roberto Trevisan. During the qualifying race, the Toyota engine had lots of electrical problems. I'd go out on the track and immediately have to return to the pits. The mechanics changed wires and even the wiring harness itself, then sent me right back. With only a short time left, we still hadn't solved our problems and to make matters worse, the car was understeering and unable to take the corners.

While the Toyota mechanics were busy working, I was talking to an engineer from Ralt named Damon Chandler. He was nicknamed, Uuuuunna Matita, because of the stilted way he spoke Italian. Each time that I mentioned understeering, Chandler would say to the mechanics, "Preload the front springs." Preloading slightly compresses the springs, and the initial movement of springing back into position requires additional power. This minor modification is only a temporary solution because it tends to lose efficiency very quickly. It is like showing up to paint the Duomo in Milan with a tiny paintbrush.

5: Racing in Formula 3 and 3000

At one point, I came back to the pits to find the engine was finally working. I gave the Toyota mechanics the thumbs up and called Roberto and Chandler over to the cockpit. Chandler asked how the car was handling. He had already preloaded the springs six times. I said, "The engine is all right, but the car is still understeering." Chandler turned toward the lead mechanic, Poncho (who could eat 18 baked potatoes in one night!) and told him, "Preload it again." I couldn't stand it anymore and told Roberto, "Chandler here—with his two preloads—is really pissing me off. Give me three holes in the front wing and increase the incidence, and lower the incidence on the rear wing. Give me four new tires and let's go for it, then he can do whatever he wants."

I went out on track again, took two laps and got pole position. I pulled into the pits, lifted my visor and said, "Now you can give me as much preload as you like." Chandler, still not happy, preloaded the springs again, obviously without any results. It didn't matter because I had pole and was thrilled. During the race, I had the same electrical problems, but not to the same extent as earlier. Coming out of the slowest corner on the track, the engine would splutter, but I eventually finished in second place. Compared to the previous years, that was a great result.

I received a third place at Magione and another second at Varano. Things were getting better. The grand prix in Monte Carlo arrived and I was racing there for the first time. Not only is this the most prestigious race but it is attended by all the Formula 1 managers. Before starting the race, Roberto wanted to talk to me. During a very long chat, he said, "Use your head. No one has ever excelled here on the first go, but I think you can. Just be careful." This advice went on through the headphones until my tires wore thin. In the decisive moments of the qualifying session, I saw P1 on the pit board while driving on the main straight. I was first! But in that quick second, I lost my concentration and crashed in the Saint-Devote corner. Even before putting on the new tires, which in Monte Carlo can earn you a second per lap, it was over for me. This was such a shame because, even with the accident, my time was sixth best. The following day, at the starting line I stalled the engine while trying to make up for the previous stupidity. Just as I restarted, Mika Häkkinen, who was behind me, bumped me and bent my wing plate. I managed a few laps, but the battered car then broke its clutch. I ended the race in a complete shambles.

Perhaps there's a kind of divine punishment that teaches you a lesson when you do something stupid. It was like this for me, so I was waiting for something bad to happen. For example after returning to the Italian Championship, the officials changed the fuel specifications. Novamotor was performing as well as before because they were tuning the Alfa Romeo engine that had a double ignition system, called Twin Spark, which could burn even charcoal. The Toyota engines, on the other hand, started breaking down. Eventually a total of 13 Toyota engines broke. I was still going fast enough to get pole position at Pergusa, but during the race a piston broke and I ended up in fourth place with a cockpit full of oil. After the race, a Sicilian fan wearing a white dress asked if she could take a photo with me. Not a good idea given that I was head to toe in grease!

From then on, things got even worse. In an attempt to enhance the reliability of the engines, we reduced the horsepower. But this really gave us a handicap at a track like Monza. It was no longer realistic to climb to the top position. In addition, we were the first to feel the ramifications of Zamagna's bankruptcy. He had not paid anyone since mid-season and, unknown to us, Roberto and Daniela had been covering the costs. They never said anything until the end of that year in order to keep up our morale. It was a shame. We had to start tightening our belts, and I didn't know why certain cutbacks were happening. By the end of the season I could no longer depend on Zamagna, so I decided to stick with Roberto and Daniela. I was Zamagna's wife's chauffeur in Bologna. I often did errands, picked up the children and babysat in the afternoon. They had a wonderful daughter, Mavi, and a son, Paolo, who had just started racing karts—my father had looked after them for a while. Zamagna's wife was very fond of me and distrusted her husband's business dealings. One day she said, "Here is your contract. You cannot be bound to such an idiot." My contract had been signed for five years so having it back lifted a heavy burden from my shoulders.

The situation was really getting bad, but finally there was light at the end of the tunnel. Roberto Farneti had a Formula 3000 team, but his driver was a disappointment and therefore had difficulty finding sponsorship. Roberto decided to invite me to Misano for a test. It was my first time in a Formula 3000 car. I went so fast that Farneti himself decided to finance me, inviting me to the last race at Digione instead of pulling out of the championship. That was the year that Irvine, Comas, Bernard and Alesi, who later won, were all racing at Digione. I showed up in France with no knowledge of the track or experience with the car. After 25 minutes of timed practice, I passed in front of the pits and saw P1 on the pit board. I was the fastest on the track! Then I crashed the car again with a huge bang. But nonetheless at the end of the session, I still came fifth. Emanuele Naspetti, a great fighter on the track but a gentleman off it, came to me and said, "You go so fast—you're out of your mind. If you go on like this, you'll definitely win on Sunday." We examined the car and, as well as the new damage, the engine was on its last leg and the suspension was completely out of alignment. We needed another engine, but Farneti had only brought one good one, given that it was the last race of the season. On the truck, however, there was the spare engine for the test car. We installed it on Saturday and during the preliminary session, I came in a mere 13th place. I was even slower during the final session and was passed by everyone on the straight, once again finishing in 13th place. It was absolutely pathetic.

From there, the whole relationship crumbled with Farneti because he had no money to fund a team in 1990. I, too, was broke and without a car. I went out with Roberto and Daniela for a pizza. We all felt very down, realizing that we had lost any chance of racing together, even with a second-hand engine and chassis. And we had no alternatives. Roberto and Daniela still had debts from Zamagna, who had fled the country, and we couldn't even get any more out of our used parts to help out. In addition, Roberto was being pursued by Osella to become a Formula 1 technician. Daniela, who was an excellent organizer, was offered a job in the Formula 3 Association. Formula 3 had become huge and needed a more efficient structure. They needed staff to manage the fuel supply and tire suppliers and to oversee all of the tests on more than 50 cars.

Ernesto Catella came to me with a proposal. He was a very nice man and an ex-driver who founded RC Motorsport, together with Carlo Migliavacca and Francesco Ravera. They were all very enthusiastic, but hadn't yet managed any results. As it was my only offer, I decided to give it a go. They not only let me race in Formula 3 for free, but added 30 million lire for my expenses. With Roberto's blessing, we went our separate ways. I started racing again with Novamotor engines provided by the Pedrazzani brothers. The 1990 championship was very strange. My direct rivals and I all had a good time and would give each other the lead. At the end of the year, Colciago won the title with just 39 points. I was right behind him, having incurred just as many faults. After the Formula 3000 race, I became rather bigheaded and thought that I was too good for Formula 3. That was a big mistake.

I raced the season without the enthusiasm and passion that separates the champions from the Sunday racers. I must apologize to my team because, although I gave them some incredible performances, I counterbalanced that with some very stupid mistakes. Despite the fact that we didn't have the best engines and had all made mistakes, I might have won the championship. Instead, I wasted a lot of races and a lot of time. I had many pole positions and won two races (Varano and Vallelunga), but there were quite a few bitter experiences, too. Like Pergusa, which I always considered my home track. Even to say, "this is my track" is a bit of a weakness. It's not that you have a magical recipe on your home track, but the fact that you can't repeat this same magic on other tracks that makes it special. For me, Pergusa was special. There was a double bend with a very fast section at the rear of the track that I would take in fourth gear in a Formula 3 car. I looked insane. I had a way of taking sections of the track on the curb, thereby gaining an incredible advantage on the others. At that point, I was able to gain increasing distance on the other drivers.

Ironically, it was this fearless quality that paved my way into Formula 3000 in 1991. Raul Gardini was pushing his son-in-law, Giuseppe Cipriani of the Cipriani family in Venice, to stop Formula 3 racing because the Montedison Group was looking for a manager for a new Formula 1 team. Montedison was already sponsoring the *Moro* racing boat in the America's Cup, and they had just started a Formula 3000 team. Cipriani became the new manager and quit Formula 3 racing. During that time, Formula 3 had so many cars that the practice runs took place in two sessions. Cipriani wasn't in my session and would instead study how the competitors took the corners. In Pergusa, Cipriani came to me with eyes wide open, "Tell me, how on earth did you take that corner? I timed everybody and you are eight tenths of a second faster than your closest competitor—it's unbelievable." At that time, none of us could imagine that we would be working together as a team by the end of the year. I was so distracted by his flattering compliments that during the race I smashed the car and damaged the wing plate on the first stretch, jeopardizing an easy victory. With a bent wing, which did everything but produce downforce, it looked like an opened umbrella. I finished in fourth place with the fastest lap of the race. Things like this were common during that season.

Another lost opportunity was Monaco, but this time it was the team's fault. Thanks to the previous year's experience, I managed to take pole position using new tires and without tasting the guardrail. We were the first to create a torsion bar that connected the shock absorbers, creating a type of mono-shock arrangement. This solution would work well with the Michelin tires used in the Italian Championship. We also mounted the bar in Monaco. In dry conditions it worked well but in the wet we might as well have shot ourselves in the foot. Well, it started raining. The team didn't want to reveal this secret at the starting grid so, rather than lift the cover of the engine, they made me start with a connected bar. The car became too rigid and was skidding all over the place, going from oversteering to understeering in a split second. I did a few laps, but with everybody overtaking me, I pulled out of the race. I was bitterly disappointed.

On the very long trip home in the car, no one said a word. I always hated trips home like this. When I used to race karts at the international level, I would always say, "I'd better do well because I can't face 13 hours of traveling in a foul mood." Perhaps this is why I've always done well in Australia and Hong Kong. Anyway, it was very difficult. I had started the race on pole position, in front of all of the Formula 1 team managers, and ended up chucking it out the window.

I went back to the *Tricolore* again and, between a series of good and bad races, eventually competed for the title in the final race. The second to last race should have been in Mugello, but they were modifying the circuit, so the last two races were moved to Vallelunga, near Rome. I won the first race in the rain, and re-opened the doors to the competition. Until then, Colciago and Angelelli seemed unreachable, but this victory made it all possible again. At that point, I had to beat everyone in the last race. Jacques

Villeneuve was in pole position and I was next to him. Colciago and Badoer were in the second row. Badoer had a suspicious start, but Villeneuve anticipated it and jumped the starting grid at the same time. The judges only saw Jacques and gave him a one-minute penalty. Although he had a great advantage, this penalty forced him out of the competition. But Badoer, who was racing with a year-old Ralt, was incredibly fast on the straight. I raced behind him but couldn't even hang onto his slipstream. Although I had the fastest lap and could have passed him, it would have been very risky. The real problem was Colciago being in third place. This was the first time I was rational and waited to observe the other driver's strategy. If he had lost third place or pulled out, I would have tried everything to pass Badoer and get second place in the championship, but nothing changed in the race. Colciago finished third and won the title, and I had to accept the outcome. Amen.

The Formula 3 European Cup took place in Le Mans that year. This race had lost a bit of its prestige over the years, but it was still important because the winner would be given the super-license to race in Formula 1. At that time, you needed several requirements to race in Formula 1, either a Formula 3 national title, or the European Cup, or to be in the top six in the International Formula 3000 Championship. Le Mans was a good opportunity, but only 18 cars showed up. In addition, Michelin was offering standard tires while Bridgestone had superior ones. Although Angelelli and I were faster than the others, we were the only ones using Bridgestones. We had agreed to develop the tires for Bridgestone in exchange for exclusive use. Michael Schumacher, who raced for Willi Weber's team, felt undermined and got Mercedes involved so that he could have the Bridgestones. I remember the Japanese being very embarrassed because they didn't know how to explain the situation. Schumacher used those tires very well and grabbed the pole position, while Angelelli was second and I was third. Schumacher started badly and Angelelli and I were on each side of him. But coming up to one of the features, the German bumped both of us—one to the left and one to the right—and sent us off the track. Then Angelelli turned and hit Schumacher, sending him off as well. At that point, the championship was over for me and I jumped out of the car. Michael realized that the race wasn't going to be stopped so he jumped in the car, parked it in the middle of the track, took the steering wheel off and left. This way the race was forced to stop.

I returned to the pits and managed to get the spare, but by then it had started to rain. In a rush, one of the pit guys had forgotten to change the rear wing to the one for wet conditions. We didn't realize this until the second start, but it was too late to rectify the situation and I had to start with the wrong set-up for wet conditions. It was exhausting, but I managed to fend off my opponents and come in second. Schumacher had an easy game and won. After the race, Guido Forti, manager of another Italian team said, "It doesn't matter now because we're out of the race, but if I was you I would file a complaint. Schumacher won with an Opel engine while his original car had a Volkswagen engine." It is against the rules to have two different types of engines. Even the officials didn't notice this when the car was checked. Only after checking the type of engine was Michael disqualified.

The funniest part of the story was the way in which we gathered the information on Schumacher's car. Catella had this idea that if he could get a picture of Schumacher's engine, then we could prove his theory. He went to Michael and asked him, in his clumsy English, "Can I have a photo of you, the new European champion, next to your car?" Catella came back to us with his Polaroid, but we couldn't see the engine's details. So he went back to take another, saying to Michael, "Can we take it again a bit more to the right," in order to secretly snap a photo of the Opel-Spiess insignia on the engine. It was hilarious, but soon became quite serious. The officials initially laughed when we showed them the evidence, then half an hour later they disqualified Schumacher. I became European Champion, although this is not the title I'm most proud of. Years later in Formula 1, Willi Weber saw me and said, "Do you remember, Le Mans 1990?"

Catella really made me laugh … and what a generous guy he was. At Imola, he showed up with a brand new Mercedes 300 CE, threw the keys at me and said, "Take the keys, drive it home, and show it off to your friends." But it wasn't all fun and games, and the whole Montedison team worked very hard. The crew would put 36 hours of work into a 24-hour day. They often slept in the garage, yet never stopped enjoying their work. Over the years they refined their technique and brought home many Italian championships (and the German one) and became a very important team. But we should have won the 1990 Italian Championship.

The mistakes I made that season proved to be useful in the years to come. The average driver is someone who always does his homework and is popular with the team manager because he doesn't do any damage. But the average driver is also someone who fails to push the envelope or invent something new. In the beginning of my career, I made many avoidable mistakes. I could have won more races, but I wouldn't have improved my skills as I managed to do.

So, 1990 ended on a fairly mediocre note. But most of all, there were no prospects for the following year and I knew that I couldn't stay a fourth year in Formula 3. The only ray of light that year was my romance with Daniela. No matter how hard we tried to hide it, we were clearly fond of each other and in 1989, we kissed for the first time. I was mad about her and couldn't think of anyone else. It is difficult to describe how huge this emotion was. She not only inspired me, but also gave me tenderness and security at the same time. She is very strong, ambitious and handles pressure incredibly well. She only needs to say a few words to get her point across, whereas I handle pressure very differently. She is admirably lucid and articulate, and I've seen businessmen completely silenced by her intelligence and business acumen. But she is also a very sincere person, just as I thought when I first met her. I'm certain that my wife has never lied to me, although she probably can't say the same about me. To her, sincerity is a fact of life. I am a tough guy and throughout my career, I've had to overcome challenges and disappointments, but I never gave up—even in the most difficult situations. I have needed someone to lean on, and having Daniela by my side enabled me to detach myself from things. She is still this constant source of strength. My friends often say to me, "Daniela has square balls!" which is a common saying in Bologna meaning someone is a very strong character. Anyway, a wonderful relationship started and, for some reason, remained hidden for a long time. It's a bit like smoking; if someone finds out, it doesn't make a very good impression. We could have revealed the truth about our relationship in the beginning of 1991, but she became my team manager in Formula 3000, so we had to keep it secret to avoid the appearance of a conflict of interest.

Going back to December 1990 when my career was once more at a dead end, it was Daniela who really inspired me. When I feel frustrated, I am remarkably good at becoming a lazy slob. I was in Daniela's office with my feet on the desk, doing nothing. Usually, with that kind of depression, I woke up at midday and remained unshaven and sloppily dressed. Then, starting to feel like crap, I decided to do something. So I put on a worn-out tracksuit and ran for ten kilometers. A little bit like the film *Rocky*, with the hood on my head, running through the countryside. Afterwards, I went home, showered and shaved and felt like a new man. That day Daniela, seeing me worse than ever, realized I was alone and without a future. I had a taste of Formula 3000, but it had become a financial impossibility. All of the teams that I had talked to wanted between 800 million and one billion lire. I didn't have a penny, was driving a Golf with a broken exhaust and being supported by my parents. Those were not abundant years. At the end of 1988, I had even gone back to kart racing and won the *Avenir 135* class at the Grand Prix in Hong Kong, bringing home a prize of around seven million lire. For me that was big money— enough to even consider replacing the Golf.

On that rainy day in December Daniela said, "Do you know that Giorgio Breda and Giuseppe Cipriani are putting together a Formula 3 team—with sponsorship—and perhaps you should give them a call?" I wasn't too sure. Breda was an excellent Formula 3 technician, and I remembered what happened at the double corner in Pergusa. I said, "Maybe they will consider me." I didn't have Cipriani's phone number, but I found Breda's. At the time I was in Padova where Daniela lived, and Breda was 25 kilometers away in Mestrino. I called Breda and, coincidentally, Cipriani was with him discussing a few ideas. I made up an excuse and said that I was "just checking his availability" for Formula 3, but in fact I was really hoping to speak to him. Breda said he was no longer interested in Formula 3 but perhaps he could make me another offer. He put me on the speakerphone and explained, "Giuseppe Cipriani and I are putting together a Formula 3000 team and sooner or later we will need a driver. Do you want to talk about it?"

It was like asking a cat if it liked mice. I said, "Guys, I'm not going to lie to you—I'm telling you now that I don't have any money. I've had some offers, but I don't actually know how much I can give you. I can bring you great enthusiasm, and I'll put my heart and soul into the team because I believe in it." They told me that the money might not be a problem and asked, "So when can you come see us?" I replied, "I'll be there in 20–30 minutes!" They had a standard contract in a drawer and by the evening, I had signed the deal. At that time it was common practice for a driver to contribute money. Therefore the typical contract had a clause in it that listed everything the team had to do from a technical point of view, and what the driver had to do in terms of his responsibilities, "The driver will offer his services and make a financial contribution of X amount in exchange for the team's services." I remember that at the end of my contract, the X amount was "to the driver's discretion" plus VAT. Throughout the meeting, Breda was telling Cipriani to "sod off and eliminate the clause altogether," whereas Cipriani replied, "No, no. I really like the way 'to the driver's discretion plus VAT' sounds!"

That's how our relationship began. Within a week, we set some meetings with Lola and Reynard, the companies that built Formula 3000 chassis in England. Reynard later became fundamental in my career. At the time we all preferred Lola, who had a stack of orders. Cipriani found out that Montedison's chemical industries were Lola's sole suppliers of composite material. Thanks to Cipriani we were given a second-hand Lola chassis for the winter practice sessions, along with a promise for a new one after the second race, and a new one a week before the championship. This meant that we would have started practicing with just one untested new car between two drivers. We were a bit discouraged but, like everyone else, we wanted the Lola chassis.

Since we were in England, we decided to go ahead and see Reynard too. I knew Rick Gorne, commercial director of Reynard, and set up a meeting with him. We arrived and he welcomed us with open arms. He showed us the plans for the car, but it didn't exist yet. They were looking for a way back into the competition after repeatedly losing that year. So, although they only had a design, we were impressed by Rick's enthusiasm and competitiveness. He told Cipriani, "You made the right choice for a driver." Needless to say, I've liked him ever since. In addition he said, "You have money and everything you need to win. With a good run of winter testing, you can win the title. You are very important to us, and therefore we are ready to give you chassis numbers 2, 3 and 7 for this new car." They had promised to deliver all of the cars in mid-January. Giorgio Breda had a close look at all of the modifications in the drawings and thought that they had been done extremely well. On the trip home, we thought about it a lot. I said only a few things, but they were all in favor of Reynard. We impressed Rick Gorne and he impressed us, so we ultimately decided to go with them. We had all of the sponsors from the Montedison Group and a hefty budget. Cipriani was able to put together a proper team and proved to be an excellent manager who could make brave decisions. Even our image was different. Apart from the very appropriate team name, the "Rampant Baron," we were the first to have a motorhome and stylish team colors.

Back from England, I pursued Roberto Trevisan and Daniela because we needed capable people to run the organization. They accepted my offer and quickly became vital to the team's success. Roberto became my personal technician, as he was in Formula 3. We had other good people, in particular my chief mechanic, Roberto Fassina. He was very shy and later got fed up with racing, but he really was an exceptional mechanic. He had worked on Marco Apicella's car for the Leoni team, called "First Racing." I shared his opinion that Marco was a great, but very unlucky, driver. He always went on about Marco, calling him "The Professor" and making comparisons between us. I spent the entire winter practice with The Professor in my head. I wanted to win a place in this mechanic's heart because I really admired him.

One day we were doing a preseason test at Vallelunga. The pole position had been around 1 minute, 6.2 seconds the previous year, but we knew that this track was notoriously faster in the winter. So it wasn't unusual to see a Formula 3000 lap time at 1 minute, 5 seconds. That day, my average lap time was 1 minute, 5.8 seconds and Fassina said, "We'll see how well you do at the first race, but if The Professor was here he would race below 1 minute, 5 seconds." I went back to the track and my lap time was below 1 minute, 5 seconds. Fassina said, "Well, the track conditions are good, but if The Professor was here, he would do around 1 minute, 4 seconds."

I jumped in my car and did around 1 minute, 4.7 seconds. Fassina then said, "The track and car seem fine." This was actually the first time that we drove the Reynard, thrilled that they made such a great and fast car. I drove in the low 1 minute, 4 seconds range, but that wasn't enough for Fassina. He was being a real pain in the ass with the story of this Professor. So I managed to drive 1 minute, 3.5 seconds, which was an outstanding time. Despite this feat, I went home with his voice in my ear, echoing, "We'll see how you do in the first race when everyone is serious—you'll be lucky if you qualify."

We practiced the whole winter. Finally the first race arrived in Vallelunga and although I started in second position, I won! It was an incredibly rewarding victory, but it was really the team behind me who helped me reach this level. I kept my head on straight, remaining calm and focused on the next race—and on Fassina. The second race of the season was at Pau, a very different street circuit. On certain corners, for example, you have to brake on the inside of the hairpin and watch where you place the wheels. There are several other details to remember—in other words, it is the expert's paradise. The Vallelunga victory was magical … I was holding my breath as I made the final laps and tried to get my head around the fact that I had scored my first Formula 3000 victory. But once off the podium, Fassina gave me some advice. "Well, you clearly know this track, and Reynard has delivered a great car. Let's see if you're lucky enough to qualify in Pau."

That year, there were just two 40-minute qualifying runs, both of which were valid for the starting grid. A 40-minute run was nothing. In addition, Pau was a short and narrow circuit and thus they had to divide us into two groups, giving us one qualifying time instead of two in order to avoid confusion. I had a lot of doubts, but I kept concentrating on my job. This time when I saw "P1" (i.e., first place) chalked on the pit wall, I didn't crash the car and instead got pole position with more than a second advantage on the next car. I was thrilled. I went to the pits and received countless pats on the back. I went to the garage and asked Fassina, who was working quietly on an engine, "Did we do well then?" He said, "Well?" This went back and forth until he replied, "Is 1 minute, 9.48 seconds good here? No, 1 minute, 9.48 seconds is unbelievable!" Finally he was pleased with my performance. I was over the moon, but to prevent bad luck I said, "There are still 40 minutes to go for the other drivers." Fassina lifted his eyes and put the wrench on the floor, saying calmly, "The others could spend a week here and they'll never come in at 1 minute, 9.48 seconds. Today you have replaced The Professor's position in my heart." He took his wrench and went back to work without saying another word. And he was right, even the fastest of the second group, Montermini, was more than a second slower than me.

Throughout the year I started in the first row eight out of ten times, and my worst result in practice was fourth place. Apart from my performances, it was qualifying races at Pau and Brands Hatch that put me in the limelight. This last track is considered impossible for non-British drivers. It is a very difficult, undulating track with fast bends and blind corners. I got pole position again, a second faster than Damon Hill who started next to me in the line-up. But sadly I didn't manage to complete the following lap because I crashed the car at Dingle Dell, a very famous chicane. The car was utterly demolished. Although I had the best time among heavy traffic on the track, I kept pushing and insisted to Trevisan on the radio, "There is still more, I can go faster. What should I do, stay on the track for another lap?" He answered, "No, we are fine like this—you have the pole so come back in."

There was still five minutes to go in the qualifying. "Come back in," he said. This is typical of my character, I always try to reach my limit without considering the ramifications to others or myself. So ignoring the pit instructions, I launched into that lap and crashed. I've never seen mechanics so willingly work through the night on such a heap of scrap. That year, I had a feeling that my guys were happy to go the extra mile. Everyone was ecstatic when the telemetry revealed that I had nine tenths of a second advantage on my fastest lap. If I had not crashed, I would have had two seconds on everybody. But I overdid it—I wanted too much. That was one of those things that young drivers try on the ovals, it is mathematically possible but in reality, highly improbable.

Returning to Pau, I started badly and was positioned second behind Montermini (who then broke down) when a driveshaft broke. In the third race in Jerez, we miscalculated and unloaded the aerodynamics, ending up second behind Christian Fittipaldi. The fourth race meeting was at Pergusa, "my" track. I had a fantastic pole, but I got heat stroke on the Saturday afternoon and by the evening I was feeling terrible. On Sunday I woke up with a deliriously high fever. They gave me an antibiotic intravenously when I arrived at the track, but I didn't get any better. Daniela didn't want me to race, and Roberto was uncertain. But I wanted to go at all costs. The local doctor, who was a huge race fan, gave me the okay. I told the others, "Now don't piss me off—I'm in pole position and I'm racing." And so I did.

Unfortunately the fever caused me to have a delayed reaction at the green light and I didn't take off until the sixth row passed by me. I had to fight back but after six laps, I was in first place. Suddenly I felt a hell of lot better and my clear mind gave me an incredible advantage on everybody. But just before the end, I blew a tire. I slid off at the chicane, skidded into the sand and completely damaged the car. I was about to stop on the side of the track when I realized that if I placed the car in the middle of the track, like Schumacher did, then the race would be stopped and I could still win. Like an idiot, I only put it partially on the track. The only thing I gained from this was a series of insults from *Autosprint*, which described me as a cheat who couldn't handle losing. From a certain point of view, the critics were right. On the other hand, the nicest compliment came from Daniela who said, "Even before you explained to me whether you did that on purpose or not, someone with a fever as high as yours, who drives such a good race, destroys the competition and at the end, despite the blow-out, has the guts to do what you did, is still a hero in my eyes." Roberto, on the other hand, was crying. He came to hug me, "Don't worry, we're going to win the championship because we're stronger than misfortune." Let's hope so, because losing two races in such a ridiculous manner wasn't making things any easier.

Luckily I dominated the next race at Mugello. Although my teammate, Bugatti, was very fast, I took both the pole and the victory. Apicella (aka The Professor) passed me at the start, but I overtook him in the following lap and never saw him again. The next race was at Hockenheim in front of a Formula 1 audience. There was just one qualifying session, and I took fourth place. But then I spun out at the motordrome during the warm-up lap and had to start in last place. Trying to make up for time, I did a video game-style attack at the first chicane. I passed ten cars, but then missed the corner and spun out of the race. At Brands Hatch I had a disastrous start. In the first lap I was in eighth position, but soon recovered and finished second after Naspetti. At Spa we were once again in front of a Formula 1 audience. There was a downhill start, so if one foot is on the brake and one is on the clutch, how can you accelerate? You invent a handbrake. We found a bike shop and bought some wire and everything that we needed to build the mechanism. It was a wire with a little ring by which you would press the brake with the foot, pull the wire and hold the brake on with a finger. On the starting grid, you would let go of the wire and shoot off like a rocket. I was third on the grid, but by the first bend, the famous *Eau Rouge*, I was already in the lead. Luca Zanella, the mechanic who invented this solution, was absolutely delighted. But I didn't win. Back then, as in Formula 1, there was special fuel that could greatly increase your speed. Although

Monteshell sponsored us, we hadn't managed to produce any special fuel. At one point Cipriani, given his friendship with Flavio Briatore, managed to obtain some race gas from the Benetton team. But when we tested this, it literally destroyed an engine. On some race tracks, for instance in Spa, it gave us a disadvantage. Naspetti caught up with me, and although I tried to fight him off, he quickly left me behind and ended up in second place. At that point, Naspetti and I were at the top of the championship, and Fittipaldi was in third.

That same weekend at Spa, something happened in Formula 1 that would eventually involve me. Jordan was launching Michael Schumacher, who was undoubtedly making a splash and impressing everybody. Some days later Benetton offered Schumacher a contract to substitute Moreno in the team alongside Piquet, literally stealing him from Jordan. The unsentimental German didn't give it a second thought. On the Thursday before Monza, Benetton's sporting director, Joan Villadelprat, called me. I couldn't believe it. "What? Me with Benetton?" They took me to the motorhome and said, "We took on Schumacher, but it's a messy situation. It's very likely that he won't be able to race with us but whatever happens, we don't want Moreno anymore." They wanted to place Moreno with Jordan and keep Schumacher on standby until the waters calmed. The discussion concluded with, "If Schumacher doesn't race, we want you in the car." This seemed surreal. I went to the pits and was secretly fitted for the seat.

A short time later, Maurizio Arrivabene from Marlboro called me. He always did what he could to promote young Italian drivers and said, "Look, Jordan wants you to race." I thought he was mistaken. "You mean Benetton?" "No, Eddie Jordan himself." I was totally confused and went to the autodrome with Arrivabene to meet Jordan. "They stole Schumacher from us and they would like to give us Moreno, but we want you," Eddie said. I was really torn and explained, "This is a secret, but I have to tell you that

Benetton's made me the same offer. If Schumacher doesn't race, they want me. But if Schumacher can't race for either of you, what will I do—I clearly can't race for you both?" I was both embarrassed and overwhelmed at the same time. I went from a disheveled, jobless loafer to a racer sought after by both Benetton and Jordan Formula 1 teams. I was only 24 years old and needless to say, it was difficult to keep my feet on the ground.

I left the track and after a few minutes, my phone rang. I remember that I had one of the first mobile phones, a half meter long. With this in my pocket, I walked worse than I do now! It was Villadelprat, "Thanks very much, but everything is all right with Schumacher, so we don't need you." I thought to myself, perfect— I have a solution. I immediately called Jordan who said, "OK, if there aren't any problems, you come here tomorrow morning at six and we'll get you ready to drive." I went back to my hotel and a barrage of phone calls began again. Jordan started saying, "Tomorrow you will drive for us, but be psychologically prepared because you're only going in the car if you sign a contract, so if you have a lawyer bring him with you." Obviously he was burnt by the Schumacher affair, but I was already annoyed by the tone of his words. Briatore called me next.

The situation was getting more complicated. Moreno had very cunningly got an injunction with the labor courts which would force Benetton to take him back if he could justify his claim. Benetton was faced with either bringing back Moreno or dropping out of the race. Briatore suddenly became very ingratiating and asked me not to commit to anybody. Now I can see that it was the opportunity of a lifetime and I should have waited for Benetton's offer. But I politely replied, "Mr. Briatore, this is such a fantastic opportunity to race and I just can't say no to Jordan." Briatore responded, "Fine. Do what in the hell you want" and slammed down the phone. Two minutes later, he called me back. "I'll make you an offer. You'll immediately become this year's official test driver, and next year's, and you also race in Formula 3000. Then in 1993, you will be Benetton's official Formula 1 driver, but tomorrow you will not drive for Jordan." I tried to be as polite and convincing as possible. "Thank you very much for your offer, but I'm going crazy here. Until yesterday, I only dreamed of racing in Formula 1, and now two big teams are fighting over me. But Jordan is asking me to race now, so try to put yourself in my position." Briatore shouted, "You don't understand a goddamn thing!" and slammed the phone down again. Two minutes later I received another call from Cipriani. "I'm here with Briatore discussing your situation, and you'd better listen to him." At this point I went mad, "Cipriani, I really care about you. You let me race in Formula 3000, but you shouldn't get in the middle of this." We discussed it a bit more and then he put Briatore on the phone again, "Don't you understand who I am in Formula 1? If I want, I can kick Piquet out and put you in the car tomorrow!"

The situation was becoming more and more surreal. "Mr. Briatore, I really don't know what to say, but if I was stunned to be fought over by two such prestigious teams as yourselves, you can imagine how I feel when you suggest replacing Piquet, a three times World Champion, with me. That said, if you are serious we can talk about it, but I've already accepted Jordan's offer and I'm not going to pull out of the deal." He got really angry and started being aggressive. He was telling me what I should do, as if he were my father. At that point I stopped the conversation. "Listen, I'm really flattered by your interest but with all due respect, we've never even had a meal together—yours are just words. Now I have to go to dinner, get up very early and then prepare myself for the test drive, so goodnight." And then I waited for Eddie Jordan's phone call—which never came.

Unknown to me, Briatore and Cipriani had been to see Jordan. Briatore told him that I had a contract with Cipriani and warned him, "If you make Zanardi race, we'll take you to court. Cipriani decides what Zanardi does." That wasn't true, but Jordan believed it and never called me. The next morning I showed up at the track and saw Moreno driving the Jordan. After free practice I went to the motorhome to look for Eddie. He came out screaming at me. I was stunned, but the misunderstanding was soon cleared up. In reality I did have an agreement with Cipriani, which allowed me to race in 1991 in exchange for a share in my future profits. And that's all. But the damage was done and I was screwed. I quickly tried to forget about it and jumped head first back into Formula 3000. What a nice dream this was while it lasted ….

CHAPTER 6

Formula 1—At Last

I put the dream of Monza behind me, but Formula 1 soon lured me back into her arms. The incredible Formula 3000 season attracted the attention of several grand prix team managers, including the illustrious Eddie Jordan. I was at practice in Le Mans, preparing for the penultimate race of the championship. While chatting with Roberto about the car's handling, I was called over the loud speakers to go to the steward's office to take a phone call. It was Eddie Jordan. Even with my broken English, I managed to understand what he wanted when he said, "Take the first fucking plane and come and see me." The negotiations were very quick. Eddie was very tough and in a foul mood because I'd got "on the second fucking plane," instead of the first. At the end, I signed a contract for the last three grand prix races of 1991. He wanted me to race in Portugal as well, but I couldn't because of a conflict with the last Formula 3000 race. He was pissed off and thought that I should do whatever he said, whereas I was just trying to win a championship that I'd pursued for the entire year. He was really aggressive and from that moment on, I knew he would even be telling me when to go to the toilet. I wasn't very happy and he said abruptly, "You'd better make a choice because guys are lined up out there waiting to race for me." I calmly replied, "Thank goodness, I would have felt bad about saying no if I were your only choice." I wasn't playing games with him—I was actually quite sincere. Jordan took it the right way and said, "Listen, take this contract with you, read it properly and sign it tomorrow." He wanted an option for five years. It would have expired at the end of October, but I asked him if it could be changed to October 23 to coincide with my birthday, thereby giving me a birthday present each year that he decided to extend it.

The Jordan team wanted to organize a test drive before my debut at the Spanish Grand Prix, but there was no time. I was in France for the Formula 3000 finals, so they had to check the equipment for the upcoming race in Portugal without me. Meanwhile, I got ready for my main duty that season—the Formula 3000 title—feeling great about my ticket to Formula 1 in my pocket. Theoretically, the winner could have been confirmed by the penultimate race. Had I won and Naspetti retired, then I would have automatically become the Formula 3000 Champion and the same for Naspetti if the situation had been reversed. Christian Fittipaldi would have to rely on our misfortune in order to get back into the game, and that's exactly what happened.

Ten minutes before the start at Le Mans, there was a downpour. In the supplementary warm-up, my car was very fast. I was flying and more than a second ahead of everybody else. I didn't have a terribly good start and was third on the grid, but that changed in just a few laps. Then things turned for the worse. The alternator broke down, the battery started discharging and the injection system began to falter. Probably the injectors had a delayed opening and closing which made the engine flood. On the straight, the engine would misfire, but while coming out of corners, it would splutter and not accelerate. So I started taking the corners in a lower gear than usual, thus keeping high revs on the engine. The engine was running smoothly and burning off more fuel which helped to reduce my handicap. Driving on a wet surface with such a handicap was extremely difficult, and the fact that engine power delivery and weather were highly unpredictable made it even worse. It was agonizing, especially in the last four laps. Then everybody caught up with me, the engine blew on the last corner and I was out. In addition, I was at the farthest point from the pits, in the middle of a downpour with no one to fetch me. Fittipaldi was now back in the game after Naspetti and I had pulled out. The Brazilian finished second without really deserving it, having been able to improve his position thanks to others' misfortune. But this is irrelevant, because all that matters at the end of the day is the name of the winner.

With only one race left to go, in France, Fittipaldi was in first place in the standings. We arrived at Nogaro, where the officials discovered that the fuel in Naspetti's car was irregular. He was prevented from using it and disappeared from the competition. Meanwhile, Fittipaldi's team showed up with superb fuel for his Honda engine and blew us all out of the water. There was no competition. He won and I was second, exactly how we finished in the championship. I was very disappointed. I had felt that I should have finished as champion and instead, I had a bitter defeat and lost the title.

I didn't have time for disappointment, though, because I had to focus on my Formula 1 debut. I hadn't even seen the car before arriving in Barcelona. Fortunately, Montmeló was a new circuit for everybody, so we were all given an extra hour of practice time on the Thursday before the race. But things did not go as expected that weekend. Jordan had an excellent car, but its unique qualities didn't necessarily adapt well to all tracks. For example, when Schumacher was racing for Jordan, the car performed so well that he qualified in seventh place at Spa, and de Cesaris was very close to winning the Grand Prix. But at Barcelona, for example, we qualified in 20th and 21st positions because the car wasn't suited to the Catalunyan circuit. During the race, the car performed better and after overtaking several drivers, I ended up in ninth place.

What surprised me on my debut was the number of useless people around a Formula 1 team. Who knows what they actually did, but they seemed to keep themselves busy with the strangest things. They are the experts at "giving advice" and like to buddy up to the new drivers, especially when no one else is around. Most of these unlikely advisors had warned me, "It will be very hard—100 km longer than Formula 3000—and you will need a lot of fluids." My head was spinning with their useless comments. There were numerous things to get used to: a new car, a new track, a more powerful engine and carbon brakes. But the biggest problem was not to dehydrate. Because of this fear, I drank so much that as soon the green light came on, I wanted to take a piss. Years later, I learned to wee in the cockpit, but at that time I held it, avoiding the ridged curbs because the vibration made it worse. Nevertheless, I finished the race and everyone was satisfied, except Eddie Jordan, who was probably expecting a miracle performer like Schumi.

They were at least two very proud people, my parents. Many things had changed since the happy years of karting, and inevitably my move to cars had burst the bubble. The moment came when I, like all teenagers, looked for some independence from my parents. My mom has always been a woman with an unusual quiet inner strength, whereas my father was a time bomb. When he was angry, nothing could hold him back. He'd always say how he felt and I had to listen. This is why our relationship became strained over the years. Mom would try to convince him that I was an adult and needed to get on with things, but he wouldn't change his ways. So he followed me around, trying to participate in my life. "Come on, tell me what's going on," he would say. It was like a break-up, with one person drifting away while the other clings on. This wasn't our only problem. One year he came to Vallelunga to see one of the Formula 3 races. When everything was going OK, I was very happy for him to literally lift me out of the car to celebrate, but when things were not great, if something wasn't perfect, he would go on and on—like he did during the karts—shouting and screaming, which was totally unacceptable. A spin, an accident, a technical problem and one of my first thoughts would be, "Let's hope Dad won't make a scene in the pits." As I got older, I often found myself hoping that my parents wouldn't show up, and as a consequence my attitude at home was less than encouraging. Strangely, though, they were always the first people I would call if a race went well. The fact that they always answered on the first ring, waiting to hear my results, somehow still made me feel guilty. I'm sorry for cutting them out, but that's life and is nobody's fault.

My best memory of Barcelona goes back to them. I had forbidden my parents to show up in Spain, "Papa, this is my Formula 1 debut and I can't drive worrying about what you may say if someone hits me or something breaks." I could picture him insulting Eddie Jordan himself, shouting, "What did you give him to drive?" So I asked them, "Please, do me a favor and watch the race on the television." He came anyway, and during the slow-down lap after the checkered flag, despite 80,000 people in the stands, he managed to make himself noticed by climbing a fence some six or seven meters high. I spotted him waving his hands victoriously when I finished the race in ninth place, which, in his mind, was a great result. In that moment his paternal pride was irrepressible. I was so touched and remember saying to myself, "I love you, Dad." It was a very sweet moment.

Jordan had a partial revenge on Briatore during the following grand prix in Japan. On the Friday, I qualified seventh at Suzuka on a new track (for me at least). That night, Eddie was in a good mood. In the free practice on Saturday, I went even faster and everything led us to believe that I would do well. We would receive two sets of tires for each timed qualifying session, but I wore them both out because of the congestion on the track. I would often see drivers exiting the pit lane and trying to avoid me in fear of getting stuck behind a new driver. I was completely shut out and not able to do any better and fell to 13th position even though the car was handling extremely well. This car, even when loaded with fuel, came in sixth during the Sunday morning warm-up. Trevor Foster, my engineer, told me, "Go out with a full tank so that you get used to the car—we don't have to prove anything to anybody—just take a lap." That's what I did and I was unbelievably fast. I even overtook Prost in the Ferrari. I'm not bluffing—I was really fast. While I was walking in the pit lane with my helmet in my hand, I came across Mariani, the engineer for Scuderia Italia who asked me, "How much fuel did you have? Five liters?" I replied, "No, I had a full tank." He started laughing, but then became serious, "Boy, if you were really full of fuel, you will have a fantastic race." Off I went and that's what happened. In six laps I went from 13th to 5th place. Berger was leading, followed by Senna, Mansell, Patrese, Prost, Martini, Schumacher and me. It was when I overtook Michael Schumacher that Eddie Jordan got his small revenge. People told me that Jordan leaned from his pit to Benetton's and called out, "Briatoriiiiiiiii" and gave him the finger. Unfortunately that gesture brought us bad luck because while I was coming out of the hairpin, the clutch froze in first gear. That problem had happened before, but this time it put an end to my race.

During these few laps, I passed my teammate de Cesaris who was battling with Morbidelli in the Minardi-Ferrari. Coming out of the 130 R corner, they both moved to the right so I threw my car to the left (more to avoid them than to pass them). But because they were obstructing each other, they were really slow and braking too early. I quickly accelerated and at the last moment, spontaneously passed both of them from the outside. I went past the chicane and suddenly saw the green of the other Jordan spinning behind me. De Cesaris made a huge scene after the race, like in a Western. He said that I was a disgrace and that I didn't respect him, blaming me for taking advantage of the situation with Morbidelli and causing him to spin out. Eddie Jordan and the other people on the team were rolling their eyes. I was really sorry about it because in those days, we often went out together and he always made me laugh. I didn't want to reply, but he kept going on and on and he finally pissed me off, "Maybe I'm the new guy, but let's not fool ourselves. You're the one who will look ridiculous if you keep on complaining like this." He never mentioned it again until three years later in Hungary during another one of his scenes in the paddock. At the end of the race, JJ Lehto, who had been following me and de Cesaris in the Scuderia Italia car during that lap, said to me, "I heard that de Cesaris was giving you a hard time. I wanted to explain to Eddie that I saw the whole scene because I was right behind you, and you passed him in the cleanest possible way." Actually, when he spun, Andrea also took out Lehto and his teammate Emanuele Pirro!

I missed a great opportunity at Suzuka. My lap time had really been impressive and comparable to Senna and Mansell, who were racing for the title. At that moment I was faster than Berger and Patrese, who finished third. Mansell ended up pulling out at the end, so maybe I could have been on the podium. Anyway, my performance attracted the attention of several team managers. At a press conference at the end of the year, a journalist asked Ron Dennis why he had never hired an Italian driver. "I don't have anything against Italian drivers, but if I had to bet on anyone today, it would be Zanardi, who seems very fast." So although Suzuka ended badly, I was rather proud of my performance.

Two weeks later, we arrived in Adelaide for the last race of the season, and that's where our little game stopped. Suzuka had gone to my head, but it was the installation lap that really threw me off my equilibrium. The installation lap is when the car is checked to ensure that everything is mounted properly. I saw Senna shooting up behind me in the rear-view mirror, but made sure he could pass without any problems. He suddenly seemed much farther away and I thought, "He's given up," but he hadn't. Instead, he was directly behind me again. Then I realized why he had backed off—there was a bend right in front of us that I clearly wasn't taking. I desperately pounded the brakes, but ended up smashing the car against the wall. I felt so stupid. I was sent out again in the T-car and tried a move that I hoped would bring a smile back to everybody's faces. Over the years, I'd learned to disconnect my emotions when racing and to rely on my brain as much as possible, and this was one of those days that taught me the necessity to disconnect. After just two laps, I crashed the second car into the wall.

In Adelaide, I had only completed three and a half laps on what was a difficult and new track, and the team was not smiling. I had been advised in several different languages to take it slow, and then told, "We'll allocate a set of tires for qualifying and another set of race tires so that you can take a few laps and learn the track." Slow and calm were the passwords. I entered the track and shot off after the first corner, but on the straight, while changing from third to fourth gear, the stickshift (the box was a traditional H pattern) broke. The bolt connecting the two pieces of the linkage snapped and instead of going into fourth gear, the car slipped into second. In third gear, I'd revved up to 13,200 revs, and I don't even want to think about the number on the rev counter when it was in the wrong gear.

Jordan had just warned me, "Be careful and don't do any damage, and don't over-rev because the Ford people will charge me a fortune." The Ford technicians later stopped by to compliment me because 16,900 revs in second gear was a new record, but I don't think Eddie found it very funny. The engine made a terrible noise and everything unfolded right beneath the team's eyes. The engine was still running and so I asked on the radio, "What should I do—stop now or come back to the pits?" My engineer said, "Go slowly, try not to change gears and bring it back to the pits." But on the radio Jordan himself intervened, saying, "That's it, that's it!" He thought that it was my mistake. Until they found out about the bolt, the pit team looked at me worse than my father did when I flipped the car. While they were checking the car, I took a chance and broke the silence, "I also have this problem with the handling," and they linked the cause to the effect right away.

After the mechanics solved the problem, Trevor Foster showed a bit of compassion and smiled at me encouragingly. I raced five very bad laps. Trevor came to me with this crazy idea and said, "So you feel like going fast? You'd better be sure because I'm putting my career on the line, and if you crash the car again, I'm finished." I didn't give a damn about his possible unemployment and pushed the car like crazy, but it went really well. Trevor had a lively discussion with the Ford people who did not want me back on the track, convinced that the engine would blow up after the over-revving incident. The discussion went on for quite a while, and then during the calm in between the first and final qualifying, I was sent out onto the track. The engine was working fine, although they told me to be prepared to put my foot on the clutch and switch off the engine if there was any sign of a problem. But the engine held on and I had the eighth best time, even faster than my teammate. Then everybody went out with their second set of tires and I fell back into 11th place, which still wasn't too bad given the situation. The team congratulated me and Trevor Foster became my hero.

The next day in the free practice, I had the fifth best time. Trevor asked me, "How's the car doing?" He had a big smile from one ear to the other. I said, "Good, but I couldn't go as fast as I wanted." He looked at me like I was an idiot so I said to him, "Believe me, if they hadn't blocked me in on the last part of the track, I would've done much better." At that point he stopped smiling, "What do you mean, much better?" "Seven or eight tenths of a second faster," I explained, "and I could go even faster." He thought I was exaggerating and was almost angry. Doubtful that I could go any faster, he sent me out with a new set of tires. Trying to prove that I was right, I pushed the car a bit too much and crashed another car into a wall. This was disappointing for everybody. The team's morale was down, and mine was even lower. Although the computer measurements weren't as accurate as they are today, they saved my skin. When the individual sector lap times were officially announced, we saw that I had the third best time in the initial sector; the second best time in the second sector (only one two-thousandth of a second slower than Senna); and in the third and last part of the track, I had the 18th best. I'm not kidding— it could have been a super lap and possibly my second or third best time with a Jordan. When they realized that I wasn't lying, they cheered up, "OK, he broke another front suspension, but it doesn't matter, we've got spare parts." Moments before qualifying, it began raining and everything started going pear-shaped. The track eventually dried, but they didn't let me go out (probably to prevent me doing any more damage). Also, they didn't believe I'd do any better with the track in its present condition, but that wasn't the case and the other drivers went on the track, someone beat my time, and I fell back to 13th position.

That grand prix went down in history because it was stopped after 15 laps due to a torrential downpour. The race was officially over after the 14th lap when Mansell had an accident. This created a lot of controversy. The rules say that the classification is based on the position of the driver when he crossed the finish line on the previous lap. Mansell, and a few other drivers who had already gone out, were recalculated into the results and I ended up in ninth position instead of fifth, losing the first points I'd gained in my Formula 1 career. In fact, just before the red flag was waved, I passed two cars, including Stefano Modena who was driving a Tyrrell-Honda. This was one of the craziest things I've ever done. I had been following him for a while and gaining speed, so much so that in the technical sector of the circuit, I almost tripped over him. I couldn't see where I was going because of the spray off his car. On the straight, with water like that, I couldn't get into sixth gear and drove in fifth with a feathered throttle to avoid the risk of hydroplaning everywhere. I was groping my way through the spray and could only see while braking in the corners. I could see Modena as I entered the corner, 90 yards in front of me. At one point I got tired, wedged open the visor of my helmet and concentrated on the noise of his car, trying to assess his speed by sound. I couldn't even see his red rear light, so I had to rely on following the noise. I heard him decelerate, hit my brakes and when the wall of water disappeared, he was right in front of me. Two corners later, I passed him and after another four corners, I overtook de Cesaris and Pirro, whom Modena had been battling with for several laps. But it was insane—I was practically relying on sound to guide me while going at 160 mph on a river. It was a very wise decision to stop the race, but unfortunately it made my feat of double-overtaking completely redundant. My only consolation was setting the fifth fastest lap, behind Berger, Senna, Piquet and Mansell

The season was then over and I had done OK. Although I had caused a lot of damage to the cars, I was soon forgiven because they were always trashed by the end of the season. Unfortunately the Jordan team was broke, but it survived thanks to special insurance with Lloyd's of London arranged by Eddie Jordan. He made a bet that his team would be classified in the top five in the Constructors' Championship; if this happened Lloyd's would have to pay an enormous sum, almost half of the budget required for the season. And that's exactly what happened. Despite this things were financially difficult. Towards the end of the championship, Tyrrell was about to pull out of the scene and their main sponsor, Braun, was now available. There was talk of Braun wanting to personally sponsor Stefano Modena, so Jordan signed him. Jordan was convinced that signing Modena would also secure Braun, but it never happened, and Jordan ended up with another driver, a real driver, to finance. Jordan put me on hold—with the help of that famous option in my contract. But he kept me involved in all the winter tests with the Yamaha motor, the new substitute for the Ford Cosworth HB V-8, as a sign of good faith. After a stalemate with our contract negotiations, he asked me—extremely politely this time—to extend the deadline. I thought of him as a saint as he was the one who'd given me a start in Formula 1 and kept me behind the steering wheel, therefore I didn't hesitate to extend. With hindsight, I should have insisted on a signature, given that other teams were interested in me, but once again I was too impulsive.

Jordan couldn't find any financial backers, so I was on the sidelines the whole winter. He even asked me to help him look for sponsors in Italy, but I couldn't even find the money for an ice cream. A few weeks before the beginning of the championship, IMG, a big American management company, closed a deal with Sasol—the South African oil company which would guarantee a certain financial coverage. At the same time, IMG requested that their client, Mauricio Gugelmin, serve as the second driver. Jordan, with his back against the wall, quietly accepted. I started suspecting something, but I kept hoping that the situation would evolve in my favor.

With the championship approaching, I'd decided that I had enough, so I called Ian Philips, commercial director of the team, and said, "I don't know what's going on, but this is my life and I need to know if you've signed Gugelmin. There is just one week until the championship and I want to resolve this." Philips responded, "Alex, this is not official, but if I were you, I'd start looking for another team." I realized that it was over and it was the Saturday before the first race of the season in South Africa. As soon as I put down the phone on Philips, I called Ken Tyrrell, whose team was the only one still looking for a second driver. I spoke to his son, Bob, but didn't get anywhere. I was very depressed and then Roberto Trevisan (my F3 and Formula 3000 technician) gave me some good advice: "Go and get on a plane and go and see Tyrrell." "But they told me that they weren't interested in me," I said. Roberto insisted, "Just go and make them understand how much you want to drive their car." So I did. They were very surprised when I turned up, but at least they took the time to see me. We started talking and after ten minutes, the tone of the conversation changed dramatically. They weren't crazy about me, but they were impressed that I'd taken the initiative, without a manager. They were really honest and said, "We have ongoing negotiations with de Cesaris, and have asked him to make a financial contribution because we need it. But at the moment we are still far from closing the deal. If we wanted a driver as an investment, we'd prefer to put our bet on someone as young as you. Now go to the workshop for a seat fitting and we will register you on the entry list for the championship. Then we'll wait to see what happens, but if by Monday, de Cesaris has the cash, you're on your own."

Much to my surprise, they registered me. When number 4, Alessandro Zanardi, appeared on the official International Federation list, a few eyebrows were raised. Unfortunately, on the Tuesday morning, de Cesaris's backer came through and the situation changed. Tyrrell called and said, "I'm sorry. To be honest, we'd started hoping that no one would sponsor de Cesaris." I finished the phone call and thanked Tyrrell for his kindness. He was known to be tough, but he was very honest with me. I remember when the phone call was over, Daniela said, "Alessandro, I don't know if you've realized it, but you really are out on your own." It was her comment that woke me up to the situation. I found myself staring at the ceiling for hours on end. The day before South Africa—watching the qualifying on television—I was feeling very down. I'd thought that I would definitely be racing for Jordan and so hadn't started any other negotiations. Shortly after the season began, I received an offer to be a test driver for an Italian team, Scuderia Italia. Even Cipriani called me, saying, "I told you—you didn't listen and now look where you are." He was still in touch with Benetton and added, "I spoke to Briatore and if you're up for it, he's still interested in you as a test driver for them." At that point, I decided to listen to him and accept the offer, apprehensively.

This move to Benetton really annoyed Maurizio Arrivabene of Marlboro, who had gone to a lot of trouble to find me the place with Scuderia Italia. Briatore, who had made me fantastic offers before Monza, offered me £300 a day plus expenses to be his test driver. I just sat around doing nothing until June—they seemed to have forgotten me. Then, Alfa Romeo invited me to take part in the *Superturismo* race at Imola with a 450hp GTA, along with Larini, Nannini and other drivers. But two days before the race, Benetton called and wanted me to test at Miramas on that Sunday. Miramas was an airport where I would drive back and forth on a straight track for a couple of hours. I couldn't believe it. I had been twiddling my thumbs for four months and now, when I could have taken part in a race and been paid ten million lire for each stage of the competition, they needed me. Also, I really needed the money to help open up some opportunities for the future. Alfa was very understanding and allowed me to race on the Saturday—Giorgio Francia raced on the Sunday—and then I left for Miramas. It went on like this for most of the year; the inactivity gnawed away at my motivation and I needed something to re-infuse my enthusiasm. When I was left without a team in March, I honestly wasn't that disheartened. I was happy to stay at home and take a break for a while. The Formula 3000 had been hard, but total dedication is necessary for Formula 1—mere talent is not enough. In addition to races and tests, there were other marketing responsibilities to juggle. You have to forget about a normal life and learn to live out of a suitcase. In the beginning, I didn't worry about my career coming to an end—I just considered this a well-deserved rest—but after a while I started getting restless. To make matters worse, I was only the test driver on paper, but not so much on the track, which meant just a few bitter trips to England. There, I had to go back and forth on the straight at Kemble, an RAF base near Oxford. I was working with technicians whom I hardly got to know, before they returned to the factory and disappeared. These were the people who generally didn't go to the grand prix. On one of these occasions the car was loaded with sensors that were sensitive to water and therefore couldn't be tested in the rain. I had to wait three days just to drive a couple laps on the asphalt around the airfield. I was stuck in a small hotel room, with a tiny television, while it pissed down with rain. Alone with nothing to do, I felt very depressed. From a racing point of view, this period did nothing for my career and the fee, a little more than £300 a day, was pathetic. It wasn't at all the situation for which I was hoping.

When I finally returned home, I couldn't wait to see my friends. They liked to go out quite late, but I've never been into clubbing. The few times that I did go, I felt like a complete misfit. One Saturday in July, the usual bunch took me to a club and I had a good time, especially after dragging them out for a late night cycle ride through the park and then having breakfast down at the seaside. The following day I was at Chicco's house, half-asleep, in front of the television. It was the French Grand Prix and during Saturday's qualifying, Christian Fittipaldi had an accident in his Minardi. He had damaged his vertebra and was forced to pull out of a couple races, including that one at Magny-Cours. The commentators were discussing his injury and although my head was still foggy from the night before, I thought, "I wonder who will substitute for him?" In that very moment the phone rang and it was Giancarlo Minardi—the great opportunity I was waiting for had arrived. I was very excited, and Minardi seemed so sincere. He explained that he could have given the car to someone with a sponsor, but he wanted to invest in me instead.

It didn't go terribly well though, and I'm still sorry that I failed to live up to his expectations. I did all right, but I wasn't fit enough and paid the price for my months of inactivity. In addition, there were some unfavorable circumstances. I hadn't raced since the Australian Grand Prix in 1991, and the upcoming race was to be held at Silverstone, which was one of the most physically demanding tracks on the calendar. Not only was the car hard to drive, but I also failed to give it a hundred percent and didn't qualify. My teammate was in 25th position on the grid, and I was 27th just four tenths of a second behind him. The guy between us, who got the final place a tenth ahead of me, was Damon Hill. The following race was Hockenheim and I was around 24th at the start. Morbidelli was less than a second behind me, but during the second lap of the race, my clutch broke. Then in Hungary, I made a complete mess of things. During qualifying I went off the track, but without too much damage. The officials arrived, gave me a push and I drove the car back to the pits, but this wasn't allowed and I was prevented from going out again in the T-car, so I didn't qualify there either. Minardi was disappointed, and so was I. He was a very good person and I would have liked to have done a good job, but we were both dreamers, and over the course of my career I have learned that only the best cars make phenomenal drivers. Ending this chapter, I went back to my semi-jobless life thinking that I had missed my chance; I was wrong.

Well into September, Benetton had to test their active suspension. Martin Brundle was out of the game because Benetton had replaced him, and Schumacher was ill. They had to test a prototype system which the team felt needed a lot of work and then remembered that they had a test driver, and called me for three days of work at Silverstone. It went surprisingly well. I drove at a very respectable 1 minute, 24 seconds, which was quite good for the circuit and would have put me 11th on the grid for the grand prix there. But more importantly, I offered some very crucial suggestions. The first evening, I stayed back with Pat Symonds to discuss my reaction to the test drive. He was Schumacher's engineer, but was already the leader of the technical group. I answered questions using terminology that was comprehensible to an engineer and this impressed him. During the second day of testing, he radically modified and reprogrammed the set-up of the active suspension after thinking about what I'd said. The results were so good that we jumped ahead with the maximum performance possible. Although the car had newly introduced technology, it was going surprisingly fast. They weren't expecting this, and realized the driver had a big part in it. My technical explanations were very good and my levels of speed impressive. From then on, Benetton completely changed their attitude towards me and started taking me to every test. It was worth it, they told themselves.

I started to integrate with the team and had some really good days, free from the pressure of having to win for any reason other than my own pride. Finally at the last test at Castellet in France, I started to get noticed by other teams. Benetton took two cars to Castellet and asked me to join Schumacher and Riccardo Patrese, as the new driver for 1993. Patrese was allowed to join us from Williams, with whom he still had a year-long contract. He was scheduled to drive the car set up for Michael. Patrese didn't have a good feeling about it and was complaining, asking for setting modifications. In effect, Schumacher preferred a car with a slight oversteer and a very free differential. As soon as you touched the steering wheel in fast corners, the car would turn in like a bullet. If you could manage to drive the car that way, it was certainly faster, but you needed to get used to it. I, too, had a hard time with it but soon realized, by watching the times, that indeed this was the fastest way. Patrese, on the other hand, wanted the car to be his own way and didn't want to drive it the way it wanted to be handled. He eventually got annoyed because the team had put him under pressure, giving him a new set of tires and asking him to drive three fast laps. He was probably right, as it did seem that they said, "Go out there and show us what you're made of." But the Brits are a bit like that; so much so in fact, that they even said, "If you want, we can start a grand prix simulation." He was already pissed off, "I should be skiing with my children, and I don't give a damn about race simulations. You have a test driver here—use him." I think the attitude was taken badly because Pat Symonds turned to me and said, "Do you want to do the grand prix?" I jumped at the offer.

Before the simulation began, Symonds himself told me, "Go out with the tires that we had fitted for Patrese—they've only been used for three laps, you drive for another ten and we'll fill the car with fuel and you can begin." In that period, I didn't need an invitation to go as fast as possible. I used to take every corner with the fighting power and passion of someone chasing a carrot that he's never tasted. While taking enormous risks, I drove four super laps that were two tenths faster than Schumacher, who held the lap record. My lap was the fastest of the day among the Benetton drivers.

At the end of the simulation, Michael came and gave me a two-handed pat on the back, "You're an ugly bastard, but you sure went fast today!" I was wearing a windbreaker that the team had given me. I was very proud of it, and couldn't wait to go back to Castel Maggiore and show it off at Bonini's. But Michael had put an egg in my pocket so that when I was congratulated and patted front and back, it would obviously break. I swear, the joke was intended to be funny, and I tried to laugh, but I was gutted. I started chasing him, but couldn't catch him as he was as fast on his feet as he was in the car. But I took my revenge on the next day.

Michael was getting ready for his grand prix simulation. At that time you had to go for the warm-up and wait at the starting line for the virtual alignment of the other drivers, allowing for the most realistic time. At the red light, you'd go into first gear then take off at the green. While Schumacher was at the starting line simulating the time and waiting for the other drivers to arrive, I called him on the radio, "Michael, look what nice colors are on the flag." I had gone into his motorhome and taken all his clothes and his brand-new Boss shoes, and attached them one by one to the flagpole. Jacket, shirt, trousers, socks and shoes were all hanging in front of the starting line. He pleaded, "You bastard, take them down!" But he had to start anyway because he wasn't yet "the famous Michael Schumacher," and could not interrupt the simulation to save his clothes. Therefore, each time someone asked me about the egg stain on my jacket, I would delight in retelling the story and enjoying the subtle taste of revenge.

Despite this relaxed atmosphere, that test was very important because Peter Collins, the Lotus team principal, was in the paddock. I didn't know him and assumed he was a mechanic, so when he asked me if I wanted to join him for a cup of tea, I nonchalantly agreed. A few hours later, while walking around the paddock, I went to the Lotus area and he repeated the invitation. When I saw how relaxed he was around the team, I quickly figured out who he was. I understood even better when he sat down and so did Peter Wright, a long-standing Lotus technician who had a very famous history. Collins introduced himself and in a few words said, "We are 99 percent certain that we have sold Häkkinen to McLaren, so we need a driver for next year. Do you want to race with us?" What a question! With Lotus! My answer was the same as my father's when Mantese offered him the 25 million lire, "Sonofabitch!" When I told Briatore, who had started to like me, he was not very happy. He was very honest with me and said, "I'm not going to lie to you—I don't think I can offer you a place for 1993. I have every intention of keeping Michael as long as possible. Patrese has a two-year contract, but he is tired and we need to see if he gets motivated, so you never know. Stay with us as a test driver, and I'll let you race in Japan in the Formula 3000 so that you can earn some money [I'd been offered $250,000], and then we will see. I can't make you any promises, but the best possible promise is my enthusiasm. The team has changed its attitude towards you. You're doing really well, and providing really useful technical suggestions." He had been realistic and sincere. But when I tried to explain that I wanted to go to Lotus, he said, "Zanardi, in life we have to make difficult decisions. In my opinion, you'd be better off staying with us." Maybe Briatore was right, who knows, but I wanted to race ... so that's what I decided to do.

CHAPTER 7

The Lotus Years

I was very excited about Lotus and decided to go with them. On the night that we signed the contract, I stayed at Ketteringham Hall, the team's historic headquarters in Norfolk. I was fascinated by everything, including the story of the ghost of Colin Chapman, the team's founder, who'd died ten years earlier. The outlook was good. The team had had an excellent season in 1992, and I wanted to remain in the UK because I had usually driven for British teams in F1. From the moment I entered the front door of Ketteringham Hall, I was overwhelmed with emotion.

Collins offered me a three-year contract and $100,000 a year with an annual option. In two seasons, however, I saw less than $50,000, including personal expenses. Lotus sent me $10,000 when I signed, which together with my savings, took my bank account to something like 38 million lire (approximately $35,000). I suddenly felt rich. It probably doesn't seem much for a Formula 1 driver, but for me it was a lot.

My bank manager suggested I should buy some shares of stock. I touched my balls for good luck and asked, "Are you sure?" and he replied, "Yes, the fund is a safe investment with a large growth margin." I invested in the suggested shares, valued at 16,500 lire each. The following week, still feeling rich, I decided to buy myself a motorbike, the beautiful Cagiva Elefant 900, which had just come on the market. It cost around 5 million lire with discount. I called the bank again asking, "Do I have the cash or is it all tied up in the shares?" The bank manager replied, "I bought the motorbike for you because the fund shares are now worth 18,900 lire each." So I suggested, "Let's sell everything immediately." He said, "No, let's wait—these should reach at least 20,000." However, they plummeted to 3,200 lire each and today are still only worth around 5,000. I lost everything. I never invested again, not even during the 1990s when everyone was making money. That experience taught me a lesson. I still have those shares, somewhere around here, but they have to get back to at least 16,500 before I'll sell them back, even if they are shares that "should reach at least 20,000 ...."

Apart from my financial misfortunes, my professional choices seemed to be going well. I desperately wanted to race in a grand prix and had waited far too long. Team Lotus was convinced that the new car could compete with Williams. The 1992 chassis was very good, and they intended to make further improvements. And although the engine was still a Ford Cosworth HB V-8, the active suspension was ahead of its time. I was ecstatic when I laid my eyes on the car for the first time—it appeared to handle beautifully. In the workshop, the technicians had attached a tube which generated the same pressure as the engine-driven pump, and with a computer, they could set up different parameters. One of these parameters controlled the ride height and using sensors and taking into account the stiffness of the various car components, together with the compression of the tires, the computer would continually calculate the ride height of the car, keeping it as constant as possible. The only problem was caused by the speed of the compensation. When the system acted too slowly, the performances of the car suffered and the car seemed soft and heavy. On the contrary, when the compensation happened too fast, the flexible components of the car became energized, and would make the car unstable. To demonstrate this theory, they ran this unbelievable test. They set the parameters to maximum, and then touched the rear wing with a finger. The system read the vibration and started to move the active suspension, "chasing after" the tire compression. The reaction increased and began vibrating even more, making the wheels almost lift from the ground! You could take the rear wing off the car and move it around the workshop like a hovercraft. I was shocked, yet imagined the potential. The problem was that the technicians were so fascinated by this new system that they overlooked other aspects of the car, including the crucial aerodynamics of the time. Ultimately, the complexity and fragility of the system sent us back to the drawing board.

That year was full of ups and downs. When the car was going well, especially in the first part of the season, I encountered more misfortunes and hitches. For example, during the qualifying session of the South African Grand Prix, the acceleration sensors couldn't be mounted directly on the bodywork. Instead, they had to be applied using material similar to earplugs, a high-density foam rubber which, after being squeezed, slowly returns to its original shape. But it was also very temperature sensitive. In the winter at Silverstone, the material became very rigid; in the summer heat of Kyalami, it became very soft. So here we were with a car that was impossible to keep on the road.

I was desperately trying to give some helpful feedback, and then by accident knocked one of the sensors, which vibrated three times before stopping. I asked Peter Wright, "Is this reaction normal?" He immediately realized that we had set up the car based on recordings from a sensor that was giving completely different readings in the heat. It was as if it was reading the odometer six times higher than it actually was—a real mess. We made all the calculations again, changed the sensor support material and on the day of the South African race, I was 11th on the starting grid.

In the race I passed various drivers until I reached Damon Hill, who was debuting in the Williams. Williams had won the championship the year before. I passed him four times, and he passed me four more times. At the fifth attempt, I failed to pass him and we both ended up going out. It was a real shame because at the finish line, Blundell, who'd been behind me, ended up third.

At Barcelona, the engine blew up during the next-to-last lap when I was in fifth position, giving the points to Berger who was behind me in the Ferrari. At Imola, I was stupid enough to be pushed out by JJ Lehto, who slammed on his brakes right in front of me when I had fourth place in my pocket. At Monaco, I went from 20th to 5th, only to get tangled up with Berger and Hill at the Loews Hairpin. I got jammed between them, wasting a minute before the officials came to free up the track. Meanwhile, Fittipaldi and Blundell passed me and I finished in seventh place.

At Silverstone, the car was very fast and on Friday's free practice, with a wet track, I had the third fastest time. I went out for another go, more fired up than ever, but as I approached Stowe Corner, I ended up having a colossal crash. I was still light-headed after such a big shunt and shouldn't have raced, but foolishly I did.

While my races seemed to end under a black cloud, my teammate Johnny Herbert was steadily collecting points. By the middle of the season, I only had one point from the second race in Brazil, whereas Herbert had ten. I started to go mad—a good result was not enough anymore, nor was just one little point. I was racing for the podium. I started having a series of rather serious accidents, culminating in a monumental one at the fastest corner at Spa, *Eau Rouge*, which was due to an active suspension failure.

It was during Friday's free practice. The car was set up to run on hydraulic actuators which basically worked according to the pressure generated by the engine-driven oil pump. A leak caused the car to sink. There were security springs, but they were only sufficient to counteract the downforce over 70 mph. In case of a failure, the car would bottom out. A yellow light would come up if the leak was small, but if the leak was big the alarm would sound once the car was already flat on the ground. In fact, when I started spinning, the yellow light came on and although I can't remember much, I'm sure that I let slip a dry "Fuck me!"

I received a blow that was beyond human limitations. When I hit the guardrail head-on, the telemetry recorded an amazing deceleration and everybody thought I was dead. This was my second brush with death before the Lausitzring. As soon as they took me away in the medical helicopter, the team gathered the remains of the car and shipped them out of the country, in case I died and the car was impounded. When the medics arrived, I was still moving, but unconscious. Even Senna, whom I almost hit as I flew across the track, stopped to help me. I can still remember the feeling I had, which I've never had again, even when my wife took me from the Berlin hospital in a wheelchair with machines still connected to my body. When I came to in the helicopter, I instinctively remember thinking the sky was bluer and the trees greener than I'd ever seen them, and I wondered why I'd never appreciated them before. Seeing this just made me happy, and I thought about the futility of racing. I thought about how silly the game was—the chess game with death. That feeling didn't last long. I would see more wonderful skies and trees, but I never stopped racing.

Daniela arrived at the hospital that morning and was very worried of course, especially given what I said as they lifted me into the helicopter. Apparently, I said, "Daniela, I love you and I don't want to race anymore. Let's get married and have children." Daniela told me she was extremely worried and thought I was seriously ill to have said those things. In fact, as soon as she arrived, she asked me to repeat what I'd said earlier, but I couldn't remember a thing. She said, "Are you still sure that you want to quit racing?" and I answered, "No, if they tell me I can drive tomorrow, I'm up for it." She immediately felt relieved and concluded that I wasn't going to die.

When I finally came to in the hospital, I was in a very bad state. I couldn't move and was completely exhausted. As soon as I moved a finger, I felt excruciating pain. A doctor looked at my test results and came to me with a superficial smile, saying, "Everything is fine. You can go home and even race tomorrow in the grand prix." I couldn't believe it. I asked, "How is it possible?" I felt dreadful, and obviously didn't race, but I left the hospital on Saturday. We had traveled by car to Spa, so Daniela had to drive the entire way back. I had a terrible headache, nausea and hallucinations. Many of the capillaries in my eyes had exploded, so my eyes were completely bloodshot.

We eventually arrived home after a painfully long journey. I was so relieved, but everybody was worried about me because I was clearly still out of it. Chicco came to see me and I babbled a few words to him, "Oh Chicco, did you see my crash?" I then immediately fell asleep and mumbled the same words when I woke up. It went on like this until I saw Drs. Costa and Bollini. They gave me an intravenous drip and I started to bounce back, but after about ten days, I lost movement in my left arm. A painful follow-up exam revealed that I had stressed and strained a spinal nerve—the one that controls the muscles of the chest, the shoulder, the back and my left side—and I was paralyzed. The nerve was sending impulse signals, which meant that it was still attached and working, but I had no control over its movement. Dr Bollini explained, "The seat belt caused the damage. If you want to race at Monza, you'll have to consider that the seat belt passes exactly over this nerve. Maybe you'll be all right, but if you take a sharp corner the nerve could break, and if that happens, you won't be able to move your arm again. You might have some recovery, but it will take time. Instead, if you stop for a couple of weeks, you can recover fully." I reluctantly agreed to pull out of Monza.

Instead, I went as a spectator as it would have obviously been stupid for me to race. Even Peter Collins agreed, but for different motives. "It's better if you don't—you haven't recovered yet," he said. He let the Portuguese driver Pedro Lamy race in my place and they put him in the car with some additional sponsors stickers on the bodywork. I quickly picked up that they weren't just interested in his driving. Lotus needed his money. The following race was in Portugal and the usual journalists were telling me that Lamy would race at Estoril, his home circuit. I didn't believe them because I thought I'd be ready to race by then, but that's exactly what happened. In the meantime, Collins sounded like the same old record, "Look, Alessandro, it's for your own good. There is a long period between Estoril and Suzuka, which will give you time to totally recover. You had a big blow and you think you're all right, but you're not. In a Formula 1 car, you need to be both physically and mentally strong, or you'll never know what might happen. Suzuka is very important for us. We have a lot of Japanese sponsors and I'm under a lot of pressure from the directors, so I need a great performance from you in order to keep you in 1994, so take the time to get in shape." I believed in him and was soon persuaded. In the meantime, Trevor Foster, my engineer from Jordan, had become the Lotus team manager. A week before leaving for Suzuka, the team organized a test session. I thought that this was a test to re-acquaint me with driving again, and took it for granted that I would be the only one racing in Japan. The evening before leaving for Japan, I went out for dinner with Collins and Foster. It seemed like a completely normal night, chatting and joking … the usual shoptalk.

At the end of the dinner, which I paid for, they suddenly said, "Sorry, we have to tell you something. It isn't easy to say, but we don't have any alternative. It's for your and the team's own good. This year you've had a lot of accidents, and we have enormous responsibilities to our sponsors. You have been very fast, but Johnny has collected more points and you haven't performed as well as you could have." Peter took a breath and said, "Next year you will not drive for us." I was in shock. Even though the doctor had given me the all clear to race, I agreed to skip three grands prix because they asked me to do them a favor. If I had taken advantage of my contract, I could have raced but didn't—and this is how I was repaid. They pulled this stunt the day before my official return to racing. I didn't hide my bitterness, "I can't believe what you're saying. I don't have anything to say. You've totally screwed me around. I never believed the rumors that I was hearing because you were telling me the opposite. I trusted you, but I've been an idiot to trust you and play your game." They told me they'd turned down $2 million to have Martini or Morbidelli in the car at the beginning of the season, and scrambled for something to say, "No, it wasn't like that—you need to think about the situation and circumstances." I left feeling desperate. I drove around Silverstone in my rented Ford Fiesta for hours that night. I even managed to cry because I was so tired.

The following day, I went to the test with very low morale, but was determined to prove myself and ignore what the others thought of me. I exited the pits and during the first fast lap—who knows what I was thinking—I spun out at the fourth or fifth turn and was out. They came to bring me back to the pits. Collins wasn't there and Trevor asked me to get out of the car. I got out and went with him to the truck. While I had been on the track waiting for the tow truck, he called Peter. Together they decided that I shouldn't continue with the tests. "We are convinced that you haven't recovered psychologically from the accident and that you should stop now rather than hurt yourself and cause further damage to the car." I lost it and started screaming. Trevor suggested a conference call on the mobile with Collins. I hoped that I could change their minds, but instead, I had to endure them using my psychological state as a justification for their decision.

I went back home and watched the last two races of the championship on the television. I felt better when I received a surprise on the Friday before the Japanese Grand Prix. Because of the time difference, I was watching practice at five in the morning, when the mechanics from Lotus held up a placard with, "Happy Birthday Alice" (Alice was my Lotus nickname). It was indeed my birthday, and that thoughtful gesture really cheered me up. The winter passed without any other offers and I was feeling quite empty. I didn't pursue any other opportunities, feeling very wounded and unmotivated after what had happened. I was far too easy on Lotus, even though they were having financial difficulties which unfortunately became worse.

Peter Collins encountered many obstacles that year. In 1991 he'd put his personal and financial life back together and had come back to the team which he'd managed for many years in the 1970s and early 1980s, and invested all his money, only to lose it all again. I couldn't hold a grudge against him because he was acting in good faith and trying his best. Maybe he wasn't savvy enough, but he was never dishonest. In the end, Lotus offered me a position as a test driver. With no other options, I accepted. That was my job for the first months of 1994 and this time, contrary to what happened with Benetton, I was frequently on the track. They trusted my technical knowledge, so naturally I was on the track more than Lamy. This created a tense atmosphere until a near tragedy struck.

There was a three-day test planned in May at Silverstone with two cars. Herbert was going to drive the whole time, and I was driving the first day, and Lamy the other two. Lamy was complaining about not having enough time to test, and not finding an affinity with the car. The team explained that they were using me more because I could give good technical advice. I drove the first day and Lamy was already grumbling. Wright told him, "Tomorrow, Alessandro will start again because he's testing an important aspect of the car and has to make a crucial evaluation. After he's driven ten laps, you'll take the car." I stayed on the track all morning and afternoon, and also on the morning of the third day. I started the test on the afternoon of the third day, and ended up doing another 25 laps before they stopped me. There were only two hours left, so they changed the seat and seat belts and Lamy took the wheel. Until that moment I had driven 394 laps in that car. He went out and during his first fast lap, lost the rear wing and had a terrible accident. In the straight leading to Bridge Corner, the car took off and flew into the underpass beyond the fence. I was in the pits and there were rumors that Collins wanted to replace Lamy, which I secretly wished for. When I saw the red flag stopping the test, I thought, "Let's hope that he's done something silly and is up to his neck in sand." But Herbert, who was following Lamy, started yelling on the radio, "Pedro is off! Pedro is off!" He stopped when he saw what had happened, and we immediately knew it was far more serious than a sandpit.

I took my Ford Fiesta and drove round the service road to the scene of the accident. When I arrived, I found the smoking engine in the middle of the track under the bridge. Nothing else was attached—just the engine. I turned around and saw dense, black smoke pouring out of the pedestrian tunnel. I got out of the car and heard Pedro screaming and screaming. I had chills and felt horrible for wishing him bad luck. At that moment I said, "God, if you exist, I'm sorry for what I thought—please let him be OK. Please hang up my career right now and never let me in a car again, but save him." That was the most I could give in exchange for his life. Flames were shooting out of the tunnel, but they were quickly put out by the emergency services. It was a pedestrian passage used to cross beneath the track and was a couple of meters wide, surrounded by corrugated steel. It went underground and came out the other side and in the middle there was a thick steel handrail. Pedro's car had landed in the underpass and the handrail had destroyed the chassis, breaking his legs on impact.

Destiny. If I had remained on the track, it would have been me. It wasn't his fault that the wing broke off—it was his destiny. It was really a terrible period for Formula 1.

7: The Lotus Years

Ten weeks before that dramatic afternoon at Silverstone, there had been a tragic weekend at the San Marino Grand Prix at Imola which took the lives of Roland Ratzenberger and Ayrton Senna. I was watching qualifying at the Variante Bassa area of the track on Saturday, April 30, with my father. Suddenly, Roland Ratzenberger had an accident and the red flag was waved to stop the session. Later we found out that Roland had died.

It seemed impossible, but the weekend got worse. On the first lap of the grand prix on Sunday, Lamy hit Lehto's stalled Benetton and sent a wheel flying into the stands, seriously injuring a spectator. After Senna's fatal accident on the fifth lap, nobody could understand what was going on. I was watching that race from a friend's house in Bologna. My friend, who was working in medicine, said, "It depends where they take him. If they stay at Imola it's not serious, but if they come to Bologna, it's very grave. And if this is the case, we'll know it because we'll hear them fly right overhead." Two minutes later, we heard the chopper above our heads, and the rest is history.

When something like that happens, everything seems unreal. Drivers are reckless, not courageous. You know that there is a possibility of a bad accident, but you convince yourself that it is an extremely remote chance, and even if it does happen, it won't happen to you. But that weekend it seemed that divine punishment took away the best of all, Senna.

Ironically, that was one of those events in life that can give you hope. No matter how tragic it may seem, from my point of view that weekend in Imola was a sign of hope for humanity. It made me believe that it wasn't just an accident … that perhaps something more powerful exists. What happened during those weeks in Formula 1—the chain of events, the tragedies, the fear—was not coincidental. It was as if a hand from above was reshuffling the cards to remind us that we can't control everything. That period showed me that we are small and insignificant bystanders in this life and that someone more powerful exists above us.

I took Lamy's place five races into the 1994 season, starting at Barcelona, which had been the stage of my debut in Formula 1 in 1991. Before this, I'd been testing the Lotus 107B and it was not going well. In practice, we found numerous problems with the stiffness of the chassis. The new 109 was ready before Spain, but there was only one available and it went to Herbert. I didn't care what I drove, I just wanted to race.

The 109 was a vast improvement. Had we been able to couple it with the latest Mugen-Honda V-10 engine, which arrived at the end of the season, we would have had a fantastic car. But we ran out of time, and therefore it was sheer chaos the day before the grand prix. I was very fired up and couldn't wait to race, despite the fact that a small drivers' strike had been organized until a chicane was installed.

There had been another threatened teams' strike over a disagreement about the sudden introduction of new rules, like the elimination of diffusers following the terrible accidents in the previous race. Nobody had had time to adequately test the new requirements. Safety was the main issue, so the organizers eventually agreed to put a chicane in the track. It was made from tires and put in the middle of the straight, which was unbelievable. After many threats and discussions, we were able to race.

I finished the grand prix with the car in ridiculous condition. But the race was a mess and the changes ruined our season. Even when we had understood the problem, we didn't have the money to fix it, and even when we had money for new parts, we never got them in time. We spent the whole championship in pursuit of our rivals, collecting useless ninth-place positions. Both Herbert and I failed to do anything, but at least Johnny got noticed.

Throughout 1994, I was constantly in England trying to help and look for money that never came. I was broke. I even drove my diesel car all the way to the German Grand Prix in order to save money. After the British Grand Prix at Silverstone, there were a couple of practice sessions at Snetterton and when the test was finished, I drove all the way from Norwich to Padova. Despite everything, I felt happy and optimistic, and didn't feel that my career was going downhill. Roberto Trevisan, whom Collins greatly respected, came to Silverstone to help me, which infuriated the team engineers. He offered great suggestions and the car improved, but something broke during the race. It seemed impossible to be competitive. The last dream was Monza.

We had been talking for ages about a great new engine that Mugen-Honda was supposed to deliver. It finally arrived in time for the Italian Grand Prix. I tested it at Silverstone, and hell was it fast! It was 1,000 revs faster, and the car handled brilliantly and I had the fourth best time in the test. It was a triumph for us. We arrived in Monza, and I started hearing the first strange comments, "You know there was only one engine available. We don't know whom to give it to, but as this is your home circuit, we'll think about it." And so on. I started getting worried—I'd heard all of this before. A representative from Honda tried to explain that it was a difficult situation to juggle. It wasn't a matter of favoritism, but logistics; they needed a spare engine for both qualifying and the race. In addition, Lotus had built a new gearbox for the new engine.

In the end, I found out that there were enough engines but the truth was Peter Collins and his crew were not able to produce new gearboxes in time because money was so tight. I made a scene trying to find an engine, calling Japan and ranting all over the place. That was the only time that I made a scene, but nothing was resolved and I ended up looking silly.

Herbert was racing with all the new kit. I asked if at least I could have a new engine for qualifying, saying, "It doesn't matter that I can't race with it tomorrow. If Herbert blows his engine, you can take the new engine and I can go with old one, but at least we can have two decent qualifying." That was when I learned about the lack of gearboxes. Herbert ended up qualifying 4th and

I was 13th. Comparison of the telemetry results showed that in several sections of the track, especially in Lesmo Corner and in the chicane, I was clearly much faster. Monza suited me and later that day, either out of rage or who knows, I had an incredible result. Just as at Lesmo, I was nearly six tenths of a second faster. After comparing the qualifying results, Peter Collins ate his words. Johnny was 490 thousandths of a second slower than Alesi, who had pole. Between my car and Herbert's, there was almost half a second gain, thanks to the power of the new engine. If you added the one tenth of a second that I'd gained on the corner, it was clear to everybody that I could have been on pole. Who knows, maybe the car would have broken down during the race as it always did, but it would have been a big coup for Lotus to have pole, and maybe something would have changed in my career. It would have undoubtedly changed the team's history and helped them to find an important sponsor, but that didn't happen.

Sadly, the 1994 season started looking like the previous year's. While in Belgium, 15 days before Monza, the team substituted Philipe Adams, an unknown Belgian driver in my place. In Hungary, Collins took me to one side, "You will not be in the next race," he said confidentially. I already knew from past experience what he would say. "I have to let him drive because the team needs the money," he said. But at least this time he sweetened it with lots of compliments because I was driving so well and I was a completely different driver from the previous year. He blamed the car for the fact that I didn't have any exceptional results. He also said that I was better than Johnny, but at the end of the day the Brit was the more prestigious name and had grown with the team. It would have been much less painful to leave me without a car than Johnny, which would have really pissed off the sponsors.

This was all true. I somehow digested the news and wasn't too upset. I calmly said, "I don't know what to tell you. Once again I have to step aside for someone else. I hoped that you'll at least pay me a bit of what is owed with the money that Adams brings in." He agreed, "You've got my word. I'll transfer $50,000 to you on Monday." I never saw it. Shortly after, there was a management takeover as the penniless team went into receivership. Ultimately, Adams did two races (Belgium and Portugal, where he was painfully slow) and did not pay the money. They made fools out of all of us. I only needed a little and took great pleasure out of seeing a banner in front of the pits at Spa saying, "We want Zanardi back." That was all I needed.

Right after Portugal, Briatore made an offer to take on Herbert's contract. Herbert was more than happy to leave Lotus and the administrators agreed he could go as the move involved financial compensation. Johnny raced in the European Grand Prix at Jerez driving a Ligier, which at that time was also controlled by Briatore. He drove in the last two races of the season next to Schumacher in the Benetton.

In the meantime, there was an internal division at Lotus as Peter Collins had been stripped of his decision-making power. At the same time, even my track engineer changed and I was assigned Jock Clear, who later became Jacques Villeneuve's technician. Jock and I had a lot of laughs and I became number one on the team that would soon be extinct. We hired Eric Bernard, a Frenchman from Ligier, as our second driver for the Jerez Grand Prix. He was a mediocre driver and I was in front of him the whole weekend. In Australia and Japan, Lotus hired Mika Salo, who knew the Suzuka track, having raced there in the Japanese Formula 3000 Championship.

Towards the end of May 1994, my father had started having some problems with prostate cancer. After hearing the news, my mother and I forced him to go to see a specialist, who said, "It's operable—men no longer die from prostate cancer, especially if it is caught in time, and we have caught yours in time. You can have surgery with the health service, but this will take a while, so I'd suggest that you go privately. Come to my clinic and we can operate immediately." My father came home and explained everything. We said, "Get this operation done right away—even if we have to sell the flat—we will find a way." So, at the beginning of July, he had the surgery. Everything seemed fine, but at the end of August, he went for a check-up. His doctor was on vacation, but the clinic prescribed some cortisone and told him not to worry, "It's just an inflammation." On the starting grid at Monza, I sent him a message via the television, "Get out of bed—there is nothing wrong with you!"

The truth was that he'd just been re-admitted to the hospital for observation, but unfortunately the tumor had spread. The doctor told us his liver was riddled with inoperable cancer. We never told my father. A few days later while taking a walk, with an eerie calmness he started giving me instructions for the future. Looking back, I realize he understood everything. He was more lucid than me.

Although I knew my father was going to die, I was hoping it was all just another one of his practical jokes. Even when he closed his eyes for the last time, I was expecting him to open them and shout "Boo!" He was my fearless father, the one who carried me on his shoulders when I was young, and the one who protected me. Mom is affection, love, and education, but Dad was the wall that no one could destroy: the perfectionist who dotted the "i," and who had led the pack. I'd always seen him as an infallible machine that nothing could destroy. But the illness had left him weak and humiliated. The dignity of such a strong and lovely man was completely trampled on, making him bedridden until he slowly passed away. It was terrible to watch. It is always difficult for a son to watch a parent pass away because the child is used to being protected, rather than doing the protecting.

My father showed his strength all the way to the end. One day on the way to the hospital, my mobile rang and it was Peter Collins confirming I would race in Japan. Given my father's condition, I hesitated. My father overheard the conversation, "Whatever happens, you have to go. This is your career." I cut it short, but he insisted, almost angrily. During his last week, he found it difficult to speak and was disoriented. He would just stare at me with his vacant eyes, saying nothing. All of sudden, he snapped out of it just to tell me, "Don't be silly, whatever happens, you go to Japan, and try to go fast, will you?" Then he went straight back to his catatonic state. He died on October 27, 1994, and I had to leave for Suzuka on the 30th.

Sometimes I wonder if my father wanted to get out of the way so that I would race in that grand prix. It took a lot of time, but after the pain and sadness, the best and real memories slowly started coming back. I was able to understand many things, including his behavior, and even more so since Niccolò was born—when I look at my son, I understand perfectly what my father wanted from me. I can only imagine how proud and happy he was when he saw me winning a race. The memories of those times together still comfort me. My father was an incredible person, as is my mother, and that will always stay with me. Two days after my father's death, I looked my mother in the eyes and knew that she would be okay on her own, so I left for Suzuka.

That grand prix in Japan was emblematic of the whole 1994 season with Lotus. I was really hoping things would go well after qualifying 17th, two seconds faster than Mika Salo. I drove like mad in the beginning in order to gain an advantage; then it started raining and everybody stopped to change tires. A few drivers spun out and the safety car was deployed. I went to the pits to refuel while everyone started to slow down. This was the correct strategy because I was able to maintain my position with a new set of tires and a full tank.

All of a sudden the car started losing downforce at the rear, and when I went in for the second pit stop, I realized the undertray was coming loose. Two laps later, I lost a rear-view mirror. I was calling the team on the radio, asking what to do. Their response was, "Keep going—you never know what may happen." I was going four, five, six seconds slower than the others, the radiator was leaking, the belly was coming undone and then the other mirror flew off. I wanted to stop because it was too dangerous. At one point, I was on the main straight and heard on the radio, "Ohh, watch out, watch out! Hill and Schumacher are right behind you." They were racing for the championship. I started panting, "Oh my God, Oh my God, Oh my God!" I could already see myself pushing them off the track and being criticized by the whole world, so I started scrambling to get out of the way, but they never caught up with me. They had already crossed the finish line. "Where the hell are they?!" I dragged myself all the way to the end, and I came in 13th even though Damon had lapped me twice.

In Australia, I qualified 14th with more than two seconds on Salo. I soon gained position and fought tooth and nail to move to seventh. I started fantasizing, "Maybe I'll get some points this time and save the team." I arrived at the first chicane and the accelerator stuck, sending me bouncing over the curb. I completed the first lap by connecting and disconnecting the electrical contacts until I could get to the pits for a check. They sprayed a bit of oil on the wires and I started again. It didn't look like much, but the fault happened again exactly at the same point, and I went over the curb again. I went back to the pit and had to stop because the accelerator cable was broken.

I pulled out on lap 40. I was wandering around the paddock, sad and depressed, when Jock Clear came looking for me, "You think that you've been unlucky, don't you?" I said, "Of course, I had to pull out over such a minor problem, and this was our last opportunity." He took me behind the car and showed me that the two rear wing mounts were completely cracked. If I had gone another lap, the wing would have come off as it did with Lamy.

Had that happened on the very long Dequetteville Terrace straight at Adelaide, the car would have catapulted into the air.

And so everything finished like this. That is to say, badly. I'd been so busy dwelling on the fact that I was with Lotus, who were going bankrupt, that I had no chance to look for another team. The reality was that although I drove very well that year, I did nothing to improve my image. In fact, it was quite the opposite. Without knowing the facts about my performances, new teams simply didn't find me appealing. Lotus dropped out of racing and I was out on my own again and quickly running out of time. David Hunt, James's brother, took over Lotus, but his attempt to salvage it failed. I still had the guts to ask Peter Collins where was the money transfer which was supposed to have arrived on Monday? He justified it by saying, "I am so stupid that I didn't transfer any money to myself, either." I don't know if that's true, but I do know he only paid me a total of $48,000 in two years, which had to cover all my costs of European travels and risking my life at Spa. The receivership administrators paid me nothing.

CHAPTER 8

Time Out, and an Introduction to IndyCar

I was waiting for a miracle that obviously never happened. When Lotus closed down, I tried with little conviction to find another team, but nothing came of it. I still remember a phone call to Peter Sauber, who owned his own team. "I'm Alessandro Zanardi, can I speak to Mr. Sauber," I said in my broken English to his secretary. After two minutes, he came to the phone. I said, "Hello Mr. Sauber, do you speak English?" He said no, and that ended the conversation. That phone call made me feel even worse, confirming that managing myself was not a good idea. I was washed-up in Formula 1 and the door was now firmly shut. Unless I could find a big personal sponsor as a sort of dowry, I was out, and I knew from past experience that asking for money was not my strength.

The 1995 championship started and I was once again without a team. I had been to England to see Rick Gorne, who'd become a friend since we met at Reynard. I spoke to him regarding opportunities in the prestigious Japanese Formula 3000 series, where drivers can make a lot of money and Reynard was making chassis for some of the best teams. In reality, I think I was hoping to remain jobless, as living in Japan was not my ideal move. On the other hand, I knew that I should take whatever I could find given that my career was at a delicate crossroads. Rick said, "To see you like this now, looking for a job, is very sad and a waste of talent. But I can't magically create a position. This year is difficult, but I'll let you know when you can come to a couple of races in the United States, and something may come out of it." I asked, "What do you mean, in the United States?" "Yes, IndyCar in the U.S.," he said. It was such a fantastic idea, but I'd never even considered it. I had completely forgotten that Reynard was a supplier for that championship too, and therefore Rick and Adrian Reynard were much respected there. I asked Gorne, "Do you think that I have any chance in IndyCar?" He said, "Not this year—the pieces are already in place. But if you trust me, we can try next season." He continued, "You know about Gil De Ferran—he came to several races and we introduced him to a few people, and then Jim Hall gave him a test, and now he'll be racing next year. Also, his experience will be important for you; if he has a good season, he will open the way for other drivers like you to move into IndyCar."

With hindsight, Rick could not have predicted a better outcome, but nothing happened in 1995. So I had a year of complete rest apart from a Porsche Cup race supporting the San Marino Grand Prix at Imola, which I won. I passed the time trying to keep fit in case somebody called, which did me good. After my father's death, I was depressed and tired of investing in and focusing on myself. I wanted to slow down, stay close to my mother and go back to my roots. I wanted to plan some holidays with friends, ride the motorbike, the usual activities of a young man. It was a great year and very helpful. It allowed me to recharge my battery, which I really needed. Although the outlook wasn't too bright, it didn't get me down. I never worried about the day after tomorrow. During that break, I found a new equilibrium, reorganized my life and got back to important friendships, like Filippo.

Filippo Zanelli deserves his own chapter. He really is the nicest and funniest person that I have ever met. We lost and refound each other in the most serendipitous way and I am grateful to destiny for reuniting us. I was driving around Bologna, when in the rear-view mirror, I noticed someone flashing their lights behind me. Some generous honking followed this, so I slowed down. At that time, I was driving rather carelessly and often annoyed other drivers with my reckless maneuvers. Therefore I thought that this driver was following just to tell me off. This went on for a good kilometer until I stopped at a gas station and got out of the car, ready for a fight. Incandescent, I yelled, "What's the problem!?" I didn't swear because out of the car stepped a guy twice my size. "Zanardi, it's Filippo." I didn't recognize him, "Filippo who?" "Filippo Zanelli!" The last memory I had of Filippo was from high school—he was a thin, tall, long-haired hippy wearing tight jeans. They were so tight that he had to use a tablespoon to help push his feet through the ankles. Now I had in front of me a tanned, chiseled, short-haired fellow, dressed in a dark suit with chic glasses that made him look like a successful manager. I finally realized who it was when he burst out laughing and I immediately recognized his chortle. Two evenings later, we were sitting together in a restaurant on the base of Bologna hills, telling stories about our past. Between two dishes of pasta and a glass of red wine, we rekindled a friendship and have been inseparable ever since.

Filippo and I met at the Galilei Technical School where my parents sent me to high school. He arrived a couple of months later after being thrown out of another school. We were the only ones in the class who were not behind academically, and therefore we were always hanging out together. We attended the first, second and third years without any problem, but then at the beginning of the fourth year the school went bankrupt. We went our separate ways and I started at a new school at Pacinotti. Because I was out karting so often, I failed my course. So I quit school and started working with my father, then eventually went back to school. At this point I had two options, either go to a fourth year in a public school, or go for fourth and fifth together at a private school. So I ended up going to the private school on the other side of town.

The first day of school, I saw someone on a Vespa PX who looked familiar. It was Filippo. Of all the possible choices, we ended up in the same school once again, and although I knew from an academic point of view it was bad news for both of us, I couldn't have been happier. I remember that I asked him why he had substituted his pokey 50cc scooter for a Vespa 125. He replied, "With a 50cc motor, you stay a virgin because you can't have a passenger." While laughing, I asked him if anything had changed, and he replied, "Well give me a chance—I've only just bought it!"

We started a year of lots of laughter and very little studying. Sitting next to each other, we kept our heads buried in our desks chatting away while the teacher explained the lesson, especially when it was the Italian literature teacher, whom we nicknamed Camomile, because he put everybody to sleep. He was very passive and hardly ever disciplined us, and we rarely studied. He was a retired teacher (and a typical private school teacher) who was working for money rather than the joy of interacting with the students.

But one day, even Camomile showed he had a heart. It was during a written essay when he'd given us a choice of three subjects. A very nice black kid named Akim Seyum was sitting next to Filippo and me. But Seyum had gone to the john for a cigarette while Camomile explained the essay. When he returned, he asked us what the subject was that we had to write about. As a joke, we told him it was entitled, "The last happy day that you spent with your mom." The poor guy wrote a very long and detailed essay. The following day, when Camomile handed out the results, he yelled at Akim, "What the hell is this all about?" Our eyes bulged, but Camomile was smarter than we thought and burst out laughing, having figured out our little prank.

I passed the final exam, despite having completed two years in one and coming from a private school. I chose current events as my subject and it went okay, as did the construction technology exam. I had to take two oral exams, one covering all subjects, and the other one covering two specific topics. The first was a disaster—it started really badly with Italian literature and went downhill from there. (Later, when Daniela introduced me to her mother, who was an Italian literature professor, I told her about my poor results. She wasn't impressed and I am surprised she let me continue to date her daughter.) The second exam was specifically on legal studies, and that went really well, and I finally received my diploma.

Filippo, however, failed the exams and went on to night school. By his own admission, he has always been an incredible liar, so I wasn't surprised to hear that he was a car salesman. He tries to justify his actions by explaining, "I don't know why it happens—I can't help it. For instance, the other day I told a client that there was a big crash at the crossroads. Well it didn't actually occur, but for some reason I felt compelled to invent this story." When he met his future wife, she introduced herself as a graduate of foreign languages. Filippo said to me, "What was I supposed to say—that I don't even have a diploma? So I told her that I was a surveyor. Theoretically I am." But when she went shopping for her wedding dress with his mother, she found out that he didn't have a diploma. So she confronted Filippo when he got home, "Explain something to me—are you a real surveyor, or just one in theory?!" He managed to calm her down and explained the situation.

That is my friend Filippo. In 1995, I was unemployed and really enjoyed going out with him. All I had to do was keep fit in case a team contacted me, so it didn't matter how late I went out. We went out almost every night—doing nothing particularly special—just going out to eat, to the gym, or to shoot pool. We'd play the Bolognese way at the Bar Sport in Castel Maggiore and met up with Chicco, Bonza and the guys. To liven up the evening, we'd often go to Dante's bakery. He'd just be waking up and getting ready for work, so we'd have a joke and a very early breakfast. When we were around, there was rarely enough bread to sell in the shop first thing in the morning.

Daniela was very busy and often away for the Formula 3000 races. All I was doing was working at the driving school—the fast driving school, obviously. Siegfried Stohr, a former grand prix driver with Arrows who later became a friend, asked me to be an instructor at his Safe Driving School. Understanding the theory of safe driving later helped me master safety both on and off the track. In addition, it was a nice place to work with a great group of guys. During the years of my American races, these guys were always there to send best wishes as I crossed the finish line. I could picture them in front of the television cheering after each victory.

That was the only job I had for the whole year. I tried to do some Touring Car racing, and even went to Spa for the traditional 24-hour race in order to speak to the BMW Motorsport manager, but he deliberately avoided me. I arrived on Thursday and by Saturday, I decided to go looking for him. I saw him coming down the steps of the truck near his motorhome. He noticed me from afar, but didn't know that I saw him roll his eyes to the sky as I approached, probably thinking, "Oh, here comes that pain in the ass again." Nonetheless, he greeted me with all smiles and asked me to have a chat. I wasn't surprised when he came out with the usual bullshit, "You're a great driver, but we are full at the moment and BMW is reducing its number of cars. I know that we are missing an opportunity, but there simply isn't space for you." Without much hope, I asked him if they needed anyone for the next 24-hour race. I really wanted to do that race—and I needed the money. They race twice a year and pay up to $15,000 per race, which was equal to one whole year's salary. But he didn't even consider it. I was miserable when I left Spa and on the way home, all I could think about was, what I was doing with my life.

Meanwhile Rick Gorne, who'd not gotten back to me yet, suddenly phoned me the day before I was leaving to go on a trip with friends to Sardinia. I received the call on my infamous 20-pound mobile, which Michaela used to call the Flintstone telephone. He explained, "There could be a possibility—if I were you, I'd go to Loudon." Loudon is a circuit in New Hampshire, USA, where they race IndyCars, or CART as the series was also known. "Oh, shit," I thought as I hung up the phone. I had been sitting around doing nothing for six months and now an invitation arrives right before my holiday. I was thrilled about the opportunity, but I went to Sardinia and kept in touch with Rick by phone. I spent the entire week going back and forth to the only telephone box because the Flintstones mobile had no signal. Instead of carrying around a 20-pound phone, I was carrying around 20 pounds of change in order to call Rick. He was in Cleveland, and I wanted to talk to him about the race at Loudon and the contacts that he had for me. My buddy, Stefano Friso, nicknamed Titano (Titan), always accompanied me on those trips to the telephone box. He was a huge racing fan and was anxious to hear about what the future held for me.

There were quite a few of us on that holiday. Titano was a huge fan, analyzing everything and wanting to know every detail. He was interested in details; he could spend the whole day trying to understand how a car was taking a certain corner. He was in love with the idea of my future in the United States and shared my hopes. When you have an opportunity and a dream, you tend to travel with your imagination, starting to believe it is a reality. I was already studying the Indy races on television, doing technical analyses as if Gorne was going to call any minute with a contract. Titano and I were often on our own and had time to fantasize about this American dream.

I had met Titano in 1991 at a Formula 3000 race. He was an ex-school mate of Roberto Trevisan. A few months later, I decided to go for a spin in some karts at Jesolo with Chicco. Trevisan and Titano showed up, and we invited them to join us. To be honest, I couldn't stand Titano when I first met him. He looked like an accountant, with a ring of grey hair around his prematurely balding head. He really kept to himself and was very shy, at least in the beginning. To be shy and timid is a Padovese trait, but over time we got to know each other.

But the real spark happened at the end of 1992. Daniela wanted me to meet her friends. We had been dating for a while, and each time that we were in Padova, we always went out alone. She wanted us to go out with her group of friends, but she didn't want to ask me because she thought I'd feel out of place. That was her decision. All at once, she did a 360-degree turn and wanted me to go skiing with Titano, and her friends.

While staying at Titano's ski cabin, I saw that he was much more at ease in his own home. We bonded over that trip and realized how much we had in common. In addition to cycling, he plays guitar really well, and we would stay up singing until four in the morning. We'd be up the next morning by 11:30, have breakfast, shave and shower and at exactly 12:30 pm we were on the slopes again until 4:45. We'd wait until everybody was off the mountain, and then take the last run all the way down to his garage. He would say, "Look, we're like two Titans—you and me alone on the mountain." From that holiday, we called each other Titano One and Titano Two. Out of respect for his age, I was Titano Two.

The following summer, I retired from the role of Titano during a holiday in Crete. The sea was so cold that despite the wet suit, I couldn't stay in more than hour. I wore my robe and lay in the sun, but my lips were still blue for some time. Titano would stay in the water, thinking nothing of the cold. The girls and I would go home, and Titano would still be in the water until I returned to fetch him. I would need a fleece, whereas he was still in his trunks, cleaning the fish that he had caught. I was freezing just looking at him. That's the night that I announced, "You are now officially the only Titano. I resign my claim."

That was a great holiday, traveling around the island in an Opel Corsa listening to 1970s music on a radio with only four buttons.

There was only static on the medium-wave radio, which got louder as the engine got louder. We had a great time simulating a rally race with Titano navigating and me driving, with the screeching static as the sound effects.

Over time, we really got to know each other. Titano worked in Bologna as a pharmaceutical representative and asked to be transferred there because he was going out with a girl named Susanna. On the weekends, he'd return to Padova. Despite our compatibility, our characters couldn't be more opposite. I'm very precise, but only when I need to be. I'm very practical, and also very quick with manual labor. For example, if I need to finish something very quickly, I'll take a big file and scrape away three millimeters in one go; Stefano, on the other hand, will take a tiny piece of sandpaper and meticulously rub away. He is very obsessed with details, and is basically a pain in the ass. Over the years, as a joke, I have made up a lot of songs where he comes off as the ass. For example, there are lots of switches on our boat that I always keep on. Titano boards the boat, thinks he knows everything and starts switching them all off without even thinking. He'd unknowingly switched off the john, and Trevisan had to go back and forth 18 times carrying a bucket of crap before we realized what had happened. You could hear Trevisan screaming all the way from Corsica to Padova.

There are thousands of anecdotes about Titano's obsessions. Filippo knows better than anyone, because they often had to share a room as they did when they came to Berlin, to what was supposed to be my deathbed. Filippo said, "After Titano's been to the bathroom, it's so clean, you could eat an egg in it." When Filippo's been to the bathroom, it looks like there's been a battle in it! There is not a speck of dust in Titano's house. He also has an amazing way of packing clothes. After a month on vacation, you actually have to smell his luggage to tell which clothes are dirty and which are clean—he doesn't even sweat! During the summer, he rides his motorbike in a very elegant linen jacket that never seems dirty, creased or wrinkled. Not even the flies stick to his bike. Not to mention how determined he is. He can spend ten hours under the scorching August sun just to catch a tiny sole. He'll then light a fire to cook that one little fish. When we came back from the boat excursion I suggested we quickly rinse the salt from the boat, but there was no way that he'd settle for that. He'd get out the soap, bucket, rags and scrubbing brush, which he always checked to make sure it had sufficient bristles.

He and Susanna were together for several years, but then they broke up and went their separate ways. In 1998, he came with us on holiday on my first boat, *Hakuna Matata I*. I invited a girl to join us named Nicoletta, whom I met while racing. She was single and already knew Titano, so I asked her to come along, almost as a joke. Titano and Nicoletta flirted like teenagers and something must have happened between them, because Titano came back every weekend and eventually he didn't need his own cabin anymore.

Titano and Nicoletta have been together ever since. A couple of years ago, Nicoletta convinced him to shave his head, eliminating the few hairs that he had left. If you compare the present Titano with photos of him when we met, you wouldn't recognize him. You'd never guess that he's 47 years old. He's incredibly fast on a bike, and it's the same with tennis, which he plays like a professional. He's very athletic and has a permanent tan. Even now he seems ten years younger than he did back then. When we introduce ourselves, everyone assumes that we went to school together and that we're basically the same age. Maybe one day he'll have a rapid decline, but for now, I'll have to accept that he's annoyingly fit.

Returning to the summer of 1995, I left Sardinia four days early and went to America with my old karting friend Glauco. Glauco had the time to accompany me, and wanted to visit New York on his return. This trip was an important experience, but rather depressing from a practical point of view. I wore out my shoes walking back and forth in the paddock looking for an opportunity. I spoke to several people, including Chip Ganassi, the owner of the team for which I'd later win two titles. I gave him my business card, but later saw him throw it away. I still give him a hard time about that even now. Everything seemed to be a waste of time. I found myself staring vacantly behind the net fencing of the track, thinking about my life. I didn't feel I had achieved much and had probably reached the end of the line. It was clear that I had to look for something else. But, as always happens in my life, I didn't dwell on it too long and a minute later, I was back to my usual, optimistic self, certain that good news was just around the corner.

In fact, something did happen, and at the end of the three days, Cal Wells took an interest in me. Wells, a California businessman, was organizing a team with Toyota. Toyota was new in the category and would be the technical partner and sponsor. This could be a good opportunity, regardless of Toyota's inexperience. I liked Wells immediately, and had nothing better at that time. But let me re-emphasize that I liked him and he proved to be a real gentleman. I went to Wells's motorhome, which he had borrowed because he didn't have his own, and he was very honest with me. He said, "Reynard told me good things about you. We want to organize a serious team, but I can't promise you that we'll win races. Next year we'll have a new engine and therefore it'll be tough to have the top position. It's going to be a lot of work, maybe taking two or three years to get to the top." For me, this was more than I'd hoped for and we agreed to continue talking.

Glauco and I went to New York, but without speaking much English, we became a bit depressed and decided to go home. I missed Daniela and Glauco missed his home. We tried to change our flight, but couldn't, so we stayed there, rather pissed off, and almost ended up arguing about it. Finally, we departed. On the plane we were in between two other people, sitting right in front of the television. At one point, while trying to get comfortable, I accidentally hit Glauco. He was half asleep and looked at me and said, "I hate you," and turned away. After that, we had many other good times together, but at that moment, we had really had enough of each other. When we arrived back in Milan, we got in our own cars and went our separate ways. We didn't even think about doing the journey together, or stopping off for a coffee along the way. We just said a quick goodbye and left.

That trip also took its toll on my finances. Rick Gorne and I had planned to go to that race and return to the last one in Laguna Seca. Before Loudon, Gorne had been very enthusiastic, but now he was getting embarrassed by the reality of the situation. The fact that I was an ex-Formula 1 driver didn't impress the people in IndyCar. In the United States, they don't even know who Schumacher is, so perhaps Rick had unrealistic expectations. When I asked him if I should go to Laguna Seca, he replied, "Well, it's up to you." I decided not to go because of the costs and to avoid any more disappointments.

It was Daniela who changed my mind by saying, "If you don't get out of the waiting room, you'll never know if your train is arriving. You decided to go, so stick to it. Just have a good time, after all it's a nice place. Why don't I buy another ticket and come along?" she asked. We went together and had a great time. The area of Laguna Seca, 90 miles south of San Francisco, is rather similar to Tuscany. We visited the city, had a few relaxing days and then went to the race circuit. I started wandering around the paddock while Daniela waited on the grass area. There was a bridge across the track that accessed the paddock. I think I walked across it at least 30 times. My feet were aching but I said to Daniela, "I'm going for another walk to see if I can find Rick. Maybe something will come out of it." I remember how supportive she was, and could see in her eyes that she was telling me, "I hope something happens for you—you deserve it. You've worked so hard for it, it would be such a shame if it finished like this."

As I reluctantly crossed the bridge for the umpteenth time, I saw Rick Gorne running towards me with his tongue out. "Where in the hell have you been? I've been looking for you—Ganassi is waiting for us!" I asked, "Chip Ganassi?" He said, "Yes! I can't explain now, but he's crazy. But maybe if you go there, you'll get a contract. Just sign everything that he asks for. This is a chance you can't miss." I was a little confused, but on the way to the motorhome, Rick explained exactly what had happened. Ganassi had just had an argument with his driver, Bryan Herta, and had accused him of being too slow, saying, "I can accept that you're too slow, but I can't accept your bad attitude." It was the last race of the season so he fired him on the spot.

Ganassi then asked Gorne, "Do you have another De Ferran?" De Ferran was the Brazilian driver who'd left European F3000 to join Jim Hall's CART team and started winning right away. Gorne replied, "I have someone who is even better than De Ferran— Alex Zanardi." Chip said, "I've never heard of him; bring him to America right now." Gorne then told him I was already there. Chip said, "What do you mean here? All right, I want to meet him in my motorhome in half an hour." Gorne found me just in time.

Chip sat down and started talking immediately. I was expecting a conversation about racing, but he asked me about what music I liked, my zodiac sign, and then went straight into hypothetical questions like, "If you were one of my drivers, and you were in the lead with only two laps to go, and then I told you to come back to the pits, what would you do?" I responded, "I'd ask you to explain." Chip said, "What do you mean, explain?" I said, "I'd think that you were crazy to ask me to come in." Chip asked another question, "Let's change the scenario. We are second in qualifying and you are going for the flying lap, and there is only one car in front and you know that pole is yours, and I tell you slow down, what do you do?" I said, "I ignore you." Ganassi replied, "No you don't!" He was trying to explain the importance of radio communication in the States. On an oval, if the yellow flag is waved as you come out of the corner, you don't know what is ahead. You have to trust unconditionally your team manager. At least I'd showed him that I was open to his ideas and could understand his reasoning, which I know was important to him. I think that he began to see me as one of his creations. I can teach him, shape him, and control my little toy. I made a couple of jokes, and he concluded, "If you can drive as fast as you can make me laugh, then I think you'll be racing for me next year. How about we organize a test in October and see you there? Now I have to go, goodbye." And then he disappeared, typical of Chip Ganassi.

I left feeling a bit anxious and asked Rick, "What should I make of this?" He replied, "You have no idea what just happened—next year you'll race with Ganassi." He was really excited, which got me very excited, too. Gorne had no doubts, and always believed in me; "When you do the test, you'll eat them alive." I then went to find Daniela, who was lying on the grass smoking a cigarette. When she saw me almost walking on air, she understood what had happened. It was difficult for me to contain my enthusiasm, but I stayed committed to my plans to see Cal Wells in San Diego. His offer was more than a possibility; he had formed a team and invited me to test in October.

In the meantime, Chip Ganassi called everyone on the team—the managing director, Tom Anderson; the team manager, Mike Hull; and the technical director, Morris Nunn. He told them, "Guys, I want to test someone to replace Bryan Herta. As we are all equal partners, you have the right to a choice. Mine is Zanardi, but you can test whomever you like." Anderson replied, "I want to keep Herta," so Ganassi kicked him out. Then Mike Hull said, "I know Jeff Krosnoff. I think that he drives well, but has never had a chance in the United States. He races in Formula 3000 in Japan, and I'd like to invite him." Chip agreed. Then Morris Nunn said with his British coolness, "I read in *Autosport* that there's this chap named Norberto Fontana who has won 11 out of 14 German Formula 3 races. He must be fast, so I'd like to see him." They contacted Norberto, who had already been offered a test drive with Sauber in Formula 1 and therefore wasn't interested—unbelievable ....

The test was between me and Krosnoff, although it hadn't been explained to me in those terms and I didn't realize I was competing for the position. I thought it was just a session to test me in the car. Anyway, we were scheduled for four days of testing on the brand-new track at Homestead, near Miami. It was the first time that anyone had driven on the circuit. For two days, the track was set up as an oval and for two days as a street circuit. Jimmy Vasser, the main driver of the team, spent the first two days on the oval, testing the new Honda engine, which proved to be excellent.

The track was then converted to the street circuit and we started the test. It was scheduled to take place on the third day, and if necessary, on the fourth. Vasser went out in the morning and set a time around 1 minute, 19 seconds. The track was newly surfaced, so it was cleaning up from minute to minute. For this reason, Jimmy's time was not representative of his actual speed. It benefited us for him to go out first because it was easier to get a good time with a clean track. We started with an advantage and everything looked good. I jumped in the car and suddenly rain clouds appeared—the typical Florida clouds that look like they'll downpour at any moment. Nonetheless, they let me complete around 30 laps and it went really well. Morris Nunn, who at that point was one of my enemies, insisted that he had never seen an Italian win a title in a Formula 1 championship. He thought that Italians have always been fast and have driven the best cars, but when it came to dealing with the pressure, they can't cope. The British, according to Morris, were a completely a different matter, of course.

Before I got in the car, Morris called Ganassi from the pit and said, "Do you see that corner there? [This was the hairpin before the main straight.] You'll see that bloody Italian will come out of it in second, accelerate to the max and spin the wheels." And when Chip asked why, Morris explained, "Because Italians are like that at the wheel, they exaggerate, go fast, but don't care about the car." During my racing career, I couldn't have been more opposite. It's not surprising that they called me "The Parisian." I always had a very polished style, so when they saw me coming out of that hairpin on the first lap, accelerating and giving the tires as much as they could take, but not spinning the wheels, they were surprised. It was Morris who was first to change his mind. I gradually lowered the lap time from 1 minute, 19 seconds to 1 minute, 17 seconds. They were very impressed. They also liked how I gave interesting technical feedback that often helped improve the car, and that when I realized I was wrong, I was always humble enough to stop and say, "No, you're right. The change that I suggested will not get us anywhere."

During those 30 laps, my time progressively decreased. They finally made me stop because it looked like it was going to rain, and they still had to see Jeff Krosnoff. I was under the impression that it had gone well, and Morris's change in attitude reflected that fact. Chip asked Morris to have a chat with me in order to evaluate my technical background, but he avoided me by hiding in his motorhome. But after seeing the atmosphere around the team change, I felt confident about my chances. Even Tom Anderson, who had preferred to keep Herta, came to congratulate me.

Krosnoff drove well, but obviously had a lot of pressure to out-perform me. He didn't make any major mistakes, but he was inconsistent. He would go from 1 minute, 24 seconds to 1 minute, 18 seconds and then back again. It never rained, so he completed 70 laps with new tires and managed to drive faster than me with 1 minute, 16.8 seconds, but that didn't seem to matter because it was clear to everybody the track was improving. It was more about the way I handled the car and the feedback that I gave to the technicians, so I assumed that everything was all right.

I was already on the phone to Daniela when suddenly Anderson came over and said, "Alex, we need you again." I told Daniela that I had to get off the phone. When I arrived at the pits, they said that Chip wanted to see me again. I thought, "Oh shit. What does this mean?" and then I felt the pressure. I'd already been making plans and now I had to go and play the game again. I went out on the track with the tires that Jeff had been using and was immediately faster, around 1 minute, 16.5 seconds, but this wasn't the point. The point was that my hands were shaking and I was nervous. I stopped the car and went back to the pits and Chip asked, "Why did you stop?" I muttered, "Well, the problem is that I desperately want this job and am driving with my heart instead of my head. I'm very sorry, but I have to stop and get my bearings back." It wasn't a ploy, it was the truth, and Morris was very impressed. In the meantime, they gave me new tires so that I had the same chance as Krosnoff. With the new tires, I did 1 minute, 15.7 seconds, then 1 minute, 15.5 seconds and finally 1 minute, 15.1 seconds which was the unofficial lap record for the track. I was being compared to Penske driver Emerson Fittipaldi, the former F1 and CART champion who was a legend in racing and had set an official time of 1 minute, 16 seconds, which was great publicity for me. All of this happened on October 18. They said that they would let me know, but the team's enthusiasm was obvious from the series of pats on my shoulder.

I was very optimistic and rushed to the hotel to call Daniela again. On the way, the police stopped me for speeding. The police don't mess around in Florida. As I got out of the car, they pointed their guns at me and started screaming at me not to move. They asked me for my documents, and as I went for the back pocket of my trousers, they pulled their guns out again. They soon realized I was an ignorant Italian who didn't know that in the United States, you're supposed to remain in the car. Fortunately, they were huge racing fans and when they heard I was coming from the circuit and that I would be racing in CART, they let me go. At that moment, I'd taken more risks there than I did on the track—they'd pointed their guns under my nose, and they weren't joking.

The following week I was supposed to test for Cal Wells. Mike Groff and I were competing for that seat. During the days before that test, we started talking with Chip who was asking for references. He insisted that he couldn't make a decision and that I needed "this person or that person to call me as a reference." I think that he'd already decided before the test to keep Bryan Herta, but after I'd driven so well, he was torn over what to do. To satisfy Chip's concerns, I asked Peter Collins and Briatore to contact him. I learned that Peter wrote a wonderful letter to Morris. Briatore tried, but couldn't reach him; anyway, there was a lot of hassle. Chip was being very difficult and the time was passing quickly. Finally Wells's team arrived at Homestead, so I went to have a seat fitting for the upcoming test. That evening, they invited me to dinner. As I was getting up from the table, they said, "Wait—there's something else." I sat down again and then the "Happy Birthday" music began and they all started singing. It was October 23 and they had remembered it was my birthday. They organized a party with a cake and candles and I thought, "This is the team that I want to race with for the rest of my life."

When the party was over and I went back to my hotel, I received a message from Ganassi. I called him back and heard the usual crap, "Tomorrow you won't test for Wells. Just get Briatore to call me." In the beginning I went along with him, but his arrogance really started to piss me off. I had one of those reactions that throughout my career closed many doors but opened some others. I said, "Listen, Chip, with all due respect, something's not right here. You're simply not convinced, or we wouldn't be having

17. The only photograph I have of me passing Bryan Herta in the "Corkscrew" at Laguna Seca in 1996. This last-lap pass won me the race and lots of fans in the U.S.

18. In Japan during our honeymoon. From the left: Asaka, Daniela, a Honda PR executive, Kawamoto, me with my birthday cake, Amaniya and Ganassi.

19. Daniela and me with Morris Nunn
and his wonderful sideburns in 1996.

20. Leading teammate Jimmy Vasser in
the Turn 1 chicane at Surfer's Paradise,
Australia, in 1997. By starting on pole
in this race, I set the CART record for
consecutive poles (six), which I still
hold today.

21. Setting up a photoshoot after winning my first CART championship in 1997 with, at the front, Ganassi, Jimmy, me and Joe Montana.

22. With the guys at the traditional end-of-year CART banquet in 1997. Top, from left: John Wayne, me, Ricky, chief mechanic Rob, and Mike Hull. Bottom, from the left: Simon, Doug and Mark.

23. Providing feedback on my car's handling to the team engineers during a preseason practice session in 1998.

24. Celebrating a triumphant victory at Long Beach in 1998—one of the most spectacular races of my career.

25. On the road to another CART series victory in 1998. After starting fifth on the grid at Portland, Oregon, I passed Vasser on the outside in the hairpin during the first lap and went on to win the race.

26. Jimmy holding Niccolò when he was just a few days old, with a proud dad keeping an eye on them.

27. A pitstop at the Elkhart Lake race in 1998. Despite a collision with Al Unser Junior, I managed to finish second.

28. An end-of-season photoshoot in 1998. Me with my 1997 and 1998 PPG Cups (on left), Jimmy with his 1996 PPG Cup (on right), and Chicco (in front).

had a conference call with Wells who was in his
California. After I explained everything, he had
reaction that made me realize that these Americans
people, "If I was there, I'd kick your ass to make
assi right away. Ganassi is offering you something
better than we are, so you have to sign with him.
could win in that car. You won't with us, so go,
. But if something goes wrong, we'll still be here
We were really interested in you and you were our
d we'd still love to see you in our car." I went to see
verything went well. I called Wells and told him,
I'm happy for you." At that point they invited Jeff
est in my place, and found another driver to take
place.

antime, Ganassi made me work for that signature.
picked me up at the airport, took me to the hotel
dinner with his wife. We drank, told stories, and
following morning, he came to pick me up again and
he contract. It seemed that the American dream was
fore my eyes. My contract was for three years, earning
the first year—the kind of money I'd never imagined.
I hoped that I could "steal" some prize money. I had
self psychologically, and the prize money was the only
ntended to negotiate. At the time, Formula 1 drivers
a percentage of the prizes, equaling around 5 percent.
ly asked for 15 percent hoping to meet somewhere
percent. But he showed me a 40 percent base right
sing to 50 percent if I won the championship. There
g left to complain about. Finalizing the contract, the
ve clause that I naïvely overlooked was in terms of
an prize system. The ceiling on the prize money was
or the first year, and everything else above that would
ssi. He later explained to me that he had to account for

29. Greeting reigning World Champion Mika Häkinnen during my Formula 1 debut for Williams at Melbourne, Australia in 1999.

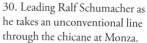

30. Leading Ralf Schumacher as he takes an unconventional line through the chicane at Monza.

31. My season with
Williams was a major
disappointment. My car
seemed to break down
more often than teammate
Ralf Schumacher's.

32. Attending the
October 2000 CART race
in Fontana, California,
during my sabbatical year.
By this point I knew I had
to get back to racing.

this discussion. As a ma
take me on because you
accident. If you're not co
try again in the future." C
with me?" I said, "Are y
but it is obvious that you'i
that I'm not certain, it's ju

At this point I said, "C
not clever enough. You're i
your victories to sell their c
recommend the first idiot
them, who can you trust?"
continuing, "Why do you
don't even know them. Evei
does that change? If you do
Gorne, who stand to direct
do you believe? I'm going to
tomorrow I have to drive on a
It's 11 pm, and I have to go t
you again soon." He said, "Fii

That was the end of our
until he called back again. "I
want you get on a plane to Pitt
to sign here." He had finally m
first thought was about what I
impatient, "You need to know
was right, so I agreed to go to Pi

The following morning I w
about Wells waiting for me to
remember how many times I'd
so even if I did the same to some
of the world. I spoke to Jeff Tenze
was completely unprepared for

his vehicle and
headquarters ir
an unexpected
are very good
you go to Gan
a million time
Next year, you
and good luck
for four days.
first choice, ar
Ganassi and
and he said, "
Krosnoff to t
Mike Groff's

In the m
He came anc
and then to
laughed. The
showed me t
unfolding be
$150,000 in
In addition,
prepared my
issue that I
were offered
So I cheeki
around 10
away, incre
was nothin
only negat
the Americ
$150,000
go to Gana

149

"all the potential damage that beginners make when they start." That didn't sound unreasonable, but in reality, it was a joke.

Prizes are very hefty in the States and after two races, even without doing anything incredible, I had already reached the ceiling. Jimmy Vasser, my teammate, who later became champion, cashed in something like $3.2 million dollars that year. I came in second with prize earnings equaling something like $1.9 million. Had I been able to have the whole 40 percent of it without the ceiling, I would have earned $760,000 dollars. Instead, I got $150,000 and Ganassi made $610,000 from me. Indeed, he changed my life. I want to clarify this because later, Ganassi made me a decent offer, but he loves deal-making and getting the best possible share of someone. The more naïve you are, the more fun it is for him. He played hardball in every negotiation, but he's always honored his word, which is a rare trait in motor racing. But when I understood how things worked and what the other drivers were making, I was a bit pissed off. I never told Chip though, because I was so grateful and happy to be racing for him.

Over time, I had many disputes with Chip. We never seemed to agree on anything and we had some pretty big blow-ups. Arguing was his hobby and his passion, and since I would never give in, he just loved it. Thanks to this, we have some very vivid memories of one another. We never held anything back—so it was, and so it had to be. Despite a few harsh words, we became very good friends and I worship the ground he walks on. He's the man who saw something more in me. In the end, he was the one who finally took a gamble on me and this proved to be very good intuition. I thought it was by chance that Ganassi had found me, and as a consequence didn't think much of my own talent; only later did I realize that it wasn't luck, but his cunning foresight that had made him choose me. I was very proud of his decision.

CHAPTER 9

A Good Start in CART, and Marriage

I went to back to Italy with my contract in hand. I felt like a hero, but kept a low profile because I'd been kicked too many times and had learned my lesson. I was thrilled to have number 4 on the car. Numbers 4 and 12 had been assigned to the cars several years before and Jimmy Vasser was number 12, and as number 4 I was beside myself to see my name so high up the list of drivers. Little did I know that my name would eventually climb up the rankings and that I would eventually have the number 1 on the front of my car.

During winter testing, I slowly developed a great relationship with Morris Nunn, my new engineer. Morris had been a star in Formula 1, and founder of the Ensign team for which Chris Amon and Clay Regazzoni had once raced. In 1963 Morris started as a driver, and won a few races in Formula 3 with Team Lotus. Then he stopped racing and built a Formula 3 car in his garage in Walsall. In 1971, the car proved to be a winner.

At the end of 1972, Rikki Von Opel, heir of the German carmaker, commissioned Morris to build a Formula 1 car to debut at the French Grand Prix in 1973. Opel and Nunn started a long but ultimately unsuccessful relationship that survived Regazzoni's dramatic accident at Long Beach in 1980 from which he emerged paralyzed. They also had many incredible and funny adventures. But Morris never had any money, so in 1983, he sold the team to Teddy Yip, a Hong Kong millionaire who was a huge racing fan, and moved to the States. After working with Bignotti, Newman-

Haas and Patrick, Morris collaborated with Emerson Fittipaldi who won the title and the Indianapolis 500. In 1992, Morris moved to Ganassi's team.

Morris was 58 years old by this point, and after all those years of racing, was ready for his retirement. He was never very enthusiastic about Bryan Herta, whom he had been looking after, and Morris was looking for a new challenge, hoping to find it with me. Nonetheless, he was very dubious in the beginning, primarily because I was Italian. Whenever he had the chance, he would test me. Once again, I was trying to win over my engineer, as with Fassina and his Professor, but this time with more at stake. I learned a lot from Kathyrin, Morris's wife, who was very good fun.

Morris began to change his attitude during our negotiations back at Laguna Seca, and then, after the first test at Homestead, he called his wife and said, "For once in my life, I must admit that I was completely wrong." She couldn't believe her own ears, and started teasing him, "Oh, I can't believe it. What happened that was so important?" He laughed, "We tested an Italian and I've never seen anyone drive so fast and so flawlessly. There is still a lot of work to do, but if today's results are any indication of the days to come, we've got a great future. Today we really put on the pressure and he clearly wanted to impress us, but he never lost his head. He drives in a surprisingly polished way, but also very efficient, never going off his line. He gives the wheels exactly what they can bear, nothing more or nothing less than the required load. This guy really has traction-control in his foot. Peter Collins said so, but I didn't believe it. But it's true. He respects the car's functions and is fast, fast, fast. In addition, he gave us very interesting feedback, which surprised us." Not a bad first impression.

From then on, Morris tried to ignore his prejudices and became more open-minded. I enjoyed going out with him and was fascinated by his stories. I've always been passionate about the era of 'real racing' when you had to say a prayer before getting into the car, "Lord, I hope that I get out of the car on my own two legs." Or, you could smoke a cigarette and drink some whiskey before jumping in the car. Morris was racing back in those days and had amazing stories. I never got tired of going out to dinner with him, always had a great time and enjoyed his typically English humor.

Morris and I got along really well and complemented each other: when one stopped, the other would start. We cemented the relationship during the winter testing, when I was competing with my teammate, Jimmy Vasser.

Jimmy was very fast and had won the championship, but he was also very generous to me. The first race in the championship didn't go that well for me. I had the typical misfortune of doubting myself. When you trust yourself, you also become lucky and then nobody can stop you. Jimmy was always incredibly nice to me, but I couldn't help wonder if it would be the same if the situation was reversed? I had come from a European school with great friendly rivalries, but I never hid information about the cars or pulled any tricks. My philosophy has always been, "If I have talent, I will go fast and at the end, it will show. If I haven't got it, I'll go home and become a plumber." In terms of Jimmy, I'm ashamed to have doubted his motives, because when the positions did change, he was better to me than I'd ever been to him. We started a wonderful friendship that still exists today.

Winter testing had given me hope. My lap times were always very competitive, especially compared to Jimmy, who was a candidate for the title. But the ovals were a real unknown for me. In CART then, they alternated between classic circuits and oval tracks of various dimensions. In fact, there were three, the short ones—one mile long—like Nazareth and Milwaukee; the long ones at a mile and half, like Brazil or Homestead; and the super speedways such as Michigan and Indianapolis. These are truly temples of speed where you drive at 220 mph, and it is not unusual to go over 250 mph while running in somebody's slipstream. Such a variety of tracks tends to flush out the good drivers. This is one of the reasons why Jimmy started the season so well, winning four of the first six races.

On the other hand, I was rather unlucky. While Jimmy was winning the first race at Homestead, I made my debut by crashing into a wall, thanks to a loose wheel.

My chief mechanic, Rob Hill, was new to the team. He'd arrived from Bobby Rahal's team and was excellent, both in terms of his professionalism and character. The other guys were all exceptional mechanics. In addition to Rob, there was Brad, Steve, John Wayne (his real name), Simon, Norm, Wayne and Ricky. It was Ricky who'd left me with a loose wheel in Homestead. Many in my place would have made a huge scene, but I didn't say anything as I was still happy with things. I only started in 14th position because I had been told to take it easy during qualifying, but during the race, I went up to 5th position and things were going well until the crash. I wasn't scared, but was hoping it wasn't my fault. When I saw the wheel move in a completely different way than the car, I thought, "This can't possibly be my fault." When I went back to the pit, I did something that seemed quite normal and that the team really appreciated. Instead of blaming Ricky during my television interview, I said, "We're a team, and one day we will win. I made a lot of mistakes during practice, so nobody saw them. Unfortunately, today you saw a superb member of our team prove he was human. These things happen."

I then went to Ganassi and repeated the same words. Meanwhile, Ricky was very sad and felt under a lot of pressure. I hugged him and said, "I'm not cross about losing the race. These things happen. And now I know that I can really count on you because you'll try your best to not make any more mistakes." That day, a seed of a very happy relationship was sown. My mechanics realized that I wasn't the typical Formula 1 driver who looked down on them, collected their million dollars and then flew off in a private jet. I obviously hoped that I'd earn that much money one day, but I wasn't there just for money. I was doing that job out of my passion for driving and the relationship with the team. That episode helped me break the ice with them. I'm not comparing myself to Senna, but I felt that the team respected the way in which I dealt with the situation. In addition, because I now lived in Indianapolis, where the team had its headquarters, I always tried to spend time with them.

The second race, in Rio de Janeiro, became another important step in building my relationship with the team. Right before the race, Morris set up the car, based on his considerable experience with poorly paved Brazilian tracks. We only had drawings of the track because we knew that the oval had just been resurfaced. So when I saw the chosen set-up, I was a bit concerned and asked, "Morris, why is the car so soft? After all, it is an oval and a very new, smooth track?" He replied, "Smooth? With Brazilians?" He laughed and started telling stories about his past experiences in Rio. "You'll see when we get there. If the track is smooth, then I'll buy you all dinner for the rest of the year." Obviously I had to buy Morris dinner and in fact, the road was so bumpy that it was difficult to see where you were going, despite the track literature boasting of its "superior technology."

Morris created a fantastic car, thanks to the addition of a superb Honda engine. We had a terrific advantage, especially in qualifying. Even on Thursday's free practice, I came in first. It seemed like a dream. I was first on Thursday, had an even better time on Friday, had the same on Saturday morning, then finished first in qualifying on Saturday afternoon. Jimmy's set-up was completely wrong, and at the last moment, they changed it to match mine, without even testing it. Jimmy immediately improved and then had the best time. Back then, the qualifying sessions worked like the current-day qualifying in Formula 1. I was scared shitless, thinking after having helped him set up his car, he'd steal pole from me. I barely managed stay in front, but got pole back. Jimmy came to congratulate me and confessed, "I swear, for a second I thought that I'd stolen pole position, but you made this car perform like it did, and so it wouldn't have been fair."

The race itself went badly for both of us. I was ahead for the first part, and then the team made a mistake and called me in for refueling. Until then, each time a yellow flag was waved, they called me in and everybody followed suit. This time, a yellow flag was waved, but no one followed me to the pits. After the pit stop, I went down to 24th place. I called Ganassi on the radio and said, "Mr. Ganassi, I don't understand this American strategy—how is it possible that I was first and now I'm 24th?" His rather confused reply was, "But now we have a full tank."

A few laps later, there was another yellow flag and everyone else went in to refuel except me, and I ended up in first again. This time I radioed Chip with a lot more confidence. To be honest, I often pronounced his name as "Cheap" and he was always correcting me. Ten laps later, another yellow flag was waved, I was called in and I was last again. So I said, "Cheap, how does this fit with your strategy?" He said, "It's Chip. Alex, the good thing is that we now have enough fuel to get to the end." I immediately replied, "Cheap, do the others have to stop for fuel again?" Chip replied abruptly, "All the others have enough to finish." There was a long moment of silence. "Cheap?" I inquired. "My name is CHIP!" came the reply. I said, "I don't understand. I was first, then I was last, then I was first, now I'm last again, and you tell me that everyone has enough fuel. So as far as I can see, it's the same as it was in Europe. If I want to be in front, I have to pass as often as possible." He replied innocently, "You've got it right, man." Therefore, 18 laps before the end, I pushed as hard as possible and went from 24th to 4th, finishing just inches behind Scott Pruett.

On the journey home, Nunn was a bit embarrassed about what had happened. I didn't blame him, but rather assumed I was still being tested and after such a performance, my conscience was clear. I couldn't care less about the title because I never imagined that I'd be racing in the first place. In addition, I had a great time with all of the passing, comebacks, and exciting finale. When Mo realized I wasn't angry with him, he relaxed and said, "Well boy, today you really did well. Despite our mistakes, you drove a fantastic race. Are you sure that you're Italian? Are you sure you don't have even a smidgen of English blood in your veins?" I couldn't have asked for a better compliment.

After Rio, a series of blunders followed me. In Australia, I was in the slow drivers' session, which gives the first drivers an opportunity to clean the track for the quicker ones. In my group, I had by far the best time, and Vasser immediately gave me another great compliment, commenting on how I had driven the car with good control and with slight oversteering, just missing the walls of the track. I practically drove a lap sideways, almost skidding and letting the car bounce like a pinball. Jimmy approached me, gave me a slap on the shoulder and said, "That was a spectacular show." But then the bastard took pole from me! Even Pruett managed to go faster. During the race, I was hit by one of the typical flaws of circuit racing—the clutch broke and I had to pull out halfway through the event. This was especially difficult on the mechanics.

I felt exasperated when I arrived at Long Beach. I had been so close to victory, but hadn't managed to collect many points. In the first free practice session, I had the third best time and everyone went ballistic. There was this theory that it was impossible to go fast on a new track, and everybody kept reminding me about this, but I've always been able to learn a track in just three laps. So, on Friday afternoon, I got the preliminary pole, which was amazing. The following day, I came in second after the Brazilian, Gil De Ferran.

At the beginning of the race, he sped ahead, but I stuck to him like a pit bull. We managed to keep a significant gap ahead of the others, but he wore out his tires in trying to block me and had to go into the pits. I still had fuel and could stay out a bit longer.

In this situation, whichever driver enters the pits first for refueling and new tires must then drive a lap with cold tires while the others are at full speed. When this happens, you can gain four to five seconds after the pit stop and get in front of your opponents. With a little experience, you can keep the opponent behind until the tires reach the optimal temperature. So basically, whoever enters the pits last automatically passes the others unless he makes a mistake. This is why strategies are so important in the States, not just in terms of managing the race, but also for planning the maneuvers, based on the pit stops.

When De Ferran rejoined, I was clearly ahead of him, but when I was trying to increase the gap and exit first from the pit stop, I was immediately stuck behind two cars which had been lapped, Teo Fabi, who was substituting for Mark Blundell, and Bobby Rahal. We arrived at the first corner and Rahal braked so hard that I thought that he was letting me pass. I was still racing with a European mentality that requires the lapped driver to give way. This doesn't happen in the States. Rahal took his corner and ran over the nose of my car, forcing me to pull out. I thought I had the right to be pissed off, but the people in the pits looked at me as if I'd done something really terrible.

To be honest, I didn't understand their mentality yet. If you are about to be lapped, but manage to keep in front of the leader when a yellow flag is waved, you can make up the lap because the leader has to slow down and nobody is allowed to pass. This completely changes the fate of the race. I discovered this on the same circuit two years later in 1998 when I exited the pits and tried to fight off the leader, De Ferran, blocking him several times in order to defend myself. I managed to keep him from passing for a lap and a half.

This time, in 1996, De Ferran ended up having a problem with his turbo, Tracy hit a wall and my teammate Vasser finished first. I still felt that I was being tested, and effectively this was the case. If Ganassi wanted to, he could have fired me, and I think that race created some question marks about me, even though Vasser won. Once again, Jimmy had taught me how to drive in that championship, and the pressure was mounting.

Apart from my racing results, that was a wonderful time for me. Back from Long Beach, we started decorating our rented condominium. Daniela and I started looking around town for furniture. Our "nest" was in Indianapolis, just outside the Route 465 ring road in one of the nicest areas of the city. There was a pond outside the house which was filled with very chatty ducks. For the things we needed to set up our household, we of course went to the local Target store—our team's sponsor. With our 10 percent associate's discount card, we loaded up everything we needed. The condo had two bedrooms, giving us ample space for the many friends and family who came to visit us. My life still felt unsettled, just as it always had been. My main wish was not to win, but to have Chip say, "I'll keep you next year." The following year, I stood to earn $500,000, which would have set me up for the rest of my life.

We arrived at Nazareth, a short oval, which wasn't our ideal track. Although I occasionally beat Jimmy, he was driving with his head, whereas I once again made the fatal mistake of driving with my heart. I was trying to accomplish completely impossible things, and if I had continued like that, I would have ended up against a wall. That's exactly what happened at Nazareth and Milwaukee. On short ovals, there is a completely different way to set up the cars, but in those years, they didn't know a thing about it. We finally solved the problem and in the winter of 1997, two modifications gave us good results. Jimmy and I spoke with Mo, tested the changes on the track and through race simulation, and found out that we had gained an incredible amount of time. It was brilliant when Jimmy won the race at Nazareth in 1998. I was happier about his win, and my second place, than all of my own victories combined because it was a true team achievement. I think that Ganassi had the great ability to create a team where everyone worked for the benefit of the group, a bit like the Japanese. I felt that some of Jimmy's victories were mine, and I'm sure that he thought the same about me. I was never more satisfied than during the last race of 1998, when Jimmy won and I took third place at Fontana.

Nazareth was very traumatic. I was fastest during the first practice, but as soon as the others stopped for refueling, we found ourselves in an unexpected position. I was no longer in the first ten, and then it started raining. Although the track eventually dried up, I managed to find a wet patch and lost control of the car. I smashed into the wall and damaged another chassis. The race went just as badly, and after a fuel feed problem, I ended up in 13th place, just short of winning a point. The booby prize, so to speak.

Then came the U.S. 500 at Michigan. For CART, this represented the Indianapolis 500, which was to be taken off the CART calendar later that year. Tony George, owner of the historic Indiana circuit, had decided to pull out of CART. They were always patronizing him, so Tony made the Indianapolis Motor Speedway the foundation for a rival circuit, the Indy Racing League (IRL). CART responded to this with a new race on the Michigan oval, almost at the same time as Indianapolis, which they called the "Real 500." At the time, that was absolutely true in terms of participants. As at Indianapolis, qualifying was held 15 days prior to the race. In order to create interest in the track, there was a big promotion with the most famous drivers—Andretti, Fittipaldi, Unser—along with us new drivers.

But despite all the effort, we were unconvincing, even to ourselves. Target was the official sponsor of the event and fronted most of the million-dollar prize money, generating substantial media interest. I went to the race with a bit of fear and reverence, but I wasn't about to give up. One afternoon before the race, I was in the workshop with Morris when our managing director, Tom Anderson, arrived and told us that he'd found a new turbocharger. That particular year, it could be any size. A bigger one had fewer benefits at high revs and caused problems while accelerating at low revs, but on the super speedway, it increased the speed of the cars and would have been useful on the Michigan oval. Morris said, "OK, when do we get them?" Tom replied, "I've only found one." Morris replied, "What do you mean, one—what are we going to put on Jimmy's car?" Tom was talking to Morris as the team's technical director, and Morris was talking to Tom as the engineer responsible for my car. Tom said, "It's for Jimmy's car, but you can put a 28 on Alex's, which is equally as good." Mo replied, "It's not equally good or we wouldn't be here doing all this work." Tom admitted, "Sure, it will have three of four less horsepower, but it doesn't really matter because Alex is just learning at Michigan." At that point Morris did something that really made me feel proud. He took off his glasses, slowly put them on the table and said confidently, "You'll see where my driver will be when the green flag is waved. And if nothing goes wrong, you'll see him right near Jimmy Vasser at the end of the race." He said it with such conviction, that he instantly won my heart.

Every now and then, Morris had one of his rants in order to fire me up. But mostly, he told me to be humble and respect my opponents. With this in mind, I was preparing to do my best. Then on the Sunday, it was up to Ganassi to fire me up. He was on the radio directing my race, and when I passed the way he wanted, he "loved" me and didn't do anything to hide it. His enthusiastic coaching was typically American, "You're the man! You can do it!" This usually happened during the last lap when I should have been concentrating on the fast lap rather than his noisy chants, but

Chip was like that, and I think his excesses, together with Morris's, got the best out of me.

Ganassi is also a very intelligent and intuitive man. On several occasions, he could predict what would happen and adapt his strategy. Thanks to his intuition, we sorted out obstacles that initially seemed insurmountable.

Going back to Michigan, Morris was right. I was fourth in qualifying, only pushing it when necessary. I had my rookie orientation for the super ovals, which was the test for beginners who had never raced on that type of circuit. To be honest, it was a completely different world. During that test, I was instructed via radio to try three laps at a given speed, then faster, then slower. They wanted to be sure that I could manage a situation. Clearly that was not the end of it, and it certainly didn't teach you how to drive on such a fast oval.

After passing the orientation, I was left to my own devices, but I kept going slowly. All the others were averaging 143 mph, while I was terrified to do 135. I couldn't feel the car—I was already pushing like crazy and was still only in third gear, and I couldn't reach the rev range to move into fourth. I slowed in the curves, but if you don't keep your foot on the accelerator, you can't reach enough speed to change to higher gear. I was driving in third, telling myself, "I should be in sixth gear and I can't even get into fourth." As it happens, gears on the ovals are different, and third, fourth, fifth and sixth are very close to each other. For instance, sixth gear is just 200–300 rpm above fifth. The entire experience was traumatic for me.

I stopped and told Morris, "I'm not going anywhere—the car feels too light." He replied, "All right, Alex, now we need to start unloading the car. The car is loaded aerodynamically and that's why you're not going fast enough." I couldn't believe it and thought he was crazy. I begged him not to, because I was certain that I'd kill myself on a curve if that car was any lighter aerodynamically than it already was. But he said decisively, "Alex, trust me. Leave me to take care of it and don't worry, you just go out and drive. If it doesn't go well, come back and we'll set it up again. The most important thing is that you go out and do what you can do." I went back on the track and as if by magic, unloading the amount of downforce generated by the wings increased my speed on the straights. The wings, even with less incidence but due to the increase in straight line speed, were able to push down the car and produce a much stronger level of downforce that kept the car close to the ground. I was left with a much faster car on the straights, and more stability in the curves. I started enjoying myself and going for it. On the radio, I yelled, "Damn Morris, unload, unload, it is perfect!"

I was very humble when I started my first race on a super oval, doing exactly what I had been told and nothing more. I was in the lead after five laps, but despite this, I felt very insecure during the lapping and heavy traffic. I lost some positions, then regained them, and it went on like this.

In the beginning, it was all very dramatic. When you drive at 250 mph in someone's slipstream, the car vibrates as if it is on a cobblestone street. Then if you move out of the slipstream, you get a gust of wind as on a highway when you exit a tunnel with a trailer attached during gale force winds. But as a matter of fact, if you are calm and controlled, the car does exactly what you want. It doesn't matter that you're going at 250 mph; the car is made for that speed. It's up to you to relax and handle it gently.

Throughout the race, I became more confident and more daring, and ended up back in the lead. I was in the lead for quite a while, and after the first 30 laps, I was the undisputed leader, until returning to the pits. Everything was going really well, but then I had a small problem during refueling when a wheel wouldn't fit. The wheel was fixed and I rejoined the track, falling back into seventh position. But I was so fast that after just three laps, I was leading again. I began to have the situation under control and handle the car perfectly, despite the crazy speed and the fact that it was my first race on a super speedway, supposedly the most difficult race I would face that year. Just when I thought everything was fine, the engine blew on the 148th lap, with 102 still to go. The Honda technicians later explained that it was a pin, hardly worth a dollar, which had broken. It was probably faulty, because the engine wasn't under any particular strain at the time. The failure of this insignificant piece, which just holds a part of the oil pump in position, had interrupted the lubrication of the engine, thus causing it to blow. At least I was given a point for being the driver who was in the lead for the majority of the race.

I received a lot of support and encouragement from everyone, which made me feel better. But frankly, I would have rather won and taken home a million-dollar prize (even though this would have been in Ganassi pockets thanks to that ceiling in my contract). But it wasn't really about money. Even though my recent streak of bad luck was frustrating, I'd had a great race. I wished that I were as lucky as Jimmy, who was doing surprisingly well. Right in the middle of that 500-mile race, he lost a lap because of a problem during refueling and appeared to be out of the running. But in this type of event, it's relatively easy to rectify a situation—yellow flags, neutralizations, refueling, everything can change the stakes and get you back into the game. You can still win, even if the stakes appear to be working against you, which is what he managed to do. He took advantage of the others pulling out, and more importantly, used his head when making choices. I heard that Jimmy had won while driving back to Indianapolis with Daniela. When I left the circuit, he was "nowhere" as they say. I couldn't believe his luck! Although I was a bit envious, I called Jimmy that evening to congratulate him, wondering again if he would do the same for me, but throughout the years, he proved to be much bigger hearted than me, or anyone else that I knew.

Milwaukee, another very short oval, followed the Michigan race. It went as badly there as it did at Nazareth. During the practice, I had an accident that left me very disorientated. Chip was furious, and rather than give me the usual encouragements like, "Don't worry, these things happen," he said, "If you ruin another car, you're fired. You've crashed one in every race." I tried to defend myself, "Don't forget that the first time that I crashed, you'd sent me out with a loose wheel." He said, "I don't give a shit—if it happens again, you're out." He probably didn't mean to sound so harsh, but this telling off reminded me that ultimately, I was a nobody and still had a lot to learn. I couldn't pretend I was going to become an expert after four laps—the other drivers were the real experts.

The following day, I had a terribly stiff neck from the accident and came in 13th. While I was either pulling out of races or failing to get any points, Jimmy was going for the championship. But halfway through the season, at the eighth race, Detroit, things got difficult for him, and he didn't make the top ten in qualifying. During the warm-up Jimmy had a terrible crash, smashing the rear of the car again.

The Detroit Grand Prix, as they called it, was equally disappointing. Not that I was doing any better. During that time, the race organizers were trying to organize how to restart the race after a yellow flag in order to suit television requirements. They decided that after a neutralization, the lapped driver should give way to the leader. The rule was later reviewed, but at Detroit no ruling had been made and so they were still experimenting.

The first part of this race was on a wet surface. Although we were the first to change tires, our strategy was sabotaged by a yellow flag. There were many more yellow flags. At each restart, there would be five or six drivers, but I'd have to go back and let everybody pass because of the new rule. I think that I overtook P.J. Jones at least seven or eight times, but it didn't get me anywhere. Towards the end of the race, I was 11th with Jimmy right behind me, and Chip said to let him pass because he was fighting for the championship. I asked, "Why should I let him pass at a time when I could also use the points?" and Chip replied abruptly, "Do whatever you want." So I stayed in front of him. At that moment he had 100 points, almost 50 more than his closest rival, and I was in desperate need of some.

Halfway through the season, Jimmy was still unchallenged, whereas I only had 17 points. Rio and Long Beach would have been within my reach had things not gone belly-up.

The ninth race of the year was scheduled for Portland. Our team's publicist was Mike Knight, whom I immediately didn't like. He introduced himself with his loud voice, "I'm Mike Knight and I've worked with Nigel Mansell, Mario Andretti, etc." I thought he was bragging, but he wasn't. I now admit that my first impression of him was wrong, as it was with Morris. Eventually, I learned he was a very funny and kind person with a great heart, and we became good friends. "Don't worry, my friend, you'll see that your real season will begin in Portland," he said. I nodded, more out of good manners than believing in what he said.

In the meantime, the mechanics had started to call me Pineapple, which is what they call annoying children where Morris comes from. I would spend days with Morris because I was fascinated with the technical side of racing. After the mechanics had finished working, I would often return to pits with an idea, saying, "I know what we have to change in order to win tomorrow." Morris usually got rid of me by saying, "Pineapple, shut up!" But sometimes he would genuinely use some of my ideas. My mind never stopped ticking and I was completely dedicated to my work … it was my real passion. I would be thinking about the car set-up while having a shower, I would kiss Daniela, still thinking about the car, and I would often leave dinner early in order to chat with Morris. Sometimes, during a team dinner, I'd even try to convince Morris to go back to the circuit and fiddle with the set-up. Sometimes I succeeded, but mostly I got, "Pineapple, you think too much!" We eventually bonded however, and he respected me for this dedication.

That Friday night at Portland, I wanted to change the gear ratios, making a total change at 10:30 pm. As usual, he said, "Pineapple, shut up! You can't bother me now—the chaps have to go home and can't open up everything just for you." All of the other mechanics started taking the piss out my nickname, so I went to the truck and found some felt-tip pens and drew a pineapple on my helmet. I wore it during qualifying on the following day and Mo and the guys got a real kick out of it. I took pole position and dominated the race on the following day. That pineapple became my lucky symbol and I never took it off again.

Portland was fantastic. I started on pole, took the lead, and after a few laps in dry conditions, I had an enormous advantage. But it was too good to be true. I was afraid of the usual bad luck, even though things were going so well. The first stop was as smooth as oil and I had a 30-second advantage. Everything was going perfectly, so even before I had time to think, "Who's going to take this race away from me?" it started to rain. I began to see huge drops on my visor and my Bolognese cursing was interrupted by Chip on the radio, calling me back to the pits for refueling. I made it back to the pits hoping that someone on the team would know what tires we should use. I saw that they were preparing the slick ones for dry conditions. It had just started to rain and I didn't know how to help the team. Then it started to really rain, covering my helmet. There's a famous photo of me at the pit stop, holding my hands together with my eyes towards the sky. It seemed that I was praying, and all the newspapers printed the photo, saying, "Zanardi only needs to pray to win." But to be honest, I wasn't praying—I was swearing, "Damn it to hell, doesn't anything ever go right for me!?"

I thought this was a perfect way to lose a race which thus far, I had dominated, as I went out on the track with slick tires, certain that I'd be screwed. But it was dry on the farthest part of the circuit, which allowed me to push hard and warm the tires so that when I arrived on the wet part, I was able to stay on the track. Meanwhile, De Ferran, who was second, spun off onto the grass. The same thing happened to Vasser, who stalled and pulled out. I was struggling to maintain the lead, until Al Unser, Jr., who had rain tires, passed me. It then stopped raining. The track was already dry in some parts and as a consequence, I made up the five seconds that he had on me, passed him and won the race. Our random choice of tires just happened, thankfully, to be the right one. There were a few yellow flags, two of which were at the end of the race and could have been used to the other drivers' advantage, but that never happened. In both cases, I was so fast on the restart lap, that they couldn't catch me even with my cold tires. I won with more than a ten-second advantage, which I managed to accumulate during the last 15 laps.

It was a dream come true for me. The previous year I was only a driving instructor and now I had just won my first CART race! During the victory lap, a million things passed through my head. I still remember something my chief mechanic had said, "When you crossed the finish line, I saw an ugly, black monkey flying away from your car." My English wasn't that great at the time and I thought that I'd had a mechanical problem, but then it was explained to me that he meant my bad luck had lifted. Morris limited his comments to a laconic, "Good job," whereas Ganassi was jumping up and down in the pit lane, and Jimmy came to congratulate me after the race. I'd waited far too long for that moment.

Then there were the various phone calls to Italy. Portland is on the West Coast with a nine-hour time difference so the race had finished around two in the morning in Italy, followed by the various press conferences, parties and so on. I managed to call home when it was 4 am in Bologna. My grandmother Gisella answered the phone. I thought that I'd woken her up, but it was quite the opposite. She started screaming with delight and wouldn't let me get a word in. She gave me a blow-by-blow account of the race, explaining it as if I wasn't actually there. She even told me about what happened after the race, including the "red men" (the mechanics) and how pretty Daniela looked. She finished by saying, "The race was so emotional. If I didn't die today, I'll never die." To be honest though, she said that every time I won. She then started to say, since I never stopped surprising her, how she wants to live just to see what else I could do. Fifteen minutes later, I was finally able to talk to my mother who was anxiously waiting to congratulate me.

This was my first victory at such a prestigious level. The round-trip flights to Indianapolis were never-ending. I was traveling in economy class, squeezed in like cattle. I even went to Australia in economy. I took the red-eye flight from Portland. We had a long stopover and an unbearable cabin temperature, but that didn't bother me because I'd just won a very important race. I was too pleased to even think about the next race. But then I realized that this victory meant that I was back in the game, so I'd have to start working hard.

Then there was Cleveland, which would become one of my favorite circuits. I qualified on the first row next to Jimmy, who had pole by one four-hundredth of a second. I went wild during that race. I had broken the ice in Portland and felt much stronger from a psychological point of view, but I needed a supernatural force in order to really turn things around for the best. Initially in the lead, I didn't receive enough fuel in the pit stop and had to stop again. I rejoined, giving the lead to De Ferran. I had four or five faster laps, caught up with him and then passed him. With only two laps to go, I skidded and couldn't pass him again and I ended up in second place, which was still a terrific result.

The next race meeting was in Toronto where Ribeiro was on pole and I was second. At the first turn, Ribeiro slowed down so early that I thought he had broken something. I passed him on the outside, assuming that it would be an easy win. But I didn't win. In hindsight, I'm relieved because it was the race in which Jeff Krosnoff, the driver with whom I'd competed with for the Ganassi seat, died in a tragic accident. He was racing for Cal Wells and died in an absurd incident, like the one when I lost my legs at the Lausitzring. Jeff didn't make a mistake but was bumped by another driver and hit a concrete pole, after literally flying off the track. I was in second place when the race was suspended with a red flag. At first, we didn't understand what had happened, although we knew that it was serious when we saw what was left of his car. When they told us to return to the pits, we immediately knew what it meant. I was in shock. I'd just met Jeff's wife and seen photos of his children. I took a moment to think about the ridiculous risk that I was taking, but then, as with all drivers, I put that risk out of my mind as quickly as possible.

After Toronto, we went to Mid-Ohio and Max Papis came to replace Jeff. Max had always been a very sensitive person and found it difficult to accept the job, primarily out of respect for Jeff. But he knew it was a very important opportunity. Max had been outstanding in the 24-hour race at Daytona, in a Ferrari sports prototype, and again at Sebring. I was the one who convinced him to do it, knowing it was the chance of a lifetime. Considering how things had worked out for me, many other European drivers were hoping they might be equally lucky. You'd always see a long line of them hanging around the races looking for the same chance.

The fact that Wells had called Max, and no one else, should have alleviated any doubts that he'd had. Max had made a big impression in Daytona, but not a lot of people knew he'd raced in Formula 1 in 1995 with Arrows. I kept explaining to him, "I'm not just a good driver, but I was lucky enough to end up with Ganassi. You have to realize that this doesn't happen to everybody. They're offering you a way in and although you don't have a great car, it will give you a chance to make yourself known."

He decided to accept the offer, and ironically, they asked me to be his examiner at the rookie test, which I had just taken a few months earlier myself. The Thursday before the race, the test managers allowed him to have some additional free practice. I instructed him via the radio, "Now go out and do two laps in 1 minute, 20 seconds, and then one in 1 minute, 15 seconds, and then I'll tell you when you can go for it." At the end, I went to Wally Dallenbach, the race director, and told him that Max was ready. I must admit that I felt rather cool, even though I myself was only a beginner driving with three fluorescent stripes representing "L" for learner. Max did well, but didn't finish the race because the engine blew. Compared with the other Toyota drivers, he was doing exceptionally well. Little did he know that he was starting a career which would eventually bring him great results and many victories.

At Mid-Ohio, I took pole after a hard battle with Jimmy. Towards the end of qualifying with his last set of tires, he took the best time from me with an incredibly fast lap. In a final attempt to regain pole, I went for an all-out super-lap and beat the track record just as the checkered flag was waved. With a three-tenths faster lap than Jimmy, I now had pole position. Jimmy was already being interviewed about the pole and he came over to hug me, saying, "Ugly bastard, you stole the pole—I was already doing interviews when I saw you streak by and snatch it from me." This confirmed what a sincere and kind person he really was. Other than one hairy moment when I lapped Moreno, the rest of the race went smoothly and I maintained the lead until the end. I brought home 20 points and finally started to go up the ranks in the championship. I stormed through the second part of the season, getting first place at Portland, second place at Cleveland and Toronto, and first at Mid-Ohio.

I then arrived at Michigan for another long-distance race, the Marlboro 500, which I blew by not listening to Morris. I was in the lead after dominating the first part of the race, but the car started oversteering and De Ferran was closing on me. Stupidly, I refused to give up the lead and with a typical European stubbornness, I pushed the car to the max and crashed into the wall. It all happened so quickly, in something like three or four seconds, maybe less. After the race, I took a moped to measure the distance of the accident, and it was over 800 yards! They say that in that length, you can regain control of the car and have time to brake, accelerate, or whatever you like. Instead, in what was almost a half-mile, I couldn't keep hold of the trajectory. I went on the slippery part of the track, trying to control the car, saying, "I can do it, I can do it!" But then crash, and I thought to myself, "Shit, I can't."

The cycle of the ovals finished in a rather mediocre way. I ended up crashing the car in Michigan, just as Ganassi had predicted. I should have listened to Morris again, "In a 500 miler, you should never compare your performance with a rival. The only thing that you have to do is stay in the lead, hold on to the car and decide what you're going to change in the following pit stop. When you go for the last refuel and final laps, then you start racing. You stop driving and start racing."

A week before the Elkhart Lake race, they allowed me to test. Morris relentlessly lectured me about making the most of it, not to mess around, and to memorize the circuit because it was a difficult track. In fact, it was 4.65 miles long. He said, "If you are two seconds behind at the beginning of practice, don't assume that you're far from the others, because that's like half a second somewhere else. Instead, modify the car, put on new tires, and make up for the time. You have to take it step by step. It is a complicated track to memorize with lots of blind corners, so during the first morning if you are two seconds behind Jimmy, I would be very happy." He said this right in front of Jimmy, whom he asked, "During your first couple of laps, can you give Alex a hand and show him the right racing lines?" Jimmy was confused, but agreed to do it. Coincidentally, Jimmy had an electrical problem on the first lap and was forced to stop, so I drove on my own. In a couple of hours, I was already doing quite well; the stopwatch said that I was the fastest, almost two seconds ahead of the driver behind me. Jimmy used to carry around an Italian-English dictionary and phrase book. He looked up how to give me some advice in Italian and found a line from a conversation with a taxi driver, saying with a Yankee accent in Italian, "Can you please go more slowly?" We had a good laugh about it.

When we went back to Elkhart Lake for the race, things didn't go so well. Towards the end of qualifying, De Ferran had pole and it looked like everything was over. But on that particular track, the timing line does not correspond with the finishing line, so when I passed under the checkered flag, I still had a lap available for qualifying. I kept on pushing, despite the fact that Ganassi had forgotten about the issue of the non-coinciding lines. I had to keep driving with him in the radio going on and on about the qualifying classification, unable to interrupt until he was done speaking. I was busy driving and listening to his endless rant of calculations. When he finally stopped talking for a moment, I told him to shut up, but he didn't understand. When I was on the final straight, he said, "OK, Alex, good job. P3," and then he added, "I'm coming down from the pits, I'll see you later." Right then, I crossed the finish line and saw my name at the top of the time list. I then heard Chip shout, "You're first, you're first!" He was great like this, and in the following years, I really missed his words of encouragement.

Chip "called" my race and always went wild on the radio. Tom Anderson "called" Jimmy's race and managed his strategy. When I arrived in the team, everybody told me it was Ganassi's toy and we had to let him do what he wanted. At the beginning, I believed his success was a matter of luck, but that wasn't the case. Chip was very honest—you could argue quite aggressively without him holding a grudge. He was open to confrontation, which was amazing given he was the owner of the team. I later missed his exuberance and his cheers when I did well, and making him happy really encouraged me. If I achieved the fastest lap during a race, he would charge me up with words like, "You're the fastest on the track, nobody can stop you!" We had very opposite characters. Although I am very energetic and a bit of a show-off, I tend to hide my true feelings. Chip, on the other hand, wears his heart on his sleeve. I'm the first to admit that I like to be praised and hear, "Bravo," just as much as the next guy. Elkhart Lake exemplified the dynamics between us. Chip jumped in the pit lane and was laughing hysterically after I got pole. During the race, De Ferran and I bumped each other at the second turn. De Ferran was out and I had a bent suspension, but I went back on the track with it and finished the race in third place. Thanks to Al Unser, Jr., who blew an engine just before the end and had to pull out, I was on the podium.

I was fighting for the title with Jimmy, Unser Junior and Michael Andretti, but in Vancouver my hopes were quashed. I had a great pole and during the race, I took the lead, gaining 15 seconds in just ten laps. I lapped a few cars until I reached P.J. Jones, the son of former Indy legend Parnelli Jones, who blocked me. It was easy to overtake in a city circuit, but he blocked me for three laps. Halfway through the third lap, I complained to Chip. He said that the race officials had been informed and they would ask P.J. to move over.

We arrived at a right-hand double turn; the first was fairly open, whereas the second was a tight hairpin. You would stay on the inside for the first corner and then move to the left to enter the second. Exiting the fast one, he moved to the center of the track, as if he were offering the ideal trajectory to overtake him. In addition, he slowed down very early so I interpreted his move as a belated courtesy to me. I moved to the outside but right at that moment, he drifted towards me. I don't know if he did it on purpose, but I was fooled by it. He squeezed me towards the wall and I was forced into the escape lane. I was really furious. I passed in front of P.J. Jones's pits where Dan Gurney, the head of the team and himself once a great Formula 1 driver, widened his arms and said, "I'm sorry." He realized what a stupid thing his driver had done. That year, they had a Toyota engine that kept breaking down. The only thing I could think of saying was, "Your driver is even worse than your engine."

After accepting that I had lost the race and the chance of the title, I cooled down and acknowledged that anybody can make a mistake. I wanted to give P.J. Jones the benefit of the doubt and assumed he would apologize, but he never said anything to me, which was very surprising. Each time that I ran into him, I looked at him like I was saying, "Go on, tell me something." But he never did, he just lowered his eyes whenever he saw me. I never put down P.J. in the papers or on television as he was expecting me to do. As a result, he thought I was just expressing my superiority and got angry. He started throwing me dirty looks on several occasions—clearly he really hated me. The irony was that I no longer cared; after all, it was his fault. P.J. Jones was probably just frustrated because I continued winning, while he became more and more bitter.

You could compare my frustration to racing a bicycle. It was as if you'd closed the gap on the leader after 125 miles, and you knew your legs were able to win the sprint, but then you got a puncture 200 yards from the finish line. That year, I never thought I could have competed for the title, so it was a real pity to actually win and then have things end the way that they did.

Before Vancouver, the next-to-last race of the season, Daniela and I had gone to San Francisco with her best friend and her husband from Italy. We visited the usual tourist sites and while I was driving, the husband saw a green NSU Prinz car (in Italy, *Prinz* is slang for bad luck). He couldn't believe it and "passed" it to me, "The Prinz is yours!" Oh shit, bad luck before Vancouver! I turned to him and told him off, "Listen, it's bad enough to see a Prinz in San Francisco, but then you decide to 'pass' it to me right before I have to race—you must be mad!" He was mortified and apologized. I was joking with him, but he took it quite seriously. So when I had the run-in with P.J. Jones, he felt terrible. In Italy, people feel dreadful if they think they have brought you bad luck, and boy did I have bad luck at times.

Fortunately, a week later in Laguna Seca, lady luck was on my side. I did a maneuver that changed my luck, and not just from a career point of view. It wasn't just a matter of calculating the limits, grip and physics of the car. A lot of it was due to fate, and my father always told me that luck helps the fearless, and I was damned fearless in Laguna Seca. I took pole, stealing it from Bryan Herta on the very last lap, with Chip's usual cheering and the ecstatic mechanics in the background. I knew that I could win and end the season on a fantastic note.

There was another reason to do it. In CART, almost all the teams have two cars per driver, and each driver has his own group of mechanics, with a maximum of six mechanics during each refueling and wheel change. In addition to the chief mechanic, there are two mechanics—one for each chassis. It is also the norm to name each car. The first one in 1996 was called Betsy and the other one Old Midnight, because each time we raced her, for one reason or another, she would have problems that kept the crew working until at least midnight. If it wasn't an oil leak that forced us to change the engine, it would be damage to the chassis. The head mechanic for Old Midnight was named Brad Filbey, a very funny, huge fellow who always had a smile on his face. That year I won two races in Betsy, but unfortunately for Brad, none in Old Midnight.

The day before Laguna Seca, Brad kept repeating, "I can feel it—this is the one." I had had an accident in Old Midnight in Vancouver, so they had to stay up late again. When I took pole with Old Midnight in Laguna Seca, Brad was very excited. After the first pit stop, a blister had formed on one of the tires and the car started vibrating, and Bryan Herta was able to catch up with me. He passed me while I was trying to defend my position and make it to another pit stop. After the pit stop and with new tires, I pushed like crazy and recovered the ten seconds that Herta had on me and I was right behind him. There were 20 laps to go until the finish line. Each time that I passed the line, Brad screamed, "Come on, Old Midnight", come on!" But as the laps passed, I was still behind Herta. At Laguna Seca, there was a huge screen from which the teams could follow the race, so everyone was glued to the action. As we approached the last lap, the team began turning towards Brad, shaking their heads. He was proud until the end, saying, "You never know." They kept watching until the last lap, holding their breath.

That glorious day is one of my fondest memories of America. I kept trying to imagine what my friends in Italy, the mechanics and fans, were thinking as they watched the last lap of the race. They naturally assumed that it was all over. I would have given anything to see my mechanics' faces when I passed at the Corkscrew just three turns from the finish line. The Corkscrew is an S-shaped part of the track, and so-called because it really looks like it screws into itself. I dived inside Herta by outbraking him on the left-hand side, ran inside across his nose and into the dirt on the outside, but kept it all together to grab the lead. The mechanics put their hands in their hair, then started screaming, hugging and patting each other on their shoulders. Brad went crazy, and in the ten seconds before the checkered flag, he started jumping back and forth in the pit lane singing the glory of Old Midnight.

I was absolutely delirious, and still have the whole event on tape from the camera in my car. On the tape, you can see Brad pounding on my helmet as I arrived in the *parc fermé* area after the finish line. I love reliving that moment and listening to my friends' various reactions, like Filippo, for example. He was in front of the television with his brother-in-law, who was smoking a cigarette and repeating, "There's no way that he's going to overtake Herta." When I finally did, Filippo screamed so loudly that his brother-in-law almost swallowed his cigarette. Mike Knight explained that I did something so special that a year later, there would be a million people who would claim that they were there when I passed Herta at that corner, when there were actually only 2,000 spectators. That tells you the power of what I did that day.

I felt really proud of doing such a courageous and spectacular move. I had no idea how many people would talk about it in the years to come. And the timing was so perfect—it was the last lap of the last race of the season, with nothing ahead for the rest of the winter, so there was nothing else to talk about. Unfortunately, there was some animosity with Herta, even though I apologized to him on the podium. He said, "Hats off to you. I didn't see you coming and I can't believe you did what you did, but you were lucky. I think I drove a perfect race, and I still came in second." I thought it was over, but throughout the winter, the press fueled rumors that I was the hero and Herta was the fool, which slowly created bad feelings between us.

The incredible finale at Laguna Seca helped change my contract situation, but it didn't seem to help Ganassi make my negotiations a priority. In August at Mid-Ohio, after the pole, Ganassi wanted to renew the option (the deadline was August 31). I was really pleased at the time because I had received a load of offers from other teams. But what really made me happy was when Chip said to me, "I want you to know that I would be crazy not to keep you, and since you've proven to be a top driver, which I wasn't expecting at all, I've decide to amend your salary. I took a risk signing you, so I'll have to consider my personal stake as well. But I also want a happy driver, and you won't be one on what you're earning now. You're doing fantastic, and there are drivers who go half as fast as you and who are making $4 to $5 million. I want to make sure that you are content and motivated, and although I don't owe it to you, I think that it's the right thing to do." I was stunned and thought, "Is he God?" He then said, "I don't know exactly how much. I'll talk to the sponsor, but don't worry. We will find somewhere between your market value and what you're making now."

At that moment, I had tears in my eyes. Everyone told me what a bastard Chip was, and that he was the toughest boss you could have. But I was coming from Formula 1, where I'd encountered nothing but false promises and bosses who were entirely self-centered. I was constantly screwed, so to finally see someone like Chip standing in front of me, who wanted to share the financial benefits with me, seemed incredible.

Over the last eight races of the season, I had won three (Portland, Mid-Ohio, Laguna Seca). I started on the front row in all eight, establishing a record.

I was the driver of the moment, and finished the championship with the same number of points as Andretti, who only came second because of his better placements. Numerous teams started approaching me from CART and Formula 1, including people such as Rahal and Penske. They all started asking when my contract with Chip would expire.

Even teams from Europe started calling me. One day while I was in the car with Daniela, my phone rang and she answered. She almost fainted when she asked who was calling and heard, "It's Alain Prost." She had always been a huge fan of Prost, and was trembling as she handed me the phone. I was just as nervous—Prost had never called me before. Eddie Jordan was even more insistent, having finished a great season with Rubens Barrichello and Martin Brundle. He could now make me a proper offer as his sponsors had finally loosened the purse strings, but I wasn't interested because I was very happy where I was.

I had not heard back from Chip after his unbelievable offer at Mid-Ohio. On the way to Vancouver, I started wondering what was going on. I had already turned down all the other offers, except for Jordan's. Chip didn't say anything to me in Vancouver, either. Then on the Thursday before Laguna Seca, he invited me out for an ice cream. We went for a walk and I was expecting to hear something about my contract, but he didn't mention it. At that point I confronted him, and he tried to change the subject. I couldn't understand why he was being so evasive, and then I thought that maybe the offer was just a ploy to calm me down.

Later, when the other teams had all their drivers in place, he finally said, "Let's see what we can do." Behind his nice words, I saw an evil streak and started to doubt whether he was, indeed, a decent guy. He said, "Let's meet up in a couple of weeks in Pittsburgh, after I've spoken to the sponsors." CART traditionally holds a banquet at the end of the year to present all the various prizes. That year it was scheduled to take place one month after the last race.

When I arrived home from Laguna Seca, there were what seemed like 684 messages from Eddie Jordan. I started to give it some consideration. My American lawyer, whom I kept updated with the developments, said to me, "Look, Alessandro, if you want to go into Formula 1, you can do it at any time. Ganassi's contract is valid in the United States only, so you can wipe your ass with it if you want to. Formula 1 doesn't hold a race in the States, so your contract is scratch paper outside of here." This was something that I'd never realized.

Finally, I received Chip's phone call. He said, "I spoke with Target, and if you come to Pittsburgh, we'll have a chat." I immediately got on a plane and spent the whole day talking to him about everything except the contract. The following morning, after making me wait like a nobody for two hours, he invited me into his office. He sat me down and said, "What's up?"

I said, "What do you mean, what's up? I'm here to talk about the contract. That's why you've invited me here." Chip said, "Oh, yeah. OK, I spoke to the sponsor and they agreed to change your salary. They'll give you an additional $200,000 next year, and a further $200,000 the following. But $700,000 for 1997 is not great, so I'm personally adding $50,000 which will make it $750,000 for next year, and $1,000,000 for 1998." He gave me a big, shiny smile while I looked at him blankly. I couldn't believe that given all of the money and prizes that I'd won for him, his generosity equaled a measly $50,000.

I don't want to be misunderstood here. I appreciate the value of money and how difficult it is for normal people to earn a decent living, but I was not a normal person in this situation. I had gone to the betting table with my entire life, lost a hell of a lot, and finally had a lucky hand. I had shown Chip loyalty and talent, and although I really appreciated the opportunity that he gave me, he had given me high hopes in terms of negotiating a new deal. I just assumed that the money would come in time. But when Chip said we would settle somewhere between my salary and the current market value, and then he offered practically nothing, I was really offended. I thanked Target, who didn't owe me anything, but I thought he was pissing on me with that offer, especially after Mid-Ohio.

To make matters worse, he started saying strange things like, "This is what I can give you." He said this two or three times until he added, "What can you offer back?" I was speechless, and didn't know what to say. He explained to me, "You can give me your time, another year on your contract, $1.5 million for 1999 and another option on a season." That really was the epitome of insult. Why would I accept only a $50,000 increase for 1997 when in reality, once my contract expired in 1998, I could ask for at least $5 million, which was the going rate for drivers such as Andretti? Plus you never know what might happen in life—there may be an accident, and so on. It wasn't right that he could decide my future, and this was the straw that broke the camel's back. When I realized how selfish and egomaniacal he really was, I decided that I would no longer race with him, even if I didn't have an option from Jordan. I stood up and said goodbye. I went to the airport, called Daniela and caught the first flight from Pittsburgh to Italy. I wanted to get back home immediately.

The following week, I went back to the States with Daniela for a series of meetings with the sponsors, concluding with the famous banquet at the end of the season. We arrived at the Westin Hotel in Detroit after the usual photographs and publicity appearances before getting dressed in black tie and tuxedo for the evening. I called Chip and said, "Do you have time for me to buy you an ice cream?"

We sat down and without many words, I said, "I'm not racing for you next year." He laughed at first, "What do you mean you're not racing for me?" I replied, "I was very offended by your offer, so it's not important what I'm going to do, all you need to know is that I'm not racing for you next year. You've made a fool out of me for too many reasons." He said angrily, "We have a contract, so you can't quit." I said, "I never thought I would get into a legal argument with you, but I'm ready to do it if necessary. According to my lawyer, if I decide not to race for you, there's nothing you can do. You can come and get me in Monaco, but it wouldn't do you any good. But that's not the point. The point is that I don't want to race for you. That's all you need to understand."

Instantly, he changed his attitude and starting sobbing like a child, "You're right—I've become a son of bitch. I've always had a problem understanding other people's feelings because I was born with money, and always felt that's why people were interested in me. That's a huge problem for me. Also, my wife and I are separating. On top of that, I have to deal with the responsibility of the team, and I never know if I have a real friend in front of me.

I'm trying to keep all the pieces together and sometimes I have to be heartless. But it was wrong what I did to you. I should have known that you were different. I tried to find the most convenient way to keep you with me, but everything that you said is right. I've been an asshole, but I swear it wasn't malicious. From what you've told me, although you have a winning career in front of you, you're ready to throw everything away out of principle. I really appreciate this. Tell me if there is something that I can do to fix the situation. In you, I've found an incredible friend, as well as the best driver in the world."

I was obviously very touched by what he said, but had to stand firm, "First of all, you can begin by making me a decent offer. Let's forget about the issue of the fourth year—that was just a complete joke—and let's pretend that we are at Mid-Ohio and take it from there." Chip asked, "What do you mean by a decent offer?" I told him, "Chip, you opened the discussion, so you know what to say." He replied, "Instead of getting into an argument, just tell me what you want and I will say yes. Don't put the screws on me, but think about it and I will say yes." I was caught off guard, but proposed the following, "I want $1.5 million next year and then $1.5 million for the year after that, because I know that if I were free to negotiate a new contract today, I could ask even more than that. But I'm not greedy, and without an American passport or title yet, I'm not that interesting to the sponsors. But if Michael Andretti or Unser, Jr., can earn $5 million, then I should be able to ask for $3 million. I deserve it, and you need to give me at least half of what I am worth."

He thought about that and said, "That's right, you haven't won a championship yet, so let's do it this way, next year you will get $1 million and if you win the title, you get another half-million; in 1998, you'll get an unconditional $1.5 million." I said, "What about the salary increase that you promised for this year?" Chip yelped, "What are you trying to do, bleed me dry?" I snapped back, "Chip, these were your own words, so all I want is half of the prize money that I lost." After making a few calculations, we figured out that it was around $250,000. He accepted this and gave me a check of $250,000 for Christmas, along with everything else that I'd asked for.

I was genuinely happier about him acknowledging my principles rather than just offering me more money. We jotted down the agreement on two napkins and both countersigned. He kept one and I kept the other. Only later, while in the elevator going up to my room, did I realize just how much more money he was paying, but I believed he was a thousand times happier to save a friendship by signing a check. I saw how sincerely sad he was over our disagreement and how relieved he was to come to terms. At that moment, he didn't seem concerned about the money as much as salvaging our friendship.

I pushed the button for the 36th floor and when I entered our room, Daniela immediately said, "How did it go?" I looked like Donald Duck after he's been smacked in the face. (Little Duck was her nickname for me.) Given how angry I was when I left and how quickly I'd returned, she was certain that Chip and I had told each other to piss off, and so I told her everything, "This year, he raised my salary by $250,000; next year, I'll get $1 million, and another half-million if I win; and the following year, an unconditional $1.5 million." She was stunned, "Holy shit, the little duckling must have really been pissed off." Without a manager, lawyer or anyone else, I was able to get exactly what I deserved. We went to the banquet and had a fantastic time. The team gave me a huge cigar, on the label of which they had printed a little design of my helmet. I smoked it all and then puked. A little from the booze and a little from the tobacco, and boy did I feel sick.

There was another reason to celebrate. A few days earlier, Daniela and I had gotten married. We were on tour visiting the sponsors, the so-called "Thank you tour." She came with me everywhere, first to Vegas, then Japan and then to Detroit for the final banquet. After a tour of Minneapolis, where Target was based, we went to Las Vegas. We spent five days there before departing for Japan via San Francisco. In Vegas, we found a church called The Little Church of The West, where motorcycle champion Mick Doohan had also gotten married, and we just loved it. That year, we went to quite a few weddings and listened to our friends' endless complaints. Titano was bothered because he had other plans for the day of the wedding, or didn't want to buy presents, etc., etc. So we decided to get married in Vegas, and organize a dinner back in Italy to let everyone know about it. We went into the church, got the necessary information and were married on the same afternoon. We then went to see Jimmy Vasser, who lives in Vegas, to tell him the news. He congratulated us and said, "Why didn't you tell me, you bastard—I could have been your witness. So where are you going on your honeymoon?" I said, "What are you talking about? We have to go to Japan in three days, don't you remember?" Jimmy said, "Well you have two days then." We wanted to go to Sequoia National Park, which was on the way to San Francisco. He said that he would organize a stay for us in Yosemite and called his travel agent.

The following morning, we left for Yosemite and when we reached the mountain pass, we found out that it was closed because of snow so we were forced to turn around, and go via Los Angeles in order to reach the other side of the park. We arrived at the bungalow around 4 am. It was a wonderful room in a warm, cozy mountain resort with fireplaces, big rugs and champagne on ice. That was our first night as a married couple, and after such a long trip, it was just perfect. Although it was far from a typical honeymoon, I took Daniela on my trip to visit Honda in Japan. We were both incredibly happy on that trip, and her happiness made me realize not only that she loved me, but that she felt loved.

CHAPTER *10*

CART Championship
Victory Number One

The next year, 1997, couldn't have started on a better note and I went on to win everything, literally dominating the second part of the CART season. I also won over Honda, who initially had opposed me joining the team. I also held all of the records—consecutive starts on the front row, pole positions and laps in the lead, beating Nigel Mansell's previous record. In addition, my renewed contract gave me plenty of personal and financial security. Daniela and I decided to settle down and look for another house. Adrian Reynard, my car constructor, had bought one in Indianapolis that had belonged to Derek Daly, ex-Formula 1 and CART driver. Adrian would have liked to have lived there with his family, but his business headquarters were in England, so the house was sitting empty. He had offered to let me stay there in the past, so I asked him if he would consider renting it. We quickly agreed and although it wasn't cheap, it was fully furnished and had everything. I went to see it and fell in love with it. It was a large house, surrounded by wonderful trees and flowers on the banks of Lake Morse. From that moment, everything changed and I suddenly felt very American. When I had a few days between practicing and racing, I would hurry home to work around the house. From flowers to furniture, we spent a load of money making it our home.

The weather in Indianapolis is similar to Italy, but the terrain is flat from north to the south with no mountains. The weather changes so quickly that there is a saying in town, "If you don't like the weather, stick around because it'll soon change." I remember some days we'd wake up to a blizzard with winds blowing snow horizontally across the sky. Then a couple of hours later it would be sunny and the snow would stop. By the evening, it would be completely dry. In the spring, Indianapolis tends to be as calm as Northern Italy. It was exciting to live there, but there were a lot of sacrifices. I missed my friends and I'd think about going home whenever my schedule would allow, just to hang out with Bonini in his workshop or Filippo at his car showroom. Ironically, now that I am back in Europe and can do all these things, I miss the United States.

Daniela had an allergy—an allergy to the American lifestyle. She found it difficult to get used to their mottos like, "Live and let live" and "An eye for an eye." These kinds of attitudes are only slightly accurate. At first I thought that the Americans were superficial—they meet in an elevator, two minutes later are friends and are having dinner together that evening. For someone like me, who was far from his own friends and family roots, this seemed rather strange. I frequently saw people change their lives—from where they live, to how they hop on a plane in the same way that we would hop on a bus. This is why they socialize with such ease.

I now understand how sincere Americans can be, and feel badly that I judged them too quickly. They were always so supportive and warm whenever I needed something and they definitely make friends easily, but they also commit to keeping them. With time, I learned a lot from them. I met men and women who showed very strong values and I'm glad that I got to know them. I definitely feel closest to Jimmy and I still care about him a lot. Although we are now physically far apart, we were like brothers when I lived there, which is unusual among teammates. But after my accident, many of my racing friends came to my side and sent money to the foundation that we eventually opened. They would send as much as $5,000 or $10,000—anonymously. They are very generous people.

10: CART Championship Victory Number One

That year, I was incredibly focused on my work and my dedication reached its pinnacle. I often went to the workshop to have a coffee with the mechanics, while Daniela was in the office chatting with the girls of the team—for bureaucratic reasons. During early spring, I would sunbathe on the pier or read a book until Morris called to say, "I'm home." I would always reply, "Switch on the coffee machine—I'm on my way." Morris and his wife Kathyrin lived just across from us on the opposite end of the lake, so I jumped on my jet ski to go to see him. While he explained to me what happened in the workshop, Kathyrin would make a fantastic espresso. La Caterina, as we used to call her, was a very sweet and charming California beauty with blonde hair and blue eyes. I was their official supplier of Italian coffee. When she whispered, "We're almost out of coffee," I'd promise to smuggle in Italy's best products during my next trip home.

Morris would then start telling stories. They were always so entertaining and original that I could listen to him for hours. I loved his story about the Le Mans 24-hour race. Morris's idol had always been Colin Chapman, the founder of Lotus. Chapman was racing with an innovative car that had very thin bodywork. On the nose of the car, painted in front of the driver's seat, there was a mysterious black circle about a foot across. During the practice sessions, people kept wondering what was the purpose of the black circle; they soon realized its purpose at the start. At Le Mans, the drivers had to run across the track and jump into their cars, starting the engines and then taking off. Jim Clark, the Lotus driver and later a great World Champion, ran across to his car, jumped and put his foot on the black circle and landed directly in the driver's seat, therefore getting a substantial lead on everybody else. Under the circle, there was a support to prevent him from busting through the bodywork. Utter genius.

I loved listening to Morris's stories and would completely lose all track of time. Between one story and the next, we would talk about my car and come up with ways to improve and enhance its performance. In CART, some teams would conduct expensive wind tunnel tests or develop the shock absorbers and the engines, but Chip always thought this was a waste of money. In some respects, he was right. Our strength as a group was the perfect synergy of each individual, which allowed us to take advantage of both our own equipment, and that provided by Reynard. But the organization was impeccable and structures like those aren't born everyday, and this was thanks to managers Tom Anderson and Mike Hull, and obviously Chip. Tom was serious and cautious—sometimes his obsessions were annoying—but he was the bricks and mortar of the organization.

I arrived in the team when it was at its best. Everyone was doing his or her own distinct task, and everything fitted together perfectly, creating the most productivity in the shortest amount of time. This made a big difference to our performance. For example, if we had to test ten new changes, we would always end up with a clear idea of what worked well and what didn't. At the end of the day, I was part of a well-oiled, professional machine. But we also had a lot of fun.

Some teammates were very funny, while others became the butt of others' jokes. I remember when Doug, the telemetry technician, who always had a computer in his hand, became the next target. It was during a practice session in Firebird, Arizona. Each time I went back to the pits, I'd careen towards Doug who would run off jiggling his big belly in search of a place to hide. He'd wait behind the truck until I was safely in the tent before approaching the car to download the data. But he didn't take into account how sneaky I could be. When you stop a car with a turbo engine, it is best to leave the engine idling for a moment and wait for the turbocharger to stop. Poor Doug didn't realize that the engine was still on and, feeling safe, finally reappeared. I winked at Rob, my head mechanic, who already knew what was going on, and put the car in first and did a wheelspin. Doug's eyes popped like Wile E. Coyote's and he ran off screaming that he'd quit.

I was really happy in the team; we enjoyed our work, we had a good time together and everyone was professional. Morris, despite his British humor, was having just as much fun. He always knew how to put me in my place, not offend anybody, and get everybody back to work.

I had endless ideas for developing the car, but I wasn't focused enough and needed Morris's cautious eye. My enthusiasm, coupled with the team's constraint and insight, created excellent results. I found myself trying to push Morris into modifying the car so that it would go faster. The following day, I would show up at the pit and find that the set-up scheme had indeed been changed, but only slightly, a quarter change to the camber of the wheel, a 20-pound shift of load from one tire to the other, a half a degree change to the toe-in, and a slight modification to the pressure of the tires. I would say to Morris, "This isn't a change, is it?" and he'd say, "Just get in the car and drive it." So I did, and the car was incredibly fast, and I'd often win this way.

My suggestions gave him a lot to think about, though I understood the problems and was able to isolate what was holding me back from getting a good time. Just tackling one issue was often enough to get myself back on the track. I really liked the Reynard-Honda and adapted really well to it. There were a few occasions when I had to drive a different car during practice, but despite this, I was always able to get a result during the race. Everyone did their part, Morris gave me everything that I needed in technical support, the team was exceptionally organized, and for my part, I was able to adapt my driving style whenever required.

I remember reviewing the tape recording of a race that I'd won. I'd entered the pit in third position and left in first, gaining two places thanks to my mechanics. Ricky, the mechanic who'd left me with a loose wheel at Homestead, was interviewed after the

of time, I was very pleased with my performance on a track that had seemed very intimidating on paper.

The second race was in Australia, at Surfers Paradise where we staged a great battle for pole. Just when I thought that I had nabbed it, Paul Tracy pulled off a fantastic move and beat everybody. I didn't give up though, and regained the pole at the last moment of the qualifying. I was thrilled, especially because our PR man, Mike Knight, had already prepared a poster for our pits with Andretti and Sullivan's names crossed out and in their place, "New record of consecutive poles—six—by Alex Zanardi!" I'm pleased to say that I still hold this record, as well as the one of consecutive starts on the front row. I was delighted to get this record in Surfers Paradise, which was equivalent to Monaco in terms of how it allows the drivers to dictate the outcome.

Although the race was exciting, I was not terribly happy. I had problems with the tires, giving Tracy a chance to pass me. After changing tires, I tried to overtake him and got in slightly deep. He tried to resist and we ran into each other. He went out with a bent suspension and I spun twice and ended up in the tire barrier. I had already undone my seat belts when the officials arrived, saying, "Stay there while we push you." That may sound incredible, but the car was not damaged, so they pushed me back to the pits. There, I refastened my belts before rejoining the race. With 18 laps to go, I went from last to fourth place. Ganassi was instructing me over the radio, when the officials waved the white flag to end the race. When Ganassi realized they'd ended the race at the wrong time, he started yelling like a madman. But he was thrilled when I passed De Ferran and Ribeiro and went from sixth to fourth. It was reported to me that De Ferran told a journalist, "When Zanardi comes up behind you, it's better to get out of the way because he'll move right into you. And besides, he cuts the chicane."

In Australia there was an agreement that if you cut the corners, you had to allow the driver whom you had passed to pass you. This happened to me with Rahal, to whom I promptly gave back his position. The following lap, I passed him in the same place, but on TV, you could only see me cut across the chicane and then, a lap later, I was in front of Bobby. De Ferran probably looked at the race on TV and didn't have a clue as to what had really happened, and instead, went around falsely accusing me.

In April, at Long Beach, De Ferran was on pole and I was next to him. Before the start he said, "Have a good race." And I said, "Have a good race, my ass. It's better you engage your brain before speaking—and learn to mind your own business. If you think that I've been wrong, make a claim, but don't speak on TV. But if you see me in your mirror, be sure that I'm going to try to pass you, because that's my job. And anyway, when I do pass, I'll finish the race. Quite the opposite to someone else. Have a good race." It was a straightforward race, which I went on to win once I passed the Brazilian during a stop. Besides this small argument, we have been good friends, and I greatly admire Gil for his talent.

The following evening, I went to a restaurant with Daniela where someone anonymously paid for our dinner. I later told this story to the press and they made headlines out of it. I explained that only in the U.S. do these things happen. It's a pleasure for them, but it's also the truth.

The joy of Long Beach was followed by the disaster of Nazareth. We had a horrible set-up, qualified in 21st place and finished the race in 11th. Moreover, Nazareth ended my dream of continuing to break my own consecutive record of poles and front-row starts. But on the other hand, the statistics were clearly against us. Nazareth was a short oval, our Achilles' heel, so we were philosophical about the failure.

Then we went to Rio—a track that I adore—and where I started last without a qualifying time due to electrical problems. I finished the race in fourth place, but the car was not 100 percent. Tracy spun while coming out of Turn Four, but kept accelerating.

He was spinning in the middle of the track with plumes of smoke around him when I approached him. Like a scene from *Days of Thunder* with Tom Cruise, I couldn't see anything at all and didn't have the time or opportunity to brake. I couldn't believe the adrenaline buzz when I passed through the smoke and came out the other side without hitting anything. Luckily the stewards waved a yellow flag because I was completely out of control. I wanted to laugh, but in a hysterical way. I'd never felt real fear before, but in Rio, I was completely frozen in the cockpit. Despite this hitch, Tracy managed to win and the championship was slipping away from me as he now had a ten-point advantage.

Next, it was the new St. Louis Gateway oval where we had a lot of problems during practice. Qualifying was cancelled due to rain and we had to start using our practice times. I started tenth and managed to gain some positions, battling with Patrick Carpentier. I was doing well until Raul Boesel, a lapped driver, got in the way and I lost contact with Carpentier. Towards the end of the race, the team asked me to slow down and save methanol, which by the way, I had been wasting trying to lap Boesel. In the last few laps, Tracy passed me and won, while I just made to it to the finish line, but was passed by De Ferran and arrived fourth.

Paul Tracy, who had won the last three races, further increased his advantage at Milwaukee. I, on the other hand, had a disastrous race. I qualified 17th and finished the race 13th, just outside the points zone. Jimmy had a bit more success by using a completely different technical strategy that eventually paid off, finishing in a very decent third place. The first part of the season ended in Detroit where I hoped to see the last of my negative spree. I started on the second row in fourth position, but Dario Franchitti hit me from behind at the first corner and I had to pull out.

That was a very black period in my career. Portland, the midpoint of the 1997 season, wasn't any better. Given that it was the turning point of my previous year, if not my entire career, I had high hopes for that race. But the practice didn't go well and neither did qualifying. I had a lot of problems during the race and came in seventh, and the race ended with a vicious argument within the team.

Soon after the start, it began to rain heavily but I managed to pass everyone and take the lead. Then the weather changed and towards the end of the race, the track began to dry. A yellow flag was waved, and I was the only one called into the pits for refueling. I asked the crew to put on tires for dry conditions, explaining that although it wasn't the right moment, I didn't have anything to lose since I was now in last place. But they wouldn't do it. After the race, we had a huge argument. I asked why they called me in and they said, "With the track drying up, you wouldn't have had enough fuel." I asked, "Then why didn't you put on the slick tires?" Justifying their decision they said, "The weather forecast said that it might rain again." I fumed, "Then the fuel would have been enough!" The team admitted that they weren't sure about what to do. What a mess it was. In fact, the track did dry and I had to go back for the slick tires and a tire change after a blowout when I hit Boesel. After nine races, Tracy was leading with 100 points, followed by Greg Moore with 95, Michael Andretti with 77, while Vasser and I had 69 points each … 31 from the lead.

Fortunately, Cleveland was next. I love that circuit, and easily took the provisional pole. The following day I was in the paddock with a friend, Cesare Maria Mannucci, an Italian journalist who'd migrated to the States with me. We often had a coffee together or went to dinner during the race weekends. That Saturday morning he was a bit worried. "Shit, 31 points—it's not going to be easy to make them up." But I wasn't the least bit worried. I was confident and knew that the best part of the season was just beginning. The worst was over and that from that moment on, I was convinced we would start having fun. In fact, it was not just the turning point of the year, but it was to be the best race of my life, and a couple of hitches made the race all the more memorable.

I started on pole and took the lead right away. After 20 laps I had almost run out of fuel, which meant that I was entering the so-called "window" when each yellow flag or neutralization is an opportune time to refuel. Suddenly, Richie Hearn crashed exactly at the entrance to the pits. Generally in a situation like this, the officials forbid access to the pits and request the drivers to stay in a single line behind the pace car until the track has been secured. My radio had a short circuit and kept cutting out, so I could only hear bits and pieces about what was going on. While passing the finish line, I saw a message on the team board, "Stay Out." I approached the pit entrance and heard the officials on the radio. "Pits are going to be opened on this lap," but they meant the following lap. Chip heard and started yelling on the radio, "Come in now!" By chance the radio was working, so I returned to the closed pits. Other drivers were equally misled by that message and followed me in. I refueled, went out and lined up behind the cars that had stayed out on the track. But during the following lap, with the pits now effectively open, all the other drivers went in for fuel and I found myself back in first place. Everything seemed all right but after another lap behind the pace car, Chip called. "We made a mistake and you have to return to the back of the group." I let everyone pass me, except those who had followed me into the pits and who had also been penalized. I ended up fifth to last, but that was not the end of it.

The entrance from the pit lane to the Cleveland track is not a straight one. It goes around the outside of a hairpin, stretching the length of the pit lane. If the race is neutralized by the deployment of the pace car, the rules say that a driver cannot overtake on the track. The driver exiting the pit lane must check his exact position when passing on the "blind line"—the border between the pit area and the track. Although in the pit area a driver has to abide by a speed limit, he is allowed to overtake before entering the track, where the drivers' positions are fixed. So I did this. But given that the exit lane is longer than that section of the circuit and situated right on the hairpin, four drivers passed me. I recovered the position which was originally mine when crossing the blind line. It's difficult to understand this layout. Even the race officials were confused and gave me another penalty for overtaking during a yellow flag. I tried to explain what had happened but they refused to listen.

At the end of the race, I went to complain and they finally realized I was right. Anyway, when the race was restarted with a green flag, I should have done a "drive through," which is a very slow passage on the pit lane. The radio wasn't working at all now, so I had a lot of difficulty receiving instructions. I was gutted when I saw the message on the pit board, "Drive Through." I had to take the penalty before going back on the track, with 57 laps remaining. De Ferran, who was in the lead, was directly behind me. In the United States, the races are often neutralized by a yellow flag, creating the opportunity to make a comeback. This time, however, there were no yellow flags until the end of the race.

I was confused for a couple of laps, but started focusing and pushing harder. Even with De Ferran on my tail trying to lap me, I did the 18 fastest laps of the race with the best being 1.2 seconds better than my fastest opponents. It was like a video game. I recovered the missing lap and overtook all the cars between De Ferran and me and I finally passed him with just two laps to go. I was completely oblivious—almost in a trance—and had no clue of my position because the radio didn't work. Nevertheless, I won the race. But I was so focused during this comeback that I completely forgot to drink any water. Not a wise move at Cleveland, where drivers often have to stop because of dehydration. When I got out the car, I could barely stand.

The post-race occasion was fantastic. When I arrived home, I couldn't wait to see the television coverage. ESPN showed a very good special with plenty of behind-the-scenes coverage. I could see the guys of my team high-fiving each other whenever

I passed a driver. The closer I got to the leaders, the greater the team's enthusiasm. I could even read Morris's lips as he yelled, "Unbelievable!" when I passed De Ferran. There was a message on the phone from Jimmy, who had to catch a plane right after the race, saying, "Alex, you convinced me of one thing—like in basketball, nobody moves when Michael Jordan makes a basket because he is so incredible. You are the Michael Jordan of our category. I've never seen anything like it in the entire history of CART!"

But the best feeling was simply recounting the events with Daniela on the way back in our Honda. We always went by car because we liked the experience of driving the American roads. As good immigrants, we listened to lots of Italian music, like De Gregori and Dalla, and stopped to eat at Italian restaurants. When I arrived home, I was still asking Daniela about my mechanics' reactions, especially Ricky, who went absolutely crazy every time that I passed. When I finally passed De Ferran, Ricky high-fived everyone and even kissed Chip on the lips. Chip didn't waste any time and ran over to yank me out of the cockpit to share in the celebrations.

Toronto followed Cleveland and I qualified in sixth place. I had a terrific race and finished second, just behind Blundell, who was faster that day. At the end of the race, Tom Anderson congratulated me and said, "Today you raced like a champion. You gave it your all without jeopardizing the points for second!" Tracy finished tenth, decreasing his advantage over me to just three points.

A few days later, Titano arrived with his girlfriend, Susy. They had been to California on holiday and would now be spending some time with me. After my race in Cleveland, Titano left a message on the answering machine explaining that in order to watch the race, he had to go to a bar and order numerous gin and tonics, and drank so much that he ended up getting incredibly drunk. I missed my friends during this time. Filippo and his wife came over for the Michigan 500. He was supposed to land on the Friday morning before the race, so Titano offered to pick him up, but he was so enthusiastic about the upcoming race that he opted to watch the practice instead of fetching Filippo. Daniela picked them up instead. We needed a bigger car for six people, so I traded my Honda SLX for the team's minivan so that we could go back and forth to the race.

The reunion was very emotional—the three of us together in the middle of such a different place. I found them tickets for the grandstand where they watched me qualify in seventh position. They didn't want to miss a thing, so on Sunday morning, they came along to watch the warm-up. They even argued with the girls, who didn't want to wake up early just to watch a half-hour warm-up. Titano and Filippo told them to take a taxi. That was one of the rare occasions when they showed them who really wears the pants!

Our team was starting at around 7:30 am. The grandstand holds around 250,000 spectators, but at that time in the morning, Filippo and Titano were the only two people there, jumping and screaming as I passed. Jimmy had heard so much about these two friends that at one point he looked at the grandstand and said, "Those must be your friends." I burst out laughing when I saw them. Later, Filippo asked, "How were you able to see us?" I laughed, "Good God, how could I not—it was just the two of you!" During the warm-up I went to say hello to Target, our sponsors, who gave me a pen and a stopwatch. Much to the delight of Titano and Filippo, I grabbed a couple extras for them, too.

Apart from the race, the real show was in the grandstand. I would have loved to have been both in the grandstand and on the track. Filippo, who doesn't speak a single word of English, somehow managed to chat with a few Bobby Rahal fans and before realizing he was Italian, they offered him a beer. When they learned he was a Zanardi fan, they started giving him a hard time, not only for the fact that my car wasn't going well at the beginning, but because I was penalized with a "drive through" for over-shooting the pit stop and entering Jimmy's pit, hitting his air pump. After that, I had to fight tooth and nail not to be lapped. Rahal's fans gestured to Filippo. "Where is your Zanardi now?" But then I started a comeback after a few pit stops had enabled me to sort out the car's set-up. There are several things that you can do to the aerodynamics and after a few tweaks by the mechanics, I eventually found the perfect set-up. Halfway through the race, it was over for everyone as I seemed to pass each driver at the speed of light. Then it was Filippo's turn to ask the Rahal fans what they thought, doing so with exaggerated gestures and loud exclamations like, "Fenomeno!" (phenomenal). As if that wasn't enough, Bobby Rahal took a turn the wrong way and crashed against the wall. At that point Filippo imitated Bobby with broken glasses and a dizzy expression, which didn't really amuse his fans. During all this, Titano spent the whole time clocking the race on his stopwatch, giving Filippo a running commentary. Given that it was a 500-miler, you can guess that this was a very demanding afternoon.

Then I delivered a huge adrenaline rush for the fans. When I arrived behind Christian Fittipaldi and P.J. Jones, who had been battling for about ten laps, I slipped into their draft. When they opened up to overtake one another, I stormed through the middle without them even noticing. The image of that move was used in the years to come as a race introduction. Filippo told me how absolutely amazing it was in real life.

Anyway, I won and was on the podium surrounded by a sea of fans, holding a trophy that weighed nearly 50 pounds. At that moment, I saw this massive figure coming out of the crowd; it was obviously Filippo, who shouted, "Do you want to see Bobby Rahal's face when he came out of the car?" And once again he did his now-famous impression. I laughed so hard that the trophy fell on my head.

It was a fantastic victory, especially on such a long and fast oval, proving that I could win anywhere. During the press conference one of Chip's comments went down in history, "Today, Zanardi showed up in our town, stole the horses, robbed the bank, kissed the girls and left town laughing." Not only did I now lead for the 1997 championship, but I was dominating a home-grown sport.

We returned home in the minivan. I was driving, Filippo was sitting next to me, Daniela and Titano were behind us, and Susy and Catia (the "Cat") sat in the back. At one point, a truck driver wouldn't let us pass. I pulled out to overtake him, but for some reason he blocked me so I had to back off. Three cars tried the same move, and he happily let them pass. At that point we realized he was just messing around with us. I tried a few more times, but to no avail. When we came up to a junction, I put on the indicators and took the exit, crossed the overpass and re-entered the freeway in front of the truck. We were all in hysterics, but the truck driver was furious.

We later stopped for food and fuel, and Titano jumped in the van saying he wanted to drive. After a few miles Filippo casually asked, "What if we see the trucker again? Will he take it out on the driver?" Titano was petrified at the idea. "Hey, let's not joke." It wasn't what Filippo said that was funny, but his way of saying it. "What if the truck driver stops and gives Titano a couple of smacks on the head—would you laugh, Alex?" I was already laughing, like everyone else. I don't know if it was out of fear, or the lunch, but Titano had to pull over immediately and find a john. He ran in, but returned just as quickly. "There's no toilet paper. Does anyone have a napkin?" Filippo and I went to the toilet and saw Titano with his trousers around his hairy ankles, and couldn't stop laughing. Then some mechanics from the PacWest team entered the toilets; they recognized me and started complimenting me on the race. While we were chatting, Titano—because of his tummy troubles—let escape a few too many noises. The whole thing ended up with the mechanics encouraging his shots: "Come on, come on!" He was mortified.

Overcoming this obstacle, we returned to the car and arrived home in the middle of the night. I had asked Titano not to mention the size of my house to Filippo. When we drove up the driveway, Filippo looked puzzled. "Are we visiting someone?" I explained that this was my house. He gasped. "Holy cow—you've gotten out of the gutter!" That house was beautiful. He was amazed at the beautiful rooms, the fireplaces, and the upstairs. The bathroom downstairs had a car theme with black and white tiles like a checkered flag, a car seat toilet and so on, thanks to Derek Daly. Filippo wandered around the house, opening doors and yelling to his wife, "Come take a look at this!" They went to the kitchen and admired the central island, which isn't so rare now, but then it was very impressive. Finally, I opened the sliding glass door and switched on the lights to the garden with its lovely terrace, immaculately groomed lawn and private pier on the lake. They were speechless. We went on the lake and drank beer and talked rubbish until 3 am.

There are moments in your life that you remember taking for granted and not until later do you realize how incredible they were. This was not like that. I knew instantly that that night would remain unforgettable and it was a very special period. "Guys , this night will undoubtedly go down in history for us." I think that that evening was one of the best moments of my life. I had won the 500-mile race in Michigan, I was leading the championship, I was married to a beautiful woman, had a fantastic house and terrific friends, and I had earned a hell of a lot of money. I was on top of the world. Filippo stopped the magic, by saying, "It may be a fantastic evening, but if we stay all night on the water, we'll no doubt spend all of tomorrow on the john!"

We had a fantastic time together, playing water sports during the day and having barbeques in the garden at night. We often invited some of the team to join us. We were completely surprised by Filippo's knack for making conversation, regardless of the fact that he didn't speak a word of English.

Two weeks later, we went to Mid-Ohio where, like the previous year, I won again. Herta had the pole position and tried to resist, but I was simply too fast. I stayed behind him just to save fuel, knowing that he was burning through his trying to keep ahead and would be forced to stop for more before me. But right before refueling, he burst a tire and I just managed to avoid hitting him. Once Herta was out, there was no stopping a victory for me. After Michigan, I had taken the championship points lead and we began the team's most favorable phase of the season.

Elkhart Lake was the last shot for the other drivers, and Paul Tracy's last chance to re-enter the championship. If I ended up pulling out, and Tracy gained some points, we would be neck and neck for the championship. We did qualifying on a dry circuit but then it rained, the track flooded and we had to wait to hear if we could race. At the last minute, the officials decided to go ahead. I was third during qualifying, and Mauricio Gugelmin and Blundell were on the first row, both racing for PacWest.

We started on a wet track and I remember the commentators insisting, "Tracy must stay in the race at all costs, as you never know what could happen to Zanardi, which would re-open the race for the title." But Tracy stalled moments after he started the race. It wasn't his fault—a driver spun out in front of him— so he didn't even complete the first lap. I drove very carefully throughout the race. I quickly passed Gugelmin and was right behind Blundell until I stopped to change tires. After my boys worked their magic, I took the lead, retained it for the rest of the race and won. Filippo had just returned to Italy, so I called him on the phone. He assumed the race had been postponed due to rain, so he was thrilled when I told him the news.

We went to Vancouver, the third-to-last race of the season. I had a theoretically open run to the championship. Among the opponents, De Ferran was at the top of the list. He's a really good driver, but talks too much. It was another intense race, comparable to Cleveland. 1997 was the last year that we raced on that track at Vancouver as we would be changing circuits in Vancouver due to too many complaints from the drivers about the difficulty in passing there.

Anyway, I was starting on pole and immediately nabbed the lead. On the corner after the starting line, I arrived too deep because of a problem with the brakes. One of the discs had become warped and began vibrating. Since a warped disc tends to push the pads back, you have to slightly pump the brake pedal with the left foot, closing up the pads so that when you arrive at the end of the straight, the pedal is hard and ready to brake. If you don't do this operation correctly, there is more brake pedal travel when you brake—we call it a "long" pedal—and your right foot tends to touch the accelerator and you just go straight on. In that instance, I also stalled the engine. The officials pushed the car to restart it, but I couldn't get back on the track until last because all the other drivers were approaching.

Everyone assumed it was over for me, but I didn't let that bother me—I was leading the championship and at that point, just wanted to collect some points. I started to focus, achieving the now-customary 15 fastest laps of the race, and catching up with everybody. On a track on which most drivers consider passing impossible, I passed the field by actually braking longer in the turns than my opponents. While passing, a driver usually brakes and the other driver brakes a few moments later, so that there is a difference in relative speed, which allows you to see one car passing another. During this particular race, the speed difference was tremendous. It looked like a video game because the other drivers were braking while I was braking for much longer than the usual fraction of a second.

I wasn't Superman at Vancouver in 1997, but I had a great car and was doing incredibly well. I even passed Gugelmin who was first, but then I arrived too deep into the corner again. I still had the problem with the brakes, and during that lap, I didn't pump the pedal, and I went straight on the same corner. I said to myself, "Zanardi, from Castel Maggiore—you're an idiot!" I stalled the engine just as before and once again the officials pushed me until I restarted, during which time I was lapped. There were 20 laps until the end and Herta was leading, but he was due for a pit stop anytime. The real leader was Gugelmin who was behind me. If I was able to block him and take advantage of a possible yellow flag, I could make a comeback.

I resolved the problem without a yellow flag as I out-braked Herta, and when he saw me arrive in his mirror, he did the worst thing he could have done by trying to squeeze me when I was already alongside him. If you squeeze an opponent on a straight, there is nothing that he can do, but if you do it while entering a corner, an accident is inevitable. Your opponent can't brake anymore than he already is—as a matter fact, he is praying that he'll stop in time to make the corner.

Herta was more concerned with not letting me pass than being the leader of the race, and even less concerned that I'd already been lapped. A lot of bad blood had brewed between us, and he obviously didn't want me to pass. I moved towards the wall to avoid contact, but I was going very fast because I had delayed braking, so I touched the barriers and bounced back against him. He absorbed the energy of the impact and went directly into the tire barrier, while I made the corner.

I felt bad, but I couldn't stand all the subsequent complaints. Everybody clearly saw what had happened. Herta didn't want to let me pass for personal reasons, deciding that he would rather crash than be overtaken.

De Ferran piped in after the race, telling the journalists what an idiot I was. "Zanardi's doing anything he can to lose this championship, and it looks like he's succeeding." I replied to his insult: In my opinion De Ferran should be more concerned with trying to win rather than worrying about what I'm doing." I had somehow managed a comeback and during the last 12 laps, and had gone from last to fourth. If I hadn't stalled the engine twice during Vancouver, I would have won the race and the championship on a nearly impossible track.

So the celebration was delayed. At Laguna Seca, I came in third and captured the title. It was a great race, made all the better by Jimmy taking the win after a rather lackluster season. Bryan Herta started the race on the pole and took the lead. I started from second and was behind him for many laps until he had some tire problems. At one point, I tried to overtake him from the outside and was in the process of passing him when he pushed me on to the grass. The race officials clearly didn't like me and issued a statement. "We have examined the video playback and Herta's contact was accidental." It was the opposite. I recovered the lost time and was behind Blundell, who was second, but then ended up in the grass again. I was coming up fast and tried to overtake him as he exited from a pit stop, but he blocked me (although I don't know if it was deliberate or not). Blundell ran away from me, but I finished third with the fastest lap of the race.

With the 1997 Championship in hand, the celebrations began, made unforgettable by an accident with Jimmy in the parade lap. We were so happy with the team's results that after the checkered flag, we started joking and pretending we were bumping each other's wheels. Closer and closer until BANG! We bumped each other and I "parked" Jimmy on the side of the track. I can't tell you how surprised the team looked when they asked me what had happened to Jimmy. I was in stitches of laughter under my helmet.

Everybody was thrilled—the team had now won two championships. Chip was so happy that he almost squeezed me to death, while the ever-reserved Morris never praised me directly, but instead, complimented me to others. I could see in his eyes that he was proud of me. He treated me like a son, and perhaps I was attached to him because I saw a fatherly love in him. I still care about him despite the fact that we had some bitter episodes. He was never particularly generous with his words, but one compliment from him was worth a thousand from others. One evening at dinner he said, "There are drivers who endure problems and others who tolerate them. At Elkhart Lake I saw Alex, drenched in rain with a broken automatic accelerator, manage to change it manually, releasing it with his foot and then accelerating while changing gears. He didn't waste a second and immediately adapted to the situation on a very difficult track." That was an incredible compliment for Morris.

I went back to Europe to enjoy my victory before heading back to Fontana, California, for the last race of the season. Once again, Chip proved to be an incredibly lucky genius. During Friday's free practice, I had four new tires and drove a full lap with a low downforce set-up in order to simulate qualifying. I came out of a corner at about 240 mph right when Chip was yelling on the radio, "Yellow flag, yellow flag!" hoping to slow me down. Right in front of me was the wreckage of Carpentier's car, with both suspension units detached. I had two options: steer to the left and risk the car understeering into the wreckage head on, opening the bodywork like a tin of anchovies; or go to the right and hit it with the left flank of the car. I would have hit him in either case because I couldn't have changed trajectory at that speed. I went slightly to the right and hit the wreckage with the left side of my car. At that point, all that remained of my car was the cockpit. I then crashed against the wall, scratching it for nearly 900 yards and making a huge hole in the bodywork through which I could see the wall. The only good thing left of that car was the steering wheel, but luckily I didn't injure myself.

I staggered out of the car and went for the mandatory medical check-up, where they gave me the go-ahead for practice. I went back to the pits and apologized to Chip for crashing the car. He looked at me sincerely and said, "Don't worry about the car. The only thing that matters is that you're not hurt."

I returned to the track with the spare car but after only five minutes, an oil pipe broke and lubricant splashed on to the back wheel, causing me to spin. I was halfway round a corner and ended up smashing against the wall at an incredible speed. I passed out and was taken by stretcher to the medical center. When I regained consciousness the doctor, Steve Olvey, told me I wouldn't really feel the impact of the accident until later that evening, so they would decide the following day whether I could race or not. There was only one other car available—Jimmy's spare.

Meanwhile, Chip called Arie Luyendyk to enquire, "If Zanardi can't race, can you?" That night at the hotel, I told Daniela the same joke about 25 times, so she called Steve Olvey and said that I shouldn't race. The title was mine anyway; so it wasn't worth risking it. Luyendyk raced in my place and on the 39th lap, he crashed into the wall while trying to avoid a driver who'd spun out in front of him. He was taken to the hospital and didn't come to for five days. Another car was destroyed, so I told Chip, "I am sorry for destroying three cars in a day and a half." He was very calm. "Don't worry, as long as the both of you are all right."

I couldn't believe that he was so relaxed, until Mike Hull shed light on it. "Look, Chip has just sold three cars to the insurance company." Chip would be reimbursed for the price of three new chassis, minus the deduction, for cars that he didn't have to use again because the season was finished. This would total something like a million dollars at the end of championship, when in reality they were probably only worth $50,000. Nothing illegal—just very lucky. He also still had Jimmy's chassis for winter testing—perfect. Jimmy finished second at the Fontana oval and finished the championship in third place. That was his goal, so it was a great season.

With the 1997 season over, Chip and I didn't have to discuss the future because my contract was already finalized. "I reread the contract and just realize that you've won $500,000 for winning the title. Does this mean that next year you'll slow down because there is no incentive in the contract?" This made me laugh. So, as a symbolic gesture, we agreed on a deal. "If I win the championship again, you give me a car." And that's what happened, so at Team Ganassi headquarters, my Reynard-Honda waits for me to collect it.

That year, I received even more offers from Formula 1 than the previous winter. In addition to Jordan and Prost, Ferrari also approached me. I spoke to sporting director Jean Todt, who has always been very nice to me, but I was happy where I was. I considered myself well paid. Chip Ganassi had changed my life and my career, and it was right that he would have a driver racing who was making less than he really should. This was the least that I could do for him. He hired me when the others kept me in the waiting room and now that everyone wanted me, the pleasure was in saying, "No, thank you." You don't live for this type of revenge, but after so many difficult years, I was enjoying my moment in the sun. The objective was now to win another championship. It seemed impossible. I was already proud to have a back-to-back team sticker, therefore we jokingly said, "If we win next year, it is going to be back-to-back-to-back."

All the members of the team had been confirmed and the only problem was Morris. He'd bought some land in Florida and wanted to build a house and move there permanently. Ganassi explained, "Each year, Mo talks about retiring, but he really just wants a pay raise." I thought Morris was serious so maybe he hadn't quit completely, but he was already thinking about continuing as technical director during the races only. Perhaps it could have worked that way; the team was really good on its own and Morris could work via fax.

But we still needed someone to run the workshop and keep track of developments during the various tests. Morris had an idea: "We should find a young guy who wants to keep the books. I'll work on the car and he can learn from me. Then midway through the season, he can do everything and I can stand back until you need me to intervene." I suggested Roberto Trevisan as the ideal person for this transition. I knew he would never be competitive with Morris and would thrive in this symbiotic kind of relationship. I started mentioning it to Chip, who was somewhat skeptical. Quite frankly, he was terrified that Roberto and I might start speaking Italian in a panic situation. Morris and I could talk about cars over dinner all night, but Chip couldn't accept that I would do the same with another Italian. One day, Tom Anderson said they'd hired a candidate called Steve Clark, an ex-Ligier engineer. I didn't like him from the moment we first met. Not only because he wore socks with Smurfs on them, but also because he took his shoes off and put his feet on the table, and burped all the time.

Joking aside, I'd had a great relationship with Morris and didn't want to lose him. My objective was to keep him and for this reason, I never really gave Steve a chance. In addition, Steve didn't understand that Morris was his best ally because he wanted to work less. Instead, he took an obviously competitive attitude towards Morris. He was hired just before the beginning of the 1998 season, and because he didn't have experience of the ovals, I practically acted as the engineer for the first two.

In the third race at Long Beach, Steve took over and did a good job. I made Morris think the situation was fine with me, as it is useless to run after a woman who is trying to leave you—you will only tire her out. With Morris this was the right approach. I wanted him to believe I could do it without him ... that his son, so to speak, could manage on his own. After all, looking at my new car in the workshop, I told myself that the number 1 on the front of the car was there because I put it there.

CHAPTER *11*

CART Championship Again, and a Son Is Born

It was to be the best year of my life in 1998. Born an optimist, I always believe there is something better ahead, but it would be really difficult to top those 12 months. A few minutes into the New Year we conceived our son Niccolò, and I woke up in the morning of January 1 with a very strong certainty. It's not always easy to conceive a baby. While some manage the first time, many don't. We'd tried for a while, but nothing had happened. I wasn't worried, but I'd wanted to be a father ever since Ganassi had signed me and given me the peace of mind and financial security I needed. From that January day on, I started tormenting Daniela to take a pregnancy test, but she kept telling me to be patient. I don't know why, but I was certain of the results and had convinced Daniela of the same. So we were both delighted, but not surprised, when we saw the positive sign on the pregnancy strip. I proudly announced the news to the team while at Phoenix, during a photo shoot. They all took part in suggesting names for the baby. Then Ganassi came out with his suggestion, "Hey Alex, why don't you call him Alex Junior." I said that I could at least come up with something more original than that. He said, "Original—then what about Chip?" That was never an option.

Returning to racing, I didn't just have to deal with the Morris situation. At the beginning of the 1998 season, something worse was happening: there was hostility mounting against me among the other drivers and even some officials. This often happens when you start to win a lot. People tend to judge you from the outside, especially if they are a bit envious, but it's normal for a young man who suddenly finds success to become somewhat big-headed and although he might try to remain humble, he can become excessive. Thinking about it today, I realize why things happened the way they did, but at the time I was shocked to hear what was going on around me.

After the race at Vancouver in 1997, the one with the accident with Bryan Herta, I was put on probation and fined $15,000. I thought this was totally unfair. Not because I didn't deserve the punishment, but because the decision stemmed from envy. Even the other drivers started going against me. For example, after the Vancouver accident, nobody defended me when Herta said on television that I had been a complete idiot. Maybe he shouldn't have risked resisting my attempt to pass because I had already been lapped. In addition, other drivers started to complain about my driving. At that point, I got pissed off and started getting into useless arguments that would end up the focus of our driver briefings.

Wally Dallenbach, the CART race director, couldn't keep things under control and wasn't respected. Although I promised myself that I'd keep my mouth shut, I couldn't help it and would always end up in arguments, but I was never as articulate as my wife was. The tension of the previous season subsided when the championship came to a close. At the final banquet in 1997, the usual charlatans showed up to congratulate me and say how great my victory was. This annoyed me at the time, but looking back, I should have been proud; but it wasn't easy to work in conditions where the racing directors were so heavily influenced by the negative atmosphere. I'm also sure that the decision to put me on probation was partly due to this general feeling.

I didn't mind the punishment, but they should have at least disciplined Herta for what he'd said about me on television. That never happened. Instead, I could tell by people's behavior that things weren't going well. At the end of 1996 Dennis Swan was substituted for Dallenbach, but Swan later had a heart attack and Dallenbach returned to the position. At the 1996 banquet in Detroit, when Ganassi and I renewed my contract on a napkin, Dallenbach had come over to hug me. "You have been the year's revelation and the overtaking at Laguna Seca was the most incredible move in the whole history of IndyCars." I thanked him and said that I was lucky. "In life, you always need some luck, but you took a chance and made a great pass." He kept complimenting me, so I told him, "Some think that I crossed over the line."

Dallenbach was an ex-driver and quickly picked up on what I was referring to. "If I had been the racing director at the time, I would have said that you completed the maneuver before the hypothetical crossing that you've been blamed for. You passed and ended slightly off the track, but you didn't take advantage of this and the lap time proves it. You didn't pass by cutting the corner. You overtook, arrived slightly deep and went off the track, but if Herta had been slightly faster, he probably would have passed you again. That move was actually to your disadvantage. If Herta had been clever enough, he would have passed you, but he was taken off guard by your attempt." I was very grateful for this and appreciated the sincerity of his compliment.

Given what Dallenbach had said, I wasn't expecting him to criticize me a year later at the drivers' meeting in Laguna Seca. He started saying, "This year, we won't tolerate any cutting in the Corkscrew. In the past, we've been too generous. I wasn't the racing director, but now we will take disciplinary action if anyone cuts it again." I looked at him incredulously. He couldn't look me in the eye, which was a clear sign he not only remembered what he'd said a year ago, but also was embarrassed by his "new" attitude. By this time, I was convinced that the negativity towards me had gone beyond the cockpits.

I'm not playing the victim, but I really had to struggle against a very negative attitude. Winning in such an explosive way—and rising to the top more quickly than everyone had imagined—made the situation even more difficult. In the beginning, when things weren't going so well, everyone was happy. But halfway through 1997, when I destroyed the competition and was within reach of the championship, the only thing that they could do was attack me. They tried to ruin my results by accusing me of racing improperly, taking enormous risks and basically being crazy.

Some drivers still tried to fly these rumors towards the end of 1998, by which time I had learned to control myself. I simply told them to read who was on top of the list of most completed laps and number of miles—I was far ahead of everybody else. It was true that I took risks, but they were calculated risks and therefore I made few mistakes. Apart from Motegi, where I hit a wall, I finished 18 of the 19 scheduled races in 1998. I was on the podium 15 times, obliterating the existing record. "Take that!" I said to the critics. I could handle the criticism because you need to be tough in motor racing. If you're overly enthusiastic, you can make a mistake and therefore you have to accept the consequences. But I couldn't stand the way that much of this criticism came from envy.

I am glad that not everyone was like that; during a couple of briefings, I was defended by Jimmy Vasser and even more so by Greg Moore. Greg became so fed up with these attacks that he finally said to the other drivers, "You are all real pains in the ass." And to think that he was one of my main rivals …. He had arrived on the scene at the same time as me and had competed for Rookie of the Year in '96, and for the title during the following two years. Greg died in an accident at Fontana in 1999. He was one of those drivers who fought like mad in the car, but was the first to congratulate the winner. I don't feel obliged to say something pleasant about him, but I'm saying this because he was a real gentleman. Anyway, after winning the 1997 championship at Laguna Seca, it seemed the criticism was over, but in reality the critics were just waiting to spark the fire again.

1998 started well. I qualified sixth at Homestead and was in the running to win the race. Twice during the pit stops, my mechanics were so good that I was able to pass Michael Andretti who was faster than I was. Moore was even faster and ended up passing me and came in second, just a few centimeters behind Andretti. I came in third, which was great given that Homestead-type ovals were not our forte.

Then we went to Motegi in Japan, which was a Honda circuit despite their history of bad luck there. Honda spent loads of money creating a fantastic circuit, but had never managed to win at home, and that year was no different and we failed to put an end to their bad luck. I crashed into the wall after just a few laps and was out of the race. The only positive aspect of the trip was the karaoke in the hotel, because the rest of the week was just crap.

We went to Long Beach, the third race of the season, with a few uncertainties. I had an unimpressive 7th place in the first day of qualifying, but then dropped to 12th on the following day. Steve Clark didn't have an explanation. I remember that I spent the whole night thinking about the car's handling. The following day, I spoke to Steve at length and convinced him to make some daring changes to the set-up. Unlike most drivers, understeer always bothered me more than oversteer. On that occasion, connecting the rear anti-roll bar and keeping the front disconnected, together with some minor adjustments, improved the car even though it was exactly the opposite of what is usually done. In general, one drives with a disconnected rear anti-roll bar to give freedom to the suspension and a connected front anti-roll bar to stabilize the car. I did exactly the opposite because I wanted to solve the problem with the car's chronic understeer.

Without wanting to sound too grandiose or to broadly equate myself with a superior athlete, my driving style is similar to Schumacher's. I probably learned this technique from him while test driving for Benetton. With a bit of oversteer and a very precise front end, the car is more difficult to drive but much faster. I set up the car in this particular way, in clear contradiction to Morris who took one look at the set-up and grumbled, "Well, Pineapple, good luck!" My answer to his skeptical comment was to drive one of the best races of my career.

During the Long Beach race, I was passed by Tracy, who bumped Fittipaldi while trying to pass him, putting them both out. Immediately afterwards, there was a multiple accident at the hairpin with Bobby Rahal and another driver who blocked me. Pruett arrived on the outside and literally drove over the nose of my car. Scott hit my left front tire with his rear right tire, damaging my suspension and making a "u" in the wishbone. When the stewards enabled us to continue, I was the last car they restarted—I could do nothing but return to the pits. Chip said on the radio, "Bring it in. We'll have a look at the car." While traveling at 45 mph in the section before the pits, I asked my chief mechanic, Rob, "Why don't you try to straighten the wishbone with your hands because the rest of the suspension seems all right."

During the pit stop Rob did just that, his arms pumping while the suspension arm fought against his strength. He finally succeeded and I started again at the back, without much hope. We decided to concentrate on recovering the lap in order to earn a few points. Because of the forced pit stop, my tank was full. This extra fuel would give me the time to eventually regain the lap in case of a yellow flag, but not enough to finish the race. A few laps later, there was a yellow flag and everybody went in to refuel, but I had enough to stay out.

I was almost driving on fumes when the officials announced another neutralization. During a neutralization, the leader will still be accelerating and can lap you, so in theory, you should wait for the group to line up behind the pace car rather than go immediately to the pits in order to regain precious time. But for some strange security reason, the officials closed the pit lane, so I had to wait for a green flag before making a pit stop.

I finally went in for my last refueling. As I exited the pits, De Ferran, who was leading the race, was right behind me. I drove a couple of laps, defending my position by pushing the regulations to the limit. In Europe, I would have lost my license for this behavior, but it is allowed in the United States because the unpredictability of the outcome justifies the action. I thought to myself that De Ferran had a lot to lose and would think twice about lapping me, therefore I could push harder and make up for the lost laps. I started pushing and luckily didn't need to stop again for refueling, whereas all of the others needed a splash and go. A driver can lose 15–20 seconds during a splash and go, and that is exactly what happened. I worked my way back to tenth position while my opponents stopped to top up their tanks with the few gallons needed to finish the race. I was then fifth with five laps to go. In the first two, I passed Scott Pruett and Adrian Fernandez, ending up third, behind Dario Franchitti and Herta. It was easy enough to overtake Dario, who had lost both of his mirrors and therefore didn't see me enter his slipstream.

At that point, something happened that shocked me, requiring all the self-control I could muster. More than 100,000 spectators were cheering me on so loudly that I could hear them scream even in the slowest part of the track. This may seem normal, but I can guarantee that it wasn't, especially given that I was wearing special radio-linked earplugs to protect me from the deafening engine noise. Although the fans were rooting for different people, at that point everyone wanted me to catch my prey. At that moment it didn't matter what the passport, nationality or fan club was— everyone was rooting for the same outcome—and nothing could change that. I made the comeback from hell just when everyone thought I was finished. Herta even admitted during the press conference that his team told him that I was out.

I eliminated the remaining opponents and with only three laps to go, I was miraculously racing against Bryan once again for the victory. I was a good distance behind him as I approached the straight, but I could see him turn red in his rear view mirror. At the end of the straight, I was in no condition to overtake, but he started driving as if blocking someone who wasn't there. He knew that I was behind him and he started taking each turn defensively, giving me an opportunity to catch up with him. On the second to last lap, I could have tried to pass him at the end of the main straight, but that would have been the most obvious thing to do, so I didn't. The antagonism between us had clearly reached its peak, and I knew that Bryan would not let me overtake him at any cost and we'd both end up out of the race. He closed the gap while I faked a passing move. In reality I was getting ready to take him at the next corner, but I needed to find the best line in order to get him where he least expected it. Feeling the pressure, he crossed the chicane in a rather clumsy way. On the contrary, I took the best trajectory and aligned my car towards the exit as quickly as possible in order to accelerate and pass him. When he slightly widened his line to take the following corner, I was right behind him, and at that point, I moved in from the inside. All of this happened in a place where drivers never try to overtake. He was so surprised to see my car next to his that even Franchitti was able to pass him.

I won one of the most satisfying races of my life. It was incredibly rewarding to do so in the face of the critics who claimed that I raced with all heart and no brain, and in the face of all of those colleagues who made excuses like, "fourth place is a good result; today my car wasn't fit for winning; the circuit didn't allow passing; it was my opponent's fault; my grandmother had a cold, etc."

As had happened before, the greatest pleasure was to relive the race through those close to me. We had mounted a video camera on the flagpole of the pit lane in order to see how we could improve pit stops. At the end of the race, I took the tape to see the reaction of my guys when I overtook Bryan Herta, a scene that was also shown on television. It was fantastic to see the team hugging each other and screaming like mad. Ganassi seemed like a cartoon character and couldn't stand still. I shared unforgettable emotions with that group which was unlike anything else. Not because of winning championships, but because of days like this with spectacular moments.

To win at Long Beach in such a way is really exceptional. Even today, I'd not give up those memories for the legs that I lost in Germany. Those were immensely happy times. Of course there was the irreplaceable joy of my son, but that is something else. Those were unexpected outbursts that would arrive in a split second. Half an hour earlier I thought I had lost everything, and then I was a hero. The Americans, who are very loyal to their country, were only cheering one driver on that day. It was no longer the American versus the Italian, but a fairy-tale race where the fans only cared about a happy ending. It is only fair that someone who races like that should win.

Given that envy seemed to fuel the attacks against me, you can imagine that it reached its peak at Long Beach. I was attacked on every front. Even Scott Pruett, who bent my suspension during that hairpin accident, complained about me. Naturally De Ferran complained because I didn't let him pass while coming out of the pits. I couldn't believe it—I'd spent the whole championship in the lead stuck behind people who didn't want to be lapped, and no one did anything about that. The only time that drivers seemed to complain about it was when I adopted the technique to my advantage and ended up winning the race. I didn't let it get to me because I was mature and already had one title in my pocket and the number one on my car. I laughed about it and comforted myself with "donuts"—the smoking tire circles I would do after crossing the finish time. I did that to celebrate because I needed to release all the pent up emotions from the race. Once the checkered flag was waved, I could finally let go.

Long Beach put things back in order, especially in terms of the classification. Immediately following Long Beach was Nazareth, the famous short oval where we'd had our turning point. I didn't win, but came in second behind Vasser. Jimmy was very lucky, because he stalled during a pit stop and had to change his strategy. He loaded more fuel, which facilitated stopping later than the others did. But at the end of the race, they waved a yellow flag and Gugelmin ended up having a serious accident. It took so long to clean the track that we had to start again with just two laps to the end. Jimmy managed to save enough fuel during that long yellow flag session, that he was able to complete the race without stopping again. I didn't win, but I was happy for Jimmy, and as a team, we learned about short ovals. It was a matter of set-up, even in the details, like the tire pressure. I had an exceptional car and was able to overtake everybody on Turn Three. The others would oversteer on the outside while I took it correctly and passed them on the inside. It was wonderful to drive that car. We came in first and second, whereas the previous year we had performed particularly poorly. Overturning the situation cemented our team's spirit.

I also came in second in Rio de Janiero, but I wasn't happy at all. I had control of the race from the beginning and should have won it easily, but then a yellow flag was waved just few laps from the end, allowing Greg Moore to close the gap. On restarting, I took the lead again until I reached Arnd Meyer, who didn't know what to do. First he took the corner wide, then he closed up and eventually, halfway through the corner, he realized that he was in the way and decided to suddenly slow down. He did not realize that on a circuit like Rio, it is not possible to overtake from the outside because the corners are very narrow. I widened my line a little but couldn't pass him, and obviously on the following straight, Greg moved into my slipstream. We came up to the corner, he out-braked me on the outside—he certainly didn't lack courage—and came low looking for the only possible gap. I widened to avoid contact, he took advantage and with only two laps left, I couldn't catch up.

I was very annoyed with the outcome because I really liked Rio and would have liked to have won there, just once. I lost in 1996 due to poor strategy, and in 1997 we simply weren't fast enough. Greg took the race away from me. I felt robbed of a race that I had been dominating, but thinking back, I'm happy I "gave" him that victory. After this, Moore solidified his position as a championship contender. He was second at Homestead, collected points at Motegi, Long Beach and Nazareth, and won Rio with a Zanardi-style move, which really stung.

We were reaching the halfway point of the 1998 championship and Greg looked like my most dangerous opponent. Where I won, he was on the podium, and vice versa, but it was an honest and loyal fight. There had always been great respect between Greg and me, which was made evident at Jimmy Vasser's house at the end of the year. We often had to attend promotional events, organized by Firestone or Honda in Vegas, and we were always invited over to Jimmy's. One evening when the season was over, Jimmy invited around seven or eight drivers along with a host of other people to his house. He had a great pool table and as a joke, I explained how to play a typical Bolognese game. Greg immediately challenged me. He lost all the games and by the fifth or sixth one, he got a bit pissed off. We had each had a couple of margaritas, so there was no way to reason with him. "Give me another chance. This time I'll beat you!" I told him, "Greg, let's go outside because the others are waiting for us." He looked me straight in the eyes, knowing I would be racing with Williams in Formula 1 in 1999, and revealed his true feelings. "You bastard—you're leaving now, when I know that next year I would have beaten you. But since you're leaving, I'm going to tell you that you're one of the fastest fucking bastards I know, and I'm proud that I beat you a couple of times." This made me really pleased because he was a real fighter, one of those who would try to overtake anywhere on an oval at any speed.

St. Louis came after Brazil. It rained during practice, so we were unable to do the qualifying and started in the same position as we were in the championship. At one point during the race I was third, when everyone went in for refueling. My mechanics worked their magic and sent me out first, right in front of Michael Andretti, who was the king of that type of oval. Mario's son was the one whom Morris always held up any time he needed a comparison: "Because Michael warms up his tires this way, because Michael drives that way, etc." Clearly, Mo admired Andretti Junior. At that moment, something clicked in my head. I wanted to win very badly, which is usually a disadvantage because it clouds your focus, but on that occasion it helped me to be even more determined.

Although it was ultimately the car that made the difference, my pride helped to push me those extra yards. Michael passed me and we were very close to each other when we pulled in for the last decisive pit stop. Once again the boys performed a miracle on the car. Even the news reporters went to interview them about their pit performance. The mechanics yelled, "He's not going to give up this time!" With hindsight, it seemed as if I could hear them. After the pit stop, I kept Michael behind me for five laps, but there were still twenty to go, and everyone was sure he would overtake me. Instead, I focused and started driving against all the odds.

On the ovals, you need to let the car do 99 percent of the job, and the driver does the rest. I took the reins of the game and pushed the car to its limits. Lap after lap, I began to pull away from Michael, a meter-and-a-half, then four, then ten, then fifteen until there was a second and a half between us. It was incredible. To win at St. Louis meant that I could win anywhere and in any condition. I came in first on city circuits, street circuits, at Long Beach, on super speedways, and I showed that I could handle shorter ovals as well, but to triumph on a classic American oval like St. Louis left the crowds speechless. Everyone had expected Michael to overtake me in the last couple of laps but I held him off.

Milwaukee, another short oval, brought us back to earth. Even though the race was an improvement on the previous year, it didn't go well. I couldn't catch up with Jimmy the whole weekend. I even tried to set my car up like his, but he was still faster. To keep up with the others during the race, I used more fuel. Towards the end, I was battling with Al Unser, Jr., for the podium until two laps from the end, when Ganassi called me back for refueling because he thought that I couldn't finish the race. I was really pissed off because if they had told me to leave Unser alone, I could at least have come in fourth place, which was a hell of a lot better than the eighth place that I ended up getting. Anyway, the weekend was positive for Jimmy, who won the race and moved up in the ranking.

At Detroit, I just missed the pole—Greg Moore took it—but I was able to drive a long sequence of fastest laps. In qualifying, Morris substituted a couple of front shock absorbers and the car improved immensely. Despite the improvements, Morris still wasn't convinced about the car. On the day of the race, I went out to warm up and I crashed into the wall. Morris was already concerned from the previous day. "There's something wrong with this car—it's not normal for you to crash like this." I reassured him, "Sorry Morris, I started on the wrong foot, but today we are going to win." He was still very dubious and wanted to tweak the car, but I refused because I was certain that the car was all right. At the start, I found my concentration again, and for the first 25 laps, I literally played behind Greg, who always had more problems staying in the race. His car was clearly oversteering and ruining the rear tires, which were bald after 25 laps. I didn't even try to pass; all that I was thinking about was taking a pit stop after him, which I did.

He went in the pits on the 26th lap and I had a free track in front of me and for three consecutive laps, I took the lap record.

When I came out of the pits after my stop, I was still nine seconds ahead. It was a really easy race and he was my only competition, but eventually, other drivers caught up with him and he came in fifth. I perfected doing "donuts" on my victory lap. I was so good that the car rotated perfectly on the front wheels, and the outside wheel turned forward and the nearside rotated backwards. The spectators loved it.

From Detroit we went to Portland. I had a few problems during practice and wasn't terribly happy with the car. I still qualified fifth though and Jimmy was fourth. At the start, he wasn't great and on the first corner, I was on the inside and he was on the outside. He was able to hold on to the outside perfectly so on the following turn, he found himself on the inside in a better position than me. But Bryan Herta was in front of him and I kept accelerating on the outside, driving like a demon. I took the hairpin turning wide and passed Jimmy on the exit.

After the race, Jimmy came up to me and said, "You bastard, I thought I had you, but you returned the favor." We cared a lot about each other, but during the race, he was like any other rival. Once our visors were up, he was my team-mate Jimmy again.

During that first lap, Chip almost had a heart attack. After I passed Vasser, I started chasing Scott Pruett who was blocking me and thereby allowing Herta to keep the lead. At the first yellow flag, Herta's team took a completely wrong strategy; they let him stay out while everyone else had stopped to refuel. He found himself in first place, but with only half a tank of fuel. He took off at the restart, trying to put as much distance as possible between himself and his next rival in the hope of limiting the damage of the pit stop. But after the untimely pit stop, Herta was out of the game and Franchitti moved up to first, followed by Pruett and me.

When Pruett needed more fuel and went to the pits I had enough for another lap and at the end of my pit stop, I was still in front of him. I was second and would have to fight for the victory with Franchitti, who was stronger than me on that day. But sometimes in life, things happen exactly the way you want. How many times did I wish that I had punched P.J. Jones? But Jones was now paying me back a huge favor because he eliminated Franchitti. He pushed the leader off the track, "parking" him against the wall. I thanked P.J. and ended up winning a race I didn't really deserve, but in terms of points, it was invaluable. I seemed unstoppable, and next it was "my" Cleveland.

Cleveland excited me. I really wanted pole there because I'd never had it there before. During the free practice, I was something like eight-tenths of a second faster then Franchitti, my closest competitor. I went to study the classifications after the practice, and saw that Jimmy was in 16th place. "I'm in trouble," Jimmy told me.

I tried to help. "Do your set-up the same way as my car, which is going really well." "But my car is exactly the same, it only has a half of a degree on the wing." I replied to him, "I don't know what to say or how to motivate you. You should be pissed off with yourself, not the others, and try to figure out where you are losing time. I can understand that your car isn't exactly like mine, and that your driving style on this circuit is not ideal, but you're 1.8 seconds slower than other drivers with the same car." Jimmy lifted his unmistakable sunglasses. "You're right, bro." He scrapped the documents with the telemetric results and left the office, thanking me for his help. Well, the bastard went on to break the track record during the fourth lap of qualifying! For the entire session, the best time that I was able to get was half a second slower than his. All of the other laps were slower, but the one that gave him the pole was fantastic. I couldn't believe it.

"What did they do during that lap—put a plastic bag on your visor?" This comment referred to when I overtook Herta at the Corkscrew at Laguna Seca. At the Target party in 1996, I made a dramatic speech about how I'd prepared for that move. During the last laps, I imagined how Bryan Herta, who had achieved much greatness in his career, was feeling. The last point where I could pass him, I would imagine Herta relaxing, thinking about his friends at home celebrating his apparent victory. He would then start thinking about what he would do the day after his victory, and so on. This would inevitably make him brake early, allowing me to pass where not usually possible. I waited for my chance and was very lucky, and everything worked out very well for me. Jimmy, who was sitting next to me and had heard the whole story, stood up and announced, "I don't know what your theory is about Laguna Seca, but mine is that Zanardi had a plastic bag stuck on his visor and when he finally managed to pull it off, he found himself in the lead."

On the Saturday, although I improved my time, Franchitti qualified second after Jimmy, while I was third. Never mind, it was still a good starting position. I leapt from the grid, leaving Franchitti behind and following Jimmy, who was in the lead for ten laps. Then a yellow flag was waved after an accident and we were put back in a single line. I've always been quick on cold tires and able to obtain great results in restarts. Cleveland is built around an old airport. On the first corner, you arrive on the main runway and then enter an intersection, going from a wide entry into the corner—where it's very difficult to get a line—to a very narrow exit. Often, the trajectories crossed over. I faked an attack from the inside and Jimmy closed up on me. He arrived too deep, I went on the outside, took my corner and on the exit, I passed him from the inside. I took the lead and didn't let it go again. Fittipaldi, who had a different sequence of pit stops, was leading for ten laps towards the end, but then he had to stop to refuel so I regained my lead and maintained it until the end. I won the race with relative ease and was now dominating the championship.

After Cleveland, we went to test in Mid-Ohio. Morris thought that Jimmy was having problems because he was using his left foot to brake, whereas I was using my right foot, and therefore he was braking and accelerating at the same time. This style made him use more fuel than me and wear out the brakes more rapidly. For instance, after a 40-lap session, my car was still in perfect condition, whereas his was deteriorating. I think that setting up my car in a way that allowed me to drive the way I wanted to drive, rather than the way the car wanted to go, was one of my main advantages. I started the race with the same competitive level as the others, but halfway through, I'd often be at least a second a lap faster. This wasn't due to my speed as much as to the others slowing down. Especially with that type of powerful and heavy car, my "Parisian" style of driving allowed me to be as fast and aggressive as necessary. I used the brakes and tires properly, and consumed enough fuel to go on, but nothing more. If Robby Gordon or Paul Tracy were seen arriving in a corner, they would seem to be going incredibly fast, as if they were literally about to break everything. But then the rankings would show that they weren't actually as fast as they appeared. During the race, my smooth driving style translated into a great advantage. I learned many things from Jimmy, and he was now trying to learn something from me. So we went to Mid-Ohio for a test with the intention of studying a more efficient way of driving.

The team had hired Jeremy, a young engineer, to work on a research and development department that Ganassi wanted to create. Jeremy had to report on our driving styles, paying attention to the use of brakes, throttle and telemetry times in each corner. We finished the tests, and Jimmy was slower than I was, so he relied on the report to understand where to improve. When the results of the study were eventually completed, I was in a meeting with Morris. Jimmy came in with a copy of the report where our names were abbreviated as JV and AZ. "In this corner, JV brakes 20 feet after AZ; JV has a better acceleration than AZ; JV enters the corner faster than AZ; JV is three mph faster than AZ." Then he paused and said, "The outcome of all this is that in this corner JV is four tenths slower than AZ. How on earth is this possible?" We burst out laughing, because according to the report, it seemed that he should have been much faster than me but instead, Jimmy was losing time to me.

I continued to battle for the title in Toronto, where I qualified in second place. Franchitti only just took pole from me, but he deserved it because he was clearly unbeatable during the race. For the first part, I was following him, and then a few drivers behind us bumped each other and almost completely blocked the track. I tried to pass through the only possible opening, but the lapped driver in front of me stalled his engine, closing down the only gap available. Franchitti had been the first to overcome the obstacle, whereas I was stuck on the right until the stewards could free the left side of the track and allow the driver on the left-hand side to restart his car. At that point, the stewards focused on the car in front of me, finally freeing up an opening. While this was going on, Jimmy Vasser, Michael Andretti and Adrian Fernandez all passed me through the gap on the left-hand side. I went from second to fifth. Once I restarted, I overtook Fernandez right away while Andretti passed Jimmy, who was right in front of me.

Jimmy had been losing his position in the championship, so I gave him some suggestions before the race. We were on such good terms that we always collaborated and shared strategies. Although we were both very capable professionals, we were humble enough to listen to one another's feedback. I told Jimmy that "the best place to overtake is from the inside at the end of the straight, but people expect you to do this, so they block you. I've noticed that if you fake the move and then go all the way to the outside, squeezing your opponent to the inside, he is forced to make a clumsy exit."

Back on the track, there was a small straight that led to a 90-degree corner where it was usually impossible to pass. Using this trick, passing became almost a game. In fact, it was in Toronto where I made my moves. I was behind Jimmy, who thanks to what I had told him, knew what was going to happen. He started placing himself in the center of the track so that I couldn't overtake him. Trying to pass him, I wore out both brakes and tires and ended up spinning out, but I quickly regained control of my position.

Ten laps from the end, Franchitti spun out with a similar problem. He arrived at the end of the straight, braked, and the rear wheels locked so he spun at the first corner, stopping in the middle of the track. Once again there were two gaps, one to the left and one to the right. The first one was wide enough, but the second was very narrow. Chip started yelling on the radio, "Stay low!" Therefore I braked, took a tight corner and exited on the outside. Jimmy didn't receive the same instructions. Andretti was able to pass, but hit both the wall and Franchitti. Vasser was in the middle of a mess, so I passed him again and ended up second behind Andretti.

My car cooled down during the several laps behind the safety car, but I could tell she was in good shape when I restarted. I concentrated on passing Andretti. Two laps from the end, I faked the most obvious move by pretending to pass from the inside of a 90-degree corner. He blocked me, so I went to the outside as if I was giving up. He braked and widened his line a bit to enter the corner on a better trajectory. At that point I stopped braking, swerved to the inside and passed through a tiny gap. There couldn't have been more that a hair between the wall, Andretti and me. Once I passed him, it was an effortless win.

Daniela and I arrived home in the evening from Toronto. She could feel the baby moving, but was not feeling well. Sometimes, I'd put my head on her tummy to listen and speak to him. I had been told that if I spoke to the baby, he would recognize my voice. Despite not feeling well, Daniela brought me breakfast. I was suddenly woken up by her screams as she tripped over some luggage. It still gives me chills to think about her that moment. We went to the hospital in Indianapolis to see Dr. Mary Soper, a very kind doctor and friend of CART's doctor, Terry Trammell, who was responsible for the Facet medical equipment. It was quite serious. During the previous week in Canada, Daniela had become badly dehydrated.

I don't know if the fall exacerbated the problem, but she was having severe contractions. She was six and half months pregnant and was already dilating. Given that the baby was underweight, the doctors were concerned. "We're going to keep you here and monitor you for 24 hours, and give you some medication to assist the baby." They gave her some cortisone for his lung development, and medication to limit the contractions so that she would not go into labor until the baby had had another 48 hours to strengthen his chances of survival. As soon as I heard "chances of survival," I was really scared.

Theoretically, I should already have been in Michigan. But on the first night, Daniela threw up continuously. This went on for the entire next day until she finally started reacting to the medication. With each hour that passed, the baby's chances became greater. In that period, we used to call him Giacolo because we hadn't decided between Giacomo and Niccolò. Every once in a while, Daniela would send me out of the room. I was very distraught, but I was trying to put on a brave face for her. I even cried. I'd go to the car park and cry, "Giacolo, hold on!" I've never prayed for help before, but I looked up to the sky and said, "Lord, I don't know if you exist, but if you're there and can do something, please do because this is the most important thing in my life." I don't know if He heard or it was just a coincidence, but Daniela's contractions stopped and Giacolo stabilized.

I was very close to the guys in the team and they were very supportive. I was fighting for the championship, having just taken the lead, so the race in Michigan was very important. Chip was the first to tell me, "Do what you need to do, but don't decide now. If you decide to race, I'll take you to Michigan on the jet at five o'clock in the morning on Friday and bring you back that night. The same for Saturday and Sunday." Thursday afternoon, Daniela left the hospital with instructions to rest. A very kind girl on the team, Kim Conrad, who worked in logistics and also spoke Italian, offered to come and help her. I called Chip on Friday morning and told him I was racing in Michigan, despite not having slept for more than six or seven hours all week. I was obviously very tired, but when you are very fit and on a terrific team, you can compensate for anything. In fact, it was a fantastic race.

A new set of rules was introduced at that race to limit the ever-increasing speed. We were racing with what we drivers called "open umbrella" wings. The basic concept behind them was to maximize aerodynamic braking. This feature equalized the drivers and therefore prevented anyone from really shooting ahead. I raced very wisely and my tactic was to stay in the group until it suited me, and then 20 laps from the end, I would push the throttle and show that I was the only one with the power and advantage to take the lead. I did exactly that, then suddenly lost power when one of the oil rings blew off. Each time I feathered the throttle, oil leaked on to the hot turbo. Every time I came out of Turn Four, the car would smoke like an old Prinz. In the pits, they started getting concerned, but they told me that everything was under control and I should go on. The rest of the group caught up with me and I hid in the slipstream until the very last laps. Despite all the problems, I tried to leap ahead, but I was caught up with Vasser and on the last lap, Moore overtook both of us. Moore was first, Jimmy second and me third. I didn't get my fifth consecutive victory, but at least I was on the podium on an unforgettable day. Jimmy and I both agreed that we lost to a driver with a superior strategy. Because he kept on the outside in our aerodynamic "shade" during Turns One and Two, Greg was ultimately able to get in our slipstream and pass both of us. He was really fearless and his intuition pushed us to try things that others wouldn't on the fast ovals. Unfortunately the day arrived at Fontana late in 1999 when this fearlessness cost him his life. He was good on any circuit, but on this type of circuit, he was exceptionally strong. We managed to bring home good team results and for a third year the Target team was in the headlines.

I went back home on Sunday evening to find Daniela feeling much better. I decided to rent a motorhome for the following race at Mid-Ohio to make her comfortable and rested. I asked Jimmy about where to rent one, and he recommended a company who were actually big fans of mine and ended up not charging me a thing. In the meantime, Filippo had arrived and Titano was coming immediately after the race.

Between Michigan and Mid-Ohio we had a two-week break. We stayed at my place in Indianapolis and had fun with the jet skis and other toys. During the break, there was the prestigious Brickyard 400 race at Indianapolis. Almost the entire town attended the race. We couldn't watch it on television because at the last moment, ABC lost the transmission. With nothing else to do, I suggested an alternative, "Why don't we go shopping at Target?" I noticed a type of surfboard where you ride on your knees. With flip-flops and vests, we went to Target and bought this thing called a Cyclone. We spent the whole afternoon on the lake trying to figure out how to use it, but eventually gave up. Jimmy called to see how Daniela was doing and I told him about the Cyclone. He explained how to use it and by sunrise the following morning, we finally succeeded. I still remember how excited we were as we told Daniela and Catia about it—it was like we had just climbed Mount Everest. They looked at us like we were a bunch of imbeciles. We also had a plan for Titano. We decided not to show him how to use the Cyclone so that he could make a fool of himself while trying to figure it out. In the following days, we tried different variations, with Filippo even trying to stand on it. After several attempts, I proudly managed to stand on the Cyclone. Perhaps I sound like a child, but we had a couple of fantastic days on it.

Mid-Ohio is the home circuit of Bobby Rahal's team. This was the last year that Bobby was racing. He had already announced his retirement, so he was really counting on winning that race, as was his teammate, Bryan Herta, who was absolutely determined to beat me. During the practice I saw that Herta's fans had put up a poster with a slur against me. That same evening, I went for a tour around the track on a moped with Filippo and saw the poster at the end of the straight. There was a group of four or five big camper vans with about 20 people having a barbeque. There was a copy of the Target logo on the poster with my name in the middle and an arrow with Bobby's name on it. On another poster was written, "We Hate Zanardi." Some of the fans, who had already had a few beers, asked what we wanted. So I started chatting with them and asked, "Why do you hate Zanardi so much?" A fellow slurred, "Because we are Rahal's fans." One of the more lucid members of the group was staring at me. "Aren't you Alex Zanardi?" I laughed. "Yes, it's me. And now that you recognize me, should I get lost?" They were so impressed that they offered us a couple of beers, and we ended up spending an hour chatting with them. During the practice on the following day, I saw that the two posters had been substituted with, "Alex, You Are the Man!" and "We Love You, Zanardi!" I waved at them and they waved back enthusiastically.

Qualifying didn't go so well however. I had several problems with the engine, then spun out, and was grouped with the slow session. I ended up in eighth position, which wasn't great, but at least I had a chance to do something during the race. At the start, I immediately positioned myself behind Michael Andretti. I tried to stay as close to him as possible in Turn One in order to pass him at the end of the straight, but I slightly lost control of the car, hit a curb and went on the grass. I drove a quarter-mile on the grass, which went down in history. Halfway through the race, I also burst a tire while overtaking P.J. Jones, who had been lapped but was blocking me. We hit each other's tires and I lost control of the car, causing me to exit the corner badly. As a result, JJ Lehto got into my slipstream on the straight. It was hell. I blocked his attempt to pass, but Lehto tried anyway and hit me, slicing my tire. His front wing fell off and landed in P.J. Jones's cockpit, forcing him to slow down.

At that time, Andretti appeared and ran into Lehto, who was trying to assess what to do without a front wing, and Jones, who was trying to toss Lehto's wing from his cockpit. Andretti tried to pass in between the two, but P.J. hit Andretti and Michael spun into the sand and rolled his car. It was destroyed, but luckily he wasn't. After the race, P.J. Jones blamed me for starting everything, which might have been true, but Andretti hit P.J. while I was on an entirely different part of the track.

I went on to recover a bit of time and by the end of the race, I was fighting for 12th place with Helio Castroneves. During my last attempt to overtake him, he blocked me on the straight. I took the outside and then together we took the corner side by side. He came out a bit better but I had the advantage of being on the inside for the following corner. I delayed braking and he took the corner without considering that I was already on the inside, so we hit each other. He spun and hit the barrier, while I was luckier and was still able to finish the race in 12th. I thought it was a normal collision, but the race director didn't agree and I was summoned for a meeting with the officials. I gave my version of what had happened and they wanted to disqualify me. I was told to wait outside the office for the final decision, and after a couple of hours, they called me.

They said it was my fault because a piece of a wing flew off, and I was to blame for the fact that Andretti had flipped the car. They told me just to listen to the verdict, but I interrupted.

"What does this mean?" They quickly gave their verdict without my consideration. "We are disqualifying you from this race and you are on probation. We are also considering suspending you for three races."

I was incandescent. I brought up the story of the briefing at Laguna Seca, and all the bullshit that the other drivers were saying and how fed up I was. "I understand that people may be envious of how fast I'm going, and I don't give a shit if you suspend me because I'm going to win the championship anyway." I admit that I exaggerated a bit, but I went on. "I'm really getting pissed off because you are officials and you allow a couple of idiots who wish that they were in my place to influence your decision. I know that I didn't race well today and made some mistakes, but they were absolutely not intentional. I didn't plan to push out anyone, but these things happen during racing. I race in a tough but correct way. If you interpret my style as incorrect, then disqualify me, because I don't care. And if you do, I know that you're prejudiced. If you have to make decisions in this mafia-style way, then go ahead, but don't waste any more of my time. I've got to get back to Indianapolis and it's 350 miles away."

On the way home, I heard on the radio that I was on probation for the rest of the season, and that they had disqualified me from the race and had fined me $50,000—the highest fine ever given in the entire history of CART. I wasn't upset for long. Titano was arriving that night and I had just enough time to take Daniela and Catia home and leave for the airport with Filippo. A mile into our journey the police stopped us. One of the sheriffs looked at my documents and smiled when he saw my name. "You've had a bad day and I don't want to make it any worse." He handed back the documents and sent us on our way.

Dallenbach and the other officials were very annoyed by what I said, but eventually they cooled down. I accepted being punished for that race, but Paul Tracy, Robby Gordon and Gil

De Ferran had all done worse things in their careers and had not been reprimanded at all. Especially De Ferran, who did nothing but complain and then shove drivers against the wall. I bump other drivers, but never on purpose. I often banged wheels with other drivers, even on the ovals with Michael Andretti and Tracy himself, but it was a healthy fight as if to say, "I'm not giving up, so do what you like." But then if something goes wrong, you shouldn't complain. It simply happens in racing.

We went to Elkhart Lake in our motorhome and in the race I qualified fifth or sixth. During the race De Ferran hit Scott Pruett on the second corner, causing everyone behind them to brake. Al Unser Junior slammed on the brakes and I didn't have time to stop. I rammed into him, sent him off the track and destroyed the nose of my car and the tires. After repairing the car I rejoined, convinced that it was the end of the race for me and that I'd receive a black flag. I raced the entire first half waiting for them to disqualify me once and for all, but instead I finished the race and came in second.

After the podium ceremonies, the race officials called me. When I entered the room, Dallenbach greeted me with a smirk. "You're expecting me to screw you. But I looked again and again at the tape of the race and Unser braked in front of you, and you did everything you could to stop. Outside the office, there is a line of Penske guys [Unser's team] waiting for me to take away your license, but from my point of view, you had no choice. Therefore, regardless of what's happened between us, I'm calling this a classic race accident in which you have no responsibility. So as you can see, I've got nothing against you, so just get over it." I was stunned and completely caught off guard. "I always thought that there was something wrong with the way that I interact with some people, and I still think that in the past, some decisions were political. But I have to reconsider my opinion of you and admit that perhaps I didn't judge you fairly. It may sound rhetorical to say that I respect you when you've made a decision in my favor, but I feel that I should because that is exactly how I'm feeling. I apologize because a driver should never disrespect a race director, and I did at Mid-Ohio. I respect you as a person and therefore I owe you an apology, and I thank you for being objective."

Dallenbach was very honest and was getting a lot of grief for not suspending my license. Even at the following race, Al Unser, Jr., behaved liked a real bastard and I had a huge public row with him. Unser and I never really got along. I had once spoken to him in confidence about a few things, as he was the drivers' representative, and he later repeated them out of context during a briefing. After the Elkhart Lake race, I went to apologize to him. "I'm sorry, but I wasn't responsible for the accident. It's not like I tried to overtake and ruin somebody's race. Everyone stopped at once and I wasn't able to stop in time. You were in my line of vision and therefore I couldn't see the pileup in front of you and couldn't stop in time. I didn't do it on purpose, and as a driver, you should know that. I feel badly because you've had a difficult season and it was the first race where you were so competitive, and unfortunately this episode ruined it for you." At the beginning of the conversation he was a bit skeptical. "I appreciate the fact that you came to talk to me. However let me say that you're driving too dangerously." And then he started patronizing me. "I'm an expert driver and you're just a kid. I've been in your position as well, with everybody praising me and feeling invincible, but you have to remember that this is a dangerous sport." We shook hands and I thought this was the end of it.

Instead, Unser later went ballistic in the drivers' meeting, screaming at me while pointing his finger. "The whole world saw what Zanardi did on television. Everybody knows what he did today, and what he did yesterday and what he'll do tomorrow. The whole world saw him push me out of the race and the officials did nothing about it!" Vasser looked at me, amused: "He's crazy." I didn't find it funny because I took it personally. Dallenbach was so surprised that the only thing he could say was, "I must let Alex speak so that he can defend himself." I was very brief. "I don't have any problems or want to start an argument with someone who is so out of line. I thought that we had sorted things out privately, but if Mr. Unser wants and needs to open up the discussion again, I'm more than happy to. Maybe even with the race director involved. But I'm convinced that we don't need to discuss this in front of everyone, especially out of respect for Dallenbach. So I'm not playing this game with you." Greg Moore interrupted. "Apologies if I step in, but I don't think that this is how we should speak to our race director. We have more important things to discuss before tomorrow's race." I offered to stay after the briefing, but Unser stormed out. Dallenbach and I looked at each other and smiled, and that was that.

Formula 1 was pursuing me once again with the top teams courting me whenever they could. Returning from Long Beach, there was a message from Briatore to call him back. When I did, he tried to be nonchalant about what I'd been up to. He sounded a bit churlish. "How's it going this year—have you won anything?" I casually replied, "I just won Long Beach yesterday." I knew what he was up to and his "strategy" made me laugh, but I was also flattered. Peter Collins, who had been my Lotus team manager, had called Frank Williams to talk about me.

Peter had worked for Williams years earlier and suggested strongly that they should give me a test. But Frank didn't need to be persuaded because he was already interested and thus began a series of long distance conversations. He would conclude the conversation in the usual way, "When you come to Europe, we'll sit down and talk about it." Jordan came around again, and I also spoke to Ferrari which was looking for a replacement for Eddie Irvine. I had already spoken to Jean Todt in 1997 who said, "I want to meet with you. Not because I want you to race with us, but because you are a very fast driver. I want to know what kind of person you are because maybe our paths will cross one day."

When rumors leaked out about my discussions with Williams, I started getting a lot of interest. But I was only considering two options, stay with Ganassi, or go to Williams. Frank became very serious. "Well there is no reason to keep talking on the phone. Since you're always racing and find it difficult to come to Europe, I'll come see you in Detroit the day after tomorrow." I was very impressed that he would do that. As soon as I met him, I liked him and was immediately convinced I should race for him. Williams had arrived in America with his lawyer to write and possibly sign a contract, and this time I showed up with mine. We discussed the broad terms on the first day and the details on the following day. He agreed to more or less all my comments and we shook hands.

To be honest, from a technical point of view, Formula 1 wasn't any better than CART. In fact, it was probably inferior in terms of my results, the team and the element of fun and enjoyment. When it became public that I was talking to Williams, I used the usual excuses. "One needs new challenges, etc." But for me, the biggest challenge was winning and it didn't matter where or in what category, I just wanted to keep on winning.

In life we always want what we don't have. I had three wonderful years in CART, which I really miss, especially in terms of my lifestyle in Indianapolis. Today, I look back nostalgically at those happy days, but at the time I felt like I was on military duty. I missed my friends, my language, our traditional games ... everything. In addition, our life started becoming a bit more complicated. We were going to have a baby and Daniela, although she didn't want to, started putting pressure on me to go home. "Do what you want, but I wouldn't mind going home. I wouldn't mind if you stopped racing on the ovals, either, because they are very dangerous." I basically just needed to meet someone like Frank Williams to close the circle. I respect him a lot and am grateful for the chance that he gave me, and I'm sorry that I didn't perform as well as I should have done. Unfortunately, Frank, who would have given his life to his team, didn't really have a presence—in the race team—after his accident in 1986 which left him paralyzed. It was indeed a strange year in 1999 with a series of things which didn't go as planned.

We were in the middle of August and my racing future was becoming clear. I'd always been honest with Ganassi and he knew about everything, even before it was official. He realized that it wasn't about money, but about my quality of life. He confided in me. "I received the authority from Target to pay whatever was necessary within reason to keep you from returning to Formula 1." I realized that if I didn't give it a try again, I would have remained in the United States and would have never known what I could have achieved in Formula 1. A driver always believes that he is the best, and I was convinced that I could help Frank return to the top.

After Elkhart Lake, I took Daniela back to Italy in August so she could have the baby there. The due date was in October, but the doctors decided to induce her. There was very little amniotic fluid, but the baby was big enough to survive on his own once born. In fact, although he was a little thing, he didn't need an incubator. A few days before Daniela went into the hospital in September, I left for Vancouver. She spoke to the doctors who explained that everything could be scheduled so that I could race and make it back in time. They would admit her on Monday September 7 and induce the labor in the afternoon. I was due to arrive in Venice from Vancouver that afternoon—theoretically in time to see our son born. But when Daniela was induced on Sunday, Niccolò came within 20 minutes and I sadly missed his birth.

I won my second CART (1998) title in Vancouver. I won it with a very honest, but not particularly brilliant, race. I was fastest on Friday, but I only came in third during Saturday's qualifying. I could have been on the podium, but during a restart while warming

33. Niccolò and I competing for "Mr. Muscle"—but who had the bigger grin?

34. Summer 2001, Niccolò riding his toy dolphin in our swimming pool in Indianapolis.

35. My mother-in-law Gianna, Daniela and Niccolò on the way to the States.

36. Mo Nunn and I early in my 2001 CART season with his team.

37. This fourth-place finish in the 2001 Toronto Grand Prix was my best result of that fateful season.

38. Jimmy Vasser, Tony Kanaan and I during the 2001 CART season.

39. The moment of impact—the
Lausitzring, September 15, 2001.

40. On the way to the medical helicopter,
with Dr. Steve Olvey on the right.

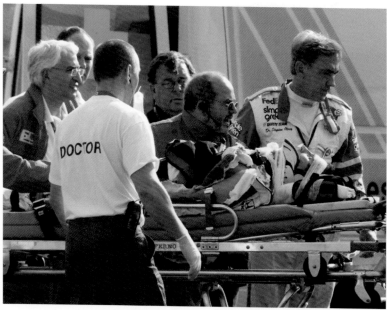

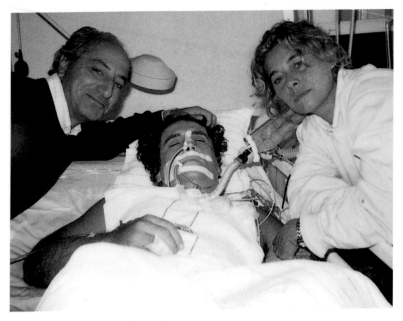

41. In intensive care in Berlin, with Sandro and Daniela.

42. Going home—Dr. Schaffartzik sends me off with a pineapple in hand.

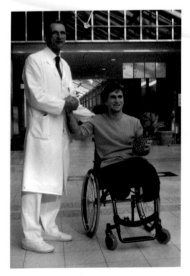

43. Dr. Franco Ferri working on my prostheses.

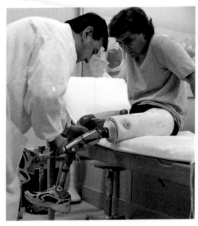

44. Attending my first CART race after the accident—in Toronto during the summer of 2002. I was glad for the chance to talk with Alex Tagliani, the driver of the car that hit me at the Lausitzring.

45. Waving off the parade lap from the tower above the start/finish line at Toronto.

46. My return to the
Lausitzring on May 11,
2003, to complete the
13 laps that I missed
after my accident.

47. Posing with the safety team that
saved my life 19 months earlier.

48. In the cockpit of the specially adapted Champ Car just before taking my 13 laps.

49. On the German oval at more than 185mph—not bad Sandrino!

50. The whole team at Costa's house celebrating the publication of the book in Italy in 2003. Clockwise, from the left: Dr. Costa (guarding his homemade salami!), me, Gianluca, Titano, Claudio Panizzi, Filippo, Sandro, Roberto Trevisan and Franco Ferri.

51. With my mother, Anna, who is an incredibly strong woman.

up the tires, I did something really stupid. I accelerated to skid the tires and clean them, but ended up spinning. I restarted last. Playing around with the strategies and passing a few drivers, I finished the race in fourth place but still sealed the championship title.

When I arrived back in Italy my brother-in-law, Sandro Giannini, met me at the airport to break the news. "You're a father—congratulations!" Sandro is a great family man whom I really care about, and I think the feeling is mutual. He considers me like a brother, and he was with Daniela throughout Niccolò's birth. He burst out crying when Niccolò was born, like he did with his own two children. I relived every single moment of the birth through him and I think that made us even closer. He is a doctor, so he was able to sneak me into the hospital that night by loaning me a white jacket and a mask. I immediately ran to Daniela and she introduced me to my son. I felt really strange. We are used to seeing parents crying for joy when their children are born in the movies, but I felt nothing. I kind of hoped that something like that would happen to me as well, but for a second I wondered if fatherhood really suited me.

But as soon as I took him in my arms, my feelings started changing, and they keep changing. Even now, when I hold him, the emotions are incomparable to anything else I've experienced. A moment with Niccolò is worth more than a lifetime of experiences. Now I sound just like the parents who used to say to me, "You'll see when you have a baby of your own …." Nothing that they do bothers you, disgusts you, and nothing is too silly or absurd. Everything they do makes you smile, and I'm so lucky to have a son like Niccolò.

After a couple of days Daniela was sent home. The next race was in Laguna Seca, so I left for California on Thursday afternoon and arrived in the evening, ready for the first practice. There I had another accident with Bryan Herta. The sessions were just finished but I was still going fast. He on the other hand was going slowly and accelerated when he saw me coming. This really annoyed me because he purposely did not let me through. I tried to pass, he squeezed me, and bang—I hit him and sent him into a wall, bending one of my wheels. Wally Dallenbach called us to hear our versions of what had happened. I was excluded from the free practice on Saturday morning, which placed me in the slower drivers section of qualifying. I eventually qualified fifth.

When we came out of Dallenbach's office, Bryan and I had a brief chat. I said, "With the microphones off, I want to tell you one thing. Everything that has happened over the years has been the result of a few comments that have escalated and created a rivalry that is based on nothing. You were going slowly today, and sped up when you saw me. When I realized that, I decided that there was no way I was going to give up. Why are we doing this bullshit? Frankly, I think that you respect me as a driver and I certainly respect you. I'm sure that you are fundamentally a loyal person and don't have anything directly against Alex Zanardi." We shook hands. A journalist later asked Herta about what happened. "Alex and I have never been friends, and maybe we will never be, but today we were able to sort a few things out and maybe our future relationship will be better."

The following day he started on pole and I was lagging behind him. Towards the end of the race, I caught up with him and tried to overtake a couple of times. A couple of times the race was neutralized by a yellow flag, so I couldn't pass him and so he won. He was over the moon, finally lifting the burden of an unlucky streak.

Throughout the whole press conference, he described his joy at winning against such a competitive and strong opponent. "I've been battling against a ghost—against a driver whom I've always respected but never acknowledged. I was finally able to win today and this is a great honor, because I know how hard I've been working and was able to stay in front of one of the best drivers in the world." Perhaps if we had spoken to each other more rather than to the press, we would have never arrived at such a point in the first place. Just by chance, I found myself in his way on a few occasions when he was in the lead. This particularly annoyed Herta because it was while I was making a big comeback for the title. At Laguna Seca in 1996, I had done that unforgettable overtaking move and in the following year at Long Beach, Bryan was winning when I had an amazing comeback and beat him. At Cleveland in 1997, I came out of nowhere to pass him and win.

Between Laguna Seca and the following race at Houston, I completed my first test with Williams after signing the contract with Frank. I had an unimpressive run at Barcelona. I was driving with 130 pounds of fuel and had a good time by the fourth lap, but I only improved this a couple of tenths throughout the day.

Frank's partner, Patrick Head, who was responsible for the technical aspects of the team, discussed with me who should become my engineer. "I'd like to put a relatively inexperienced person with you, because if we give you someone who already knows about F1, then we won't go anywhere. The young engineers are all about computers and nothing else. They calculate the set-up of the car on the computer, they give it to the driver to test, you then complain so they give you another half of a degree to the wing to personalize the car. But they can't do much else." He added, "It's probably true that you can't change much with the grooved tires, but you are bursting with ideas. If you work with an expert engineer, he will condition you to the way that he wants to set up the car. On the contrary, if you stay with an inexperienced person, he's more likely to be open to new ideas and experiments. You might waste a lot of time trying out different things, but at the end you may come up with something that will help improve the overall team." Everything he said made sense then. I was coming from a championship where, thanks to this kind of open-mindedness, we were able to build on our strengths, so naturally I thought Head's idea was excellent.

However, I had my first doubts during that Spanish test when I realized how the situation would be in Formula 1, only two sets of Bridgestone tires a day (Bridgestone being the only supplier); two tests on a circuit like Barcelona, where in the morning you can go a second to a second-and-a-half faster than in the afternoon. That's when the temperature rises; the heat quickly ruins the tires, making it almost useless to try new solutions. I quickly learned that having the right set-up from the beginning was the way to go. I spoke about this with Patrick Head who said, "We'll see." He was so excited about his own ideas that he didn't want to listen to anybody else.

I also wasn't very impressed with the cars. The engines were much less powerful and the cars are lighter than CART, making it easier to skid out of the slow corners. When the car is put into fifth or sixth gear on the straights, it simply doesn't shift, whereas the CART cars would continue to accelerate. I also didn't like having such a light car in fast corners, when the faster you entered, the greater would be the grip generated by the wing load. Basically, it's like being on a railway track where the only thing to do is to steer. On the other hand, the car was difficult to handle in the slow corners. You had to stop and make the car turn, and with grooved tires, you were always sliding and failing to grip the track surface. The grooved tires made it a bit like driving on a road covered with sand; you can't feel the car gripping and taking the corner, and therefore giving the sensation of being on the limit. If you push the car, the limit moves farther out; if you don't push, it is still there.

Formula 1 cars were notorious for sliding, so for a driver like me who is used to an aggressive but polished style, it was torture. I tried to slow down to make the tires grip better, but they wouldn't. The right way to drive was to enter the corner, accelerating even if the front of the car started understeering; then as the speed increased, let the back of the car start oversteering so it balanced out the understeer and somehow you came out of the corner. By then I had huge doubts, but I had made my choice, and I didn't want to admit it to myself.

Juan Pablo Montoya was at Barcelona that day. He was the test driver for Williams and hoped to become the official driver, but they told him that they had hired me. At that point, they wanted me to team with someone who had Formula 1 experience. They thought about Ralf Schumacher, although it wasn't official. They told Montoya that they would try to convince Ganassi to take him on. Frank believed so much in the Colombian that he even offered to sponsor him, so Chip agreed and Montoya was loaned to him.

I returned to Houston with Ganassi and Morris, who had come to Barcelona with me. We returned by Concorde and then took Chip's jet directly to Houston. During practice I crashed the car four times due to a gear problem. The first two times the nose came off, and the third time a suspension broke, but we were able to repair it in time for the qualifying. I had a fantastic time in the first lap of the qualifying, but then I crashed again on the second lap. I still managed to start fifth on the grid and regain a few positions during the race, but then it started to rain. I defended myself well enough and was second behind Franchitti, but the race was stopped due to the downpour.

There were 15 days before the Australian CART race, so I took the time to go to Padova. I traveled from the West Coast time zone, to the European and then to Australia in just ten days. Niccolò helped keep me awake because he never seemed to sleep. Even at five years old, he sleeps less than we do and recovers very quickly from jet lag. Whereas most children nap, he doesn't, and he's always been like this. We tried everything, including changing his milk, but he still didn't sleep. I even tried making a contraption from the cord of my bathrobe to rock him to sleep, but that only lasted a couple of nights. In order to let Daniela rest, I would stay up all night in the dark with Niccolò, cuddling him until he fell asleep. During that time, I must admit that I became an expert in B-movies.

I arrived in Australia late Wednesday night. I was exhausted by the time I reached the hotel, even though I managed to get some sleep on the plane. The following morning, I woke up feeling rested and adjusted to the new time zone. During practice on Friday, I was almost a second faster than everyone. But on Saturday the engine blew and Franchitti took pole. I was convinced I had the best car and I wanted to get the best out of it during the race. My mechanics helped me a lot, sending me out ahead of everybody after the first pit stop, and I won.

On the podium, I remember thinking that it could have been my last victory at that level. That evening, Jimmy, Greg Moore, Franchitti, Max Papis and Kenny (a friend of Jimmy's) came to pick me up at my hotel to go to a nightclub. I really didn't want to go out and suggested a paper airplane competition instead. Everybody's competitive nature was revealed and we stayed on the hotel balcony until four in the morning, cheered on by the people down below. We went out for an hour, but were all shattered and returned to the hotel.

I returned home just before my 32nd birthday on October 23, 1998. Ganassi called me one afternoon. "Alex, I need you to help out Montoya." They had planned to test him at Homestead as my replacement. The last race of the season was in seven days at Fontana, California. If I didn't go immediately, I would soon be too busy working with Firestone and Honda. This meant being away for 15 days instead of a week, but Chip insisted. "You have to do this favor for me because Montoya is scared shitless of the ovals." This was the least that I could do for Chip, so I agreed. I reluctantly told Daniela, who was not very happy.

When I arrived at Fontana, the only thing that I really helped with was a mistake in the car set up which was causing problems with the front wing. This had been set-up with a negative incidence but had not been given enough turns. Instead of giving it three degrees, they'd taken off three degrees. I corrected that and handed it over to Montoya with some fatherly advice. "Don't be afraid of speed; start cautiously and keep to the racing line," and so on. During the third lap of the test, he had the car sideways while entering the turn at 185 mph. Right then, I realized that he was very talented and would soon be winning races. Maybe he wouldn't need my driving lessons after all.

But I have to admit that Montoya pissed me off a bit. The Americans always tell you the same thing when you race on an oval for the first time, "There are two types of drivers, those who have crashed against the wall, and those who will crash." Montoya is the only driver who could have driven for two years and not crashed, but he eventually did, at St. Louis during the second year with Ganassi. He must not have been paying attention, because he'd never crashed before except during an accident with Andretti. He clearly had superior control of the car and did incredibly well on an oval. Even at very high speeds, he was able to predict a move and correct it before anything untoward happened.

I was happy to offer my services to Chip Ganassi. After my family and my parents, I am most grateful to Chip and wish that I had told him how much he impacted on my life. Needless to say, I went to drive my last race for him with a heavy heart. Even though I didn't win, it was the best race in my whole three years of CART. Jimmy, after a nasty accident in Australia, had lost his second place in the championship to Franchitti. He was rather depressed because he wanted to come in second after me, but this was impossible because Franchitti would have to pull out of the race and Jimmy would have to take his place. Before the race, we agreed not to block each other.

Joe Montana, the famous football quarterback, came with other personalities to chat with us before the race. Chip, with his usual theatrics, pointed at Jimmy and me. "You two guys do what you want, but I don't want to see "Michigan 2—The Revenge." Don't get caught up fighting each other and then end up giving the race away." This comment was somewhat prophetic because during the last three laps, Jimmy, Greg Moore and I were racing to win. I told Chip, "You're right, Chip, the situation is slightly different than Michigan. I've already had my moment of glory and won, and so now I'd be happy to help my teammate win, but there is a slight difference here—the winner gets $1,000,000. You win regardless because you get 50 percent of who ever wins, but it makes a big difference to us."

Jimmy then suggested, "Alex, if you let me win I will divide the prize money with you." I added, "That's not quite right. Why should I give up 25 percent and slow down if I'm winning? The one who always has something to gain is Chip—only if you and I block each other does he lose his 50 percent, so why doesn't he share the risk with us? If we don't block each other, then we all three should divide the prize." Ganassi, who had invited everyone to the meeting, was thrown off guard. Bob Ulrich, the chairman of Target, intervened. "This is very fair and shows the spirit of the team which we are happy to sponsor." But Chip was redder than the Target logo.

Those were 500 miles of suffering for both of us. We had to fight against the set-up of our cars, which prevented us from being among the leaders. Jimmy was the first to find a solution to modify the car during the pit stops. Halfway through the race, he was back in the lead. I was still trying to find the problem and had been lapped twice, when Morris pulled something out of his hat. I was complaining about the low speed in the straights and he, contrary to what anyone else would have done, started loading the car by substituting the Gurney flap, an angled piece on the trailing edge of the rear wing.

Luckily, Morris was right as usual. I stopped losing ground and started passing the drivers who had overtaken me not long before. I was able to take the turns much faster and my top speed at the end of the straights improved as a result of taking the turns more effectively. In addition, Chip called me in for pit stops exactly at the right time. He kept me on the track during some neutralizations while the majority of the drivers were stopping for fuel. It sounds easy, but the timing requires a lot of intuition and luck. On that occasion, things worked out for the best and we recovered a race that we were convinced had been compromised.

There were only a few laps to go with four of us left, Tracy, Moore, Vasser and me. Five laps from the end, there was a restart after another yellow flag; Tracy, who was leading, tried to surprise everyone with a sudden acceleration. But it went horribly wrong and he lost control of the car, smashing into a wall on the inside of the track. The officials stopped the race again with another yellow flag, but the race was already coming to an end. Chip called me on the radio. "The officials have decided on a green and white flag together." This particular combination meant that we would restart the race at the beginning of the last lap; 500 miles were boiled down to one lap. Moore was leading, followed by Jimmy and me. At the beginning of the last passage, we fanned open— Jimmy on the outside and me on the inside—and passed Greg after he "offered" us his slipstream, but did not have any intention of giving up. Jimmy very kindly took Turn One in the center so that I could take the turn fast and enter the straight in his slipstream. The usual practice would be to go on the outside and cut down to the inside, forcing the driver behind you to slow down. The driver in front has the clean air and while you understeer and have to slow down, he can accelerate. Instead, Jimmy left me the clean air to the inside. I could have tried to pass him, but I saw Greg gaining on me from the outside. He could have possibly passed us both, so I widened my trajectory, entering the stream of dirty air that Jimmy had behind him. The car understeered and I moved to the outside, taking Moore with me. This forced me to let up on the accelerator and Vasser took off into the distance. In the last straight, Greg was able to pass me but Jimmy was now too far ahead, and I remember how happy I was to see my teammate and friend go on to win a fantastic victory.

I have asked myself how could I be so happy despite not winning the race. I've always been so competitive and always wanted to win and beat everybody. But we had such an incredible relationship, strengthened by three years of working together, and therefore had enormous respect and loyalty for each other. Jimmy won the $1,000,000 and also took second place in the championship.

For days we celebrated like crazy at his house in Las Vegas, hardly sleeping at all. All our usual buddies were there, Papis, Franchitti, and Moore, with whom I had that famous billiards match. One night we went to a popular amusement ride in Las Vegas. After being strapped in a seat 160 yards up, you're catapulted into the sky at an incredible speed. It was the most terrifying thing that I've ever done. I've flown in Navy jets, driven several racing cars, but that was the most indescribable emotion, as had been my three years in CART.

CHAPTER 12

A Return to Formula 1

I had reached an agreement with Williams before arriving in Cleveland, but was told to keep quiet about it. Then a few days later, the news broke in *Autosport*, a weekly English magazine. Obviously, Ganassi knew I was leaving, but he was waiting for the right moment to tell the sponsors officially. This put him in a very awkward position and I felt badly about causing him any distress. I don't like to lie, so when the U.S. journalists asked if I had been talking to Williams, I confirmed I had, but that nothing had been signed. I said that if I were going to return to Formula 1, I would be honored to race for Williams, but I was in Cleveland to race and wanted to concentrate precisely on that.

It was a difficult weekend and I thought a lot about what I was leaving behind. I kept justifying my decision and telling myself that maybe I needed more time to think. But the truth was that I'd had plenty of time and had thought carefully about my decision—it was the right thing to do. When the season was over, I went home for good. Soon after Niccolò's birth, we moved to our new house in Monte Carlo. It was a lovely big place with plenty of room for a baby. I still remember the day that we arrived in the empty house with the baby crying in my arms ....

The relationship with the new team started slowly. I had my first test at Barcelona with experienced engineer Craig Wilson. He had been assigned to Ralf Schumacher, who had finally been chosen as my teammate. Wilson was very good, but was always skeptical about my ideas, regardless of my enthusiasm. In fact, there was very little for me to contribute, which convinced Patrick Head that his decision to partner me with an inexperienced engineer was the right one. "As long as we think like this, we will achieve nothing. Alex comes from a different championship and has new ideas—he's certainly an open-minded driver who wants to look for new and unusual solutions. If we give him someone like Wilson, who keeps telling him that nothing will work, we will go nowhere. Even if nine out of ten of his suggestions don't work, it's worth it if one does." So instead they gave me Greg Wheeler, a South African technician with zero Formula 1 experience who came from GT Racing.

From a practical point of view Wilson was right; it was very difficult to invent anything new, especially that year. Bridgestone was supplying the same tires for everybody and therefore there was very little development and absolutely no variation. The tire was extremely inconsistent. It had horrendous degradation in its performance from the first lap to the fourth. Once a tire was in this condition, it was impossible to keep the car on the track. It is also very difficult to develop a car with such tires. As soon as you mount four new tires and establish a lap time, then make changes and go out again, you end up losing a second just because of the tires. One can never determine if the changes are correct. This experience made me realize that Craig was right and I should have simply adapted my driving style to the optimal car set-up as indicated by the ultra-modern computer simulation.

My job should have been to exploit the new tires, do my best during the qualifying lap and focus on moving towards the front of the grid—this would have made everybody happy. Instead, I made the mistake that cost me the season. I was exhausted after a challenging championship and my wife's difficult pregnancy, and wanted to stay home with Daniela and Niccolò. I had become a father and was desperate for a more normal lifestyle. I didn't want to travel after having just returned from three years of what felt like military service in the United States. Now when I go back to the States, I feel much more at ease. I was so caught up in racing that I didn't have time to appreciate my experience ... how I would love to relive it again.

I also had to spend a lot of energy building a new relationship with the team, and found myself defending my opinion with Patrick Head. After a couple of tests I told him, "Patrick, thinking about it, perhaps an inexperienced engineer is a big mistake. I need someone who already knows how to set up the car so that I can focus on racing—otherwise it will be disastrous. The car is sliding as soon as I enter the corner, I decelerate and wait for the car to squat down, but that never happens because of the grooved tires. If my engineer is experimenting and switches the front springs to the rear during every pit stop, I will never go anywhere." He didn't agree with me and told me to wait, and then I did the most ridiculous thing—I compromised, exactly when I should have insisted on my views. That wouldn't have been difficult, as at that time I was still The Alex Zanardi with two championship titles at a time when Williams had to think long and hard about the last time they'd won a race. I was still highly respected and should have fought for what I believed. All I really needed to do was hop on a plane and go to England, spend three or four days in the factory talking through my ideas, and I would have found a different set-up. Perhaps I wouldn't have found the road to victory, but the journey would have been a lot less painful for everybody.

Instead I sat back and waited for things to happen. I can't say that I'm an entirely humble person, but I am open-minded and if you convince me that you're right, I'm the first person to change my mind and jump on board. I didn't have to be right as a matter of pride, but perhaps I backed down too easily and I paid the price for it. The world of Formula 1 is incredibly fast. A race is gone, then two, then three. At the fourth race, at Imola, I spoke to Patrick again. "Patrick, we need to do something about the situation before it's too late." He replied, "We'll see what we can do," but I could tell from his eyes that he was no longer seeing The Alex Zanardi. I had simply become another struggling driver who was being beaten by his teammate. At that point I realized the trust was fading for my main ally, Patrick. I didn't have the energy or tenacity to rectify the situation, which was clearly heading in the wrong direction. The result was a season spent chasing after the other drivers with just a few positive moments. Moreover, my car was always, always breaking down. On 18 different occasions during the 1999 season, I had a problem with the differential gear during the determining moments of qualifying or the race. This problem completely affected and altered my apprenticeship and my results.

I was always handed a car with an unbalanced set-up, and inevitably something would break after three laps. I would miss the whole session while trying to solve the problem, then go out again only to find that the car was still set up incorrectly and that I had lost a half a second. During the entire season, there were only a few occasions when things went well, as at Spa or Monza.

On the starting grid at Spa, my car broke down and I was forced to use Ralf Schumacher's test car. After a great start, I kept up with him in a car that was set up for him. This confirmed that Craig Wilson's computer simulation was capable of setting up the car correctly, and that I needed to adapt to it rather than trying to change the car. I could have finished in fifth place, but there was a problem in my pit stop with the refueling apparatus and insufficient fuel went into the tank the first time around. So I had to refuel again, finishing in eighth.

At Monza, I performed closer to my expectations for the season. The Monza circuit had just been resurfaced with new asphalt which allowed excellent drainage and minimal spray in the case of rain. That asphalt was also not very abrasive so the tire degradation was better. They lasted longer and performed more consistently. You could start with a new set of tires and over the course of 40 laps you would only lose half a second. In two days of testing, we were able to thoroughly and effectively test the car two weeks before the actual race. We evaluated several modifications and the consistency of the tires gave us a clearer picture of what was working and what was not. I obtained fourth place on the grid with that car—the best qualifying performance for Williams for the entire year, and clearly the opposite of my performance on the other circuits.

How could I have done so poorly on the other circuits and then performed so well at Monza? It didn't make sense, and I can't say that I knew the track very well. It's all just theories. If you want to row against the current, you can find many ways to do it, but you can find just as many ways to row with the current. I believe that the truth always lies somewhere in the middle. That year, my technician and I were unprepared to set up the car. But when we had the time and the particular situation to properly adjust the set-up, we realized that we weren't that far from the others. In particular, I found I went better when John Russell looked after my car, but then he left to go to Jaguar.

I started so well that I could have passed Mika Häkkinen, who was on pole, but he blocked me, and I didn't think it wise to be sent off the track at the first corner. I was running second, but after Frentzen passed me on the first lap I realized that something was wrong. The car was touching the asphalt after I apparently hit a curb, but I don't remember at all. Frentzen later told Patrick that I hit the curb so badly, that it seemed that I did on it on purpose. You do that all the time on Monza's curbs anyway. What actually happened was that the car's undertray was accidentally left loose during mounting. Despite this, I was able to stay behind Frentzen during the first 17 laps, leaving Ralf well behind me.

I was hoping the car would stop touching the ground once the tires warmed up and had reached the optimal pressure. This never happened, but at least I held on to my position. The undertray was literally falling off and when I heard a rumble from the car's belly. I could see in the rear mirrors the black dust of the carbon wearing out. This slowed me down on the straight and eliminated the ground effect, which was critical in the corners.

In the meantime, Ralf was right behind me. "He's blocking me!" he shouted to the team. They said that I should let him pass, but I pretended that I couldn't hear them because of radio interference. But when I realized that I was actually slowing him down and blocking him, I let him pass.

Frentzen won, Ralf had a glorious second place finish after Häkkinen had spun out, and I was forced to throw away a great opportunity. Maybe if my car hadn't broken, I would have been a threat to Frentzen … I was certainly faster than Ralf. What a difference between that race and the rest of the season. I believe that the only difference was in the reliability of the car—at least until it broke down—and that Monza surface which allowed me to find a set-up that I liked. If Wheeler had had a few years of experience behind him, perhaps we could have achieved the same set-up simply using the computer simulation. I was seventh at the end of the 1999 Italian Grand Prix, just short of getting a point. I wish that I could say that the season went on with more highs and lows, but unfortunately it was all lows.

I had a contract with Williams for three years. At the beginning of the negotiations, Frank suggested two years plus one with a bilateral option. This meant that if the team didn't perform well, I could pull out, and vice versa. I told him that if we didn't believe in one another, we could simply sign a two-year contract. I reminded myself that I didn't force their hand, they had sought me out and offered me a fantastic contract. Frank eventually wanted a three-year contract with no option. At the end of that horrible season, I felt I had to do something to sort out the situation. They'd made a huge investment in me and honestly, there were people inside the team who hadn't done anything to make the investment worthwhile. A few people in the team thought that CART drivers had little to offer, but over the years, they had to save face and admit that it wasn't the case. In 2001, they hired Montoya, whom Ralf Schumacher had always criticized.

Ralf had always been horrendous to me. Unfortunately, he thinks that he destroyed me both on and off the track, but the truth is he never understood a thing. Perhaps he should have had more confidence, because he is a very good driver. However, in seeing how manipulative he was, I realized how weak he actually was. His attitude didn't influence me at all—what influenced me was the mistakes the team and I both made, and my overall relationship with the team. Throughout this, Ralf was unbearable. He never missed the opportunity to throw salt in a wound or make sarcastic and cutting comments. He loved to say that Montoya, who was winning in CART at the time, was a "nobody in a championship that anybody could win." He also said that Montoya was only a test driver for Williams and not very impressive at that. James Robinson, then the chief engineer, had to explain to Schumacher that Montoya was really respected. Maybe this isn't any of my business, but I was delighted when Montoya joined the team and beat Ralf on many occasions.

The end of 1999 had seriously compromised the situation. I was lacking the determination that had helped me persevere through other difficult times in my career. The general atmosphere also contributed to this. Ganassi was particularly good at being supportive and exuding a particular enthusiasm. Although I can't complain about Frank Williams, I spoke to him a few times and he never complained about how much I was being paid for not doing much. I started to see in his eyes that he was questioning what "we" were doing wrong, and that by "we" he obviously meant me. I left Williams without providing an answer and I still feel badly because I would have loved to have done well for him. I don't think he doubted my talent, as he was always convinced the team hadn't exploited my strengths, but I didn't find a way either. Something was missing in the magic formula, but I'm sure he was one of the few who didn't whisper, "He won everything in America because he was racing against nobodies, but he didn't stand a chance in Formula 1 because all the drivers are good." Despite everything, I was eventually offered another year with the team, which I'm certain was all thanks to Frank.

Autosport was already suggesting before Suzuka, the last race of the 1999 season, that I would still be substituted regardless of my signed contract. In my last grand prix I'd qualified only 16th, but I was up to 9th place by the Spoon Curve on the first lap; then the electrics quit. At the end of the Japanese Grand Prix, we all said goodbye and we didn't speak about it again.

Then one day Frank called me. "Alex, what are we going to do about the situation? We need to discuss it and sort it out." I knew they were hoping that I'd be the one to ask for an agreement; it would have suited them financially for me to make the first move. During the winter, they tried to force my hand. They sent me to Birmingham to meet the sponsors. The journalists, fueled by rumors, asked what I was planning for the following year. The British Fleet Street journalists are notorious for provoking false statements out of you. They asked things like, "What does Williams expect from you? Your car was always broken and you were obviously treated differently from Schumacher." They were trying to frustrate me so that I'd reveal the truth.

I wasn't new to the business and knew exactly what the team was up to, but I had a contract and was intending to fulfill it. During the winter, the team didn't do anything to help. I just wanted them to say something like, "Let's roll up our sleeves and see if we can make things work." The facts followed the rumors. Williams started testing other drivers like Darren Manning, Jenson Button and Bruno Junquiera, while Ralf Schumacher, already confirmed for 2000, was constantly in the car. Meanwhile, I had the impression that they were sending journalists to me to trap me into saying something damaging. Only once they had finished the tests and found a new driver, were they ready for a new season of transition. The team started a new relationship with BMW to supply the engines. They were expecting a challenging season with lots of difficulties, but it wasn't like that because the engine proved to be very reliable and powerful.

A few weeks before the 2000 World Championship, I received a message to fly to England for a meeting with Frank Williams. Patrick Head, who was also there, had spent the winter making snide comments about me. "Zanardi has realized that it's a tough business. Instead of shaving his head and starting to work, he just made lots of coffees and joked around with the guys, and thus the situation never improved." They clearly wanted me to quit.

Patrick kept his eyes down almost the entire time, afraid of what he would say if he looked at me. So Frank did all of the talking, "We've thought about the situation very carefully. Last year there were some circumstances which didn't work, but if you really want it, and you're ready to get down to business and are convinced that we should continue, then we're happy to." I was incredibly pissed off and told him what I really thought, "Frank, the whole season has been a joke. You completely lost faith in me after only the fourth race. You were looking forward to the season to finish. You were certain that, for one reason or another, I wouldn't survive the conflicts. During the winter you criticized me whenever possible and waited for me to throw in the towel. You fed me to the journalists while you were out testing potential replacements for me. Now you realize that there is no one that great out there, and that it's more expensive than you thought to break my contract, so you're now trying to get me to do it." They had already proposed a financial solution to get out of the contract, of which I reminded them.

I continued, "You came forward with a ridiculous proposal and immediately abandoned it, and then moved on to a more vicious approach. But now that the new engine will require you to spend more time in the pits next year, you've decided that perhaps it's not worth substituting me. I understand that in every business, people are out for themselves. I'm ready to stay this year but if I do, I'm also staying the next. If you really want to motivate me, don't treat me like an idiot by saying that you're 'giving me another chance.' This is bullshit. You're keeping me because you can't afford to go down another route. So just tell me the truth. You don't trust me as a driver anymore, and this is the most logical thing to do. Tell me the truth that it's up to me to change your mind during the season. But most of all, tell me that when you chose to invest in me a year ago, you should have helped me as much as possible in order to motivate me."

Like a saturated riverbank, I was ready to burst. "Are you ready to ask me what I need to race a better season? How I'd like to structure the team? What type of test before the first race? What type of engineer do I need? If you did this, it would be irrelevant whether you're convinced that I'm fast enough. Obviously, I would love to have people next to me who can manage a smile and believe in me, but I realize that this is not possible at the moment. If you give me what I need and I can't race a good season, then you're right—that means that I am, indeed, just a complete bust. This is how you motivate me. If nothing changes, I'll still come and race on Sunday, and I'll try to do my best, but this is not the way to race. If you have passion, you can do well, but if it's a sacrifice, it's a complete waste of time. You decide, because it's not up to me at all. It is ridiculous that you're putting this on my shoulders, hoping that I'm so frustrated that I'll quit. The easier option would be to quit, but I don't see why I should do it. You wasted a season, but I came all the way from the United States where I was a super driver. And now after just one season, I'm good for nothing but picking zucchinis!"

On my way back from England, I met Daniele Audetto from Arrows, who asked me to call him. He said that they really respected me and that the Zanardi they saw at Williams was definitely not the real Zanardi. There is no way he could have known I was in a delicate position with Williams, nor could the timing be worse, because I'd have been a fool to offer Frank an escape route. My lawyer explained to me that there were certain legal complications which forced me to hold my position. So I was ready to race again and honor my contract. The only other option would be for Williams to get rid of me and then agree on a good exit clause. The day after the meeting, Frank called and was very honest. "Alessandro. You're right. I realized that the divide is too big and there's not enough time to repair it, so it is better that we go our separate ways and we let the lawyers get on with it."

It was only a matter of time before the lawyers reached a compromise. I'm not angry with Patrick Head—at least he took responsibility for his comments—but he often fails to think before speaking. Anyway I made a mistake and should have fought harder, but equally, they never motivated or infused me. As soon as the season began, and I crashed in Australia because of a problem with erratic brake balance, it was clear that they thought they'd bought a lemon and couldn't care less about how to get rid of me.

This attitude really surprised me. I went to Williams because I was convinced I had chosen a team with little politics, who cared less about appearances and more about the substance and the technical aspect of racing. Even with his disability, Frank went all the way to the United States to find me, which really impressed me. In addition, the BMW program had just been announced, which also gave me high hopes for the future. I knew that it would be difficult in the beginning, but I could have grown with the team. I was right about the BMW engine, which in my opinion is now one of the most powerful engines in Formula 1. If there is anything that's keeping the team from winning, it's the chassis. Anyway, Williams was destined to be a winning project—it was just a matter of time. I had really hoped to be part of this success story, but that never happened.

CHAPTER 13

A Sabbatical and Back to CART

So the Williams relationship ended badly. Although we reached an agreement and they paid me off accordingly, they played on my fears of not having a team for the following year. I was really disappointed by what happened, which affected my passion for racing. This, together with the fact that I wasn't under any great financial pressure, encouraged me to take a sabbatical for a year and think about my future.

In 2000, I decided to dedicate my time to my family, even though a few newspapers and magazines, including *Autosport*, said that it was a forced sabbatical as part of my agreement. It was my choice—a choice that began a very good period in my life.

I still remember how emotional I was when I returned from Japan and saw my son's room adorned in my honor. It was a couple of days after my birthday and Daniela and Titano had painted a lovely sign on the side of Niccolò's crib, "Happy Birthday Papà." In the photo, it looked like Niccolò was trying to hold the sign. I remember that I felt many things … from one point of view, I was delighted at the sweet present, but at the same time, I was sad to think how many wonderful moments like this I had lost without really appreciating them. I spent my birthday on the road and wasn't home even on Niccolò's first birthday.

I bought myself a boat, which I named *Hakuna Matata I*. I divided my days between my son, my wife and my boat. I spent hours changing the boat's oil, sanding the hull, cleaning the decks, oiling the teak wood, and making the holes to mount the tender.

I did everything that I loved and which would help me to think about anything other than racing. It may seem banal, but I really needed it, just as I needed to see Niccolò growing up, and needed to leave the luggage in the closet for a while, and wear a dirty tracksuit for three days in a row. My only duties were to visit the boat and to spend time with my friends. Those were excellent months to recharge my battery, but perhaps it wasn't the right time to make that lifestyle a definitive one.

I was slowly getting frustrated about wasting time, and worrying that one day, when I'm 50 or 60 years old, I'd say, "I had the world at my feet, everyone wanted me to drive and instead, I cleaned a boat and went grocery shopping when I could have been racing the best cars in the world." I started considering every CART team who'd called me about racing the next year. I said "maybe" when my brain wasn't completely clear. I wanted to be the center of attention again, to feel that I was still someone after such a difficult, soul-destroying season.

I felt better being courted by these teams and didn't want it to stop. I didn't have the courage to say, "Don't call me for at least four or five months." I started wavering. "Let's see, I'm not certain, I have to think about it ...." I was afraid to get my suitcase out of the closet, but also afraid that I'd regret it if I didn't. I didn't give myself enough time to reflect and instead, spent the whole year unfairly messing the various teams around. I spoke with Barry Green, who wanted me to drive the Motorola car which later went to Michael Andretti. He'd even organized a super team for me. I was primarily talking to Chip, who called me as soon as he heard that I was on the market. "Let's do a deal right away." But I think that he was being pushed by Target because he seemed to lack the conviction to take me back. He knew me well and suspected that I wasn't terribly motivated. Although I would have found the stimulus that I needed in his team, I knew his instinct about me was right. Chip tested the waters, but I made it clear that I didn't want to race, by asking for such a ridiculous amount of money. I am embarrassed about this, but I'm human and make mistakes like the next guy. At the time I thought that just because I was "Zanardi," everyone would make way for me on the track and I would sail through every race. But that wasn't the case. It was about working hard with a team—one that had the right equipment—and working hard to win. Ganassi had changed the engine supplier to Toyota, and I started saying some absurd things. "If Toyota wants a driver like me, they'll have to make a contribution. I realize that you want to pay me a huge amount—which Target is coughing up—but Toyota should help you out."

Nothing I said really stacked up. In fact, the only thing that did make sense was that I didn't want to race anymore, but I was the last one to figure it out. I remember that Jimmy called me and shouted angrily, "Alex, you're a pain in the ass. Just convince yourself that you don't want to race and get it over with!" His words entered one ear and went out the other. I was really convinced that they were the ones who didn't understand.

Even Carl Haas and Paul Newman, the owners of one of the strongest CART teams, would have done anything to have got me, but I missed my chance and they took on Cristiano Da Matta instead. Carl told me, "If only you'd decided before. I took on Da Matta because he's a fast driver but with all due respect to him, I would have preferred to have hired you." Their choice of Da Matta famously proved to be a winner. In September I went to watch the race at Fontana, and discovered that all the teams were almost complete—exactly what I needed to put the fire under my feet. My friends and brother-in-law encouraged me to go back to racing and not to give up at 34 years of age, while my wife, on the other hand, kept a religious silence. Maybe should she have said something, but she is far too intelligent a woman to have put pressure on me to stop. She, understandably, has her own agenda, but she'd learned from the last time, when the press said that I went back to Formula 1 to please my wife (which wasn't true), that I had to make up my own mind. I wanted to race in grand prix because I was looking for a new challenge, and was convinced I could win as easily there as I did in the United States. And yes, I really wanted to return to Europe.

I left Fontana feeling very discouraged, realizing that I had probably lost any opportunity that I may have had because of my indecisiveness. The head of the sports projects for Honda in the United States, Mr. Asaka, tried to find an alternative for me. Morris Nunn had created a team using Honda engines. Honda wanted Jimmy Vasser to be the second driver to Tony Kanaan, who had already been hired. Honda always respected Jimmy because he was the first driver to have steered them to a U.S. Championship, but they were trying to squeeze a deal out of him because they knew he didn't have any other offers. When Jimmy got fed up with Honda, he accepted an offer from Pat Patrick. Honda was annoyed because Jimmy never gave them a clear justification for his choice.

Morris called me at home and confided in me that the negotiations with Jimmy were over, and that I was Honda's only alternative. It had been reported that I'd refused to drive the second car for Morris because I didn't want to steal Jimmy's job. At that point, I played the game but said I wouldn't go for free. For some strange reason, I knew that I would win 21 out of the 21 races for Honda, and therefore they would have to pay a hell of a lot for it—for the image, for the package, and for guaranteed results. I asked for a hefty amount of money and was surprised that Morris could suddenly find a huge wad of cash for a famous driver, when only moments before he didn't have enough money for two cars. I'm convinced that at that point, Honda stepped up to the plate to get Zanardi. At the end of the week, Morris called me back. "We've got the money and can sign the contract."

Faced with the reality of going back to racing, I started thinking about the famous suitcase in the closet. I called Jimmy, who revealed that Patrick was now pulling out of his deal. I felt terrible that I had taken the place of my beloved friend. I immediately turned to Mr. Asaka, but he said Jimmy's behavior had destroyed any chance that he would have had with Honda. I explained to him that it wasn't Jimmy's fault, but he didn't listen. Fortunately, Jimmy and Patrick resolved their issues and signed their agreement three days later; I was so relieved. More good news arrived when Morris told me he would be my chief engineer and that he would be returning to live in Indianapolis. I was thrilled to keep the relationship with Honda, and have always been very proud to race with their engines. Realizing I had a good car, a good team, and a very experienced engineer, I decided to sign.

I few hours later, I started having doubts again. That's when Daniela realized that it wasn't a game anymore. "I never told you because I didn't want to influence your choice, but I really hoped that things wouldn't work out. The last thing that I wanted was to see you race on the ovals again." Then she started crying. I had a big lump in my throat, but managed to pull myself together, saying, "I can't give into this pressure, because I'll only regret not doing what I want to do." I'm happy I started racing again, despite everything that happened. I'm not saying this to justify a decision which cost me my legs, but because it's the truth—and I have to honor that. I am telling my story to show that drivers are not machines, but men, with both good and bad feelings. For people who want to know my story, I'm revealing moments that show all my weaknesses, fears and limitations.

At the end, I rediscovered my conviction and went head first into racing again. My agreement with Morris was very precise: "The most important thing for me is not to wear myself out. I don't want to go back to the suitcase feeling nauseous. I want to race for you, but we must both be honest about our expectations, and if it's not enough, you have to say so right away and we won't sign. I can practice and race for you, and move to America during the summer. I will commute in the first and last part of the year from our home in Monaco. I've looked at the calendar, and I know I can do it. In terms of marketing, I can offer you ten sponsor appearances—four completely free and six linked to a race or a test. This way, the marketing responsibilities will not infringe too much on my free time. If the sponsors want me, I'd expect them to cooperate." He later relayed my position to everybody and said that there were no problems. He only added, "If there are some marketing activities on the Thursday before the race, would these be considered special appearances?" I refused. "I'm not afraid to sign autographs or shake hands, but I simply want to limit the traveling as much as possible to organize my life in Europe, as well as race as best I can." They accepted enthusiastically.

That year, 2001, CART had introduced a new rule stopping test sessions during the season in order to limit the costs and reduce the amount of traveling. If there were 15 days between one race activity and the next, there would now be plenty of time to make it back to Nice in time for breakfast with my son the next day. If there was an appearance or practice four days later, then it's impossible to travel home and return 48 hours later. The new rule about the test sessions played an important and final role in my decision.

The first practice in Sebring didn't go that well. For the first time, we had decided not to practice on the ovals during the winter. The same rule about testing said that each driver could only spend ten days testing during the course of the year. On the ovals, it's the car's behavior, not the driver's, which really dictates the results. I had to rediscover how the car felt, but I didn't have to relearn how to drive. I was convinced that when I found the synergy with the car, I'd automatically remember how to drive on the ovals. In addition, the first part of the season was on city circuits, which are more demanding on the steering wheel and require you to be very fit. It was difficult for me after a year of inactivity and I was convinced that testing on road courses during the winter would accelerate the process of getting fit.

In Sebring, things were different from my years with Ganassi. With Chip's team, our engines would never break down. This was because a team had worked together for many years to find the right cohesion. In the end, you create a harmony which brings results. In contrast, Morris's young organization had several weak points, including a car that was often set up incorrectly because someone thought that someone else should have done the work, and vice versa. Many times, the car would stop because of brake problems, and we couldn't understand why. Then in the evening, the car was dismantled, the engine changed and the following day, it would run perfectly well. We would spend a whole day working on the brakes to solve a problem, ignoring the set-up, only to find out that the problem was linked to the assembly. We would change the engine and like magic, everything was all right again. This happened all the time ... simply inexplicable.

Several things didn't go the way they should have. Morris spent more time in the motorhome than in the pits, dealing with numerous calls from the sponsors. I realized he was no longer my race engineer, but now the team owner with other responsibilities. This was most obvious when we were at the circuit. In addition, he was still living in Florida and during the week, he was always going back to play golf.

It was difficult to reconcile Morris's life in Florida and his obligations to me. He did not realize we were having problems and kept repeating, "Don't worry, you're just getting your confidence back with the car, but I have no doubt that at the first race, you'll be where you should be."

There was also another big problem—my teammate, Tony Kanaan. He was very fast and had only one gear in his head—the sixth gear. Only the sixth! He always pushed to the maximum during testing, as if he were in qualifying. If he didn't have the best lap time, he would most certainly have the second best. Morris assumed we had an excellent car, despite the fact that I was telling him the exact opposite. I didn't go for super times, but I wasn't in a crisis either; I was just three or four tenths slower than Tony, which often gave him first position during testing.

Winter went by without convincing me the system was working. I could see that Morris's mind was somewhere else; he didn't even take notes about what we were doing to the car set-up. Jim Anderson, an extremely capable mechanic, had arrived, but had only ever worked on shock absorbers. Notepad in hand, he was very pleased to be Morris's new apprentice. "I write down everything that happens so that at the end of the year, I'll have so much experience that I'll be able to substitute for the great Morris."

Nearing the start of the championship, I had to confront Morris about the fact that things weren't going well. I mentioned that he was never around and that we had to start from scratch every time. There was no clear line of command, and we were never able to go from one practice to the next starting from a better point. We stood firmly on opposite grounds, but he kept repeating the same thing, "Don't worry, you'll see that everything will go well and we won't have any problems." At that point I had the courage to say, "Either you seriously commit to this or put me with Jim Anderson. Maybe he doesn't have a lot of experience, but he's in the workshop every day and really wants to do well." To my dismay, Morris was very nonchalant. "If you want to work with Jim, I have absolutely no problem."

This proved once and for all that Morris didn't really understand what the problem was. I was just trying to provoke him, but his response confirmed that he had lost his pride as a race engineer … he was now just the owner of the team. A confrontation like this would have offended him in the past, but he no longer felt like working directly with driver and car anymore. He still respected me, and later I would hear him defend me, despite some rather paltry racing and lackluster results, but Morris knew he was the person who lacked motivation, and so did I.

I desperately wanted some good results, but felt that people were beginning to doubt me again. After a season with Williams and a year's sabbatical, it was painful to hear things like, "He's got a wife and kid; he's got other things going on...." I certainly didn't have the same mental intensity and focus, but I knew how to compensate for my weaknesses with the help of my team. Instead, it was the team who expected me—as the most aggressive Alex ever—to pull the situation together.

Fortunately, Kanaan's team was working well, having been together for two years and thanks to an experienced engineer who was good with numbers. Jim Anderson was a very intelligent guy, but he never considered the car from a dynamic point of view. For example, he never thought of the spring in relationship with the shock absorber. He relied on graphs, which didn't take into account the driver's actual feelings, rather than the bigger picture.

During the tests at Homestead, I worked with Jim and was the fastest of all the drivers at the circuit. The situation began to turn around; I had usually been three-tenths of a second slower than Tony, but this time he was slower than me. I was particularly relaxed at that circuit at that time. It was as if I had decided to step on the accelerator right at the beginning of the season to infuse some faith and enthusiasm into everybody. But the real reason was that the car was finally working well and I was driving it the way I wanted to.

Paul Tracy had the fastest lap of the day—something like 1 minute, 7.1 seconds—but risked his life to get it. Tony Kanaan managed 1 minute, 7.2 seconds and I did 1 minute, 6.5 seconds. When I arrived in Monterey for the first race of the season, Jimmy greeted me enthusiastically. "Hey bastard, you did 1 minute, 6.5 seconds at Homestead—who's going to keep up with you?" I think that my opponents believed that sooner or later I'd make a comeback. But that wasn't justification for being overly confident, as I knew I was starting an uphill battle.

There was another new rule in CART for 2001. The participants in the first and slowest sessions of qualifying, who "clean" the track, were those ranking lowest in the championship. Obviously the order for the first race was based on their ranking in the previous year. Since I hadn't raced, I was placed last with Tony just a bit ahead of me. It went really badly for both of us; I even managed to waste my decisive set of tires in the traffic, like a rookie, and ended up in 22nd place on the grid.

During the race, I regained several positions and was fighting among the top ten until I caught up with Michael Andretti. After a double overtaking job which brought me up to the sixth place, I attacked Michael who was fifth. I came alongside him, but he resisted. We ended up taking the corner side by side and while exiting, I accelerated and spun out. My engine stalled and I had to be pushed, but only after the rest of the group had passed me. Without any traffic in front of me, I drove the fastest four laps of the race. Although the race didn't go well, there were some encouraging moments, especially for Tony who finished seventh. This meant he would qualify in the fast session at the following race in Long Beach, whereas I was stuck in the slow session.

I had big problems in Long Beach with the brakes. The car's wheels locked while entering corners and throughout the weekend, we couldn't solve the problem. Tony was particularly relaxed. He managed the best time during the free practice and was third during qualifying. In the race, after losing and regaining positions, he ended up third on the podium. I started my race with a car that looked fine, but I pulled out really quickly when Bruno Junqueria shunted me—something he never apologized for.

The car held up for a few laps, but the radiator was broken and the temperature was rising, giving me no choice but to retire. Despite my expectations, things were not going how I'd imagined.

Not only had I lost the first two of the 21 potential wins, but it was looking unlikely that I'd win any of the next 19 ....

The third race of the season was in Fort Worth, a new and very fast oval with super-elevated turns. I hadn't been on an oval for the whole winter and so I was a bit worried, but not intimidated, because that's not my character. I did my homework properly without taking any risks, and everything was going okay. I'd developed a car that I couldn't complain about and qualified fifth, the best for the Honda family.

As soon as the qualifying was over, an urgent meeting was called because some drivers were complaining about dizziness due to the lateral acceleration on that type of oval. They discussed the possibility of pulling out of the race because the doctors could not guarantee everybody's safety. A driver could race for almost 500 miles and maybe faint after 499 miles. Of course, if a driver faints at that speed, it would be a nightmare for him and anybody next to him. It sounded like pure science fiction; every category of racing, from CART to Formula 1, had sent out their drivers who risked their lives, and then suddenly, everyone was concerned about their safety.

The motivation was noble, but it created a huge mess, the tickets had been sold, spectators had booked vacations to attend, and CART had signed an agreement for this type of race. Now, they wanted to renegotiate everything after the safety issue had been brought up during qualifying. It was a bad move, one which significantly contributed to the eventual decline of the category. They studied all the possible track problems, and the limitations of the engines, but all these were different, creating enormous advantages and disadvantages. They could not strike a deal, the race was cancelled and my good qualifying time was suddenly good for nothing.

Nazareth didn't help us improve the situation. We had a decent qualifying, but the car wouldn't let me overtake or change lines during the race and therefore I couldn't take advantage of the most important weapon needed in an oval. I came in tenth, neither good nor bad.

In May 2001, at Motegi in Japan, there were a few hopes of a recovery. Morris was working on my car again, although only part-time. We were testing one of my theories that I wanted to implement for that race. It was an invention to assist the toe-in, which Morris didn't approve of because he thought it would make the car more dangerous. We started to test one step at a time. During free practice, the car started improving and before qualifying, I was halfway through what I wanted to do. Tony followed the same route and tried an even more extreme solution and came in third, where I was sixth. The prospects improved. Our cars were among the fastest during the first laps; but if you don't have the horsepower available at an oval, it is very difficult to pass. With another new rule that season, the races were becoming known as "economy runs." Everybody was trying to save fuel in order to make fewer pit stops. I finished seventh, but all the other Honda drivers lost positions because they were forced to do an extra pit stop. The Ford engines, although of inferior performance, were able to avoid the last pit stop thanks to lower fuel consumption. We went home feeling neither disillusioned nor happy.

It was time to move to Indianapolis for the summer. Daniela and I were looking for a house to rent and were willing to pay more for something special. The new owner of the house on the lake where we'd lived two years previously called me after hearing I'd returned to racing. She was tired of living outside Indianapolis and had restored a house closer to town where she wanted to live. I was asked if I was interested in buying the house on the lake, but I said no, although I was keen on renting it from June until August. Unfortunately, she ended up changing her mind and falling in love with the house herself. She was a real estate agent and knew a deal when she saw one, so she offered to let me have a house closer to town. I went to see it, loved it, and agreed to rent it without even showing it to Daniela. I offered $1,500 more per month if she would include the furniture. The owner shipped in all of the furniture, including the kitchen, bedrooms and living room.

I have to admit that I felt great when I left Europe with my family. Gianna, Daniela's mother, came with us, and I always tell her that she's "the nicest mother-in-law that I have!" Gianna, Daniela, and Niccolò were very impressed with the house. It was two stories, with a huge kitchen and living room, a master bedroom suite plus three additional bedrooms. The garden was huge and beautifully manicured, with a barbeque, swimming pool and a massive jacuzzi. The best part of the day was jumping into the jacuzzi in the evening, with an ice-cold bottle of American beer.

The swimming pool was fantastic during the humid Indianapolis summers. Niccolò loved it, and we spent entire afternoons splashing around and orchestrating tricks on Daniela. She was a good sport and played along. Thinking back to the day when I first put the key in the door, I was so proud. Daniela had given me little credit in describing the house, so I was very happy to see how pleased she was with it. In the following days, I realized she would be happy in our new home, and seeing her running around town with her mother, buying things for the house, confirmed that everybody was going to be okay.

Daniela had an extremely detached attitude because she didn't like the fact that I'd returned to racing, but something changed that day. She saw how much effort I put into looking for a house, getting the furniture, planning their trip to Indianapolis and for traveling to the various race circuits. She was surprised because I'm usually so disorganized. I've never been good at planning my schedule and getting the most out of my days. For the first time in my life, I was looking and planning ahead for the future. As a good family man, I was able to make our life as pleasurable and comfortable as possible, both at home and on the track.

Regarding the latter, I arranged to fly to the races on a friend's Lear Jet. While it was a little more expensive, I was able to deduct it from my taxes. Eddie, the owner-pilot of the plane, would pick us up at a private airfield near our house. At each race destination, I arranged a fabulous motorhome for the summer. Niccolò loved to sleep in the "mega-camper." We made a fantastic bed for him out of a cupboard near our bedroom. We even put some colorful curtains and cuddly toys in it to make it as cozy as possible. He liked it so much that he never came to sleep in our bed in the middle of the night as he did when we were at home. Jokingly, Daniela suggested that we take the motorhome back with us to Europe.

My newly acquired organizational skills helped Daniela realize that I was not only in love with her and our son, but also that I genuinely wanted them to share the experience with me. I needed her support, her warm smiles, and the presence of my wonderful son. I think I inspired a little tenderness in her … my heart wanted to go back to racing, but if she'd asked me not to, I would have abandoned the idea. Instead, Daniela stayed silent, closing up a little in fear that something might happen to me. Then, at the beginning of that summer, she started giving me advice and enthusiastic suggestions, which made me feel much better.

The summer was getting hot and the pool and jacuzzi started to get very popular with my friends. First of all, Catia showed up on her own. She was a teacher and therefore not working during the long summer holidays, so rather than stay with husband Filippo in Italy, she decided to wait for him in the United States. Filippo arrived three weeks later, together with my mother, and I'm sure the only reason they arrived safely was due to her. Filippo doesn't speak English and is so absent-minded that if he were in charge, they would have certainly been lost at the first stopover. A few days later, Titano and Nicoletta arrived, and the troops were complete.

We played badminton until we wore the grass thin. I beat Titano, Filippo beat me, but Titano would then beat Filippo, so basically everybody was happy. It was great fun, not to mention when Jimmy Vasser came to stay with us for a couple of weeks while in town racing. We organized a colossal badminton tournament featuring Italy versus the USA. I played in the American team since I was the immigrant, and didn't do too badly, even if my allegiance was with Italy. One evening we found a huge halogen lamp in the garage, which we placed next to the court so that we could play badminton all night. We had plenty of free time because, thanks to the jet, we saved an enormous amount of time traveling to and from the races. Unfortunately, it wasn't just about barbeques and badminton. I wasn't feeling satisfied with racing, due to some unlucky episodes. I was fifth after free practice in Milwaukee, but it rained during qualifying and the session was cancelled. As a consequence, the starting grid was based on the current rankings and therefore I started from behind. Although I gained some positions, I shamefully ran out of fuel and stalled the engine, ultimately losing a lap and coming in 11th.

I was accumulating a pile of insignificant finishes or DNFs (did not finish). This was partially due to mechanical faults, or more typically, an accident on the back row. The whole season was marred by the absence of any real results, but the worst thing was the total inability to have a decent qualifying. Objectively, we weren't that good as a team. Even Tony wasn't getting anywhere, whereas now in IRL (Indianapolis Motor Speedway owner Tony George's rival series to CART) he is leading the championship and doing incredibly well.

We had serious problems, but at least Tony occasionally had a decent qualifying. I realized I was in a bit of a mess at Toronto; I believed that my choice of Morris was correct, but I underestimated the impact of not having Morris as my engineer. Also, most importantly, I underestimated the fact that although he had put together a team backed by big sponsors, he didn't have the mental energy to commit himself to such a duty.

Between the two of us, the organization felt like a retirement home. This was not from a technical point of view because Morris was fully capable of making a valuable contribution and I could have driven like I did in 1996–98 if I'd had the same conditions, but the races don't just start on a Sunday afternoon; you have to start working toward a win well in advance of the race.

That July in Toronto, I let my pride get in the way. I finished free practice in last place while Tony was in the top ten, even managing the fastest time at one point. I couldn't understand what was going on and was tired of listening to the usual old theory, "Tony drives the car in a certain style and is able to get the best out of it, whereas you, Zanardi, have different needs and aren't getting everything out of the car." I was very pissed off and demanded the exact same set-up as Tony's for the qualifying. After pouring my soul into that, I still came in last. I kept telling myself that I couldn't possibly have become such a pathetic driver.

That evening, I asked for a meeting with Morris. I explained to him that I wanted to examine the set-up—inch-by-inch, spring-by-spring, and shock absorber-by-shock absorber. I wanted to examine each adjustment, one at a time, together with the technicians and mechanics in order to verify that the car was exactly the way it was supposed to be. The guys didn't like the idea because they felt distrusted and undermined. Nonetheless, we took the car apart bit by bit.

Finally, during the warm-up, I began to feel the car in my hands. As soon as the race began, I started gaining positions and was soon able to attack, pass and brake when necessary. Halfway through the race, I was third. After the first pit stop to sort out a tire problem, I was 11th. I fought back and moved back up to third, but after the second and last pit stop, I was once again in 11th place. These things happened, and usually my mechanics were very good in the pit operations. But I shouldn't have been sent out so late again, not a second time, because things were going so well in the race.

During the last laps, I was able to move back into fourth place, which ended up being my best result in 2001. I finished the race in Toronto feeling that I could have done even better. The winner was Michael Andretti, who was behind me for half the race.

At least I proved that the attention to detail pays off and that the strength of a team is often hidden behind small things. With Ganassi, I had a car that was set up with extreme precision and therefore very reliable. Perhaps it wasn't the fastest car, but it was consistently good from practice to the race. We always knew our starting point with Chip, but we didn't have that certainty with Morris's team. If something went wrong, it wasn't the fault of a single person but the inexperience of the overall group. Although the system was improving, it still wasn't established enough. We needed a coordinator—a role that Morris should have played. We were too young, and although we had the freedom to do our own job properly, we lacked the leadership necessary to pull the various components together. That was the main problem. I realized that if I really wanted to have a turning point in the season, I needed to do what I didn't with Williams: plant myself in the workshop and sort things out. From a certain point of view, I did this.

After a disastrous qualifying two weeks earlier at Cleveland, I asked to change some settings on the car. I ended up with an excellent car that almost carried me to a victory, but at the exit of the last pit stop, Max Wilson made a mistake, bumped me and cut my tire. I was forced into an additional pit stop and came in 13th. In anticipation of Toronto, we hoped it was a matter of pulling our socks up and organizing the team to work together.

At least I had relinquished the idea that I had become a complete loser. I was very disappointed with Morris, although I don't hold him fully responsible because some things were simply inevitable. We probably didn't share the same opinion and had a full-blown confrontation that weekend in Toronto. We were coming out of three very inconsistent races.

The bottom for our team had probably been at Portland, although now I can laugh about it. After having a run-in with Dixon, Tony hit me full center as he returned from the pits, completely destroying my car. Although I had a taste of the good old days at Cleveland, it too ended badly. The only good that came out of it was that it inspired me for Toronto, where I was very competitive. I even tried to explain to Honda what was going on, but their ideas did not mesh with Morris's or mine.

At the Michigan 500 I was forced to pull out after an electrical fire. Before the Chicago race, I again insisted I should dissect the car and reset it accurately. That race went well. Even Tony's technician followed this strategy and we were very fast during qualifying. Tony took the pole and I was fifth. During the race, I gained some positions and was battling for the lead, running second, until I tried to pass Gugelmin towards the end. I hit him, he spun out and a yellow flag stopped the race, destroying our strategy. We had just stopped to refuel, while the other drivers were still out.

In the short ovals, when you have a pit stop while the race is underway, you lose two laps that can be recovered later when the others stop. But if the others go for a pit stop when there is a yellow flag and the race is neutralized, they only lose one lap and you're screwed. I made a comeback and, trying to make a move, I messed up and let Castroneves and Kanaan pass me. I came in ninth and earned a few points, but it was a positive race because at least I fought to win. Hopefully, things were changing ….

Unfortunately, we continued to experience many problems and in August at Mid-Ohio the qualifying times were abysmal. Once again I spent the evening in the pits scrutinizing the set-up. It paid off because during the race, I made a significant comeback at a track on which it was very difficult to pass. I was the only driver to gain such positions and was still improving as I moved up to eighth place. Then during a yellow flag, Fittipaldi slammed on his brakes and I had to swerve to avoid bumping him. One of the stewards interpreted this as a tentative overtaking move and reported it to the race directors. Five laps from the end of the race, I got a penalty flag. My radio wasn't working and I didn't see the black flag until the last lap. The race director, who reviewed the tape recording, agreed that I didn't do anything wrong, but I was still disqualified for not stopping for the black flag.

We arrived at Elkhart Lake for another dull weekend. We had huge electrical problems during qualifying which forced me to start the race behind the others. I made a comeback and was in position for the podium, but during a pit stop the team decided not to change my tires and to refuel only once. I paid heavily for this mistake when I had to confront the second half of the race without new tires. I dropped from 4th place to 13th. I was incredibly pissed off and had another argument with Morris, who was responsible for the decision regarding the tires.

September started badly at Vancouver. At the beginning of qualifying, I wasted a lot of time after hitting another driver who was going slower than me. During the race, I climbed back to tenth position when the car broke down with an electrical problem. The season continued going downhill. My best result had still been oin July at Toronto—a measly fourth place—which seemed utterly ridiculous in the light of the hopes I'd had in the winter.

There were a few good aspects to the season, however. Daniela and Niccolò always came with me and the motorhome became a traveling nursery with all of the other drivers' children and track staff using it as well. Catia often came to the races with us and would look after Niccolò when Daniela needed a break. Catia, who had a degree in various languages, enjoyed practicing English with the other mothers. Niccolò had settled into this life quickly and I often took him on my shoulders to the pits to chat with the mechanics. He loved the atmosphere and watching the cars.

After the Elkhart Lake race in August we waved goodbye to everybody—the house and the motorhome—and left for Europe feeling a bit nostalgic for our home in the United States. We'd enjoyed all the many things to do for children in Indianapolis, like the Children's Museum and the zoo, where Niccolò loved watching the giraffes. The team manager was Brad Filbey, who was previously my mechanic on "Old Midnight" with Ganassi's team. We had made friends with his children, Hannah and David, who were wonderful children. It was amazing how they all understood each other even though they didn't speak the same language. Niccolò, who was always very shy, had quickly bonded with the other children. Brad and his wife had used the motorhome as their nursery, along with other children such as Michael Andretti's son. Often, at the end of the evening, I would take one of the team's golf carts and drive around the paddock with Niccolò, making him laugh by pretending to crash into the rubbish bins. I'd take all of the kids for a ride in the cart and they loved it, as we ignored the moans of the mechanics who complained that I drained the battery. Despite our frustrations from a racing point of view, it was a serene and pleasant year.

We returned to Monaco in August so that Niccolò could start nursery school in September. I was planning to go to Vancouver on my own and then return to Europe in September for the races at the Lausitzring and at Silverstone, England. I was the only driver who went home between the two races given that we lived in Monaco. I was then planning on going back to the States for the races in Houston and at Laguna Seca, then to Surfers Paradise in Australia and then the last race of the season, at Fontana, California.

In the meantime, I sold my beloved boat. I met Piero Cesana, the import manager of Fairline Boats, who convinced me to buy the latest model. At first I wasn't terribly interested, especially since it wasn't that different from mine, but when I saw the drawings of the new one, I changed my mind. He invited me to test it out in England, where it was being built and I could have one before it was offered to the public. I ordered one which was to be delivered in time to be exhibited at the Genoa boat show as part of the deal.

The Saturday of the race in Germany was the beginning of the boat show in Cannes, and Cesana had sent me tickets to attend. I was planning to go there with Jimmy Vasser on the Monday after the race. After the accident in Germany, I learned was not to book appointments in advance ....

My mother arrived to look after Niccolò while we were in Germany and England. The Tuesday afternoon before the race in Germany, the tragedy of September 11 occurred.

I had just returned home after being out shopping on the moped. I still had the crash helmet in my hand, and as soon as I saw the news on television, I was stunned. Daniela moved Niccolò into the other room so he didn't have to see what had happened. Terrible things happen all the time and some affect you more than others, but that event was one of those moments in life which touched everyone in some way or another. Brad called me right away, "Go to the track anyway, even though we don't know what is going to happen."

I arrived at the Lausitzring on Wednesday as planned, but it was all very surreal, as if the race did not matter at all. No one was interested in it. We were all busy in meetings and more meetings. We spent hours there in a very gloomy environment, both in our moods and with the weather. In the evening, we were trying to distract each other but it was very difficult to cheer anyone up.

What happened in New York shocked me, but I was ready to race if that's what the teams decided to do. Selfishly, I also knew that we had made lots of progress on that type of oval and had a chance to be competitive. I was looking for the chance to prove myself again and patch up the problems. I also wanted to end the season on the best note possible because I had no idea what I'd do the following year. The team was finally beginning to gel and everybody was pulling in the same direction. If they decided to go ahead, I knew that it was going to be an important race, so I committed to doing my best. And that's exactly what I did ....

When I lowered the visor I stopped thinking about the terrorist attacks of just a few days before. Before the race, I placed my fate in the hands of my American friends. I didn't want to wash my hands of the events, but I simply didn't feel I had the right to express an opinion. I was very upset by what had happened, but I couldn't imagine how the Americans were feeling that day. Our individual character and education have led us to form certain behaviors and attitudes, and therefore we all have different feelings about why and how September 11 took place. But it wasn't for me to make a decision about racing, but rather the American officials, whose reaction would have a much more profound meaning.

For many, it was risky because our race was the first international event for an American sport after the attack. Many Americans living abroad would attend the race, so all the eyes were on us and although interest in CART had decreased, we were on the media's lips—from CNN down to the local press. For all these reasons, we had been identified as a possible terrorist target.

We discussed the situation at length and after serious consideration, it was decided to race in order to let everybody know that life goes on. Each car carried an American flag and the majority of the teams removed the sponsors' logos. The message that we wanted to give the terrorists was, "You did not win. The flag has won and the spirit of freedom will prevail."

Once the decision had been made, we had a few weather problems. Tony and I were consistently the fastest during practice on Thursday, proving that all our efforts were paying off. It rained on Friday and therefore the qualifying was cancelled. As usual, the grid was based on the current rankings, which meant I was starting from the back. It also rained on Saturday morning and so I felt that perhaps there was someone above, saying, "Are you sure you want to race? I'm giving you an excuse not to." The rain stopped and strong winds quickly dried the track. Soon after deciding the race would go ahead, the grandstand was full.

The Germans are passionate about motor racing and especially love what was such an unusual event for them, so they wouldn't have missed this race for anything in the world.

I was very confident and calm before the start. I knew the car was in good shape and that the race would bring me some much-needed points. On an oval it's not so much about how fast the car is so much as how it enables you to overtake, change lines and move swiftly through the traffic. Uniquely, your line is dictated by the opponent's positioning rather than your own trajectory, so you need a very versatile car. Only a few gifted drivers are able to set up a car well enough to suit an oval. I was sure that for this race, my car was in that condition.

In April of that year Michele Alboreto had died at the Lausitzring, albeit not on the oval. He was killed while testing his Audi sports racer for Le Mans. I didn't dwell on that and didn't feel that it foreshadowed what was to come. Even if I did, I would have confused it with the general anxiety and anguish of that moment.

Michele's death had had a profound effect on me; we had raced together in Formula 1. It was such a stupid accident—it happened when he blew out a tire. We all know that racing is dangerous, but there is usually a safety area when you go off the track because of a simple mistake. These areas are designed specifically around the spots that are prone to accidents. On the other hand a technical problem can happen anywhere—on a straight while you are going 185 mph—and you can end up under a guardrail, like Michele did.

Regardless, I didn't consider the Lausitzring as a particularly cursed track where we Italians were unlucky. I thought it was a track where a lot of fans would cheer me on, which is what happened. Maybe because I was Italian, the Germans were more familiar with me than with my American counterparts. I felt the race belonged to me. Despite a slightly wet track, the race went ahead. I said to Tony before we got in our cars, "Today, the Uncle is going to kick your ass!" He replied with great affection, "Well, if someone has to do it, it might as well be you!" We jumped into our cars and started the race.

I had finally rekindled the passion of the Ganassi times. I couldn't wait for the race to begin, and wasn't at all bothered about starting from the back because I knew that after a couple of laps, I would be among the first. I had absolute conviction about my abilities, and by the first turn I'd overtaken three or four drivers from the outside with cold tires. Before the others had time to blink, I had started what would have been a great comeback.

During the initial laps on that type of oval, you're behind many drivers and feel a lot of turbulence. Everybody is fighting for a position, and it is often difficult to keep your foot on the pedal because of all of the obstacles. At one point during the race there were four cars in front of me. The leader tightened his line and the second driver, who wanted to pass from the inside, took a lower line while the third driver took a lower line still so that the fourth was left with nowhere to go, and simply waited for things to happen. At that point I slowed down slightly and moved to the outside, preparing to pass.

It was easy to predict what was going to happen. As a matter of fact, they entered the corner too fast for their respective lines and went understeering towards the wall on the outside. I kept enough space to accelerate and cut through the corner. I was side by side with them until halfway into the turn, when I passed them all in a split second. Each maneuver was becoming more difficult because as I climbed up the ranks, I was encountering stronger and stronger drivers.

It was difficult to overtake Max Papis, who was an extremely courageous driver in such situations. He certainly was not one of those drivers with a sign on the wing saying, "Please, be my guest." I studied him for three or four laps until a lapped driver forced him to exit a turn badly. I exited the turn more quickly and was able to enter his slipstream. He tried to keep as low as possible, as if he wanted to block me, but then I moved to the outside and the speed differential enabled me to overtake him comfortably. While I was passing him, we looked at each other and waved.

Finally I was behind Tony Kanaan, who was leading the pack. He had started in front and was very fast because he had a car as good as mine. I caught up with him, studied him and tried a couple of moves. I really respect Tony, both as a driver and as a person. He came from nothing and we have similar stories—I saw in him what I had been ten years before, and that is why I wasn't offended when he called me Uncle—I actually found it quite endearing. I was happy to be his teammate and if only he had been a bit slower it would have shown the shortfalls of the cars. At one point, I pretended I was going to pass him in a turn. I was in his slipstream and was convinced I could complete the move. I took the inside of the turn and was halfway through it when he closed in on me, forcing me to back off in order to avoid contact. I got caught in his aerodynamic turbulence and almost ended up in the sand.

Never mind … it was just a matter of time. I passed him a couple of laps later, giving him a sign that everyone assumed was a greeting like Papis's. In fact, I was trying to make an Italian hand gesture meaning, "I'm going to kick your ass," referring to our earlier joke. I couldn't manage it with one hand, so it looked like I was waving. Months later, Tony admitted that he was delighted to see "the Uncle kicking all of our asses today!" This reminded me of the camaraderie I'd felt while driving with Jimmy.

From then on I was firmly in the lead and I felt great. While trying to keep up with me, Tony consumed substantially more fuel and had to stop a bit earlier. Everyone was going to need a pit stop because there had not been many yellow flags. The only one with a different strategy was Michael Andretti, who thanks to our pit stop, would soon be in the lead. It would have been easy for me to overtake him because he was slowing down to save fuel.

The situation was turning around for the best. There was still one pit stop. I entered the pits, worried that something might go wrong as in Toronto. Not because of the mechanics, but because things happen, broken wheels or blocked fuel lines, which can suddenly change everything. When I saw my chief mechanic Donnie lift his hand and give me the "go" sign, I started off without stalling the engine, saying to myself, "It's done. Nobody's going to stop me now." Little did I know that it was not done at all.

CHAPTER 14

The Big One

I still don't know what happened. Jim Anderson, my engineer, found the telemetry analysis to be very strange. There were no signs of rear skidding. The car had consistent acceleration, but took off in an inexplicable manner. Everything led us to believe that it was dirt on the pit lane, which Franchitti confirmed when he came to the hospital. He was right behind me at the time and saw me skid, so he immediately took his foot off the accelerator before almost losing control himself. Almost certainly there were oil and water on the track. A few laps before, Tracy had gone into the pits with a smoking engine and was sent out immediately afterwards so that the engine could take some air. But this is only one theory. More likely, a support vehicle leaked some fluid from an overflow pipe. When my cold tires met this liquid, the horrific pirouette began.

In a moment, I had lost control, gone off on to the grass and then ended up in the middle of the track. Some of the other drivers were approaching, so a yellow flag was eventually shown. The first to approach was Patrick Carpentier, whose spotter apparently warned him just in time because he was able to avoid hitting me. Then his teammate Alex Tagliani arrived and hit me full on in the side. That's how it went, and there's no further recrimination. To be honest, when I saw a yellow flag, my strategy was always to push as hard as possible until the safety car came out. In that type of race, such a strategy can make a difference. If you want a pit stop, you can gain position and time and stay behind those who have also made a pit stop.

All I can say is that it was really nobody's fault—what happened, happened. Although I think that ovals are particularly dangerous, the track was not the cause of my accident. A similar mishap occurred at the 1993 Portuguese Grand Prix at Estoril. Gerhard Berger was coming out of the pits in his Ferrari (there were no speed limits back then) and the active suspension malfunctioned over a bump. He lost control of the car and cut across the track, just missing a full side-on impact with JJ Lehto and Derek Warwick, who were approaching at 200 mph. Everything went well for all of them that day, but they could have been dealt the same unlucky hand as me. Maybe worse.

How many people every day are victims of being in the wrong place at the wrong time? I'd raced my whole life, and the accident happened during what was probably going to be my last season. Was it destiny? Who knows? It happened and I move on with what I have left. I'm just happy to be here able to tell this story.

Tagliani tried to avoid me, but he had very little choice. He could have gone around to the right and passed me from the outside, but he would've probably hit my engine or crashed against the wall, which one's survival instinct prevents. The second option was to pass on my left on the inside of the turn. Had we been very, very lucky, we could have hit the sides of the cars, which would have made a lot of noise but would not have hurt anybody. Unfortunately, I did my stupid pirouette and kept spinning until Tagliani's car's nose was pointing directly at my car's "waist;" the most vulnerable part of my car was struck by the most robust and pointed parts of his vehicle. I was hit where the only protection for my legs was the Kevlar bodywork. No matter how well designed, the bodywork couldn't resist such an enormous impact.

It happened in an instant. Part of the car stayed with me, and the other part left, with parts of me in it. I can't remember anything and don't know if I realized what was happening to me. While rewatching the images from the crash I can see I tried to do what most drivers do after a minor accident, open the visor and take off my seatbelt. For a few seconds, the accident didn't seem that bad. If the car hadn't split in two, I would have had to have absorbed all the energy from the impact. Instead, the front end of the car took the impact and I hardly felt a thing—my helmet didn't even have a dent. I must have realized something though when I looked in front of me and saw no front to the car ... and no legs. Before fainting, I must have realized something. From time to time, if I really try hard—I don't know if it's my imagination or disjointed memories—but some images come to the surface in my mind. Maybe one day the whole event will come back to me. I'm not afraid of it though, because all the damage has already been done.

First aid came very quickly. One of the young officials arrived on the scene and immediately understood the gravity of the situation. He called Dr. Terry Trammell, who was responsible for the CART medical team, along with Dr. Steve Olvey. He reached Terry on the radio and screamed, "Shit, Shit! Terry come here, come here!" They were faced with an extraordinary emergency situation and were desperately trying to save a life. I was losing blood very fast, so they somehow carried me out of the cockpit and began blocking the hemorrhaging with a tourniquet. But the tourniquet kept slipping off, so they cut my overalls to make another. They desperately tried to find the femoral arteries, but couldn't. Then all at once, Terry found one on the most damaged leg and put his thumb in it to stop the bleeding. He did exactly the same on the other leg. At the same time, someone was trying to tie a tourniquet, but they kept losing grip because there was so much blood. Finally, one of the first aid guys used his belt to create a tourniquet. Every second was precious because I was dying. They were urgently trying to get me to the hospital, but in moving me to a stretcher, the tourniquets slipped off again and the hemorrhaging started again. Finally, they managed to transport me to the helicopter that Steve Olvey had organized.

Before each race, the medical team visits each hospital in the area to decide where to go in such an eventuality. They had made a decision that seemed dangerous at the time, but in fact, their foresight saved my life. They decided to send me to Berlin, which was a 55-minute flight away. The Dresden hospital was closer, but they felt that it lacked the technology to deal with such a situation. Steve insisted, "This is the only chance we have to save him. If we go to Dresden, we'll lose him." They got me ready as best they could and closed off the area around the helicopter to keep people away. The only two people allowed to see me were Father Phil De Rea, a priest/spiritual counselor for CART, and Daniela. Father Phil collected oil from the engine of my car and gave me my last rites.

Initially, they didn't want to let Daniela pass, but she wouldn't give up and got through in order to hold me for a few seconds. No one had the courage to stop her. Before I left in the helicopter, she kissed me and said, "Hold on, my love … hold on. You will make it. I can't come with you in the helicopter, but I'll be behind you in the car and get there as soon as possible. Don't give up!"

Dario Franchitti's wife, the American actress Ashley Judd, was always supportive of Daniela and stayed by her side throughout the ordeal. Ashley was deeply affected by the scene which she told us about again and again in the following months. In the grandstands, Ashley had seen a very big German fellow watching the scene without moving. When Daniela came to kiss me and hold my hand, the man started screaming. Everybody else was quiet as he shouted, "You're giving him a new life—he will survive, he will survive!" She said that the moment had been very surreal, almost supernatural: "Maybe I was seeing things, but when I looked up at him that man was surrounded by light, and I believed what he said. I really knew that you would make it."

At that point, the yellow ADAC helicopter left for Berlin. I was quickly losing blood during the journey. It was so dire that they had to give me a transfusion with what they had—plasma, which is basically the liquid part of blood, without any red or white blood cells or platelets. They kept filling me with what they had, but I kept bleeding. I arrived at the hospital with less than two pints of blood in my body. My heart stopped three times during the trip and I had to be resuscitated.

We touched down at the Klinikum Berlin-Marzahn 90 minutes after the accident and I was still holding on, just as Daniela had asked me to. They probably needed a water hose to handle the enormous blood transfusion during the operation. The doctors were absolutely incredible in Berlin and had been alerted to my condition, so everything was ready when I arrived.

They started working immediately, trying to save my right knee, which was still hanging on. Unfortunately, it was so damaged that they decided to remove it in order to save my life and what was left of my legs.

They took some risks on my left leg, which was in even worse shape. Rather than cut the leg at the hip joint, which would have made saving my life easier, they decided to leave what was left. Thanks to that brave decision, I am today able to use a prosthesis to walk, which I wouldn't have been able to do otherwise. I'm very grateful to them that I'm able to have a better quality of life and hence a smile on my face still.

The initial surgery took seven and a half hours, during which time the entire CART community came to Berlin. For more than hour, they waited for the phone call to hear whether I was still alive. Steve Olvey later admitted that he didn't think I was going to make it. "When I heard that you were still alive and in relatively stable condition, I thought that it was a miracle. It was simply amazing that you had survived such a horrific accident."

At the beginning, there was little hope of that. After almost eight hours the doctors came out and said, "His condition is stable but extremely critical. If he has no complications in the next 12 hours, we can hope that he might make it." I could have had kidney or heart failure, or my organs could have been damaged by the lack of blood, let alone by the accident. There was also a risk of brain damage, although they dismissed that almost immediately. Everyone in the medical field said that it was a miracle that I survived on less than a liter of blood.

The medical team put me into a drug-induced coma and into intensive care. My wife and Ashley Judd were the only two allowed to visit. They came in another helicopter, together with Rena Shanaman, who manages the PR for the drivers, Father Phil, and John Potter, president of the Drivers Association. John's kindness is a large as his size, and apparently it took some effort to get him into the helicopter. Tagliani had also been brought to the hospital with suspected broken vertebrae after crashing into the wall, but the x-rays confirmed it was only bruising.

Daniela and I hadn't really gotten to know Ashley until she'd begun coming to the circuits after her engagement to Dario Franchitti in 2000. During my comeback season, she used to come to the circuit with her own motorhome. We heard she was a bit reserved and we worried that she might be harassed, given that she was a famous actress, so we respected her privacy. We would meet up for a chat, but we never spent a lot of time together. But that day in Berlin, she thought she should stay with Daniela. Franchitti had pulled out of the race before the accident and therefore offered to drive Daniela to Berlin. "If we go at 150 mph, we can get you there in no time at all." Daniela managed a wry smile, "Thanks, but I want to make sure I get there." She ended up taking a helicopter, followed by a fourth carrying Dario, Vasser, Kanaan, Dr. Trammell and a few others.

Morris didn't show up until the following evening. He is a somewhat strange character, and probably felt badly. After the accident, he went back to his hotel in Dresden and stayed awake the whole night. The following day he packed his bags and drove to Berlin, but he didn't have the strength or the will to come to the hospital. He had lived through the trauma of the great Swiss driver Clay Regazzoni, who'd lost the use of his legs in the 1980 Long Beach Grand Prix (Formula 1) while driving for Morris's Ensign team. One hopes that something like that doesn't happen once, let alone twice. Nothing like this had happened during all his years as a technical director for other teams, yet as soon as he had a new team of his own, another tragedy struck. He was understandably very upset and although this time it wasn't a technical fault as in 1980, he felt responsible nonetheless.

There were handfuls of people in the hospital waiting to hear the outcome, including nearly all the other drivers. They stayed until Daniela sent them home to get some sleep. By Monday there were so many people in the waiting room that the hospital gave us their meeting room to accommodate my friends.

After a week of uncertainty, my prognosis improved and I was taken off the critical list. Although they had already told Daniela that I had a 99 percent chance of survival, they were still concerned about my kidneys, blood loss and possible embolism. And of course, there was the issue of infection in my shorter leg—the left one—which still had fragments of the wreckage in it. My temperature kept rising, reaching 105 degrees Fahrenheit—and the doctors were still quite concerned. It was a very tense situation because there was the constant need to reopen the surgery to clean the wounds.

Immediately following the accident, Daniela called my mother. She knew that the race would be shown on television with a 30-minute delay and didn't want her to see it. She hinted to my mother and Filippo, who were in Monaco looking after Niccolò, that it was serious, and then slowly broke the news while I was in the operating room—first saying that it was my foot, the ankle, and so on.

The Klinikum was very accommodating throughout the ordeal, even putting an extra bed in my room for Daniela while I was in intensive care. She could stay whenever she wanted, as long as she abided by the Intensive Care Unit's strict hygiene standards to avoid passing on any infection. Daniela stayed by my side and never stopped believing that I would make it, although she had been realistic from the start: "That's what racing is about, but accidents can also happen on the highway, and that's life."

After I successfully passed urine on day two and the doctors were happy with the kidneys and other vital functions, they continued operating on me. While I was in the drug-induced coma for three days following the accident, I had an operation every 48 or 72 hours. The first three surgeries involved the right leg and after that the stump was stitched up for good. But the left leg still needed surgery for another month.

On the fourth day after the accident, the doctors started reducing the drugs gradually so that I would wake up. When I did, I was very groggy. I saw Daniela and tried to say something to her, but immediately fell right back to sleep. I wasn't lucid at all until Friday, six days after the accident.

The doctors suggested that Daniela wait for the right moment to tell me about the amputations, when I was conscious enough to understand, but before I discovered it on my own. She asked the doctors for help. Dr. Walter Schaffartzik called her on Thursday afternoon and said it was the right time. When I opened my eyes, I saw Daniela and the doctor standing next to me. She asked him to stay so that he could answer any questions I may have had, but I didn't ask a lot when Daniela broke the news.

They told me that I wasn't going to die, and that's all that mattered to me. I only asked one question, "Is it true—am I really not going to die?" The doctor gave me the assurance that I needed. "Don't worry, you're not going to die." I was so relieved. "Well that's good, then." I felt extremely detached from my body and my emotions, like talking through a microphone while sitting ten meters away from my body. This was a terrible sensation that lasted for a long time. I was feeling so out of it that when Daniela told me about the accident I amusedly murmured, "Son of a bitch!"

When Daniela then told me that I had lost my legs, it seemed insignificant—I was happy just to be alive. I was still too preoccupied with getting better to think about the long-term impact. I was delirious, mumbling lots of words and sentences that made no sense. For example, on the wall of the hospital room, there were three paintings of flowers. When I opened my eyes for the first time, I looked at them and said, "Look at the pretty paintings on the wall. That one is Tony Kanaan, the one in the middle is Jimmy and that one is Massimiliano Papis." Daniela tried to correct me. "Those are three bunches of flowers." I got terribly annoyed with her. "What? Can't you see them! Why are you joking with me when I'm feeling so terrible?" It was so frustrating because I was trying to express myself, but only strange screams came out of my mouth.

The first real memory I have is of seeing Daniela surrounded by all the tubes, alarms, machines and noises of the hospital room. I remember that I couldn't move as she told me what had happened, adding that Dr. Claudio Costa—the famous motorcycle doctor— had been to visit. He'd put together some information about prostheses for me and was convinced I would surprise the world. As I listened to those words, I got a sense of what was happening to me. Dr. Costa's visit really helped me. He had measured what was left of my legs and already had a clear plan. I couldn't communicate verbally so I asked for a pen and paper. I tried painstakingly to write down a question, but all I could manage was a single line veering off diagonally down the page, looking somewhat like the graph of the Italian gross domestic product. I was exhausted by this effort and quickly fell asleep.

One day when it was clear to me that I wasn't going to die, Maria, the head nurse, came with a Polaroid camera in hand to take a photo of me. Daniela was worried it was for the newspapers, but Maria explained that it was for something else. "I'm taking this so that when he feels depressed, he can look back at it and see how far he has come." There's no messing around with these Germans.

The drivers, technicians and CART executives had left for the race at Silverstone, England, on the Saturday after the Lausitzring. Meanwhile, Filippo called Daniela from our home in Monaco, hiding in another room so that my mother and Niccolò wouldn't hear him. "Just tell me one thing—do we have to worry a lot or a little?" She replied, "A lot." Filippo and Titano jumped in the car and drove through the night, arriving in Berlin the following day. They were in such a rush that they accidentally filled the car with petrol instead of diesel, only realizing it once they went to pay. They then had to empty the tank, and fill it up again with diesel. They were so shocked by the news of my accident that they hardly spoke the whole journey.

When they arrived at the hospital, Titano rushed to my room and sat next to my bed, recounting the story of his life. He went on for four straight hours because the doctors said it would do me good to hear familiar voices. The problem was that he was whispering. When Dr. Schoeder came into the room and heard him, he said, "You need to speak up or it won't do any good." Exasperated, Titano yelled, "You mean I've been talking for four damn hours for nothing!" Filippo, on the other hand, did not want to see me and waited until Thursday to come into the room. "I don't feel like going in his room, and he doesn't need me anyway." He stayed in the waiting room and helped everybody as much as he could; he went to buy food, do errands, and drive people back and forth to the hotel. For the remainder of the time, he would sit on a bench in the corridor.

Finally on the day that Filippo was leaving, he entered my room. It didn't affect him at all, and actually made him feel better to see me looking relaxed and stable. Who knows what he was expecting, but he's always been afraid of hospitals. Because of the doctor's earlier advice, he and Titano spoke at the top of their lungs. "Well we have to keep talking and the doctors said we have to talk loudly!" So together they shouted, "Sandroooooooooo!" A passing doctor poked his head in to see what was going on. Apparently, I suddenly opened my eyes, but immediately fell back asleep. They were so excited that I'd woken up that they tried it again. The doctors calmed them down and explained that my reaction was a good sign of recovery, but that it required an enormous amount of effort and it was therefore unlikely I'd do it again. I have a vague memory of recognizing the voices and thinking, "What the hell? Oh, it's only you two. Let me sleep!"

On Sunday morning, Daniela's mother and my brother-in-law, Sandro, better known as the "Doctor," arrived in Berlin. He and his wife Barbara (Daniela's sister) were also invaluable. Sandro assisted me at night in intensive care. I had tubes everywhere, a ventilator, and a lot of machines monitoring my vital functions. Each time that one of my vital signs was over the limit, the machines would make an irritating beeping sound. Now, when Sandro and I meet up to smoke a cigar, we discuss how my problems may be resolved in the future as medical science evolves even more. He is a bit like my medical encyclopedia, and helps me a lot.

The second night after I came out of the coma, Sandro was napping in an armchair and Daniela was sleeping on the bed next to mine. I was usually very drowsy during the day but at night, I was wide awake and would hear nothing but this gloomy beeping noise. Sandro woke up and had a look at the machine, fiddled with it a bit and then yelled, "What the hell!" He pushed a button to reset the whole lot and then went back to his armchair. I remained still and after five minutes, the same thing happened again. Sandro looked at the machine and pushed the buttons and returned to his chair. It happened again but this time, he ignored the machine and pushed the button again. At that point I said, "Sandro, I know you're not new to this, but maybe we should call someone who knows the machine?" He ignored me but I think that he may have been a bit offended, because whenever we recount this story over dinner with friends, his final comment is always, "After I spent night and day looking after him, that's the gratitude I got from the little bastard."

I was extremely uncomfortable in those first days. The pain wasn't unbearable, but the feeling of detachment was. One of the worst moments of my life was when they removed the ventilator. I thought I would die and felt like I was suffocating as I couldn't get any air. I started crying and begged the doctors to replace the ventilator. They told me everything was fine, but I was certain that I was on my last breath. "Don't you see that I'm dying here?" Everyone around me, including Daniela and the doctors, were able to laugh when I said this for the third time. After a couple of hours of pain, I learned to breathe again on my own.

The second dramatic moment arrived when they took out my catheter. I started having pain in my bladder and couldn't pee. I told Daniela that I couldn't stand it anymore, but given that I was still pretty delirious, she didn't take my complaint that seriously. It became so bad that I begged her to call a doctor. She arrived, a little annoyed at first, but after a scan showed my bladder was as big as a watermelon, she inserted a little tube and I pissed like a racehorse. It was the biggest relief of my life. Ever since then I've refused a catheter in surgery. I'd rather spend half an hour in the toilet with Titano turning the water tap on to make me pee rather than go through that again.

I was still out of it from the drugs, but I certainly didn't lack optimism. The first step was to get rid of that horrible feeling of detachment. Then I was convinced that step by step, with the help of the prostheses, I could do everything that I did before. This optimism was helped by my ignorance, but at that moment it was fundamental in keeping me motivated and positive. I eventually achieved everything that I had hoped to do.

My initial problem was not losing my legs, but rather accomplishing the most basic things. Removing tubes in order to have a shower, for example, was particularly difficult. Daniela gave me the first shower, which left me feeling absolutely shattered but happy. It's amazing how you can get enormous satisfaction from overcoming the simplest of things, with the right spirit and attitude. Going to the john was also a huge challenge. In theory it shouldn't have been a problem; although it took awhile and was exhausting, I was relieved when I confirmed things were still working properly. In the meantime, Roberto Trevisan came to visit and immediately wanted to make himself useful. He'd already started to organize our house for my return, despite Daniela telling him not to worry about the major adjustments. If allowed, Roberto would have built a lift in the house in three days, fully equipped with speakers and music. Instead, he installed a few very practical and useful ramps to our home in Padova.

Everyone wanted to bring Niccolò to see me, believing it would lift my spirits. I was desperate to see my son, but so afraid that he would want to play or do something that I could no longer do. Sadly for that moment, I had to put myself first. I didn't need to see my son to pull me out of a dark tunnel because I never went there. I had a few moments of depression, but they didn't last long. I didn't weigh myself down with negative thoughts. In fact, ironically, I didn't feel that depressed until I returned home. At the hospital, I was fine and approached everything as an obstacle that had to be hurdled, therefore concentrating on only one thing—getting better.

Jimmy Vasser came back to see me for three days after the English race. If he'd come for a couple of hours, it would have been easy to have fooled him into believing I was all right. But he was there long enough to see my suffering. Despite being happy to have him there, it was torture to see in his eyes the worry, anguish and powerlessness over the situation. Believe it or not, I never cried over what happened. I've often cried in my life, but never about losing my legs.

To be honest, I knew that bringing Niccolò to Berlin would help him more than me, so I eventually said yes. Daniela went to pick him up in Monte Carlo. It broke my heart when she told me about what had happened that afternoon at the nursery. It had been more than 20 days since we'd last waved goodbye to him and promised, "We'll see you on Sunday." When she arrived at the nursery, he went crazy. He wouldn't stop screaming and patting her face as if to see if she were real. And then kisses, hugs and laughs and he wouldn't let go for more than an hour. Then all of sudden he asked, "When are you going to leave again?" She sat him down and explained to him what had happened and assured him, "We're going together." Obviously, nobody had told him anything, but at three years old, he had probably guessed that something was wrong. When he ran toward me to hug me, he was surprised to see me without my legs, but hugged me without hesitation.

I would like to go back and feel the way I do now to fully appreciate that moment. I was happy, but at the time it was a huge effort to play with him ... or even to smile. But he is the life that goes on, and he is more part of me than the legs that I left behind. During my many moments of solitude, I would think about my affection for Niccolò. I would imagine him at the nursery making little drawings or sculptures, and it always brought a lump to my throat when I thought about him. We'd waited until I was transferred out of intensive care before bringing Niccolò to see me. He spent the following 25 days with us in the Berlin hospital and the hotel. Sandro and Barbara bought him a small bicycle on which he rode around the park and down the hospital corridors, reminding me of that small boy in *The Shining*, riding the tiny tricycle in the huge hotel corridors.

I was getting rather used to the anesthetic that was required during my ongoing surgery to my left leg. I always had this feeling of fluttering before falling asleep, and I almost couldn't wait to have it, as the pain would disappear completely. I would be in a dream state until I'd hear Daniela and her mother talking, talking and talking. In reality, maybe three or four hours had passed by, but it seemed like days. One morning my mother-in-law said, "Look how relaxed his face is … he almost looks angelic." She came closer to my face and I jumped up and yelled, "Boo!" We both laughed. I adore my mother-in-law and Sandro and I are forever battling to win her affections. Because of my celebrity, I've often been able to say on television, "My mother-in-law is an incredible, fantastic person." A few minutes later Sandro would call me. "You're such a brown-nose!" At Easter or Christmas, I'd always toast her with a glass of wine. "Gianna, despite what Dr. Sandro says about you, you're lovely. A toast to your health."

I often felt well enough just hours after surgery to go outside into the hospital gardens. I enjoyed smelling the fresh air and racing around in my wheelchair with Niccolò on his bicycle. We would often have a meal in Daniela's hotel room in Berlin and then stroll around town before returning to the hospital to sleep. We'd take everything to the hotel—car, wheelchair and bicycle— because I had intensive physical therapy in the morning.

I had been moved from Room 13 in Intensive Care to Room 17 in the recovery ward. In Italy, the number 17 is even unluckier than the number 13. Just to be safe, I asked to have the number changed to 16B. I had three main nurses: Maria, the head nurse; Kaj; and Wim, who was Dutch. They washed and shaved me every couple of days when I was in the coma, carefully maneuvering around the tubes. This is part of the recovery. Even if a patient is in a coma, he can recognize habits of everyday life. I was very fond of all of them. They really seemed to love their careers and were incredibly patient. They tolerated all the visitors from CART, as well as the various journalists, and effortlessly managed the situation.

Many people helped us. Barbara and Sandro used up 20 days of their vacation to be with us. Together with Roberto Trevisan, Titano, Nicoletta, Filippo and Catia, they created a circle of support and affection. Everybody cried when they arrived, including Sandro, but Daniela told them off immediately. "If you do that, go home, because I don't need people who cry." Catia kindly stayed behind with my mother when Filippo came to Berlin. Even my mother's cousin, Albarosa and her husband Gianni came to mother's side. They all worked together like a team, determined to help us get through this. But one of the most dedicated people has to be my amazing mother. She maintained her calmness and dignity and most importantly, alleviated the enormous burden of worrying about Niccolò. I knew that he was in good hands. She protected him from everything and did her best to help him deal with the situation in the least traumatic way. Undoubtedly my optimism and strength come from being my mother's son. If I'd been more similar to my father, I would have been very funny and full of jokes, but definitely not as strong.

Filippo and Titano returned to Berlin a week after I came out of my coma. As soon as Filippo entered the room, he told everyone, "Go get a coffee. I'll stay here with Sandrino." I still needed assistance to get up and was still quite disoriented, but when I recognized him, I said, "Filippo, I'm here." He lay down on the bed next to me and by the time that the doctors arrived five minutes later, he was already snoring with his mouth open. The doctors looked at him and then turned to me rather amused and I smiled, "Yes, he's my assistant." He was still snoring like a bear when the others returned.

On several occasions, Sandro, Filippo and Titano improvised a picnic in the hospital café after it closed. These moments helped me a lot, especially when Sandro and Filippo performed their impromptu cabaret. Sharing a room with messy Filippo at the Four Seasons Hotel drove tidy Titano crazy. Titano would put the towels back as if they had never been used, and put the soap back into the paper when he was done with it. Can you imagine Titano's horror after Filippo used the bathroom? Eventually, everyone had to return to their lives in Italy and I missed them tremendously.

My first public appearance on television was courtesy of an interview with Carmen Lasorella. She was RAI Media's Berlin correspondent and as a fellow Italian, came to see me and to ask if Daniela needed anything. I was excited to meet her because she'd also reported my accident in Spa with Lotus a few years earlier. I remember back then having been so immature that I'd bragged about Carmen Lasorella talking to me, when the real fact was that she was only interested in an accident at 170 mph.

As soon as she entered the hospital room, I put my foot in it. I was still quite dazed, but wanted to start with a compliment. "Do you know that you're more beautiful on television than in real life?" I obviously wanted to say the opposite! She asked Daniela if we were ready to talk about my feelings. "I came here prepared to put on a brave face, but I'm relieved to see how positive he is and really think that this could uplift the public." She conducted the interview in my new room, 16B. One part of the interview was broadcast on the nightly news, and the full version shown in a special program about pain later that night. Sandro was a guest on the show, and although he often spoke at medical conventions, he was reluctant to go on television and speak about his family. He finally agreed as a favor, but his interview was the best part of the show. To put it as Filippo did, "His academic approach was very impressive." The program attracted the attention of newspapers, radio and television. The show was structured around the subject of pain and apparently I seemed to be the most positive of all.

I started talking to my doctors about going home, but they said it was impossible. Although the risk of infection was over, the left leg wound was still open and leaking blood serum. I had a drainage tube in my leg and therefore it was too soon to leave

Berlin. I was getting restless and was promised it would be a matter of days. Dr. Schoeder was disappointed to see that I was still there ten days later, after having already said goodbye once, but finally it was time to go home. My surgeon, Dr. Schaffartzik, waved a paternal goodbye as if I was his own son going off to war. Although in my heart I wanted to go home, I felt very close to those people. Dr. Schaffartzik had even allowed me to watch the Formula 1 and CART races in his office on his satellite television. They had all been so kind to me.

The last days were difficult and I couldn't wait to go home. My mother and my relatives Albarosa and Gianni all arrived in Berlin to look after Niccolò. Slowly I began to have fewer and fewer tubes and became more independent. For instance, I could easily shower and was more self-sufficient after a month and half in the hospital. Given how well I'd progressed, I assumed that things would be even better at home. I arrived there on October 30 and the trip was exhausting, but I'm grateful to Paolo Barilla—an ex-Formula 1 driver and most of all, a friend—who gave us his company jet to use. He even came in person to pick us up, which I really appreciated.

I went into the house and after a moment of understandable confusion, the door shut behind us. I sat on the sofa while Daniela unpacked the luggage. I had been waiting so long for that moment, imagining all the things I could do at home, but when I realized that the only thing I could do easily was change the television channels, we found ourselves alone, facing our problems. Those were very difficult days.

CHAPTER 15

The Road to Recovery

That anti-climatic beginning could have taken its toll on me, but I had the strength to move on and fight off the depression. When I was still in the coma in Berlin, Daniela had ordered me a car with special hand controls so that I would have something to look forward to. The evening that we arrived home, I went straight to the garage to see if my driving plans would work. She'd chosen a BMW with a small remote key that opened the rear door. I thought, "Open the back, get in, toss in the wheelchair, close the door and go. Then when it was time to stop, I would slide to the back, open the back door with the remote, unload the wheelchair and slide on to it." I wanted to do everything on my own. When I saw that it would be relatively straightforward, I felt great. I immediately went for a drive to see what it was like to use the brakes without relying on my legs.

Once I got used to the set-up and practiced it a bit, I went to the INAIL Prosthetics Center in Vigorso, near Bologna, where I would be having my treatment. Dr. Claudio Costa was there to greet me, and we immediately established a plan of attack for my prostheses. I had a check-up and we started planning for the necessary work. I met the engineer Gennaro Verni, the technical director of the Center; the physiotherapists Claudio Panizzi and Franco Ferri; and my physician, Dr. Pilla. I couldn't wait to begin. I thought that it would all be very straightforward, like driving the car, but of course it was clearly more complex than that.

In Berlin, they'd left an opening in my left leg in order to clean the wound; as a consequence, there was a hole between the muscular

311

strips. I had endured 14 operations to reduce and eliminate the risks of infection. They had inserted a drain with a pump that had to be with me at all times. Even when everything had been removed, the wound still weeped, which prevented full healing. Although you could stick a finger in the hole, I had been told not to worry; it would close in time and everything would be fine. Every doctor has his own specialization, and Professor Pilla is very experienced in amputations. He therefore knew how to prepare the stump to apply the prosthesis and therefore I needed another small operation to help close the wound. He suggested this be performed at Villa Serena Clinic in Forli, where Dr. Costa usually conducts his surgery. We set a date for November 18, 2001.

On the operating table, I was given anesthetic for the 20 minutes that the entire procedure would normally take. During the operation, Pilla and Costa realized that the bone had grown more than expected. My body had tried to repair the damage where the femur had been cut, as if it were a fracture, and the calcium within the blood had been deposited there in an unusual way. The remaining bone was searching for another piece of the bone to attach to, as it does in a fracture, but nobody had "told" the bone that the other piece was in Berlin!

The doctors quickly decided to change the type of operation because there was a protrusion at the end of the bone, which would have been incredibly painful with a prosthesis. They put me under a full anesthetic and I was in surgery for more than three hours.

I was exhausted when I woke up and once again had a leg as big as a proscuitto ham. I couldn't believe that I was back in bed and stuck in such a dreadful state. The pain was unbearable, especially when the painkillers wore off. I begged the nurse for the morphine that I had refused an hour earlier. My leg was pulsating in tremendous pain and I could do nothing but pray for it to stop. Then the morphine kicked in and the pain reduced to a bearable level. Despite my state I was able to recover quickly, and thanks to

Dr. Costa, I was released two days later. I was fed up with being in a hospital, but it was a mistake to leave that quickly. I had been well looked-after and felt surprisingly content while being confined to bed and watching television. Once at home, I had to ask for help for everything and was so frustrated that I couldn't move. The pain soon returned and I really began to suffer.

We spent two days in Bologna at my mother's house. I was still confined to bed, wriggling with pain from my leg that had swollen up again. It's funny how you can't wait to get out of the hospital when you're there, but once you're home and stuck in bed, you realize how many things are no longer accessible. It was so annoying and humiliating to have to ask my mother or Daniela every time I needed something. It was even worse when my son asked something of me and I was unable to provide it. I started to feel better three days later and I wanted to show how much progress I had made, so I suggested to Daniela that we should return to Monaco. The journey wasn't too painful, given my somewhat vegetative state. Brad Filbey, our team manager, came to visit us with his daughter, while traveling in Europe. I didn't want them to feel awkward, so I felt obliged to smile and try to have a good time.

My leg was still painful and felt very tight and swollen. The doctors said that this was normal after surgery and that I should just keep an eye on the wound. It stopped bleeding after a couple of days, which helped me feel better. "That should be the end of it," I thought to myself. But the pain was still there. It soon became unbearable—sharp pains like a muscle cramp in a leg that was no longer there—so I called Dr. Costa, who recommended a tranquilizer. The following morning, while Daniela was giving Niccolò a bath, I took off the bandage to check the wound; it was much darker in color and there appeared to be a fresh drop of blood. I took a closer look in front of the mirror and realized that it was indeed fresh blood. As I moved my leg, the disaster happened.

There was a popping noise and a huge burst of blood squirted out like an open tap. I tried to stop it with the bandage, but the blood starting gushing out even more quickly. I called Daniela, "Come here, come here, I've got a problem!" She ran to me and saw the blood on the floor. "Oh God!" she screamed. I said, "I don't know what happened, but I can't stop the bleeding." My first thought was that it was the femoral artery. I remember thinking, "I'll be dead in five minutes if it keeps on like this," but then forcing myself to realize that it wasn't possible because I didn't feel dizzy and weak. Daniela didn't panic, as that is not her style, but she also feared the worst, and she called an ambulance, called Nicoletta to take care of Niccolò, and then called Dr. Costa. The ambulance was already at our door by the time she'd put down the phone. Amidst the chaos, I tried to take off the bandage and realized the blood flow had decreased and then it stopped completely. I reassured myself that it couldn't be the femoral artery because I was feeling okay. Even more shocking was that suddenly, all the pain that I had been experiencing was now mysteriously gone.

The paramedics put me on a stretcher and took me to the hospital, where they ran various tests and scans. The emergency team was really scared when they saw me arrive at the hospital without my legs, until they realized that I'd left them in Berlin a couple of months before. They explained that after the surgery in Forlì, there had been blood leak that had created a big hematoma. The sack of blood had been putting enormous pressure on the muscle and leg, until it found a way out. I was released from the hospital, but they suggested that I stay in the area just in case anything went wrong. While I was being examined, Daniela had spoken to Dr. Costa again, who also thought that the hematoma was the cause of the problem. Costa offered to drive me back to the Villa Serena Clinic for a complete check-up, where they found that the main problem was not resolved. The hematoma had not emptied and the sack kept refilling with blood.

15: The Road to Recovery

I spent four nights at Villa Serena, where many of my and Dr. Costa's friends would come to a party in the evening. During that brief stay, I was able to read and rest up. It may sound strange, but I was almost happy to be back there because I was still not feeling 100 percent. It had felt great to go home after Berlin, but I was well looked-after at Villa Serena. I didn't feel like I was such a burden to others, and I wasn't so hard on myself, unlike when I was at home. That short break helped me to recover my strength. I didn't need any night-time assistance, but Filippo and Titano offered as an excuse to spend time with me. Filippo told me on his way out in the morning, "Oh Sandro, I left your bathroom looking gorgeous." I tried to take a look, but could not enter because of the mess—towels were on the floor and clothes were strewn everywhere.

When I was released, Dr. Costa took me to his house and then Titano gave me a lift back to Monaco, as he was on his way to see Nicoletta. My leg was not improving though, and I had three stitches that would not close and nobody seemed to understand why. Nevertheless, we went back to Italy in the beginning of December and stayed with my mother while work started on my prostheses at the INAIL Prosthetics Center in Vigorso.

I went to see Dr. Pilla again, hoping that we could finalize the plans for the prostheses so that I could start walking again. Pilla didn't think we should rush it and probably, from a medical point of view, he was right. Dr. Costa was there and although he studied traditional medicine, he is convinced that if you keep the motivation high, nature can do things that medicine ignores. He highly respected Pilla and did not want to disagree with him, but he had hoped for more from him. We needed something to turn the situation around, and that came in the form of Dr. Franco Ferri. Dr. Costa was pushing my wheelchair as we were leaving the Center when we met Dr. Ferri. He immediately asked about when we would be fitting the part of the prosthesis that attaches to the stump. Costa told him about what had happened with Pilla, and Ferri suggested otherwise. "Even if you can't be fitted because you are still bleeding, I don't need you on your feet to start working on it. You are his doctor, Costa, so if you authorize me to make his stump dirty with chalk, we can get started right away." I was thrilled. "How soon is right away?" and couldn't believe when Ferri said, "In about five minutes." We immediately returned to Ferri's office and I found my smile again. Costa knew he'd just found the most powerful medicine that he could—my willpower.

Claudio Costa is an exceptional man, both in terms of his competence and for his good heart. He is full of compassion and love of mankind, and when things weren't going well for me, he felt even worse. He really cares about me, and I'm almost like a son to him. He was empathic about my suffering and he lost sleep over my persistent bleeding.

One day, he had an intuition. After measuring the first fitting, the leg was still bleeding. We couldn't figure out why the three small wounds wouldn't heal. I generally heal very quickly, so this was quite unusual. Costa took a closer look with a scan, which hinted that something might be wrong. Then he took me to a friend who performed a Doppler scan, which gives details of the blood flow. Following the veins and capillaries of the arteries, they found the problem; a vein was still open and creating the constant hematoma. I could tell from the expressions on their faces that it was a big problem. They suggested one solution might be to have another complicated operation where they'd have to open the leg and find the problematic vein. If they did that, I'd have to stay in bed for at least a month, which was terribly depressing.

Costa must have had an awful night thinking about it, because he came up with a better solution. He repeated the Doppler scan to identify the exact point, and then used his thumb to press and stop the leak and made a very tight bandage with three rolls of gauze to block the leakage. Three weeks later, the problem was solved as the walls of the vein had healed. From then on, the wound started healing, the hematoma was reabsorbed and the stitches started bonding, finally helping the swelling to go down.

Once this problem was solved, I focused entirely on trying to fit my prostheses. The limited flexibility was the most evident consequence of the various operations, and I couldn't swing my leg more than 30 degrees. I started an extremely painful recuperation process to regain some mobility. I thought that wearing the legs would be easy, but it wasn't. In reality, I only tried the provisional legs. These were made of transparent Plexiglas which enabled the doctors to evaluate the pressure points by interpreting the color of the skin—white meant too much pressure, and red meant too much blood flow. Wearing protective gloves, the technicians warm up the legs and mold the fitting with their hands until they find an acceptable compromise. Those were very painful prostheses, but the other patients at the Prosthetics Center, to whom I listened more than the doctors, assured me it would be a breeze with the final ones with soft fittings. Maybe I was overly optimistic ahead of the start, but I was bitterly disappointed after this first fitting.

I was extremely lucky to be under the care of the two best technicians at the Center. Dr. Ferri oversaw the experimental division, which deals with some of the most challenging cases. Prosthetics is never a straightforward procedure. There are rules to follow and hundreds of adjustments to make, but on the other hand, some may get lucky and get it right on the first go. I was fortunate that this world-famous center was literally two minutes away from my hometown. I was even able to speak in my own dialect, which was fantastic.

The second most important person at the center was my physical therapist, Claudio Panizzi. I met him through the structure engineer, Gennaro Verni. Panizzi explained the enormous amount of work required for rehabilitation. "Now we start with the knee component, which is going to be an Otto Bock 3R60, then we move into the gym for the rehabilitation, and then the parallel bars, then the walker frame, then crutches—first two, then one— and then eventually, we will go for a walk in the garden." He then quietly whispered to me while Verni was distracted, "I'm going to make you work your ass off." We both laughed, which really helped to break the ice.

More than anyone else at that point, Panizzi was responsible for truly motivating me. He was able to do this almost effortlessly. If there was a tank to fill, he was the one to do it. Sometimes he would be quite tough, but always efficient. I liked Claudio from the moment I met him, and he liked that he found someone ready to take on the challenge. Having always been competitive, I challenged him to look me in the face and say, "This is enough for today." I never gave up, even when it was so painful that I had tears in my eyes and blisters from wrongly positioned prostheses. I just wanted to walk, even when that meant going back and forth on the parallel bars. When he asked me to stop I'd always plead, "One more time."

Michela, who assisted him, was a very talented girl, training to become a specialist on the use of the electronic knee. This requires a different approach. It's like driving a small car and then suddenly moving into a faster car—you need to trust someone to help you discover the limitations of the car. Michela was that person.

What amazed me was how this team of people would work for more than just their salary. They would often come to my house for my physiotherapy, such as when the center was closed during the Christmas period. Daniela, Niccolò and I spent Christmas at our house in Padova, and then I'd meet the therapists at my mother's house in Castel Maggiore. I would do my two-hour walk in the corridor and then return to Padova feeling great. Panizzi knew exactly how to encourage me. "I wonder how much we are going to accomplish with this guy?" he would nonchalantly ask Daniela. It was a bit like the cryptic compliments that Morris would give when I was racing for Ganassi. It may sound like a silly comparison, but I fought this battle by using the same enthusiastic strategy that I did in racing. They saw that I never gave up and therefore worked harder, becoming passionate about my rehabilitation.

The winter was spent with Ferri working long, arduous sessions. The third set of prostheses, which was supposed to be the most comfortable, proved to be as painful as the second set. "When in hell am I going to walk again?" I asked myself. I knew that there should be an adjustment period, but I was expecting things to develop more quickly after my early progress. Instead, we had to slow down and needed two prostheses in order to move forward. We spent long days testing the fittings with Ferri, who would adjust the mold. I lost a bit of faith in his touchy-feeling approach to shaping the fitting, but then all at once he managed to go from a bed of needles to a bed of feathers. It was mid-January and I had just made the biggest leap forward in my new life. I now understood what the other patients meant when they said, "Don't be in a hurry to try the electronic knee or artificial feet—the most important part is the attachment to the body. Once that is figured out, the rest will come together."

To find the right fitting for someone who's lost both legs is not easy. The first mold is made as you lie on your back, which doesn't actually reflect how you'll feel when walking. Over time, the end of the stump changes. The first phase was the most difficult, and then I slowly improved my ability to move. After the gym, I'd often go to the bar on the lower floor. I began taking walks in the garden, and just before Christmas, they gave me the prostheses to take home for the first time. I nagged Panizzi until he asked Verni, who finally gave his consent. I had to promise that I wouldn't walk, but simply wear them in order to keep the muscles tense and toned. Of course, I broke the promise and fell several times while trying to walk, returning to the Center with a fracture in my new right leg. The prosthesis broke and the fitting went one way, and my knee the other. I asked Ferri to repair the break, then I called Panizzi. "Claudio, I have a confession. I used the legs to walk and broke one." He replied, "Don't worry, I knew this would happen … look who I'm dealing with!"

Those were provisional prostheses, which were almost held together with masking tape. In order to put them on, I had to use a type of fabric, like a woman's stocking, but made out of slightly more durable material with two strips sewn at the lower end. You put the stocking on, leaned against a wall and pulled on the stocking and prosthesis. Then, by pulling the two strips you took the stocking out and closed the hole with a valve, creating suction. It is not an easy procedure, and many patients need assistance. At the beginning I found it confusing and complicated.

One day during the Christmas holiday in Padova, I asked Filippo to help me put on the prostheses. He started pulling the right leg like crazy, but it didn't want to position itself. The stocking started rolling up and he pulled even more. Then he stopped and with the stocking in his hand, said, "Hey, there's some blood here." I looked at the stocking and at my right leg, which was bloody. "Oh no, I can't believe it—what's burst now?" My left leg had just stopped bleeding, so I couldn't understand why the right had started. After I panicked, Filippo sheepishly announced, "It looks like it's my hand—I cut it this morning." That little jerk!

Going back a month to when we were still trying the Plexiglas fitting, I had been invited by *Autosprint* magazine to the Caschi d'Oro where I was going to receive a prize. One evening while I was recuperating at Villa Serena, Dr. Costa stopped by to have a pizza with us. He suddenly realized that he had not told his mother, who was at home alone, that he was going to be late. "Oh shit, I have to run. My mom is waiting and she'll be pissed off when I get home." Filippo gave him a hard time, "How old are you, Costa?" He said, "I'll be 60." Filippo was shocked, "You're

60 years old and you're mother is still having a go at you for being out late?!" We all laughed. Later that night, I told Costa about my latest goal. "I have a dream to go to the Caschi d'Oro on my legs." Any other doctor would have immediately said that I was crazy, but he thought about it for a while. He realized how important it was for me and that I would do anything to reach that goal, which was essential for trauma recovery. He made a compromise. "Alessandro, we will work on it. We can't promise it, but I'd say that there's a 60 percent chance that you can go." Being the optimist that I am, I took this as a definite yes and started working enthusiastically on the prostheses.

It was time for the first Plexiglas mold with the attachment for the knee, which Ferri tested on me as a provisional sample before building the final one. It could hold the load vertically, but broke if you did any lateral movement. Then the day finally arrived for Ferri to show me the components of the leg. "We chose a 3R60 knee component with a connection rod, then a carbon foot with energy return, and then this rotator which allows you to bend the leg." Ferri gathered everything. "Go on, and let's put everything together so we can get him on his feet." They nervously lifted me up on to the parallel bars for the first time. I tried to let go of the bars and Panizzi yelled, "What the hell are you trying to do?" But I tried again and managed to stand up straight on my own. They were stunned because generally a person loses their sense of balance after a year in a wheelchair. Ferri said, "Hey, you're quite tall. How tall were you before?" I said, "5 feet, 8 inches more or less." With my new legs, I was now six feet and so they had to shorten me. That was disappointing because I'd always been short, with a long chest and short legs, and I thought the new look suited me quite nicely.

After they gave me my correct height, I stood on my feet again. Everyone was still amazed by my balance. Costa winked at me. I immediately asked, "Can I go to the Caschi d'Oro tomorrow with these legs?" They looked at me in awe and Ferri turned to Costa, as if to tell him that I was out of my mind. But fortunately Costa was even crazier than me. When I was in a coma he apparently said some lovely things about me. "I can tell this man has passion and strength in him, and he will walk again. He will go skiing and play with his son. He will do wonderful things." And he was right. So it wasn't unusual for him to be controversial and go against the tide. "From a medical point of view, I have no problem. But you have to tell me if the legs are steady or not." At that point, Panizzi was happy, so Ferri asked Verni's opinion. Verni, the director of the Prosthetics Center, is a serious and austere man, but also very flexible. We all went to his office. He completely understood the situation and knew that from a psychological point of view, it would be very helpful for me. He also knew that it was a risk—one that he eventually decided I could take.

There are always two sides to a coin, and accepting me at the Center for the rehabilitation was no exception. If everything went well at the Caschi d'Oro, it would show the sponsors of the Center that everything was well managed, as well as provide very some very good media PR. On the other hand, if the prostheses broke and I fell on my ass in middle of the event, it would certainly turn out to be a drama. Verni finally agreed at around six o'clock that evening, so we postponed the preparation of the wheelchair and the rehearsals until the following morning. They wanted to make sure I understood what I was going to do, where to position myself, who was coming with me and how he should prevent me from falling.

Panizzi was on the stage with me, and I could feel his hand on my back holding me. It was a very emotional moment for everybody when I went through the curtain and stood up to speak. I was so nervous that I even joked about it. "I'm so emotional that my legs are shaking." I knew that the audience could sense my need for a comeback and when I saw their reaction, everything welled up inside of me.

15: The Road to Recovery

From a psychological point of view, the Caschi d'Oro was a very important event. Those were very hard months because of the incredible pains I had to endure. I couldn't sleep at night because I felt as though my legs were still there and were sending sudden contractions, like electrical shocks, apparently a common thing with people who've lost their limbs or become paralyzed.

In addition, since Berlin I had become accustomed to taking sleeping pills and a powerful painkiller each night in order to ease the pain. I decided that I wanted to stop taking them, and because I am like a kamikaze, I did it all of a sudden. Obviously that didn't help much. As if this wasn't enough, I found it rather depressing when the boring routine kicked in once again after the excitement of the new prostheses and the Caschi d'Oro. During the journey home, I'd often see someone going out for a jog in the winter evenings, when it was pitch dark, at around 5:30 pm. It was a stab in my heart as jogging alone on foggy dark nights, unwinding the mind, was one of the pleasures in life I'd never experience again.

This was definitely not one of the easier periods in our lives. To top it off, Daniela started feeling acute pains in her back and in one leg. During the journey home from Berlin, she made a strange movement while trying to get Niccolò out of the plane. The pain became worse and worse, so we asked Costa about it and he directed us to Dr. Bollini at the Bellaria Hospital in Bologna. Bollini, an exceptional character, found a herniated disc in Daniela's back. After physical therapy failed to improve the situation, she had to undergo surgery. Now we were both forced to stay in Bologna. She was admitted to the hospital for surgery and was put in a single room in the men's wing, because there were no free beds in the women's. The day before Daniela's surgery I went to visit her, and the nurse came in and in a rather annoyed tone said, "Visitors are not allowed to lie on the beds." To this I replied politely that I was there just to give Daniela, who was the actual patient, a hand, but she didn't believe me and stormed off.

I left the hospital around midnight to go home and get some sleep. I would have to wake up early the following morning because Daniela was going into the operating room around seven am. As soon as I arrived, my mom told me that Niccolò had just gone to sleep, complaining of an earache. I went to bed and tried to go to sleep, but it was difficult because of the ghost limb pain.

I was about to fall asleep when Niccolò woke up screaming, calling out for his mom. It was three in the morning and I tried to give him some medicine, but didn't have much success. After 40 minutes of him waking and crying, I really had had enough. I was there, without legs, while Daniela was in the hospital about to undergo difficult surgery and Niccolò was crying his head off at three in the morning. I lifted my eyes towards God, up in the sky, and in exasperation. "You're really annoying me. If this is a test, well then—I've failed. I surrender. I give up, that's enough."

I don't know if someone heard me, but Niccolò turned his head and fell asleep and didn't cry any more. I have always been very open about God. To me He is love, our ability to be good, tolerant and united. After all, God is deep within all of us. I try to disturb Him as little as possible, but it was an exceptionally stressful night.

Daniela's surgery went well and she started her rehabilitation right away. But unfortunately she had to go back to the hospital twice more within the following three months for more surgery to the recurring hernia. If she had had to go back there again, she would have ended up in the medical books as an exceptional case. Her second and third operations were not so stressful for me, as I was much more independent.

One evening just before the second operation, for example, I was forced to use the stairs because the elevator was broken at the hospital. As my grandmother Gisella puts it, "To go uphill, all the saints help." Therefore I started up the stairs in earnest, staggering one step at a time while holding my crutch in one hand, and the banister in the other. Suddenly, a lady came running towards me and asked, "Are you Zanardi? I really must apologize because when I heard your story on television, I had hoped you would die, because, I thought, 'What kind of life could it be without his legs?'" I responded by asking for permission to touch my own balls to counteract the bad luck. She replied in dismay, "No, I didn't wish you bad luck—it was a compliment!" It was extremely funny.

Step by step I continued with my rehabilitation while Daniela recovered from her surgery. Niccolò suffered from the situation because he had always had a lot of attention. My career had always enabled me to spend entire days with him, where I'd spend hours with him on my shoulders or going for a walk. We were always together. Niccolò had to accept that for the time being, neither Daniela nor I could take him in our arms, and that was a traumatic experience for him. I felt so strongly about this that at the first interview after the accident, talking about my hopes for the future, I said, "My biggest desire is to be able to carry my son on my shoulders again." For quite a while during my rehabilitation I doubted that I'd ever be able to, but happily I can now.

Dinners at Riva, Costa's place in the hills around Imola, were crucial to maintaining my good humor throughout the difficult periods. Riva is an inspiring place where Costa goes to take a break from everything, to meditate as he puts it, but for me it represented a fundamental stage in my recovery. The entire group—me, Titano with his guitar, Costa, Filippo, Ferri, Panizzi, and even Doctor Amadesi, the beautiful PR director of the Prosthetics Center—would meet up at Riva. The best time to go was when the locals would slaughter the pigs and have an incredible feast. Costa rears pigs and personally feeds them with a soy, salt and chestnuts mixture—his own special recipe. He then tests them to see how they progress by measuring the cholesterol content in their blood. If they are too lean he feeds them more, otherwise he puts them on a diet. He even gives them some digestive liquor. Costa almost exclusively makes salami from his pork, although sometimes he makes a culatello. But he never makes prosciutto, because, he says, to mature them is an art, which he hasn't mastered. Obviously, he does not waste the excellent meat of the pigs' legs, so his salami is phenomenal. Costa also makes incredible cotechini, lard and pork scratching. One evening Filippo had two cotechini by himself (they are as big as a small salami) so the next day he rode his bike for 80 miles to feel better. He has never been so fast on a bike!

Costa loves his pigs. One time, one of them was ill, and instead of killing it, he took care of it as if it was his own child. He even named it Rosario. He grew so fond of Rosario that it is now five years old and weighs 1,100 pounds. Costa usually pays a farmer to feed the pigs when he is away. But since it costs a fortune to feed Rosario, Costa's mom, who is not nearly as fond of the pig, and a bit more practical, went to see a vet to ask for how long pigs usually live. The vet didn't have a clue, because usually people, he explained, "do not keep pigs as pets!"

My first interview with Carmen Lasorella was broadcast during the period I was traveling to and from the Center. It stirred a lot of interest and I started receiving hundreds of requests from TV, radio and newspapers. I think the public expected to see me depressed, so they were taken off guard by my level-headedness and sense of humor. At first, I was not able to say no to anyone, then I learned to be selective so that I could have time to spend with my family.

I had also started charging to participate in certain events in order to raise funds for the Alex Zanardi Foundation we'd set up after the accident. Many people happily made a contribution. For instance, CART gave me a $25,000 donation to participate in a gala in Toronto during the summer of 2002. In addition, both CART and Pioneer offered generous sums for me to drive the 13 missing laps at the Lausitzring. The first donation by the foundation resulted in an $85,000 check being handed over to Prince Albert of

Monaco in support of his charity AMADE (Association Mondiale pour l'Aide des Enfants), which was founded by his mother, Princess Grace (Kelly). Foundation money has also been used in Madagascar to build a school with a pediatric clinic. As most of the money came from American donors, I thought it would be appropriate to choose a charity created by an American citizen.

My recovery made a great leap forward after I tried the third pair of prostheses. I started taking the legs with me to Monte Carlo and was able to walk with them for two consecutive hours. This helped me to assess any problems and utilize the good manual and technical skills that I had learned in the past years. I am relentless; instead of driving more than 300 miles back and forth to the Center whenever a problem arose, I always tried to solve the problem myself. If the prostheses were too tight, I would take a cup and push it against the fitting to determine whether it could be modified. I would then try to create the right pressure inside the fitting by warming it up with a hair drier, carefully molding it so that I could walk again. I also tried to modify the set-up of the knee using the screws in it to fit the ever-changing stump.

Although after a while the changes in the legs slow down considerably, at the beginning, changes were happening all the time. Therefore, there is no such thing as a perfect prosthesis. For instance, the bottom cheeks, which support the prostheses, become very toned due to the activity. In my case, the first fitting for my left leg that I took home was huge, but then the stump reduced in size quite considerably. At that point I should have gone back to the Prosthetics Center to have the fitting done again. Instead, I took all the molding material that belonged to Niccolò and put it in some cling film and around the inside of the fitting. Then I put the leg on and the heat of my body molded the material to fit the shape of my stump perfectly. I kept adding the material until the situation stabilized, and only went to the Center when they were able to prepare perfect prostheses. In my ignorance, I thought the prostheses would be supported directly by the stump; but this is impossible (unless the rotula is still there), because the bone keeps growing and causes incredible pain. The main support is the bone of the pelvis, which sustains almost 70 percent of the weight.

It would have been much easier to have relied on a wheelchair, but I never gave up and worked very hard on perfecting the prostheses. It was almost a full-time job, given the amount of time that I spent working on them. It would also have been much easier if I'd still had one leg, or if both stumps were the same length. The fact that I have a longer stump on the right than on the left does cause a few problems, and even now the muscle in the left stump isn't developing as it should because I tend to rely more on the right leg. When I walk my right step is great, but I still limp on the left. Despite all the progress I've made, I still give a sigh of relief every night when I take off the prostheses, knowing every minute I spend on them is an achievement. I still remember when I called Costa to tell him how great it was to feel the drops of sweat on my forehead after having walked from home to Cap D'Ail and back—2 miles—in 51 minutes. Claudio was so excited about my achievement, and I felt the same sense of pride that I did when I had won a race, or ran 6 miles in less than 40 minutes. The challenge is the same, finding your limitations and trying to improve. The support that I receive from people really helps me out a lot.

Although in a lot of pain, I'd started wearing the prostheses by March 2002. I really wanted to see my CART friends, so I started thinking about attending the Long Beach race that April. But I was worried about how I would handle and react to the prostheses on such a long flight, and postponed the idea. Instead, I went to Toronto with Daniela in July. It was the weekend of her birthday, so I tried my best to find a nice present for her. During my time in America, I had been a spokesperson for Omega watches. I knew that there was a particular watch that Daniela liked, but it wasn't available yet. I called Michele Sofisti, a friend who used to work for Omega and who was now working for Swatch, to find out whether it was possible to have the watch delivered in time. He made a few calls and a few days later, Daniela's watch arrived—as did one for me as well, along with a lovely letter. During my career I only had two personal sponsors, Barilla and Omega. They were both so supportive after my accident that I understood that ours was not just a business relationship. When I was young I'd assumed I would eventually get screwed, but I was wrong—results are what matters, not behavior.

The trip to Toronto made me feel really proud of my determination. During all the flights I never asked for any help—I left home on my legs and reached the hotel room in Toronto on my legs. We only had enough time to freshen up and slip on a dinner suit before heading to the gala organized by Molson. Daniela was wearing an evening dress and looked stunning. I couldn't help myself and told her, "There's only one thing missing from your outfit—a watch suitable for the occasion," as I slipped the present into her hand.

We had a great time during the three days in Toronto and were escorted everywhere. The people of CART completely exploited me, in the best sense of the word. Despite everything, I owe them so much. Other people have been important in my professional life, starting from Mantese and Papis's father, but the two most important people were my father and Chip Ganassi. They changed my life.

It was terrific to see so many old friends again. Morris organized a dinner for us on Friday night, and all of the drivers and friends came along. My best friends Jimmy, Max and Tony were all there, as well as Paul Tracy. I'd always had a love-hate relationship with him, until we stopped being rivals and we started trying to understand each another. Alex Tagliani showed up as well, and I was really pleased to see him. We spoke on the phone several times after the accident. His voice would always tremble, regardless of how many times I reassured him that it wasn't his fault.

Sunday was the climax of the trip. I had been asked to wave the flag both at the beginning and at the end of the race from a tower above the finish line. To access the tower, I would have to climb up a vertical ladder. While checking it out on Saturday night, I saw four workmen building an eight yard-long platform to take me up. "Are you crazy? If you have to make it so difficult, let's just forget about it," I said. But they insisted, so I asked them to show me the ladder. I took hold of the ladder rails and, climbing one rung at a time, I reached the top of the tower. Rena Shanaman began to cry, but I didn't think I'd done anything exceptional. The crowd obviously thought differently because on Sunday, when they saw me crossing the pit lane with my crutches, the TV camera zoomed in on me and they started applauding and cheering me.

As soon as the crowd saw me approach the ladder and leave my crutches on the ground, they fell silent, as if they were thinking, "What the hell is that crazy man doing?" Once again, one step at a time, I reached the top as 40,000 people stared up at me in silence. I opened my arms as if introducing myself on a stage, and all of a sudden it was mayhem. Despite the hot weather and sweat dripping down my face, a shiver went down my spine. The same scene was repeated when I descended the ladder three-quarters of the way through the race to use the toilet. The crowd assumed I was leaving and cheered so loud, I couldn't even hear the noise of the cars. But as soon as they saw me wave and enter the toilets, they all burst out laughing. It was then time to leave Toronto. During the flight my left prosthesis started expanding and I was worried that I'd lose it, so I kept contracting the muscles to keep it on. It was exhausting and it looked rather ridiculous, so I decided to take it off. I couldn't wait to get home and finally relax.

It was the middle of summer and I started spending a lot of time on the boat. It didn't require major adjustments because it already had handrails and grip bars. This holiday coincided with a big step forward in terms of my rehabilitation. I really missed swimming and it was the only instance when I thought, "Look what a situation I have ended up in." On one occasion one prosthesis got wet and the knee seized up. During the summer it was clear that I would, as suspected, suffer terribly in the heat. Someone then explained to me that the prostheses don't let the skin breathe and given that the blood takes less time to circulate in my body, it doesn't cool down as quickly. They also say that the legs, and the feet in particular, are the radiators of the body; therefore my blood is much warmer than the average person's with legs. The summer is particularly tough and that's why the boat is my saving grace where I can take off the legs and jump in the water to cool down.

We had the first holiday on the *Hakuna Matata II* with Sandro, my brother-in-law, his wife Barbara and the two kids Nicola and Francesco. In the evenings the Doctor, who is really fond of me, lit a cigar, drank a good glass of wine and poured his heart out. Tears would come to his eyes as he recalled the difficult moments that we'd been through … and how far we had come. But I still had more work to do and have since made incredible progress. I am now very agile and completely independent. It was wonderful to be able to take everybody to Corsica for a week, as well as to go diving and fishing, although it was extremely difficult because I could only use one arm to swim underwater and obviously didn't have any fins. Later that year, Ferri created a pair of prostheses with fins, which allowed me to swim like a dolphin. The second trip on the boat was off limits for kids, so I was finally able to rest, as up until that moment, I hadn't stopped.

I honestly never shed a tear over what had happened, and I don't know whether this is good or bad. Maybe I need to do it, and there have been times when I thought that I might cry, but never did. One evening I was leaving the Center. It had been a particularly hard day and I couldn't wait to get into the car and let off some steam. While opening the door, a fellow in a wheelchair stopped me and asked for my autograph. I signed it and asked him how he was and he said he was all right. But then he added, "You're lucky to have some of your legs left so at least you can walk, whereas I don't and will have to be in a wheelchair forever." I thought to myself, "What the hell am I complaining about?"

On a similar note, one time I was very tired and couldn't attach the prosthesis. It was so painful, and I was sweating and swearing and was pissed off with the entire world. We were in Padua at the time, so I stormed off to my room to be alone and find some peace. I was very close to a good cry when Niccolò switched on the TV. I could hear that the program was about Wayne Rainey, the former World Champion motorcyclist, and the amazing things that he has accomplished as a quadriplegic. I looked up and smiled. "Will the moment for a good cry ever come?" I then realized that if Rainey could give me the strength to carry on, then perhaps I could do the same for other people.

CHAPTER 16

The Race Completed

I was feeling better and was starting to think about driving again, or maybe I should say—it just happened. It was the end of May 2002 and I wanted to know whether it was possible to organize a car for the Lausitzring, where the CART race would take place again in September. I first asked Ganassi, who still owed me Old Midnight, but it didn't work out. Then Tom Elliot, the United States director for Honda, suggested I should talk to Morris, which naturally made the most sense. Mo asked me what I needed, so I explained what I wanted, a hand accelerator, and hand clutch, but most of all, hand brakes. The brakes were the main obstacles, because with those types of cars you generally have to push very firmly on the pedals. We started thinking about a solution, but in the meantime I had other more pressing problems, like my rehabilitation. Not only did I have to learn to walk with the new legs, but also follow the evolution of my body and adapt my entire life to it.

To put it simply, I had to re-educate myself to on how to do the common daily chores, like taking a bath and so on. The idea of driving again was captivating and I wouldn't give it up, but at the same time, I wasn't putting all my heart into it. A few weeks later, the German promoter of the race went bankrupt and the race was cancelled, but given everything else that was going on, I was not too disappointed.

In September of 2002, exactly one year after the accident, I decided to attend a fundraising kart race in Monaco that had been organized by the All-Star Team. I hadn't planned to race, but the team director, Mauro Serra, asked me, "Why don't you race as well?" I agreed with a simple, "All right." "What do you mean, all right?" he asked, surprised. He certainly didn't expect me to accept the offer. "If you can get a kart with hand controls, I'll race."

The modified kart, with a Saetta engine and Parilla's Italsystem chassis, was delivered in time for the practice. Simone, who was responsible for assisting the drivers, started working with me on the kart, cutting the seat and replacing the controls. Even before I drove a single meter, the news started to spread and all sorts of publicity appeared. After the first day and despite the rain, I obtained the fifth best time. People started claiming it was a miracle. To tell the truth, although I was happy about my performance, I was also slightly annoyed. I kept saying to myself, "What do you think— that I hit my head? I am the same as before. Give me a system that allows me to accelerate and to brake, and I will drive exactly as I used to." I was convinced that although people admired me for my courage, they thought that I would be living in fear after the accident and no longer able to drive. Nothing could have been further from the truth. When I was spending four or five hours a day working with the prostheses, how could I possibly think about driving? As a matter of fact, at that point in my career, even with the legs, I would have been thinking about retiring anyway. Actually, I never started the race. On the warm-up lap I brushed a barrier, and that dislodged my left leg, so I had to stop!

I enthusiastically accepted a second offer to race a kart at the motor show in Bologna. I told Parilla, who was once again providing the karts, that "I will race for no fee, but I want a kart that performs well and that I can drive. I also want all the drivers to be in technically equal positions. We need a weight check; some of the drivers come from the 125 motorbike races and barely weigh 80 pounds when wet, which gives them a great advantage. Everything should be equal." Nevertheless, neither request was met. I came in fourth during practice, just a few thousandths of a second slower than Vincenzo Sospiri, Andrea Montermini and Stefano Modena. I knew that I could win after all three of them, for one reason or another, ended up off the track at the beginning of the race. But after eight laps, I began a terrible slump because I couldn't brake anymore. At first I had cramps in my forearms, then everywhere else. This was caused by the fact that the actions I would usually do with my feet were now simply connected to the steering wheel. The crowd was thrilled when I finished in sixth place, but I was very disappointed. I was convinced that if Parilla had done the modifications for which I'd asked, I could have won easily.

I was still going to the Prosthetics Center, but I was becoming much more independent. I always drove on my own and would often travel in the evenings in order to spend as much time as possible with my family. I also met a lot of very helpful people. I finished physical therapy and only needed to see Panizzi for the more specialized controls. Meanwhile, I became much closer to Ferri, who tried to create a pair of prostheses that I could wear while bathing. Unfortunately, it didn't work. The prototype was made of fiberglass, but there were no waterproof knees available commercially. He tried to isolate the knee using a silicone sheathing and mounting a few other components, but ultimately he had to cover the foam rubber parts with a special waterproof stocking which made the whole thing rigid, nullifying all the benefits that we were trying to achieve. On top of this, the stocking made the knees become like floats. Although my first two steps into the water with these waterproof prostheses went well, my third was disastrous. Not only did I fall, but also the feet came afloat like two buoys while I was still underwater. But that was not the end of it: The stocking then broke and the foam rubber started soaking up water. By the time I arrived home, each knee weighed about ten kilograms. My legs were leaking water and it took three days for them to dry out properly. This is why I'm inventing something, and although I'm not ready to reveal the details, I may one day be able to produce it so that many other people can benefit at a low cost.

The companies which deal with accessories for disabled people form a kind of cartel. The only way to ensure decent profits in a field which luckily does not serve too many people is by keeping prices incredibly high. In a superstore you can easily buy a complete mountain bike for $200. Maybe not top of the range, but a decent one. Anyway, it is ridiculous that a wheelchair like mine costs $3,500 plus the heavy European value-added tax, when basically it is nothing more than a couple of bent pipes and four wheels, which, after one year, are already deflated. Fortunately, I have United States health insurance, which is paying for all of this. They probably organized a party to celebrate the money that they were going to save when I announced that I was going to do my rehabilitation in Italy! If I'd decided to do it in the States, it would have cost a fortune. For example, I once went to the emergency room in Indianapolis and spent $640 on a simple antibiotic prescription.

These have been the real humiliations which I had to face because of my disability. It's sad that there are companies which speculate on the need of a few unlucky people who, despite everything, have to buy their products. I'm Alex Zanardi and often people recognize me, but despite this there have been times when I did not have the courage to dive in a swimming pool from the wheelchair, like a bag of potatoes, to play with my son.

I discussed the swimming problem with Roberto Trevisan and discovered what material we should use, thanks to our knowledge from motor racing. The next step was to build a pair of legs that could be used in the water. We did this with the help of my guardian angel, Dr. Franco Ferri, in collaboration with the Prosthetics Center. With these legs I'm not only able to walk well, but I can also go swimming without worrying about the components becoming rusted. What makes me most happy is that now I can satisfy one of Niccolò's wishes and swim with him. He has recently learned to swim and wanted to play in the water with his father. It's rather infuriating to think how relatively simple the solution was. There are numerous companies in the business that could have reached the same conclusion, but instead, they put very expensive prostheses on the market that seize up with a couple of drops of water.

But there is even more to this. Initially, whenever I lost my balance, I would fall and rip my pants. The other patients at the Center asked, "Do you have the Otto Bock 3R60 knee? Because if you do, you're guaranteed to rip your trousers if you fall."

Nothing was more humiliating than to listen to some idiot with his legs, who packs his stuff up and goes home at 4:00 pm, tell me that I have to learn how to fall. Incredible! I don't think about how I'm going to fall—I obviously fall when I lose control. So I decided to take the knee, flex it and round all the edges, but it still appeared useless. Then Ferri used the same prosthesis material to make a cover that would screw on to the knee. I threw myself on to a concrete floor and my pants barely got dirty.

That's all it was, after being sold a $4,000 knee which rips your pants. They hadn't take into account that you probably spent the entire day looking for the right pair of pants to hide the prostheses, and that trying on each pair is extremely painful in cramped changing rooms—and then they rip! This really pisses me off. Perhaps one day, when the stage lights are off, I'll be able to transform this into a business. Not for charity, but a proper job which doesn't take advantage of anyone.

In the meantime, the Lausitzring event was put back in the program for 2003 and the original idea of me finishing the race I'd started in September 2001 was revived. It was not a happy time for CART and its president Chris Pook. He was searching for anything that could give the series some good publicity, so when the race was officially reinstated, he immediately called me. "Are you interested? Do you still want to go for it?" At the beginning I was a bit skeptical. I have always been a bit of a show-off, but not at any cost. The fact that CART had lost Honda to the rival IRL series made it all seem a bit excessive. But Pook didn't want to give up and contacted Pioneer to see if they were up for it, and whether they would paint the car as it was in 2001. He told me, "Both CART and Pioneer will benefit from the publicity if you drive, and are willing to give you a financial contribution for it."

At that point I had an idea. "If they're willing to pay, I don't want anything for myself—make a donation directly to the Foundation." Pook very generously told me that Pioneer would contribute $10,000, and CART, $50,000. Real money to make a real difference. Things started looking good from various aspects. I had decided that I wasn't going to take it easy on the track, but would really go for it, thinking how it would hopefully inspire others in similar situations.

I wanted to prove that the past wasn't holding me back and that I was still able to go fast, despite the fact that racing wasn't my passion anymore. I had to play the part of the hero who frees the beautiful princess from the castle; but ironically, this hero is no longer interested in the princess. In this fairy tale, the hero would take it easy, stay out of the castle to play cards with his buddies and not worry about the princess. Only after being accused of fearing the dragon would the hero fight and defeat it. Then he would go back to play cards with his buddies, in order to prove that he was sincere. My decision was taken. Everything was now down to solving the problem of adapting the car.

The main issue was adapting the brakes. We analyzed the problem, and CART assigned the task to Adam Schaeckter, one of the technicians on Morris's team. This was a bonus, because we already knew each other. He started working on it and came up with countless questions. He even asked Ford for help, but we were running out of time and not much progress was being made.

16: The Race Completed

Then my brother-in-law serendipitously led me to the solution. Near Padova there is a small circuit named "Safe Two Wheels," where kids go to learn how to drive mopeds and motorbikes. Sandro and I took the kids to drive karts one day. My nephew Francesco—who is not yet five—showed that he has the talent to become a great driver and that he could pass, like me at the Corkscrew at Laguna Seca, each time he is on a kart. That kid has no fear. Niccolò's cousins are the only pair of siblings where the older brother, when fighting at school, will say, "If you don't stop bothering me, I'll call my younger brother to beat you up!"

Anyway, back at the track in Padova, we were busy preparing Francesco's kart. Because he was the shortest and couldn't reach the pedals, we had to move the seat. The other kids were still listening to my advice when Francesco sat on his kart. "Uncle, can you move out of the way—I have to start!" My brother-in-law then wanted to a have a go. I couldn't help but give him a hard time, "Doctor, you're pitiful." He replied, "I would like to see you. You're lucky that you can't drive or otherwise, I'd destroy you." I warned him, "I could stay in front of you even without my legs!" I sat in the kart and the manager of the circuit suggested that we tie my feet to the pedals with a strap. I thought it was going to be one slow and simple lap. But as soon as I went on the circuit, I realized that although I couldn't drive properly, I definitely had a certain sensibility through the feet.

There was just a month and a half to the race at the Lausitzring. After returning from the kart day with the kids, I called Adam. "Hey, I think I've found a way to brake. If we leave only one pedal, which holds my foot so that it doesn't slip and position it away from the bottom of the chassis, I can brake by moving my hip." Adam was skeptical. "I don't know … you need to calculate how much pressure you could apply. Do you know anybody with a racing car in which you can sit and measure the braking pressure using the telemetry?" Fortunately I did. "I have the telemetry! Wait a minute … ." I went to the bathroom, rested my back against the bathtub, placed the scale vertically against the wall and pushed on it with the right leg. Without any effort I achieved 110 pounds of pressure; pushing harder I reached about 230 pounds. I made a quick calculation to convert it into pounds, went back to the phone and told him triumphantly, "I can produce more than 200 pounds!" I explained to him how I'd done it and he laughed, but that homemade method proved to be very efficient.

In a couple of weeks, Adam developed several of the ideas that I'd drawn on a piece of paper and sent to him by fax. He designed everything, then had it produced and mounted in the car in the States without me test-driving it even once. I never had any doubts on my side; the only thing that I worried about was being able to get into the cockpit, which is very narrow and made to fit a very thin driver.

Next, I had to go to the Prosthetics Center and ask Dr. Ferri to build me a pair of thin "racing legs." In the top part of the prostheses there are internal and external edges. These components can be painful if you're sitting in a tight place as they tend to squeeze the two legs together against a man's jewels, and it is no fun at all. I asked Franco to build the legs with a very low edge. They weren't terribly comfortable for walking, but I only had to walk a few meters back and forth to the car. Ferri designed the prostheses and then his team formed the foam rubber to the shape of real legs.

CART was again coming to Europe for two races. The first was scheduled at Brands Hatch, and the second at the Lausitzring. A few days before the English race we were in Millbrook, near Luton, to test the car and fit the seat, away from the eyes of the press. Ford, which was providing the engine, uses that circuit to test its own road cars. It was an emotional moment for me to see my car, although it wasn't identical to my original. I put on my overalls and tried to get into the cockpit, but I couldn't due to the incredible pain in my testicles from the prostheses rubbing

52. Roberto Trevisan, me, and the modified BMW that I drove in my first European Touring Car Championship race at Monza in 2003.

53. The steering wheel of the BMW 320i with the specially adapted controls that make it possible for me to race. The silver bow-tie shaped lever is my "gas pedal."

54. Behind the wheel again during
the promotional day for my return to
racing at Monza in September 2003.

55. Good friends and former teammates
Jimmy Vasser (left) and Tony Kanaan
(right) just as they surprised me by
coming to Monza in 2003.

56. Talking with Dr. Mario Theissen, BMW Motorsport Director at Monza in 2003. Dr. Theissen was a key supporter in making the 2003 race and my 2004 season possible.

57. I couldn't believe how many reporters were waiting outside when the garage door went up in the pits at Monza before the 2003 race.

58. The crowd gets their first look at
my BMW race car in 2003.

59. Riding the curbs—hustling the BMW
around Monza during qualifying for the
2003 ETCC race. I qualified 11th—not bad
for my first time racing again.

60. Riding my ATV in Monaco, the fastest way to get around Monte Carlo.

61. Roberto Trevisan and I making adjustments to the steering wheel during the 2004 ETCC season.

62. Mentally preparing for the first race of the 2004 ETCC season, at Monza.

63. In the cockpit of the BMW at Monza in 2004.

64. Back on track at Monza for the first race of the 2004 ETCC season. A spin-out during the race dropped me back to a tenth-place finish.

65. Autographing copies of my book before the 2004 race at Imola.

66. Recovering from my accident and
returning to professional racing has
been my sweetest victory so far. But I
know there are many more ahead ....

against one another. Among other things, this would have severely impaired my ability to brake. At this point I made use of what I'd learned while watching Ferri and the team work on my prostheses. I "dismounted" myself with the help of Mauro Serra, who had accompanied me. I took his crash helmet, which I had given to him as a present sometime before, because I realized that his had a radio earphone incorporated, while mine didn't. Mauro and I started reluctantly to cut the casing, which give shape to the leg. Then I reconnected the shinbone of my left leg to the outside of the femur creating an X-shaped leg to make it fit into the cockpit. I also opened two more "windows" in the prostheses to gain a few centimeters, which helped me fit in the car, and then adjusted the seatbelts. I still remember how we laughed when I tried the clutch lever. Since losing my legs, I had developed two amazingly powerful arms; that day, I effortlessly pulled the lever that would have normally required two mechanics in the workshop.

The clutch was a critical feature and vital for a good start. If I let the engine stall in Germany, I would make a fool of myself, and obviously I preferred not to. The accelerator wasn't perfect, but you don't really use it that much on an oval. I put on Mauro's helmet and everybody started getting excited. When they finally fired the engine up, I realized that I was once more alone, repeating all the procedures that suddenly seemed very familiar. It seemed like only yesterday that I'd climbed out of the cockpit, which put a smile of nostalgia on my face.

I pulled the clutch and engaged first gear. The boys had bet that I'd stall the engine, but instead, I started like "The Parisian." But this style lasted only until third gear, when I slipped into my old ways. I took first and second very slowly, then deliberately made a great wheelspin all the way into sixth.

Adam asked me subtly before the run, "I'm not trying to push you, but by the end of the day it would be interesting to have a lap at 120–130 mph so that we'll have some data about the aerodynamics." I called Adam on the radio while at full speed. "Adam, do you think this speed is enough?" While I felt great driving the car again, I saw a hairpin approaching. I was so relaxed that I naturally kept accelerating until the last moment when I suddenly pounded on the brakes. When I did that at 220 mph, I realized that I didn't actually know if our homespun braking system would work or not. Luckily, I found out that it did. I was so excited that at the following corner, I went from sixth to first, locking the front wheels—what a real show-off! Everybody was astonished. I did another lap and when I was about to brake again, something happened and I went straight on. Fortunately, there was an escape route. They came to get me and once in the pits, we realized the car only had three wheels. A fastening on the front suspension had completely disconnected and gone its own way. I'm just happy that it happened there and not at the Lausitzring.

As soon as I arrived home, I started receiving all sorts of phone calls, starting with my brother-in-law. "You're crazy, the last time we had to spoon you off the asphalt!" They couldn't understand that I was doing something that I really knew how to do. I had everything under control. There was no reason why I shouldn't be doing what I had done for my entire life. Of course, something could have gone wrong with the car, but that would have been very unlikely—I wouldn't be struck by lightning twice in less than a year and a half. This is the way I saw it, but after a while, a small sense of fear started creeping up on me. Everything had to go well, and I wasn't going to allow anything bad to happen, otherwise all the cynics and critics would have a field day.

Daniela and I left on the Thursday before the race for what she now calls the "Last Adventure." My wife always accuses me of being absentminded, but that time it was her fault. She thought that our 9:05 flight to Dresden was set to leave at 9:50, so we missed it and had to fly to Berlin. As we landed I said, "Thankfully, our visit to Berlin is over this time, let's go!"

Once we arrived at the Lausitzring, several people from CART started giving me a hard time about all the interest in the race, thanks to my participation. I went to dinner with Pook and the race organizers that evening. They had planned for my involvement to remain secret until the moment I took off my helmet, but two weeks earlier, someone had leaked it to the press in Germany. The word was now out that I would drive the 13 remaining laps that I didn't get a chance to complete a year and a half earlier.

Now there was additional pressure, as the only surprise I had for the public was to show them how fast I could go. I asked Chris during the dinner if I could do 40 test laps the following night, on the QT. Chris agreed and said that I could drive from 7:00 pm on Friday for as long as I wanted.

The following day the whole CART circus was there to watch me. I was glad to see my old friends and former colleagues, and how moved they were. I knew Jimmy Vasser would be there, but was not expecting to see so many of the others, including the drivers whom I didn't know well, like Michel Jourdain, Jr., or Oriol Servia. Servia was very supportive and asked to carry the box for my helmet, at any cost. Jimmy came to my car moments before the engine was fired up. "Alex, be careful. Don't fuck up." That was his way of showing his concern. Everybody thought I was vulnerable, but they were so wrong. I felt fantastic inside the car and couldn't wait to lower the visor and set off.

The car belonged to the Bachelart Team and was in terrific shape. There were two mechanics, which was more than enough. As in a movie, Rob Hill, my ex-chief mechanic and now team manager for Stefan Johansson, and John Wayne, now on the same team, approached my car without saying a word. It was as if we were reliving the roles that we had when we were all in Ganassi's team. Rob stood in front of the car for clearance and to give me the go-ahead, while John checked the tire pressures twice. I was really touched by this.

In the meantime, the grandstands were filling up with many fans who, sensing that something was going on, decided to stay. They started playing their trumpets and singing, "Nel blu dipinto di blu" by Modugno. There were about five hundred of them who sang "Zanardi" to the tune of *Volare*. I couldn't wait to get on the track for my 40 laps. It was like being reunited with the love of your life who had been taken away for a year and a half ... very intense. I had told myself I would do everything by degrees, but feeling that everything was all right, I started pushing immediately. I took Turn One slowly on the second lap, but by Turns Two and Three, I was already much faster.

Then something magical happened. I could remember everything about the accident. I had been told the details, but there, in the car, it was like switching on the television—everything came back in front of my eyes. I remembered the beginning of the race, overtaking the four drivers all at the same time, overtaking Max Papis and then Tony Kanaan with what had been interpreted as a wave, but actually wasn't. I kept in sixth gear for all of lap three; in lap four, I slowed down only a little to take Turns One and Two, and then I took Turn Three at maximum speed. During lap five, I took Turns One and Two at the same speed and then all of a sudden, I slowed down and went back to the pits. There I spoke to Cesare Maria Mannucci, the *Autosprint* journalist who had reported on my U.S. successes. He told me that Tagliani said, "Why doesn't Zanardi go back to racing on the ovals—he would beat everybody, he is so fast!" My grin was so big that it barely fit inside my visor. The journalists all came to ask me why I had stopped after only five laps. I explained that I was happy enough and satisfied with how quickly I had regained the feeling of the car.

We all went to dinner and had a great evening. Jimmy was at the top of his form and Daniela, despite her extremely tough character, was equally moved by my five laps. It turned out that I was the only one who wasn't that impressed with the whole thing.

Understandably, they had all seen me being taken away from the circuit with a trail of blood behind me, and they were surprised I was so calm and enthusiastic. During dinner we all had great fun, we had many anecdotes and many stories to tell. After that, I spent Saturday with the press, giving interviews for newspapers, TV and radio. I had been given a very big room where I could rest when needed during this tour de force. It was exactly above my pit and I could see the digital clock on top of the finish line near the lights.

When it was time to go on Sunday and complete the 13 laps, I quietly changed into my gear. I had never shared or confessed my feelings with anybody about the little fears that crossed my mind. I woke up that morning and thought, "Good grief, does it have to be 13 laps? It is like tempting fate." But then I cancelled that thought from my mind, put on my racing legs and set off downstairs. I don't know why, but I thought once more about the number of laps, 13. In an attempt to leave all that behind I looked at the clock on the straight to see what time it was, and as I raised my eyes the display said 13 hours, 13 minutes and 13 seconds. I immediately touched my balls for good luck, but then I laughed about it. It was ridiculous—nothing bad could happen.

I finally went to the garage, which was supposed to be closed to keep away the onlookers. There were hordes of people, but most had familiar faces, so I was pleased to see them all. I got into the car and put on my helmet and gloves and they started to push the car onto the pit lane. As the shutter door was being lifted I could see the grandstand full of people. With more than 50,000 of them making a hell of a noise, it was very intimidating. As soon as I fired up the engine, there was a huge ovation; then suddenly, everything went completely silent. I started off and as in the good old days, it was just me, the car, and nothing else. I quickly realized that the mechanics had restored the setting on the boost limit valve. On Friday this had been set so that I could better control the hand accelerator, but it also gave me a ten horsepower advantage over the other cars. Given how I had performed on the Friday night practice, the mechanics had worked for two days to set up the car so that I would have exactly the same power as the others. Had I been faster than they were, it would have looked suspicious. I had the advantage of driving the old Reynard, which had been set up exactly as it was during the race of the accident. The others had new cars and had to use the same aerodynamic configuration in Brands Hatch and Germany. As a consequence their rear wing was not particularly suitable for the Lausitzring, while my set-up was perfect for the circuit. I knew how to drive with it and pushed hard. In the corners, I started taking the Reynard-Ford to the limit, despite the fact that it wasn't as fast as it was on Friday. I was going faster and faster and consuming more and more fuel. The last lap, which was my fastest, I completed in 27.485 seconds. If you compare this with the qualifying times of the other drivers, it would have made me fifth on the starting grid. As I crossed the finish line, Daniela and my dear friend Jimmy enthusiastically waved the checkered flag for me. It was fantastic.

I hadn't driven a race car for a year and a half and as a disabled person, I felt I'd proved something. I let many know that behind each conquest there are often very simple solutions and that some achievements, despite how magical they may seem, often have very little magic in them. I'm not Superman, I am just an optimist who is lucky enough to have a wonderful life, and still have a life. I'm here and able to appreciate what good is left. I went back to the Lausitzring because I wanted to show something to those in search of an inspiration to get back their life … to see how far I'd gone and to see how far they can go. In any case, don't take me too seriously, because maybe the real reason why I wanted to finish that race is that, like the Doctor puts it, I am just a guy who needed a grand finale for his book ….

Anyway, it was good fun, and now it's time to move on to other things ….

Afterword

Getting my life back on track after the accident has not been easy. When I stop and look back at where my life has taken me in these past three years, I feel a bit humbled by all the praise others have bestowed on me. I'm not sure I deserve it. My strength has been in the way I viewed my situation from the very start. I see what happened to me as a problem to be solved rather than something to be suffered through. During my rehabilitation, I met so many people with physical handicaps who also convinced themselves to move forward. And so many others who, unfortunately, had lost their motivation to keep going. It seemed clear that it was self-defeating to remain fixated on the day when destiny took something away from me. It's one thing to say it, but putting it all into practice is something else entirely.

I realized early on that I would never be able to rejoice in walking again with the prostheses if, mentally, I was still stuck in the days when I could run faster than my physical therapist. On the other hand, once I succeeded in adjusting my expectations to meet the events of my life today, I have found great satisfaction in the progress I have been able to achieve. For this reason I don't consider myself particularly brave. And I don't identify myself with the label of hero which so many would like to apply to me, however flattering it might be.

I had the good fortune to wake up, after being in a coma for a week, and find in myself the drive to confront the problems facing me. It's something I don't know how to explain. It was just there.

It's the same driving force I had as a child, thanks to my passion for race cars, that made me spend entire afternoons taking my little go-kart apart and putting it back together again. The same driving force that made me discipline myself to go to bed early when all my friends were going out to the disco. The same driving force that made me put myself on a diet at age 15 in order to lose those four to six pounds of extra weight so that the go-kart could go a little faster. This driving force—something I have always called passion—has advanced me in the sport of racing a thousand times more than the simple determination often attributed to me.

On the 15th of September, 2001, I was dead. My heart had stopped three times. In fact, Father Phil De Rea, my friend and the spiritual father of CART in those days, gave me the last rites. But miraculously I was brought back to life through the skill and passion for their craft of the CART medical team coordinated by Steve Olvey and Terry Trammell and by the doctors at the Klinikum Berlin-Marzahn. How could I squander this gift of life? Would it have made sense for me to spend the rest of my days lying in bed staring at the white ceiling and telling myself that it was all over? I can't blame those who do not succeed in psychologically overcoming the serious obstacles that life at times imposes on us. It's just that I have been fortunate enough to be able to put those things in the proper perspective from the very start. I hope that others can do the same.

I have succeeded in characterizing my troubles as problems to be solved. I have examined them very closely to figure out the secret of dealing with them. Unlike someone who might think he's reached a dead end, I have tried all the twists and turns that have been presented to me by life's anticipated setbacks and unexpected successes. In doing so, I've received great satisfaction. And, why not? I've enjoyed myself.

There are so many analogies for my life to be found in my racing career, don't you think? Winning a race is never easy. You beat gifted adversaries that at times have the advantage of driving a car better than your own. And only by improving the engineering of the car, by making that last minute modification that comes from a bold intuition, will you be able to achieve the much desired result. At times, it goes well. More often, it goes badly. Above all, you must believe in yourself. But the driving force behind everything is that enthusiasm for trying.

On the 15th of September I died and then I was reborn. From that moment I threw myself into my rehabilitation with the same enthusiasm that helped me win so many races. And I'm sure I did seem to rise from the dead in the eyes of many of the fans of this sport when I returned to the Lausitzring in March 2003 to finish the race I had started a year and a half before. I've always considered my most recent success to be the sweetest, because to me, deep down, there isn't a big difference between having won this latest gamble, or the time at Laguna Seca when I pulled off the "corkscrew" pass that made me famous among the fans. I am still someone who seeks out new challenges and so I guess I should say that each victory is *my sweetest victory ... so far!*

Roberto Trevisan is a friend and, as it happens, also the technical director of the BMW Team Italy-Spain that participates in the European Touring Car Championship, known as the ETCC. In June of 2003 we found ourselves at my house one night for the usual barbeque among friends. After we had eaten, in the middle of a pretty challenging game of pool, Roberto stopped himself right before sinking a ball and asked me, "Alessandro, do you feel, after your Lausitzring performance, that you've finished with racing or would you be willing to try again if I prepared a car with controls that allowed you to drive it?" I answered him simply, "Cipo (that's his nickname) are you kidding? of course I'd try. That's like asking a cat if he likes mice! But now sink this ball and concentrate because Filippo and Titano are massacring us, they are ahead by 23 points!" The good Cipo totally blew the shot, losing us another eight points. I could tell that in his mind he was already building my car.

Trevisan works for the three co-owners of the BMW Team Italy-Spain that races in the ETCC: Roberto Ravaglia, Aldo Preo and Umberto Grano. Ravaglia was the Schumacher of European Touring Car in that he had won everything there was to win. Although I didn't know him well personally, I had read a great deal about him. So I held him in very, very high esteem. Preo, a longtime friend and business partner of Ravalgia's, started three BMW dealerships with him in the Veneto region. Preo had discovered he was so clever as an entrepreneur that, in a short time, he had turned the Motorsport Group—as their company was called—into the number one dealership in Italy in terms of auto sales. Umberto Grano, another great former champion of European Touring Car, had been involved in establishing the Motorsport Group with Ravaglia and Preo, and had had a leading role in convincing BMW Italy and BMW Spain to sponsor the racing team that participates in the ETCC.

I knew Umberto slightly, thanks to a meeting that I had with him years before. It was in 1993 in fact, after my monumental crash at Spa with the Lotus, when it seemed evident that my chances of continuing in Formula 1 were rapidly diminishing. I considered trying to reinvent myself in European Touring Car. I asked a friend, Gian Alberto Coari—a big shot inside Castrol, which was sponsoring the BMW program—to recommend me for a meeting with the head honcho of BMW Italy motorsports activities. This was Umberto Grano, as I've mentioned. At the time of our meeting in 1993, my eyes were still completely red as a result of the crash at Spa which caused all of the capillaries in my eyes to burst.

Umberto, who is such a great guy, still loves to tell the story of why he didn't hire me to drive for him. He usually tells this story over dinner with friends, with a glass of wine in his hand. He says,

"How could I take on this guy who looked like the re-incarnation of Dracula! I mean I think Coari is really a great guy, but I had to say to him, Oh, Gian Alberto, look at this guy, he looks like a maniac!" Then he turns toward me and inevitably he adds, "And anyway, you owe me a ton of money, guy! If I had hired you in 1993, you wouldn't have gone on to race in America and made a fortune. So what's an honest percentage for a manager—about twenty percent? I'd say you owe me at least a million dollars, easy. When are you going to pay me?"

Anyway, getting back to the point of the story. Midway through the 2003 ETCC season, Roberto Trevisan suggested that I try driving a touring car. He was so enthusiastic that the three team owners gave him *carte blanche*. The team offered us the use of a car from the 2002 season so our work wouldn't affect the cars of the team drivers Fabrizio Giovanardi and Antonio Garcia. The close proximity of the team to the prestigious engineering firm, Fadiel, in Mestre, Italy, meant we would have access to the expertise we needed to fabricate the special controls.

I got involved with Roberto in figuring out what I would need to drive. Keep in mind that on this type of car there are no power brakes so you need to push very hard on the pedal. Roberto had assumed that all the controls would have to be brought up to the steering wheel by means of power mechanisms. At the beginning I thought so too because of the difficulty I had braking during my 13 laps around the Lausitzring. In the Reynard chassis there had been little room in the cockpit and we had built everything in a hurry. On the track I was very quick but it was on an oval where you have no need to brake hard, so I could use my leg for braking. We agreed that totally hand-operated controls were the way to go. The Fadiel firm designed a braking mechanism that was activated by a little wheel on the bottom of the steering wheel. The accelerator was controlled by a kind of a bow tie mounted on top of the steering wheel. Initially, we used a totally automatic control for the clutch: at the simple touch of the hand, a sensor, sunken into the stick shift, allowed you to shift gears.

When we first took the car on the track we were full of enthusiasm, fueled by the good will and affection of everyone involved with the project. But during the first run I realized that there was still an awful lot of work to do. The mechanism that activated the braking controls was just a little switch, and there was no way of modulating it. In other words, either I did not brake at all, or I slammed my face into the windshield. There was nothing in between. The clutch was very punishing, always grinding when engaged. I looked like a first time driver and in many ways, I was. Even the gas control was imprecise, with a noticeable lag between when I moved the control and when my speed would change. Even with all these difficulties, I remember the day with great pleasure.

After a few laps around, my friend Trevisan called for a break, and he was in tears. At first I didn't know if he was laughing or crying, and then I realized that they were tears of emotion. Because of our long friendship, he had been more touched by my accident than most people and seeing me drive again was a very emotional moment for him. His tears made many things clear. I was able to understand that people wished me well and were genuinely moved by what I was doing. I tend to look at everything I'm doing from a purely technical standpoint. I think that might be the reason why I am never completely satisfied and always want to do better. But the people who are close to me, who realize I am not a super hero, are often touched by my efforts.

Ravaglia, Grano and Preo were there with us. By the end of the day they were also amazed, in spite of all the problems with the mechanisms. I remember that I lapped the circuit in 1:27.9, which was certainly not great (on that track now we go around in 1:21 range). There was quite a lot of work to do, but everyone seemed astonished. They told me to remember that this is an old car, the brakes aren't 100 percent, the engine is too slow, and the clutch is not perfect. I was pleased, but would have liked to explain that I was losing time because I was not able to get the car to do what I wanted. But it didn't seem to me the time to dampen their enthusiasm. It wouldn't have been right, and I was afraid of seeming to be a braggart.

However, I was determined to improve the car. I began by asking Roberto about trying to rig the brakes so I could operate them using my prosthetic legs instead of with the steering wheel control. At first, he was very reluctant. "Alex, it requires a strength of pressure that you are not able to produce," he said. We knew that at BMW Motorsport in Germany there was a system available, a mechanism that was used for the 24-hour endurance races, that was able to produce enough power to enhance the driver's pressure on the brake pedal. I wanted to try it, but Roberto was still skeptical. He would only agree to it if we could install the BMW Motorsport system mentioned above. But to do this, the FIA would have to give us a an exemption.

Three weeks passed and we continued to argue about the brakes. It occurred to me, why not try measuring my braking pressure again, as I had done before my return to the Lausitzring. If I could convince Roberto that my legs were strong enough, maybe he would agree to try it. So, leaning my back against the side of the bathtub, I put the bathroom scale against the opposite wall and pressed on it with my foot as hard as I could. The results showed me that since the Lausitzring, I had become stronger. My muscles were regaining their strength. I knew that with a well-made system this problem could be solved. Next time I went to the team's racing shop I called Roberto and the others over and said, "Make me this brake, how hard could it be?" I remember their skepticism, but cleverly I had brought my bathroom scale from home .... I asked Trevisan to make the first attempt, setting two engine casings up against the wall. By pushing even half-heartedly, he achieved a force of 230 pounds. Then I tried, and by putting everything I had into it, I was able to achieve 275 pounds. At which point, I looked at Roberto and said: "What do you say? Are you going to make this brake modification for me or not?" The new brake system arrived from Germany and they got to work.

Another problem we faced was how to modify the clutch. In the end we adapted a control that Fadiel had already built by adding a little lever placed on top of the stick shift knob. With this final problem solved, we were ready to go to Misano for an open test in which all of the drivers of the championship were participating. BMW Italy-Spain would go with Giovanardi and Garcia's two cars, as well as mine.

Misano was a revelation. It was only my second time in the car, yet I was immediately comfortable with the new systems. After a few laps I was a couple seconds behind the fastest drivers, but they were driving 2003 cars instead of cars from 2002 like mine. What a miracle. It was incredible. Ravaglia could not stand still, he was running all over the place yelling, "But if we change the engine, change the brakes, modify this, change the weight distribution, we could take another 90 pounds off the car …." With Ravaglia's changes it seemed as if I might be able to put five seconds between myself and the other drivers. Unbelievable, but that was how enthusiastic we were. The test also resolved the problem of asking the FIA for an exemption for the modified brake: at one point, after returning to the pit, I said to Trevisan, "Are you sure the brakes are working? It seems really hard to push." "Yes, yes, of course," he answered. "You would not even be able to brake at all if they weren't." "Can you check?" I asked again. He laughed in my face, but lifted up the hood and realized that the brake mechanism was stuck, it had become deactivated. "Wow, you are really braking all by yourself!" Problem solved.

We continued to adapt the diameter of the brake pump and the length of the pedals. But the system achieved on that test is more or less what we still use today. In fact, today's system is nearly identical to our original design and a real testimony to how much passion we poured into it.

When you drive a production car you have the benefit of over a hundred years of development. But in the case of my car, I am a pioneer. This is because, thankfully, not many people lose their legs and have to drive a race car with above-the-knee prostheses. My BMW 320 race car has the traditional H-pattern shift configuration for which I need to use my right hand to change gears. If only we could have used a sequential gear box. That would have been a quick fix because, with the simple addition of two buttons—one for up-shifting and one for down-shifting—everything would have been just like the system I use in my everyday driving, with which I am naturally very familiar. And it is this very system which allowed Jason Watt, the paraplegic driver, to win the title in the Danish Touring Car Championship.

Obviously, in our attempts to get the car right, we did have some total failures. But with passion and ingenuity we achieved many advances. That we ended up more or less on target on only the second attempt was a great accomplishment—the product of careful reasoning, but most of all of a real desire to succeed. It just shows that if you want something badly enough, you can make tremendous progress. When you really want to solve a problem, you think about finding a solution all the time. That's also how I was able to improve my prostheses.

Strangely enough, there was a meeting of BMW Italy at that time near Misano. I was invited to a dinner which included Gianfranco Tonoli, the managing director and for years a supporter of the motorsports programs, and Marco Saltalamacchia, the then new president of BMW Italy. He had only been head of the company for a little while and no one knew how he felt about the motorsports program. Saltalamacchia, having seen how well we did during the open test, was asked by the group, "What do you think about us preparing a third vehicle for Zanardi in time for

Monza, the last race of the championship?" We immediately knew how the president felt because he had shown more enthusiasm for it than everybody else at the table. The die at that point was cast. Everyone was in favor of the idea, but there was still much work to do. It seemed almost more of a joke than an honest to goodness plan. But in my heart I had already decided. I was going to race at Monza.

Monza was scheduled for October 19, 2003. I knew that it would be a demanding weekend. In certain places enthusiasm for European Touring Car races is very fierce. Monza is such a place. There is always a huge crowd and my long awaited return only added to the excitement. Luckily, my friend Roberto Locatelli, the former motorcycle world champion, had lent me his motorhome. This helped because I was feeling under a lot of pressure—even more pressure than when I was trying to clinch the CART championships in the States. I felt like a child again, confronting something for which I was not very well prepared. I only had two test days under my belt and I was driving a car that I did not yet feel very comfortable with. Throughout my career I had always driven open-wheeled cars that have a lot of downforce. They require a very different driving style.

Driving a touring car would be a new adventure. Thankfully, I was allowed a test day before the race; this helped me a lot. To add to the excitement, we learned that at Monza, Alfa Romeo would have Formula 1 driver Giancarlo Fischiella in one of their cars. It was shaping up to be a weekend packed with events that would guarantee a sell-out crowd. In Touring Car, unlike in Formula 1, paying for a grandstand ticket enabled one to go into the paddock too. When I arrived at Monza on Friday, I saw the grandstands empty and the paddock absolutely overflowing with people. It seemed like the center of an enormous outdoor market.

On this very first day with no on-track activities, it was already difficult to move in the paddock. I had to participate in the press conference, have photos taken together with the fans, and sign my book—which had just come out in Italy. In short, a ton of people were around me. The warmth of the crowd was incredible. I hated to tear myself away from the people or to hold back from someone who wanted me to sign a photograph for their child or a dedication on their copy of the book. In short, it was exhausting right from the start.

In the middle of all of this I noticed Daniela was acting a little strange. She is the brains of the family and I gladly leave all the nitty-gritty details to her. This time, however, I had a sneaking suspicion something was up. And then on Friday, during a book signing for fans, two strange characters showed up on the pretext of getting an autograph. When I raised my head to look at them I discovered that they were Jimmy Vasser and Tony Kanaan. It was an emotional moment of pure joy. They wouldn't have missed this for the world. I think they considered the day even more important than I did. It was so wonderful to see how pleased they all were that they were able to surprise me. Daniela was laughing like crazy. They stayed until Sunday afternoon. We had a wonderful dinner Friday evening at the Hotel Fossati, a fixture at Monza. The promoters also gave me permission to take them onto the track in my car. I proudly showed them the race track, even though Tony was familiar with it already. After all, Monza is a legendary track. The only thing like it in America is the Indianapolis Motor Speedway. I showed them my home track—explaining the various tricks, the way to handle the curbs, and so forth—with great pride.

For Saturday afternoon's qualifying session, Jimmy and Tony went to the Ascari corner and sat in the grandstand, partly to stay out from under foot and partly to see how I was driving. A fan recognized them from a distance and came up to them. He started chattering on to Tony, who speaks Italian very well. "You are Tony Kanaan," he said to him, "and that's Jimmy Vasser. I'll be damned! I am a really big fan, I always watch the American races." And so on. Towards the end of the conversation Tony, who is a talkative enough guy, said to him, "And who did you come here to root for?" The guy replied, "Well, partly for Zanardi and partly for Tarquini." "And Giancarlo Fischiella?" Tony asked. "Nooooo," replied the fan flatly, "he crashes too much, too many accidents. I don't like him." Strange that a fan would complain about something like that. "No, it's not true. Giancarlo is really good," Tony shot back. "Yes, that's true," the fan reluctantly agreed. The fact is that in the first lap of the trials a red torpedo, an Alfa, crashed pretty badly, right at the Ascari corner. The fan turned from the race toward Kanaan and said, "Oh my god, it's Fischiella! Oh jeez, that was one hell of a crash, I told you!" Now don't be upset with me, Giancarlo, but that guy really saw that one coming.

That weekend at Monza was a beautiful one, even though it has its share of problems. Thanks to an adjustment that I had asked the guys on the team to make, my motorhome was hooked up to a heavy duty 64-amp electrical socket. So I had a ton of power at my disposal in Locatelli's motorhome for all of my equipment. The other motorhomes were only hooked up to about 32 amps. I heard one of the neighbors curse because his circuit breaker tripped so frequently. It seemed like everything was set for a good rest. But in the middle of the night I woke up, around 3:30 am, with icicles practically growing down from the ceiling. It was the middle of October. My wife was too cold to even get out of the trailer. So in the dead of night, on the eve of my long-awaited return to racing, I woke up and put on my prosthetic legs which had already been put into my racing overalls, and I got out of the trailer, cursing. Some clown—I never discovered who he was—had taken my plug out and hooked it up to one of the less powerful sockets, and he had put his plug in my socket, stealing my adaptor as well as my connection. What a smart ass. So my fuse box, on which my heating, my hot water and things like that depended, was shut off. We were left without light, heat or anything else. It was a night from hell.

Afterword

Though exhausted, my enthusiasm and my adrenaline kept me charged up. I succeeded in qualifying 11th, despite a few mistakes. For a first race it was not that bad. In fact, right away we received a ton of compliments. A lot of the credit goes to BMW, who had made a car, most of all an engine, that performed really well. I had a smooth enough start in race one. But at the first chicane all hell broke lose. Touring Car races are known for aggressive driving. This is because the races are short, and also because if you bump up against another car, almost nothing happens to you. (With open-wheel cars, if you touch the front end of someone's car, it immediately flies off.) Monza was the last race of the year and everyone wanted to end the season on a high note. The first chicane at Monza narrows like a funnel, and a lot of guys end up crashing. Ironically, just as I was about to make it through turn one cleanly, my teammate Garcia spun out in front of me, and I crashed right into him. I was sandwiched in between two other cars, and there was nothing else I could do. I went back to the pit pretty depressed, realizing that the suspension was broken. I was thinking that it might be all over right there. Instead, the guys on the team were really, really great. Later, even Mario Theissen, Director of BMW Motorsport and a man who did everything he could to make this 2003 race and my 2004 season possible, expressed his admiration for the job they did.

The team worked a miracle. I was able to start in Race 2, even though I was starting last. I was lucky because there was another pile-up at the first chicane, but this time I passed through unscathed. I was able to pass some cars, even though my pace was not as fast as the other BMWs. At times I benefited from the other drivers' bad luck. But I was also aggressive, battling a few of my opponents for position. I finished seventh and I even earned some championship points. It was celebrated as a great victory, since it was my first race. Honestly, I was not really satisfied. Mentally I was already projecting to Monza 2004, the first date of the new season.

After that race, BMW Italy and BMW Motorsport showed great interest in continuing our association. And since I am always searching for what could be my next *sweetest victory*, I decided to do it again. 2004 has been a difficult year. During the winter testing we had some good performances, near the top. But with the arrival of the warm weather we started encountering problems, principally involving tire wear during the race. This is mostly due to my inability to use the brakes in the best way for this style of racing. I also have to admit, although I probably already knew it, that the drivers in Touring Car are really very good.

In Europe, other than Formula 1, the only other possibility for racing as a professional driver is Touring Car. Here there are the major manufacturers, really great drivers, and a very competitive championship. The other teams have made a lot of progress as compared to last year. Such a competitive field means that any mistakes I make end up having a greater impact on my results. I need to improve my ability to modulate the braking correctly, and learn how to brake hard without flat-spotting the tires. The cars are heavy at 2,500 pounds, and once the tires have deteriorated you quickly lose performance. It's a constant challenge. For me there is great room for improvement. One minute I'm encouraged and the next frustrated. When modifications to the controls help me gain a couple of tenths of a second, it sometimes feels like these are not actual gains against my competitors but merely improvements that allow us to compete on a more level playing field.

The desire to do well is still very much alive in me—the desire to fight and to win. I believe I'll continue racing in 2005. I am convinced that if things don't turn out right on the first try, one has to try again. Only if you keep trying will you ultimately succeed. Sometimes you don't do all that well, but if you have the enthusiasm and the drive you achieve your objective. I am enjoying myself. I am very passionate about racing, even though the results this year have not been earth-shattering. BMW Italy has renewed its faith in me and, in return, I am trying to repay that faith with a certain level of success. And of course, I am also doing it for my own satisfaction. Meanwhile, my everyday life continues. I go skiing, I swim with the floating prostheses that I helped develop (and which the INAIL Prosthetics Center is beginning to produce for its other patients). This summer I made a 1,400-mile journey at the helm of my boat with my family and friends. I am watching my son grow and go to school and play. I am well. I consider myself to be a happy man. And now, as I have said once before, it's time to move on to other things.

Alex Zanardi
September 2004
Padova, Italy

Author's Note

Journalists have often suggested that I should write my life story. Although that was flattering, it seemed a self-indulgent thing to do—to write a book about a career which my fans, for the most part, knew about already. Then I had the accident at the Lausitzring, followed by the struggle to survive, the rehabilitation and finally the return to a so-called normal life—a life for a man that wouldn't feel "normal" but instead often made me feel like an alien.

Then Gianluca Gasparini entered the picture. We met during an interview in Monaco and, most importantly, he was a gentleman throughout. He tried to be very accommodating despite the fact that the situation changed dramatically when the photographer, who had accompanied him on the trip, started making a huge fuss. The photographer wanted me to re-enact a scene with my wife, Daniela, and son, Niccolò. When I tried to explain how I never involve my family in my public life, he went ballistic. I was very impressed by how calm and unabashed Gianluca remained as the photographer screamed into his mobile phone at some head editor in Milan about what a waste of time the trip was. He could see in my face that I had vetoed the photographer's artistic agenda, so he kindly offered to cancel the whole thing and apologized for the inconvenience.

With a bit of common sense, we decided to find a compromise and go ahead with the interview. Despite the rocky introduction, I quickly realized how very similar Gianluca and I were in terms of our backgrounds and mentality. We are both from Emilia and, despite leaving for different reasons, we are both profoundly tied to our home town. For all these reasons, when he said that I must write my memoir I started to think about it. I also discovered that his writing style and storytelling, although clearly more honed, were very similar to my own.

But what ultimately convinced me was something else. Gianluca said to me, "Alessandro, whether you like it or not, you have to tell your story and share your sense of humor with the world. Since I met you, I wake up in the morning and if I'm having a bad day, I just have to think of you and what you've been through, and that puts everything in perspective. Before I met you, I had this idea in my head that you were some kind of Superman, but now I understand that you're just a man. You know how to find the spirit to go on, thanks to your innate optimism and tremendous courage. Say what you like, but it is your duty to write the book!"

This was a wonderful compliment. I thought long and hard about it and all the people with similar problems who, during my rehabilitation, had given me hope. They made me realize, "Apart from what the doctors are telling me, I see others have already reached certain goals and although it will be tough, perhaps I can do it too." In addition, I thought about my son and how proud I would feel knowing that some day he would read about his father. So I called Gianluca a few days later and said, "Let's go for it!"

I made two points very clear, however. I didn't want the book to be full of technical jargon about suspensions, shocks and so on' nor did I want it to go on and on about the accident in Lausitzring and my recovery. As I got to know Gianluca better, I realized that I didn't need to make this clarification—his attitude about life was exactly the same as mine.

Writing this book gave us both enormous satisfaction. We had a lot of laughs and would often find ourselves nudging each other as we worked during those enjoyable Milanese evenings at his home, alongside his lovely wife, Irene. But the greatest joy was re-reading something for which we gave 100 percent of our heart and soul. When the book was released in Italy in July 2003, we never imagined that the public would respond so well. People stopped me in the street to share how the story touched their lives. It makes me very proud to hear how people—regardless of whether they like motor racing or not—enjoyed the book. They found themselves wrapped up in the story, the jokes and my life. Most of all, they couldn't believe that someone from my humble background could make it among so many people from the privileged classes.

Had I not had the accident in Lausitzring, this autobiography probably wouldn't have been written. One of the other reasons for writing it was to show that the accident was only an episode in my life, but not my whole life. I've now returned to skiing, swimming and underwater fishing, and am racing in the European Touring Car Championship with a BMW. When people ask if I'm afraid to take risks again, I tell them that life is full of risks and we have to take risks if we really want to live fully.

That said, I still hold on for dear life! But I also know that people ask me this question as they think I'm vulnerable because of my disability. In other words, why didn't anybody ask me this before the accident? I absolutely know that I'm not immortal. But neither am I weaker than other drivers. Stronger in some ways. So if I should break my leg today, all I need is a four-mm Allen wrench and it will be repaired in just two minutes ....

Joking apart, life goes on and, fortunately, I'm still here to enjoy it. But the return to racing is not the best part, believe me. The best part is taking my son to school, seeing him grow up, making pizza on a Saturday with him while he throws flour on Daniela who grumbles about the mess in her kitchen ... the best part is teaching him to swim, reading him a bedtime story and watching the same cartoon over and over and laughing with him all the same. I love the photo of Niccolò leaning against my chest while I drive the boat because in it is a child who still sees his father as I saw my father when I was his age—as an invincible knight who loves and protects you forever.

Alex Zanardi Chronology

Childhood (Chapter 2)

1966 October 23, born Alessandro Zanardi in Bologna, Italy, the son of Dino and Anna Zanardi, and younger brother to Cristina.

1970 Family moves to Castel Maggiore, a village on the outskirts of Bologna.

1979 Sister Cristina (15 years old) and boyfriend killed in car accident.

Karting (Chapters 3 and 4)

1980 Father, Dino Zanardi, buys 13-year-old Alex his first kart as a way to help the family move on from Cristina's death. Finishes ninth in his first race at Vado, and fourth at Fossa.

1982 Scores first kart racing victory at Jesolo. Finishes third in 100cc National class in the Italian championship run-off at Parma. Earns full sponsorship from the manufacturer of Vega kart tires.

1983 Competes in his first international race at Gestaach, Germany.

1984   Joins the DAP kart team as a full-time driver, but his karts suffer many mechanical failures.

1985   Wins 23 kart races in Italy and across Europe and an international kart race in Hong Kong. Wins both the Italian and European Kart Championships.

1986   Wins the Italian Kart Championship racing for Kali.

1987   In the 135cc class, wins all five European Kart Championship races to clinch the title. Also races in the 100cc European Kart Championship, finishing second to Michael Schumacher.

Formula 3 and 3000 (Chapter 5)

1988   Graduates to cars. Joins an Italian Formula 3 team, but is disappointingly uncompetitive. Returns to karts at the end of the season and wins the Hong Kong international race.

1989   Joins a new Formula 3 team and rebounds with a very competitive season, including two second-place finishes and two pole positions before the team's sponsor goes bankrupt.

Meets Daniela Manni, the team's manager and chief timer. They will marry in 1996.

1990   Joins an established Formula 3 team and finishes second in the Italian Formula 3 championship with two wins and four other podium finishes. Also wins the Europe Cup race at Le Mans.

1991   Graduates to Formula 3000. Wins two races and finishes second in four to end a close second in the championship. Qualifies on the front row for nine of ten scheduled races.

Formula 1 (Chapters 6, 7 and 8)

1991   Catches the eye of Formula 1 team owners and is hired by Eddie Jordan to drive in the year's last three grands prix. Debuts at the Spanish Grand Prix, finishing ninth.

1992   Suffers a lean year, being traded among Jordan, Minardi and Benetton teams. Test drives for Benetton and makes three Formula 1 starts for the Minardi team, replacing an injured Christian Fittipaldi.

1993   Joins Team Lotus. Finishes sixth in the Brazil Grand Prix (earning first world championship points) and seventh at Monte Carlo.

Suffers serious injuries during qualifying for the Belgian Grand Prix at Spa-Francorchamps. Misses the last four races of the year.

1994   Still recovering from the Spa crash, misses the first four races of 1994.

Team Lotus declines into bankruptcy by year's end without honoring financial commitment to Zanardi.

October 27: Dino Zanardi dies of cancer.

1995   No professional racing position. Spends time off with old friends back home in Castel Maggiore. Only income is from job as instructor at a safe-driving school.

Invited to the United States to meet with IndyCar team owners (series name later changed to CART). Following tests with Chip Ganassi Racing, signs a contract to drive in the PPG IndyCar World Series for 1996.

CART (Chapters 9, 10 and 11)

1996 In second IndyCar race of career (Rio de Janeiro), starts on pole and finishes fourth. Scores first IndyCar win in Portland, Oregon. Also wins at Mid-Ohio Raceway and at Laguna Seca, making a spectacular last-lap pass of Bryan Herta in the "Corkscrew" for the lead. Sets rookie record for leading more laps than any other driver.

Finishes third in the 1996 PPG IndyCar World Series, and is named Rookie of the Year.

Marries Daniela Manni in Las Vegas.

1997 Wins the 1997 PPG CART World Series (IndyCar series name now changed to CART) with five wins: Long Beach, California; Cleveland, Ohio; Brooklyn, Michigan; Mid-Ohio Raceway; Elkhart Lake, Wisconsin.

Wins first two races of 1997 season, setting two new records, which remain unbroken, for six consecutive pole positions and six consecutive front-row starts.

1998 Wins the 1998 CART FedEx Championship Series with seven wins: Long Beach, California; Madison, Wisconsin; Detroit, Michigan; Portland, Oregon; Cleveland, Ohio; Toronto, Canada; Queensland, Australia. Sets many records, including championship points amassed (285 points, 116 over the second-place winner, teammate Jimmy Vasser).

Sets record, also unbroken, for being on podium for 15 out of 19 total races in the season.

September 7: Niccolò is born to Alex and Daniela Zanardi in Monaco.

Bouncing Between Formula 1 and CART
(Chapters 12 and 13)

1999   Returns to Formula 1 with the Williams F1 team. Has disappointing season, earning no championship points after dropping out of ten races. Qualifies fourth for the Italian Grand Prix at Monza, but finishes seventh after battling mechanical problems.

2000   Enthusiasm for racing is dampened after his season with Williams. Takes a one-year sabbatical from racing.

2001   Returns to CART with (former Chip Ganassi Racing technical director) Morris Nunn's new team. Despite early season difficulties, regains his competitiveness.

The Accident and Recovery
(Chapters 14, 15, 16 and Afterword)

2001   September: Anticipates a good result at the American Memorial 500 at the Eurospeedway in Lausitz, Germany. While contending for the lead, loses control exiting the pits, leading to violent broadside crash in which both legs are severely damaged.

In emergency surgery, both legs are amputated above the knee. He survives despite massive blood loss, three heart attacks and a host of complications.

December: Following a grueling recovery effort to learn how to walk again, Zanardi stands for only the second time on prosthetic legs to present *Autosprint*'s Caschi d'Oro award to Michael Schumacher.

2002   Driving a modified kart, competes at Monte Carlo and Bologna kart races.

Less than a year after the accident, travels to Toronto for Molson Indy to see CART friends. To the cheers of the crowd, climbs the 30-foot flag tower ladder as honorary starter and chief flagman.

2003   Drives a modified Champ Car for 13 exhibition laps at the Lausitzring, thus "completing" the ill-fated race of 2001. His lap times prove competitive with the qualifying times for the weekend's CART race; would have started fifth on the grid had he competed.

Returns to competitive racing at the wheel of a modified BMW sedan fitted with hand controls in the European Touring Car Championship race at Monza.

European Touring Car Championship
(Afterword)

2004   Completes a full season of professional racing in the European Touring Car Championship driving for BMW Team Italy-Spain. Runs competitively in most races, despite his need to adjust to a new style of racing.

Italy

100 km

0 |———————|

100 Miles

Monza
Milan
Mestre
Padova
Venice
Parma
Varano
Castel Maggiore
Bologna
Imola
Forlì
SAN MARINO
Florence
Vallelunga
Corsica
Rome
Naples
Sardinia
Palermo
Pergusa

Germany

100 km
0
100 Miles

• Hamburg
• Gestaach
• Bremen
✪ Berlin
• Hanover
• Lausitz
• Dusseldorf
• Leipzig
Dresden
•
• Bonn
• Frankfurt
• Nurnberg
• Hockenheim
• Stuttgart
• Munich

Index

A

Adams, Philipe, 124–125
Adelaide, 97–98, 128–129
Albert, Prince, 326–327
Alboreto, Michele, 289
Alesi, Jean, 71, 124
Alex Zanardi Foundation, 190,
  326, 338
Alfa Romeo, 104–105
All-Star Team, 333
AMADE, 327
Amadesi, Dr., 324
America's Cup, 73
Amon, Chris, 153
Anderson, Jim, 274–275, 293
Anderson, Tom, 144, 146, 163,
  175, 192, 202, 214
Andretti, Mario, 162, 168, 196
Andretti, Michael, 176, 181,
  183, 185, 199, 219, 226–227,
  232–233, 237–238, 251, 268,
  276, 283, 286, 291
Angelelli, Annamaria, 62
Angelelli, Max, 62, 74–76
Apicella, Marco (aka the
  "Professor"), 81–83, 85, 154
Arrivabene, Maurizio, 86, 104

Arrows, 172, 264
Asaka, Mr., 270–271
Audetto, Daniele, 264
Audi sports racer, 289
Australia, 74, 125, 128–129, 159,
  196–197, 286
Australian Grand Prix
  1991, 106
  1993, 249–250
Autosport magazine, 145, 255,
  262, 267
Autosprint magazine, 16, 84,
  320, 344
Azzurra racing boat, 51

B

Bachelart Team, 343
Badoer, Luca, 75
Barcelona, 93, 95, 114, 122,
  247–249, 255
Barilla, Paolo, 310, 329
Barrichello, Rubens, 181
Belgium, 124–125
Benetton, 86–88, 96, 104, 107,
  119, 125, 219
Berger, Gerhard, 35, 96, 97, 101,
  114, 294

Berlin, 115, 139, 296–297, 302, 306, 307, 311, 342
Bernard, Eric, 71, 125
Bignotti, 153
Blundell, Mark, 114, 160, 202, 207, 210
BMW, 136, 311
  engines, 263, 265
  320 race car, 355
BMW Italy, 355, 360
BMW Motorsport, 353
  Theissen, Mario, 359
BMW Team Italy-Spain, 349, 350, 354
  Castrol, 350
  Coari, Gian Alberto, 350
  Garcia, Antonio, 351, 359
  Giovanardi, Fabrizio, 351
  Grano, Umberto, 350, 352
  Preo, Aldo, 350, 352
  Ravaglia, Roberto, 350, 352, 354
Boesel, Raul, 198–199
Bollini, Dr., 116
Bologna, 5, 13, 15, 121, 132–133, 139, 170, 313, 334
  terrorist attack (1980), 16–17
Bonanno, Giovanni, 37–38
Bonini Engines, 15–17, 20, 108
Bonzagni (Bonza) (friend), 63, 65–66, 135
Brands Hatch, 83, 85, 340, 346
Braun, 101
Brazil, 114, 155, 226
Breda, Giorgio, 79–80
Briatore, Flavio, 87–88, 95–96, 104, 109–110, 125, 147, 149, 242

Bridgestone tires, 31, 38, 43–44, 49, 75, 248, 256
British Grand Prix 1993, 122
Brundle, Martin, 106, 181
Bugatti, Alessandro, 36, 85
Buratti, Mr., 16
Button, Jenson, 262

C
Cagiva Elefant, 111
Cannes boat show, 287
Carpentier, Patrick, 198, 211, 293
CART, 137, 326, 328–329, 333–335, 337–338, 340, 348
  end-of-year banquet, 216
  medical team, 348
  new rules, 272, 276
  safety issues, 277
  U.S. 500 race, 162, 166, 206
Caschi d'Oro, 321–323
Castellet, 107
Castel Maggiore, 5, 7, 10, 62–66, 108, 135, 318
Castroneves, Helio, 238, 284
Catella, Ernesto, 72, 76–77
Cesana, Piero, 286–308
Chandler, Damon, 68
Chapman, Colin, 111, 191
Chicago, 284
Chicco. See Serafini, Enrico
Ciao moped, 12
Cimatti, Mr., 36
Cipo. See Trevisan, Roberto
Cipriani, Giuseppe, 73, 79–81, 86, 88–89, 103
Clark, Jim, 191

Index

Clark, Steve, 214, 219

Clear, Jock, 125, 128

Cleveland, 17, 171, 173, 199–200, 202, 208, 229, 255, 283–284

CNN, 288

Colciago, Robert, 45, 57, 72, 74–75

Collins, Peter, 109, 111, 116–120, 123–126, 129, 148, 154, 242

Comas, Éric, 71

Conrad, Kim, 235

Coperchini, Mario, 57–59

Costa, Dr. Claudio, 116, 301, 311–316, 320–322, 325–326, 328

pigs, 326

Coulthard, David, 34

CRG, 47

D

Dallenbach, Wally, 173, 216–217, 239–242, 246

Daly, Derek, 189, 206

Da Matta, Cristiano, 195, 269

Dante (friend), 17–19, 22–27, 29, 64, 135

stammer, 22–23

DAP, 21, 38, 40–45, 51, 54

Daytona, 172

de Cesaris, Andrea, 93, 96–97, 101, 103

De Ferran, Gil, 132, 143, 159–161, 171, 174–176, 195–198, 201–202, 207, 209–210, 221, 223, 239–240

Demm motorcycle, 6

De Niro, Robert, 9

Dennis, Ron, 97

De Rea, Father Phil, 296, 348

Detroit, 166, 184, 198, 227–228

Dijon, 71

Dixon, 284

Donzelli, 54

Dresden, 296, 298, 342

Dunlop tires, 31, 38

E

Elkhart Lake, 174–176, 207, 211, 240–241, 244, 285

Elliot, Tom, 333

Empoli, 44–45

Ensign team, 153

ESPN, 201

Estoril, 294

European Grand Prix 1994, 125

European Touring Car Championship (ETCC), 349, 351

F

Fabi, Teo, 160

Fairline Boats, 286

Fano, 39

Farneti, Roberto, 71–72

Fassina, Roberto, 81–83, 154

Fernandez, Adrian, 221, 232

Ferrari, 35, 96, 114, 172, 213, 242, 294

Ferrari Challenge, 36

Ferri, Dr. Franco, 311, 315–317, 319, 321–322, 325, 331, 335–337, 340

Index

Fiat
  127, 13
  242, 47
Filbey, Brad, 178–179, 286, 313
Filbey, David, 286
Filbey, Hannah, 286, 313
Firebird, Arizona, 192
Firestone, 250
Fischiella, Giancarlo, 356, 358
Fittipaldi, Christian, 84, 92–93,
  105, 114, 204, 220, 230, 284
Fittipaldi, Emerson, 147, 154, 162
Fontana, 161, 211–212, 219, 236,
  250–251, 269–270, 286
Fontana, Norberto, 145
Fontenay Le Comte, 52–53
Ford, 98–99
  engines, 340
  Fiesta, 120
Ford Cosworth HB V-8 engine,
  102, 112
Formula 1, 11, 41, 86–89, 91–129,
  153, 255–265, 276
  Constructors' Championship, 101
  fuel, 85–86
  requirements, 75
  superlicense, 75
Formula 3, 35, 51, 55, 58,
  68–89, 153
  European Cup, 75–77
  German, 145
  Italian Championship, 70, 77
Formula 3 Association, 72
Formula 3000, 60, 71, 73–74,
  81–83, 136, 137
  European, 143

International Championship, 75
Italian Championship, 74
Japanese, 109, 125, 131
Forti, Guido, 76
Fort Worth, 277
Fossa, 20–21
Foster, Trevor, 96, 99, 117–118
Franchetti, Dario, 198, 221–222,
  229–230, 232–233, 250–251,
  293, 296
Francia, Giorgio, 104
French Grand Prix
  1973, 153
  1992, 105
Frentzen, Heinz-Harald, 259–260
Friso, Nicoletta, 308, 314–315
Friso, Stefano ('Titano'),
  137–140, 187, 202–206,
  236, 239, 267, 280, 302–303,
  308–309, 315, 325
  fitness, 138, 140
  obsessions, 139–140

G

Ganassi, Chip, 141, 143–151,
  154, 158, 161–164, 166–167,
  169–170, 172, 174–176,
  180–186, 192, 196, 200,
  201–202, 210–214, 217, 223,
  228, 231, 233, 235, 243–244,
  248–253, 283, 329, 333, 343
Gardini, Raul, 73
Genk, 52
Genoa Boat show, 286
George, Tony, 162
German Grand Prix (1993) 122

Gestaach, 36
Giannini, Barbara (sister-in-law), 303, 308, 331
Giannini, Francesco (nephew), 331, 339
Giannini, Nicola (nephew), 331
Giannini, Sandro (brother-in-law), 245, 303–304, 307–309, 331, 339
Glauco (friend), 15, 17, 20, 25, 29, 64, 140–142
Glauser, 54
Gordon, Robby, 231, 239
Gorne, Rick, 80–81, 131–132, 136–137, 142–144, 149
Gothenburg, 53–54
Graziella bikes, 12
Green, Barry, 268
Groff, Mike, 148, 150
GT Racing, 256
Gugelmin, Mauricio, 102, 207–209, 224, 284
Gurney, Don, 177

H

Haas, Carl, 269
Häkkinen, Mika, 34, 70, 109, 259–260
Hall, Jim, 132, 143
Head, Patrick, 247–248, 256–259, 263, 265
Hearn, Richie, 200
Herbert, Johnny, 114, 117, 119–120, 122–125

Herta, Bryan, 143–144, 148, 154, 178–180, 207–209, 216, 221–222, 228–230, 237, 245–247
Hill, Damon, 83, 106, 113–114, 128
Hill, Rob, 156, 192, 220, 343
Hill, Terence, 9
Hockenheim, 85, 106
Homestead, 145, 148, 154–156, 194–195, 219, 225, 250, 275
Honda, 39, 123, 166, 189, 219, 250, 270–271, 276, 286, 338
    engines, 93, 145, 157, 270–271
    SLX, 202–203
Hong Kong, 41–42, 49, 54, 63, 74, 79
Houston, 247, 249, 286
Hull, Mike, 144, 192, 212
Hungary, 97, 106, 124
Hunt, David, 129
Hunt, James, 129

I

Iame, 43, 45
IMG, 102
Imola, 35, 59, 77, 104, 114, 121, 132, 257
INAIL Prosthetics Center, 311, 315, 317, 336–337, 361
Indianapolis, 155, 161, 162, 171, 236, 278–279, 286
    Brickyard 400 race, 236
    500 race, 154, 162
IndyCar, 132, 137, 217

Index

Indy Racing Leauge (IRL), 162, 281, 338

Irvine, Eddie, 71, 242

Italian Grand Prix
  1993, 123
  1999, 260

J

Jacksonville, 52

Jaguar, 259

Japan, 117–119, 127, 187, 267, 278

Japanese Grand Prix
  1991, 95–96
  1993, 117–119
  1999, 262

Jerez, 125

Jesolo, 24, 29, 41, 64, 137

Johansson, Stefan, 343

Jones, Parnelli, 176

Jones, P.J., 176–178, 204, 229, 238

Jordan, 86–89, 91–102, 117, 184, 194, 213, 242

Jordan, Eddie, 86–89, 91–92, 94–98, 181–182

Jordan, Michael, 202

Jourdain, Michel, 343

Judd, Ashley, 296, 298

Junquiera, Bruno, 262

K

Kali team, 43–47, 52

Kanaan, Tony, 2, 270, 273–276, 281, 282, 284, 286, 288, 289–291, 298, 301, 329, 344, 357

Karting series
  Champion's Cup, 41
  Club Azzurro, 33, 38–39
  European Championship, 34, 39, 41, 43, 45, 51–53
  European Team, 36
  Italian Championship, 31, 36–37, 41, 44–47, 54
  Super License, 51
  Super 100, 31, 33
  Tricolore Race, 31, 36–37, 45, 47, 53–54, 74–75
  World Championship, 51–52, 54
  100 *Avenir*, 19, 27, 31, 33, 53
  100cc *Cadetti*, 19
  100cc *Nazionale*, 19, 29, 31
  125cc, 19–21, 47–48
  135cc, 51–53, 79

Ketteringham Hall, 111

Klinikum Berlin-Marzahn, 297, 348

Knight, Mike, 168, 180, 196

Komet engines, 52

Krosnoff, Jeff, 144–147, 150, 172

Kyalami, 113

L

Laguna Seca, 142, 154, 178–182, 210, 217–218, 239, 245–247, 286, 349
  Corkscrew, 17, 179, 217, 229–230, 339

Lamy, Pedro, 116–117, 119–121, 128

Langhirano, 61

Larini, Nicola, 104

Lasorella, Carmen, 309, 326

Las Vegas, 187, 254

Lausitzring, 1–2, 115, 172, 286, 287, 289, 293–296, 326, 333, 337, 340–346, 349, 351

Laval, 43

Lehto, JJ, 114, 121, 238, 294

Le Mans, 75–77, 91, 92
    24-hour race, 191, 289

Leoni team, 81

Lesmo, 124

Lido di Pomposa, 38–39, 54

Ligier, 125, 214

Lloyd's of London, 101

Locatelli, Roberto, 356

Lola, 80

Long Beach, 17, 153, 159–161, 168, 197, 219, 223–225, 242, 247, 276, 299, 328

Lotus, 109–112, 117–120, 122–125, 191, 242, 309
    107B, 122

Loudon, 137, 142

Luyendyk, Arie, 212

M

Magione, 69

Magny-Cours, 105

Manning, Darren, 262

Mannucci, Cesare Maria, 199, 344

Mansell, Nigel, 35–36, 96, 97, 100–101, 168, 189

Mantese, Sergio, 31–34, 37–38, 48–49, 54, 109, 329

Maria (head nurse), 307

Marlboro, 86, 104
    500 race, 173–174

Martini, Mauro, 57–59, 61, 96, 118

Masini, Walter, 40, 43

Massimo (friend), 17–18, 24–26, 29

Mauro (friend), 28

McLaren, 35, 109

Mercedes 300 CE, 77

Meyer, Arnd, 224

Michelin tires, 74, 75

Michigan, 155, 162–166, 173–174, 202, 206–207, 234–236
    500 race, 284

Mid-Ohio, 172–173, 180–181, 185, 207, 230, 236

Migliavacca, Carlo, 72

Milan, 31, 38

Millbrook, 340

Milwaukee, 155, 161, 166, 198, 227, 281

Minardi, 105–106

Minardi, Giancarlo, 105–106

Minardi-Ferrari, 96

Minneapolis, 187

Miramas, 104

Misano, 57–59, 71, 354, 355

Mita (dog), 12

Modena, Stefano, 38, 41, 100–101, 335

Monaco, 74, 114, 272, 286, 299, 313, 333

Montana, Joe, 251

Montani, Sandro, 36

Monte Carlo, 69–60, 255, 327

Montedison Group, 73, 77, 81

Montermini, Andrea, 83, 335

Monteshell, 86

Index

Montmelò, 93

Montoya, Juan Pablo, 250–251, 261

Monza, 70, 91, 104, 116, 123–124, 258–259, 356, 358, 359
Hotel Fossati, 357

Moore, Greg, 199, 219, 224–225, 227, 235–236, 242, 250, 253–254

Morbidelli, Gianni, 45, 96, 106, 118

Moreno, Roberto, 86–87, 89, 173

Moro, racing boat, 73

Motegi, 219, 224, 278

Motorsport Group, 350

Mugello, 85

Mugen-Honda V-10 engine, 122–123

N

Nannini, 104

Naspetti, Emanuele, 61, 85–86, 92–93, 195

Nazareth, 155, 161–162, 166, 197, 224–225, 277

Newman, Paul, 269

Newman-Haas team, 153–154, 269

New York, 1, 287

Nice, 272

Nogaro, 93

Novamotor engines, 59, 70, 72

NSU Prinz, 177–178

Nunn, Kathryn, 154, 191, 329–330

Nunn, Morris (Mo), 144–147, 153–155, 157, 159, 163–165, 168–170, 173, 191, 193, 202, 210–211, 220, 225, 227, 230–231, 249, 252
new team, 2, 270–275, 278, 281–283, 298–299
opinion of Italian drivers, 145–146, 154
racing stories, 191
retirement, 213

O

Olvey, Dr. Steve, 212, 295–297, 348

Omega watches, 328

Opel
Corsa, 138
engines, 76

Opel, Rikki Von, 153

Orsini, Massimiliano, 53–54

Osella, 72

P

PacWest team, 205, 207

Padova, 79, 123, 138, 139, 318, 339

Panizzi, Claudio, 311, 317–322, 325, 335

Papis, Cesare, 50–51, 54, 57, 60, 329

Papis, Massimilano (Max), 49–51, 62, 172–173, 250, 254, 290–291, 301, 329, 344

Parilla, 334–3355

Parilla, Achille, 40–42, 44

Index

Parma, 22–23, 31, 45, 48, 57

Patrese, Riccardo, 96, 99, 107–109

Patrick, 154

Patrick, Pat, 270

Pau, 82–84

Pedrazzani, Oreste, 60

Pedrazzani brothers, 59–60, 72

Penske, 147, 181, 240

Pergusa, 70, 73, 79, 84

Peugeot, 47

Philips, Ian, 102

Phoenix, 215

Pilla, Professor, 311–312

Pinarella di Cervia, 33, 50

Pioneer, 326, 338

Piquet, Nelson, 86, 88, 101

Pirelli tires, 33

Pirro, Emanuele, 97, 101

Pista Del Sole, 33

Pista d'Oro, 53

Pittsburgh, 149–150, 182–184

Pook, Chris, 337–338, 343

Porsche Cup race, 132

Portland, 168–170, 173, 181, 198, 228, 284

Portugal, 91, 117, 125

Portuguese Grand Prix 1993, 294

Potter, John, 298

Princess Grace (Kelly) Foundation, 327

Professor, the. See Apicella, Marco (aka the "Professor")

Prost, 213

Prost, Alain, 35, 96, 181

Pruett, Scott, 158, 159, 220, 221, 223, 228, 240

R

Racing for Italy brand, 61

Radio Bologna, 15

RAF Kemble, 105

Rahal, Bobby, 156, 160, 181, 197, 203–204, 220, 237

RAI, 309

Rainey, Wayne, 332

Ralt, 61–62, 68, 75

Ratzenberger, Roland, 121

Ravera, Francesco, 72

RC Motosport, 72

Regazzoni, Clay, 153, 299

Rensing, Otto, 36

Reynard, 80–82, 131–132, 141, 192

Reynard, Adrian, 132, 149, 189

Reynard-Ford, 346

Reynard-Honda, 193, 213

Ribeiro, André, 171, 196

Rio de Janeiro, 157, 159, 168, 197–198, 224–225

Robinson, James, 261

Russell, John, 259

S

Saetta engine, 334

Salo, Mika, 125, 127

San Francisco, 187

San Marino, 36

San Marino Grand Prix 1995, 132

San Pancrazio, 16, 45

Sasol, 102

Sauber, Peter, 131

Schaeckter, Adam, 338–342

Schaffartzik, Dr. Walter, 300, 310

Index

Schroeder, Dr., 302, 310

Schumacher, Michael, 48, 53, 75–77, 86–87, 93–84, 96, 106–108, 125, 128, 142, 219

Schumacher, Ralf, 249, 255, 258, 259–262

Scuderia Italia, 96–97, 104

Sebring, 272–273

Senna, Ayrton, 35, 41, 97–98, 101, 115, 121

September 11, 2001, 1, 287–288

Serafini, Enrico (Chicco), 64–68, 105, 116, 135, 137

Serafini, Michela, 66, 67

Serra, Mauro, 334, 341

Servia, Oriol, 343

Seyum, Akim, 134

Shanaman, Rena, 298, 330

Sheene, Barry, 25

Silverstone, 106–107, 113, 114, 119–120, 123, 286

Si moped, 15

Snetterton, 123

Sofisti, Michele, 329

Soper, Dr. Mary, 234

Sospiri, Vincenzo, 39, 40–41, 43, 335

South African Grand Prix
1992, 103
1993, 113–114

Spa, 85–86, 93, 114–115, 125, 129, 258, 309, 350

Spanish Grand Prix 1991, 92

Spencer, Bud, 9

St. Louis Gateway, 198, 226, 251

Stohr, Siegrfried, 136

Sullivan, Danny, 196

Surfers Paradise, 196–197, 286

Suzuka, 95, 97, 117–119, 127, 262

Swan, Dennis, 216–217

Symonds, Pat, 106–108

T

Tagliani, Alex, 293–294, 298, 329–330

Target, 161–163, 182–183, 187, 203, 229, 237, 252, 268

Tassi, Fabio, 36

Taxi Driver film, 9

Team Sfighé, 17, 19, 25, 29

Tenzer, Jeff, 150–151

Tinini, Giancarlo, 45, 48

Titano. *See* Friso, Stefano ("Titano")

Todt, Jean, 149, 213, 242–243

Togni, Holer, 65

Tonoli, Gianfranco, 355

Toronto, 171–172, 202, 232–233, 281–283, 285, 292, 326, 328–330

Touring Car racing, 136

Toyota, 141, 173
engines, 61, 68–70, 177, 269

Tracy, Paul, 161, 196–198, 202, 207, 220, 240, 246, 253, 275, 293, 329

Trammel, Dr. Terry, 234, 295, 298, 348

Trevisan, Roberto, 61, 68–70, 72, 81, 84–85, 91, 102–103, 123, 139, 214, 305, 308, 336, 349-352, 354

Tyrrell, 102

Index

Tyrrell, Bob, 102
Tyrrell, Ken, 102–103
Tyrrell-Honda, 100, 101

U

Ulrich, Bob, 252
Unser, Al, 162
Unser, Al, Jr., 170, 176, 185, 227, 240–242

V

Vado, 17, 19–21, 26–27
Valance, 52
Vallelunga, 57, 68, 73, 74, 81–82, 94
Vanaria, Calogero, 47–48
Vanaria, Giancarlo, 44, 48
Vanaria, Roberto, 45, 48
Vancouver, 176–177, 182, 207–210, 216, 244, 285, 286
Varano, 57, 69, 73
Vasser, Jimmy, 145, 151, 153, 155–159, 161, 163, 170–171, 173, 175–176, 187, 190, 194, 199, 202–204, 210, 212, 218, 224–225, 227–233, 235–236, 241, 250, 251, 254, 270–271, 281, 287, 291, 298, 301, 305, 329, 343, 346, 357
Vega tires, 32, 33, 36–38, 48–49
Venturini team, 61
Verni, Gennaro, 311, 317–319, 322
Vespa
  PX, 133–134
  125, 134
Vidali, Tamara, 36
Villa, Mauro, 41, 43, 45, 46, 52

Villa, Walter, 41
Villadelprat, Joan, 86–87
Villa Serena, Forli, 312–315, 320
Villeneuve, Jacques, 75, 125
Viverone, 36, 40
Volkswagen
  engines, 76
  Golf, 64–66, 78–79

W

Warwick, Derek, 294
Watt, Jason, 355
Wayne, John, 156, 343
Weber, Willi, 75, 77
Wells, Cal, 141, 144, 148–150, 172
Wheeler, Greg, 256, 260
Williams, Team F1, 2, 107, 112–113, 225, 247–249, 255, 257, 260–265, 267, 275, 283
Williams, Frank, 41, 243, 247, 259–265
Wilson, Craig, 255–256, 258
Wilson, Max, 282
Wilson, Mike, 45
Wright, Peter, 109, 113, 119

Y

Yamaha engines, 102
Yip, Teddy, 153

Z

Zamagna, Mavi, 71
Zamagna, Paolo, 71
Zamagna, Ruggero, 61, 71–77
Zamagna team, 72

Index

Zanardi, Alex
  amputations, 306
  bikes and moped, 12, 14, 64–66
  birthdays, 119, 148, 250, 267
  boats, 139, 267–268, 286–287, 331
  CART, 153–254, 268–292
    fastest laps, 208, 210, 227–228
    penalties, disqualifications and fines, 201, 215–217, 239–240, 284–285
    pole positions, 159, 169, 173, 176, 178, 180, 189, 195–196, 200
    titles, 2, 210, 216, 244, 257
    wins, 170–171, 178–181, 204, 207, 218, 221–222, 229, 233, 242–244, 250
  coma, 347
  courage, 5, 14, 268
  crashes and accidents, 3, 70, 74, 83–85, 98, 100, 114–118, 166, 174, 194, 211–212, 216, 219, 240, 245–246, 249, 284, 293–310, 346
  determination, 11
  driving instructor, 136, 170
  driving style, 34–35, 146, 219–220, 231, 248–249, 341
  driving test, 39–40
  emotions, 34–35, 77–78, 98, 111, 120, 221–222, 245, 254, 267, 331–332
  Formula 3, 35, 57–89, 94, 102
    European Champion, 75–77
    pole positions, 60, 69, 70, 73
    wins, 77

  Formula 3000, 71–72, 78–86, 102
    pole positions, 74, 82–84
    wins, 60, 73, 74, 82
  go-kart building, 11–12
  holidays, 16, 132, 136–1376
  homes, 5, 161, 189, 206, 236, 255, 272, 278–281
  hospitals, 115–116, 296–317
  intensive care, 300, 306
  investments, 111–112
  karting, 14–55, 62–64, 74–75, 94, 133, 333–335
    European Champion, 52
    Italian Champion, 46–47
    pole positions, 39, 40, 43, 47, 52
    wins, 29, 33, 41, 47, 52–54, 79
  languages, 30, 243
  marriage, 115, 187
  nicknames, 34, 119, 138, 146, 168–169, 186
  passion for racing, 2, 60, 264, 267, 271
  prostheses, 311, 317–322, 327–328, 331–335, 340–341
  romances, 62–63, 67–68, 77–78
  schooling, 7–9, 12, 19, 29–30, 39, 133–135
  self-confidence/pride, 5–6, 8, 52, 60–61, 68, 257–258, 282
    as small child, 5–6
  sponsorship, 31–32, 38, 40–47, 55–58
  swimming, 10–11, 331, 335–336
  Touring Car racing, 136
  trophies, 21

Index

Zanardi, Anna (mother), 1, 5, 7, 12–14, 55, 94–95, 125–127, 132, 299, 308, 310, 313, 318
help with karting, 28–29
occupations, 7–9, 30
Zanardi, Cristina (sister), 5, 7, 9–10, 12–14, 28
Zanardi, Daniela (née Manni), 67, 68, 72, 77–79, 103, 115–116, 141–142, 147, 190, 271, 278–280, 285, 287, 296–310, 313–314, 328–329, 344, 346, 357
business acumen, 77–78
friends, 137, 177–178, 280–281
hernia operation, 323–325
mother, Gianna, 135, 279, 303, 307
pregnancy, 233–235, 243–245, 256
team manager, 61, 62, 70, 78, 136, 191

Zanardi, Dino (father), 6–16, 23–31, 39–40, 42, 45–46, 50–57, 121, 132, 133, 178, 308, 329
boats, 17
illness, 125–127
inventiveness, 42, 48–49
physique, 25–26
pranks and jokes, 6–7, 29
Zanardi, Gisella (grandmother), 39–40, 170–171, 324
Zanardi, Niccolò, 1, 8, 127, 245, 249–250, 255–256, 267, 280, 285–287, 305–308, 313–314, 318, 323–325, 327
conception and birth, 215, 244–245
Zanella, Luca, 85
Zanelli, Catia, 205, 280, 285, 308
Zanelli, Filippo, 132–135, 180, 190, 202–207, 236–23752

4 Star tires, 31

Art Credits

All photos are courtesy of The Zanardi Collection, except as noted below:

Black and White Photos
Robert Laberge/Getty Images: page v (Foreword)

Color Photos
AlexZanardiMedia.com: photos numbered 55, 57, 58, 60–66
AP: photos numbered 40, 42
BMW Press: photos numbered 52, 53, 54, 56, 59
Michael Cooper/Getty Images: photo numbered 29
Jutta Fausel-Ward: photos numbered 20, 47
Greg Feistman/LAT USA: photo numbered 36
Joern Haufe: photo numbered 39
Kluetmeier: photo numbered 43
Robert Laberge/Getty Images: photos numbered 44, 45
LAT Photographic: photos numbered 10, 12, 13, 30
Mike Levitt/LAT USA: photos numbered 23, 25, 27, 32
Lesley Miller/LAT USA: photos numbered 37, 38
Photo 4: photo numbered 24
Reuters: photos numbered 46, 49
Sutton: photo numbered 11
David Taylor/Getty Images: photos numbered 15, 16
Mark Thompson/Getty Images: photo numbered 48

Cover Photos
Massimiliano Bianchi: back cover
Jutta Fausel-Ward: inside front flap (top)
Mike Levitt/LAT USA: front cover
Orsi: inside back flap
Mark Thompson/Getty Images: inside front flap (bottom)

In production of this book every effort was made to locate and obtain permission from the original artists.

Selected Books From Bentley Publishers

Driving

The Unfair Advantage *Mark Donohue*
ISBN 0-8376-0073-1 (hc);
0-8376-0069-3 (pb)

**Going Faster! Mastering the Art of
Race Driving** *The Skip Barber Racing
School* ISBN 0-8376-0227-0

**A French Kiss With Death: Steve
McQueen and the Making of** *Le Mans*
Michael Keyser ISBN 0-8376-0234-3

Sports Car and Competition Driving
Paul Frère with foreword by *Phil Hill*
ISBN 0-8376-0202-5

The Technique of Motor Racing
Piero Taruffi ISBN 0-8376-0228-9

**Driving Forces: The Grand Prix Racing
World Caught in the Maelstrom of the
Third Reich** *Peter Stevenson*
ISBN 0-8376-0217-3

Engineering/Reference

**Supercharged! Design, Testing, and
Installation of Supercharger Systems**
Corky Bell ISBN 0-8376-0168-1

**Maximum Boost: Designing, Testing,
and Installing Turbocharger Systems**
Corky Bell ISBN 0-8376-0160-6

Race Car Aerodynamics *Joseph Katz*
ISBN 0-8376-0142-8

**Design & Tuning of Competition
Engines** *Philip H. Smith*
ISBN 0-3876-01401

**Scientific Design of Exhaust & Intake
Systems** *Philip H. Smith and
John C. Morrison*
ISBN 0-8376-0309-9

**Road & Track Illustrated Automotive
Dictionary** *John Dinkel*
ISBN 0-8376-0143-6

Chevrolet

**Zora Arkus-Duntov: The Legend
Behind Corvette** *Jerry Burton*
ISBN 0-8376-0858-9

**Corvette from the Inside: The 50-Year
Development History** *Dave McLellan*
ISBN 0-8376-0859-7

BMW

**BMW 3 Series Enthusiast's
Companion™** *Jeremy Walton*
ISBN 0-8376-0220-3

**BMW 6 Series Enthusiast's
Companion™** *Jeremy Walton*
ISBN 0-8376-0193-2

**BMW 3 Series (E46) Service Manual:
1999–2001, 323i, 325i, 325xi, 328i, 330i,
330xi Sedan, Coupe, Convertible,
Sport Wagon** *Bentley Publishers*
ISBN 0-8376-0320-X

**BMW 5 Series (E39) Service Manual:
1997–2002 525i, 528i, 530i, 540i, Sedan,
Sport Wagon** *Bentley Publishers*
ISBN 0-8376-0317-X

Mercedes-Benz

**Mercedes-Benz E-Class Owner's
Bible™ 1986–1995** *Bentley Publishers*
ISBN 0-8376-0230-0

MINI Cooper

**MINI Cooper Service Manual:
2002–2004, including MINI Cooper,
MINI Cooper S** *Bentley Publishers*
ISBN 0-8376-1068-0

Porsche

Porsche: Excellence Was Expected
Karl Ludvigsen ISBN 0-8376-0235-1

**Porsche 911 Carrera Service Manual:
1984–1989** *Bentley Publishers*
ISBN 0-8376-0291-2